ROME

PLATE I   THE ROMAN TRADITION

Bronze handle of a lid of a Praenestine *cista*. Found at Praeneste (Palestrina). The *cista* was a cylindrical bronze box for keeping articles used for the bath, in the palaestra, and for toilet purposes; it was generally adorned with engraved designs, and many have been found in Praenestine graves of the 4th–3rd cent. B.C. The handle represents two bearded warriors wearing helmets and complete armour including greaves, and leaning on heavy spears (comp. pl. III, 1). They are carrying the dead body of a comrade, unbearded, clad in the same kind of armour except for the helmet and the spear. The general appearance of the figures is archaic, but they certainly belong to the same time as the engravings on the lid, which cannot be earlier than the 4th cent. B.C. The group is very impressive and may serve as an excellent symbol of Roman and Latin life in the 4th cent. B.C., when the Roman state was based on military strength and on self-sacrifice of its members. 4th cent. B.C. Museo Papa Giulio, Rome.

M. ROSTOVTZEFF

ROME

Translated from the Russian by J. D. Duff

ELIAS J. BICKERMAN
Editor, Galaxy Book edition

A GALAXY BOOK

New York OXFORD UNIVERSITY PRESS 1960

© Oxford University Press, Inc., 1960

Library of Congress Catalogue Card No. 60-15102

First Published, as *A History of the Ancient World, Volume II, Rome,* 1927

Reprinted with corrections, 1928

First Published as a Galaxy Book, 1960

Fifth Galaxy printing, 1963

Printed in the United States of America

Note on the Corrected Impression of 1928

THE changes made in the second impression of the first volume of this work (*The Orient and Greece*) are slight and of no importance, and I therefore saw no reason for adding anything to the Preface which appears at the beginning of that volume. But the changes introduced in the second impression of Volume II are more numerous, and demand a note in explanation.

These changes have been made in order to satisfy my critics (and of course my readers). I have not, naturally, been able to discard results established by archaeological researches, and to substitute for them the intuitive and romantic statements desiderated by one of my critics. Nor, again, have I thought fit to transform my History of Rome into a treatise on Roman Constitution and Law, as another critic suggested. Finally, there are certain debated questions on which I am unable to change my own views, though these views have been rashly taken for mistakes by insufficiently informed critics.

However, it has been possible, and has seemed to me desirable, to correct some misstatements, some ambiguous expressions, which might be taken for mistakes or might lead to misunderstandings, and last, but not least, a number of misprints. I am greatly indebted to my critics for drawing attention to these passages, and especially to Professor F. B. Marsh, of the University of Texas, who was kind enough to suggest to me (at my request) a list of desirable changes in the text of my book. I beg him to accept my sincerest thanks.

M. R.

Addenda

THIS book of Rostovtzeff's stands on its own merits and has not been outdated by new discoveries or research. There have been some new finds, however, and further research has been fruitful. The most important of these new points are noted below:

page 7. New discoveries show that the pre-history of Italy was much more complex than the simple scheme of the Indo-European invasions drawn in the text. Cf. M. Pallottino, *The Etruscans* (Pelican paperback translation, 1955); E. Pulgram, *The Tongues of Italy* (Harvard University Press, 1959).

page 15. Men already lived among the hills of Rome in the Bronze Age (middle of the second millenium B.C.). New excavations prove the existence of huts (of the same type as those represented by the funerary hut-urns) on both hill tops of the Palatine in the first phase of the Iron Age, that is, approximately in the eighth century B.C. The tombs discovered under the Forum, on the Esquiline Hill and on the Quirinal are from the same period. On the other hand, the Capitol became occupied toward 600 B.C., and the future Forum was paved for the first time *c.* 575. Thus, the archaeological evidence confirms the traditional date (753 B.C.) of 'Romulus' settlement on the Palatine. But a further interpretation of archaeological record, and its correlation with the early history of Rome, is very difficult and the relevant problems are hotly discussed. Cf. E. Gjerstad, *Early Rome* (vols. i-iii, 1953ff., in progress); R. Bloch, *The Origins of Rome* (1960); A. Boethius, *The Golden House of Nero* (University of Michigan Press, 1960), pp. 3ff. and 186; also, popular accounts: S. M. Puglisi, 'Huts on the Palatine Hill,' *Antiquity* XXIV (1950), pp. 119-121; E. Gjerstad, 'Stratigraphic Excavations in the Forum Romanum,' *Antiquity* XXVI (1952), pp. 6off.

page 32. The hypothesis that Quirinus was a Sabine god is unwarranted. Cf. G. Dumézil, *L'héritage indo-européen à Rome* (1949), pp. 87ff.

page 84. Only direct descendants of a consul (or dictator, or censor) were regarded in Cicero's time as belonging to the nobility, that is, to the best families of Rome. Cf. H. H. Scullard, *Roman Politics* (London, 1951), p. 6.

pages 84–85. The relations between tribes and centuries is a very complex problem unduly simplified in the text. Cf. H. Hill, *The Roman Middle Class in the Republican Period* (1952), pp. 38ff.; E. S. Stavely, 'The Constitution of the Roman Republic,' *Historia* V (1956), pp. 112ff.

page 110. The supernumerary tribes probably never came into being. At the end the Italics were distributed in the old tribes. Cf. L. R. Taylor, *The Voting Districts of the Roman Republic* (Papers and Monographs of the American Academy in Rome, vol. xx, Rome, 1960), pp. 101ff.

page 153. The extant evidence does not warrant the inference that Atticus had a publishing business. Cf. G. Pasquali, *Storia della tradizione* (1934), p. 399.

page 166. On the constitutional position of Augustus cf. the survey of recent opinions in a German magazine, *Historia*, vol. i (1950), pp. 408ff., containing an article by G. E. F. Chilver.

pages 166 and 192. A newly discovered inscription (Tabula Hebana) shows that at least until A.D. 19 consuls and praetors were elected by the people, but the people could only accept or reject the official candidates previously selected by vote of a committee of senators and knights. This complex system of election was established by Augustus. Cf. J. H. Oliver & R. E. A. Palmer, 'Text of the Tabula Hebana,' *American Journal of Philology* LXXV (1956), pp. 225ff.

page 197. Caligula demanded divine honors but did not proclaim himself 'Lord and god.'

page 263. New finds prove that Diocletian's tariff was also in force in the West. Cf. T. Frank, *An Economic Survey of Ancient Rome*, vol. v (1941), pp. 305ff., W. L. Westermann, *The Age of Diocletian* (The Metropolitan Museum, New York, 1953), p. 29.

page 319. The Hittite Empire was overthrown not by the Thracians but by the 'Peoples of the Sea.' Cf. O. R. Gurney, *The Hittites* (Pelican orig. paperback, 1961).

Elias J. Bickerman
Professor of Ancient History
Columbia University
May 1962

Contents

List of Plates

Figures in the Text

ROME

I

EARLY ITALY. SOURCES OF INFORMATION

IN the fourth century B. C., just when the Greek world, in spite of a background of flourishing civilization, was falling to pieces politically, the opposite process was going on in another part of the world. In Italy political unification was in full swing, and a powerful empire including the whole peninsula was in process of formation. This development took place, not among the Greek colonists of Italy and Sicily, who, as we have seen already, were unable to maintain a permanent union even among themselves, but among the Italian tribes, who had for a long time kept up relations with the Etruscans and Greeks and gradually adopted their culture. By virtue of this process of union, Italy came quickly to the front in the politics of the fourth century B. C. ; and from the end of the second century her voice is decisive in the public affairs of the East, and the Greeks have to obey her bidding.

This state of things, which fixed the course of man's development for many centuries, suggests a fundamental question. How was it possible, on Italian soil and on the basis of a league presided over by one of its members, to create a single power with a strong army and a rich treasury, whereas Greece, in spite of her creative genius, never succeeded in any of her attempts to secure the same result ?   In other words : why did Rome, just such a city-state as Athens or Sparta, succeed in solving the puzzle which had baffled both Athens and Sparta and even the Greek monarchies founded upon military strength by the successors of Alexander ?

The rise of this empire with Rome for its capital, and its extension over the peninsula and later over the world, was enormously impressive, as an historical fact, to the thinkers and historians of antiquity, whether they were natives of Italy and therefore themselves makers of that empire, or Greeks and therefore forced to submit to its sway. Great intellects, such as Polybius, the Greek historian who described the palmy days of Rome and her brilliant victories in East and West in the second century B. C., and a succession of prominent Roman statesmen—men of light and leading—all gave their thoughts to this problem and tried to find a satisfactory explanation. The explanation they gave was dictated by the political and philosophical ideas current at the time.

Starting from the position that the welfare of a state depends partly upon the moral qualities of individuals and partly upon the excellence of its constitution, the Greek philosophic historians attributed the success of Rome to just these two causes : the virtues of Roman citizens, and the perfection of the Roman constitution—a constitution which realized in practice the ideal shaped long before by Greek philosophers, from Plato downwards. We, however, cannot accept this explanation as sufficient. Investigation into the conditions of life in Rome and Italy have proved to us, what Polybius himself was beginning to realize at the end of his life—that the view held by the ancients concerning the Roman constitution and the moral and civic virtues of the Roman people is exaggerated and does not entirely correspond with the facts, and, at all events, is not a complete answer to the question.

It is clear that the causes of Rome's success are more complex and lie deeper ; they can only be discovered by careful study of the historic environment which moulded the course of life in Italy from remote antiquity. But of that early development we know little. The Greeks were chiefly interested in the fortunes of their own colonies in Sicily and south Italy. They knew of the Italian tribes as early as the seventh century B. C., but took no keen interest in them till two centuries later ; they were most concerned with them at the end of the fourth century and beginning of the third. It must be added that the copious historical literature produced by the Sicilian and Italian Greeks has not reached us or has reached us only in sorry fragments. The most valuable of these fragments were taken by Roman writers between 100 B. C. and A. D. 100 from the Greek historian Timaeus, a native of Tauromenium (now Taormina) in Sicily, who lived at the end of the fourth century and in the first half of the third, and collected whatever was then known concerning the history of the different Italian clans.

Historical tradition, as preserved by the Italians themselves and remodelled by Roman historians of the last three centuries B. C., is not only meagre but deliberately

2

perverted. The Italian tribes had hardly any contemporary records of historical incidents. The art of writing was late in reaching them, and was but little used to perpetuate the memory of events. There was one race, resident in Italy, which might have created an earlier historical tradition ; but these were the Etruscans, who spoke and wrote a language which was unintelligible to most Italians and even to the learned men of Rome. Nor, indeed, is it probable that Etruscan tradition went back far or deserved much credit ; for very few of the Etruscan texts preserved on stone are older than the fourth century B. C.

Such being the conditions, it is not surprising that historians were puzzled, when at the end of the third century they began to collect facts about the primitive history of Rome and Italy. Following such rules of historical research as were then known, they found hardly anything either in Greek literature or in local tradition to help them in giving a truthful narrative of events that had befallen the native Italians before the fourth century. The case was better in regard to the fourth and third centuries, when there were both in Italy and Greece persons who took an interest in Italian history and recorded contemporary events concerning Rome and the Italian tribes. Prominent among these persons were the Romans themselves. For the earlier period they had to rely upon the following sources : (1) casual allusions in the Greek historians of south Italy ; (2) conjectures by these same writers about the past of Italy, about which they knew little, and which they tried to connect with the legendary past of Greece ; (3) lists of the Roman magistrates ; but these were incomplete and inexact, at least until 320 B. C., when the college of pontifices began to bring together, in connexion with the framing of a calendar, lists of the consuls, and to add thereto notices of important events—this record being known as the ' chronicle of the pontiffs ' ; (4) oral tradition, preserved in songs sung at the tables of some ancient Roman families, or associated with the most ancient monuments existing in the city ; (5) survivals of antiquity in certain civil and religious institutions ; (6) some scraps of information derived from the historical literature of the Etruscans.

On such foundations no connected history of Rome and Italy from ancient times could possibly be constructed. But meanwhile the national pride of Rome, and the part she was

3

beginning to play in the family of Hellenistic empires, demanded that she, like the other empires and cities of the civilized world, should have a history of her own, and a history dating from the beginning, that is, from the foundation of the city. Further, the history of Rome must somehow or other be connected with the history of the civilized world, in other words, of Greece, and with the earliest episode of that history, the Trojan war itself. Rome must find a place in the poem of Homer, the earliest monument of Greek historical tradition. For the later period it was necessary to show how Rome marched from strength to strength till she became the mistress of Italy, and how her constitution, acknowledged even by the Greeks to be a model of perfection, took shape by degrees.

With these objects in view, the first historians of Rome—some of them immigrants from the Hellenized south of Italy, like Ennius and Naevius who lived and wrote during the Punic wars, while others were Romans who played a part in politics at the end of the third century and in the first half of the second, such men as Fabius Pictor, Cincius Alimentus, Gaius Acilius (all of whom wrote in Greek), and Marcus Porcius Cato, Cassius Hemina, Calpurnius Piso, Gnaeus Gellius, and Claudius Quadrigarius—created by their combined efforts a more or less accepted chronology and a fairly detailed history of early Rome, highly patriotic in its contents but resting upon very shaky foundations. As has been pointed out above, these authors had hardly any trustworthy sources for the early period. In the attempt to construct a continuous narrative of the city's development with fragments of true historical tradition, they had recourse to a series of arbitrary guesses, founded upon fanciful and unscientific interpretations, either of words, which bore reference to some ancient religious and civil institutions and which they did not understand, or of names borne by certain monuments erected in the infancy of Rome. They took on trust similar guesses of Greek historians, which aimed at a fanciful connexion between early Roman history and Greek mythology. In this way they got a more or less connected narrative, from the arrival of Aeneas, when that hero fled to Italy after the capture of Troy, down to the time when they could use the earliest more or less authentic facts of Roman history, preserved by oral tradition in a half-legendary shape, and also the earliest really authentic information on domestic and foreign affairs.

Out of these detached and half-historical facts, associated with the names of certain public men who figured in early times, but hardly ever assigned to any fixed date, the Roman historians again attempted to construct a consecutive narrative of events. They arranged their facts in chronological order, according to their own judgement ; they invented new heroes, for whom they had no warrant in tradition, and described their exploits in detail ; they told how these men raised Rome above her neighbours and devised the Roman constitution. This picture was to a large extent imaginary ; and it was sophisticated further by writers in the latter half of the second century and the beginning of the first, when they sought to find in the remote past support for the political and social reforms which they themselves advocated.

By careful analysis of these historical works it is possible to comb out some political, religious, and constitutional facts from the sixth century B. C. downwards ; but these facts are so general that it is hardly possible to build upon them a continuous and fairly complete history of Rome and Italy in the fifth century and much of the fourth. For more remote times the writings of the Roman historians are practically useless.

For this reason the results of archaeological research in Italy are of special value in their bearing on primitive times. They enable us to trace the cultural development of the country from the Old Stone Age. To connect the results thus gained with the statements of the Roman historians—especially with their account of the distribution of different stocks in Italy—is not easy. But a few points may be asserted positively ; and these few are of great importance, if we are to understand the later history of the peninsula.

Geographically and geologically Italy bears a general resemblance to Greece. The Apennine peninsula is a continuation of central Europe, which runs far down into the Mediterranean. Italy is bounded on the north by the Alps. Though the Alps appear at first sight to form an impenetrable barrier between Italy and central Europe, they are not really quite as formidable as they seem. For the great rivers of central Europe—the Rhone, with its tributaries, flowing south-west, and the Rhine, flowing north—rise in the Alps ; and it was possible to follow their courses as far as the passes which led over the Alps to Italy, and thence to descend, by the valleys of rivers mostly tributaries of the Po, into the fertile north-Italian plain. A further connexion between Italy and Gaul was afforded by a strip of coast. It was also comparatively easy to penetrate into Italy from the region of the Danube and its tributaries.

The Apennine range forms the backbone of the Italian peninsula; it runs far out to sea, reappears in Sicily, and is geologically connected with north Africa. These mountains are much less forbidding and bare than those of Greece. They are intersected by an endless number of fertile valleys, and were clothed in ancient times with forests and rich pastures available at all seasons. On the east coast the mountains come close to the Adriatic, except in Apulia, where a wide plain intervenes and affords excellent pasture for cattle and sheep. In the west the conditions are different. A range of volcanoes exists there, chiefly in Etruria, Latium, Campania, and the adjacent islands, including Sicily; and their secular activity has created on the western slope of the Apennines highly fertile plains, intersected by rivers which flow from the central range into the Tyrrhene sea. The largest of these rivers, and the only one suitable for navigation, is the Tiber. One of the valleys is divided by the Tiber into two parts—the two parts being Latium and Etruria; another valley is Campania, separated from the Tiber valley by spurs of the Apennine range which run down as far as the sea.

The extraordinary fertility of Campania has been mentioned already. The plains of Etruria and Latium are poorer in geological formation : the soil consists of a fertile stratum of porous volcanic tufa over a layer of impermeable clay, and is therefore apt to become swampy. But by dint of careful draining and persistent labour it can be made to grow good harvests, and even when partly submerged supplies good pasture in winter to the shepherds of the neighbouring upland valleys.

The Italian coast is less rich in harbours than that of Greece ; but it has, especially on its western side, a number of excellent bays. The best harbours are at Naples and Genoa ; and there are also a fair number of points where sailing vessels of moderate size can conveniently take in and discharge cargo. Thus on the whole the most fertile part of

6

Italy faces west : her most productive plains run westward ; and she is connected with the West both by Sicily, which is only separated from her by the narrow straits of Messina, and by the coast of the Ligurian gulf. Yet her connexion with the East is equally close : the Po flows into the Adriatic ; a succession of islands brings her east coast near the west coast of Greece ; and the bay of Tarentum offers free access to ships sailing from the gulf of Corinth. These geographical conditions have determined the history of Italy. She was accessible, on one side, to the tribes of central Europe, and, on the other, to the seafarers of the East. Both alike were attracted by her natural wealth, temperate climate, and rich vegetation. The herdsmen and husbandmen of central Europe were tempted by the excellent pastures and fertile fields, while the eastern immigrants sought the southern harbours, which gave access to prosperous Campania, the fertile river-valleys in south Italy, and the primeval forests on the neighbouring hills—forests which provided excellent timber for shipbuilding.

Under these conditions it is easy to understand that the early history of Italy is like the early history of Greece. Dwellers in central and eastern Europe and Asia Minor gradually came into the country from the north and from the south. The oldest inhabitants were Ligurians and Iberians, nearly related to the aborigines of Spain and Gaul ; and these were gradually covered over by tribes belonging to the Indo-European population of central Europe. The earliest settlers from central Europe were probably lake-dwellers in their own country : their villages were built over the lakes on platforms supported by poles ; these poles were driven into the bottom at some distance from the shore, and communication with the land was secured by a movable bridge. They began by building similar villages on the lakes of north Italy. Next they transferred themselves to dry land, where they made settlements protected by earthen ramparts and surrounded by a moat ; and here also the houses were placed on a platform resting on poles, and the poles were driven into the ground inside the rampart. These were the first fortified towns of the central-European dwellers in Italy. They are called in Italian *terramare*, because their ruins are full of a rich black soil (*terra mara* or *marna*). These inhabitants of the *terramare* reached Italy in the Early Metal Age—the age of copper and bronze.

Considerably later, in the Late Bronze Age when iron also was coming into use, they were followed by a number of Indo-European clans, who came from districts where there were fortified places of refuge for man and beast on the mountains and hill-tops. These men brought with them improved implements and weapons, and therefore drove into the background both the lake-dwellers and the aborigines. Mingling with one another and with the old settlers, and occupying one district after another right down to the southern extremity of the peninsula, these immigrants broke off by degrees into three groups, each of which spoke a different dialect of a language common to them all and akin to Celtic. These groups were the Umbrians, the Latins, and the Samnites. The first occupied the north of Italy and part of the centre ; the second, the lower course of the Tiber valley ; the third, the hills and valleys in the south of the peninsula.

But they were not fated to keep their hold on the coast. The Apulian valleys and the Venetian plains—the most fertile parts of the east coast—were occupied at an early date by Illyrian clans, who came from the north and east shores of the Adriatic. The strongest and most populous of these clans were the Iapygians, who occupied the south-east coast of Italy. They probably entered Italy at the same time as the lake-dwellers. The western coast, on the other hand, except the lower course of the Tiber, was conquered by invaders from across the sea about the beginning of the first millennium. In the north the Italians were either driven into the mountains or subdued by the Etruscans, one of the Anatolian stocks which migrated from Asia in the age of confusion and dispersion at the end of the second millennium. In the south the whole strip of coast, excluding Apulia in the east but including Campania in the west, was occupied after the eighth century B. C. by immigrants from Greece. The last invaders of Italy were the Celts, whom the Romans called ' Gauls '. They were nearly akin to the Italians and came, like them, from the north—partly from what is now France, and partly perhaps from the valley of the Danube. In the sixth century they began by degrees to occupy the valley of the Po, driving out the Etruscans.

II

ITALY FROM 800 B. C. TO 500 B. C.: ETRUSCANS, SAMNITES, LATINS

WE know that the Etruscans appeared on the west coast of central Italy, established themselves there, and spread into the heart of the land as far as the Po valley and the Adriatic; but the details of this process are unknown. Yet excavation of their settlements gives us a lively picture of their life, especially from the sixth to the third century B. C.; and a certain number of monuments take us still farther back—as far as the eighth century. We are still unable to decipher any part of the Etruscan texts, engraved on stone in the Greek alphabet, except proper names and some isolated words; yet the number of Etruscan monuments, preserved in the tombs and the ruins of their cities, is so great, and the monuments themselves so various, that it is possible for us to frame some idea of the political and social arrangements of this people, of their religion, habits, art, and handicrafts.

In the fifth and fourth centuries B. C. the Etrurian Empire was a league of several large cities, some of which were seaports. The solidarity of this league grew less by degrees, but was probably considerable when the empire was created. The Etruscan stock formed the highest class in the population and lived in fortified and well-planned cities. This class derived their wealth from various sources: they cultivated the fertile soil of the country and raised stock; they worked the copper mines of Etruria and the iron mines in the island of Elba; they carried on active industry, especially in metals and textiles; and they traded extensively with the Greek world and with the East through the agency of the Greek colonies in south Italy and of Phoenician Carthage. All over the Mediterranean in ancient times trade was hardly distinct from piracy, and it retained this character in Etruria till very late; in the fifth and fourth centuries B. C. an Etruscan merchant was to the Greeks the same thing as an Etruscan pirate. The highest class consisted of landowners, traders, and manufacturers; the labour was done partly by conquered Ligurians and Italians, bound to the soil, and partly (in all probability) by slaves, captured in constant warfare and piratical descents. There is no doubt that these landowners, piratical traders, and manufacturers formed the fighting force of the Etruscan league, sometimes drawn from a single city and sometimes from them all.

We know little about the constitution of the league or the government of the cities. It is probable that in primitive times each city was ruled by a king, whose place was taken later by elective magistrates belonging to noble families. Their religion and civilization were of a mixed kind. Though these were certainly derived from the East and akin to the institutions which prevailed in Anatolia about 1000 B. C., yet close association with Phoenicia and Greece gradually disguised the origins of Etruscan civilization and gave it a miscellaneous and incongruous character. It is quite possible that the Etruscan conquerors in many places admitted to their ranks the native aristocracy, who, at the time of the conquest, already possessed a well-developed culture and a language of their own, and perhaps even some notion of writing. It is very probable that the largest and richest cities contained Greek settlers, mainly artists and artisans of Ionian origin.

The life of the aristocracy in the cities was very like that of contemporary Greek cities, especially of those in Asia Minor and south Italy. From scenes which adorn the walls of Etruscan tombs, and from vases Greek in style but made in Etruria, we can see how they spent their time. They waged war ; they practised all the athletic sports customary in Greece—running, boxing, throwing the discus and javelin, wrestling, chariot-racing, hunting and fishing ; they held festivals connected with religious ceremonies. The women too, richly dressed, took an active share in these occupations. Whether life in the Etruscan cities developed on the same lines as in Asia Minor and south Italy, we do not know ; but such a supposition is in itself highly probable. We must also suppose that there were political difficulties between the separate communities and a social division in the heart of each of them. And in this way we may, in all probability, account for the gradual degeneration of the Etruscan league.

Successful excavation of Etruscan cities and cemeteries, carried on by Italian archaeologists, makes it possible for us to follow very exactly the development of Etruscan art, from the eighth century B.C. At first we find the geometric style characteristic of Italy; later this gives way to Eastern influences; at the same time Etruria becomes, and continues to be, a market for traders from Greece and the East, especially Phoenicia; and from a combination of all these elements an independent and original art is in time developed. We find it in architecture, sculpture, and painting, and also in industrial production, particularly in casting bronze, in the manufacture of jewellery and embossed metals. It cannot, however, be said that Etruscan art attained to the highest excellence. Their architecture remained for a long time archaic in style, and never got beyond modifications of Greek and Eastern models. Their sculpture, which shows high technical skill, never rose to the height of Greek achievement in this field. It long retained an archaic liking for bright colours; in one field only—that of highly realistic portraiture—it produced remarkable work. Their painting is perhaps the most attractive side of their art. Here, while following the style and method of Greek artists, they contrived to convey their own ideas by these means, in subjects taken from daily life or history or religion. The awful figures which they invented of infernal gods and demons, of death and future punishments, survived them and exercised an influence upon Roman art and also upon the medieval painting of the Italians. In design and industry the Etruscans acquired a high degree of technical skill; but their jewellery aims rather at size, weight, and elaboration than at refinement of form and ornament.

The political activity of the Etruscans took two directions. By sea they were faithful friends of the Phoenicians and Carthaginians, who gladly accepted the services of such adventurous and unabashed pirates, so long as they plundered the Greek rivals of Carthage and kept away from countries dependent upon her. For Phoenicia, and later for Carthage, Etruria was a desirable market, whence they exported metals and raw material, while they imported thither tin from Spain and Britain, silver and copper from Spain, and gold and manufactured articles from the East. The Etruscans were undoubtedly pirates rather than merchants, and Carthage had no fear of their competition: we do not know of the existence of a single colony or trading factory owned by them. But between Greece and Etruria the hostility was acute. The

Etruscan pirates, acting in concert with the Carthaginian fleet, prevented the Greeks from extending their influence to the north, or establishing their footing in Sardinia and Corsica ; and almost entirely debarred them from access to their colonies in Gaul and Spain. The most remarkable achievement of the Etruscans was the destruction in 538 B. C. of Alalia, a colony founded in Corsica by the Phoceans ; and Massilia, the chief Greek centre in Gaul, found it necessary during this century to make terms of agreement with Rome. Thanks to the Etruscans, the Carthaginians were able to check the expansion of Greece towards the west and north. It is true that the united efforts of these allies could not finally expel the Greeks from western waters. But, though the Greeks won repeated victories at sea—in 474 B. C. Hiero of Syracuse defeated the Etruscans at Cuma, and in 453 B. C. the Syracusans sent out an expedition against the coast of Etruria—yet they were forced to abandon the hope of suppressing Etruscan piracy once for all, and to be content with a share in supplying the cities of the enemy with the goods they needed.

Such was the state of affairs at sea. By land the dominion of Etruria increased steadily down to the second half of the sixth century. She showed no special activity in this expansion. She did not covet possession of the Italian mountains ; her ambition was confined to the valley of the Po in the north and to Campania in the south. The former was entirely occupied by Etruscans and remained in their possession until the Celts appeared there in the fifth century. At one time their movement to the south was equally successful : Etruscan dynasties ruled at Rome and probably in other cities of Latium ; in Campania, Capua became a bulwark of Etruscan power and a dangerous rival to Cuma and Naples, and ruled over a number of petty half-Greek cities, such as Nola and perhaps Pompeii. But this southern movement was arrested partly by Greek opposition and partly by new and important developments in Italian history.

These developments were due to the advance made in political and economic organization and in culture by two groups belonging to the Italian population of the peninsula— the Samnites and the Latins. The former had long lived side by side with the Greek colonies in the south, and had long been striving to acquire that part of the coast where the Greeks had settled ; they coveted especially the wealth of

Campania. On the east, the powerful and civilized tribes which inhabited Apulia retained a firm hold on the coast and kept the Samnites out of their country. We know little about the organization of the Samnites; but we must suppose that they were divided into a number of separate mountain tribes, and that most of them were herdsmen with no knowledge of urban life. Some of these tribes were united in leagues, which from time to time grew to considerable strength. Their expansion was powerfully promoted by one of their institutions, which was called 'The Sacred Spring'. By it all the younger generation of a given clan were sent forth by their elders to march under the banner of their sacred totem— wolf, or calf, or ox, or raven—and to conquer for themselves new pastures and fresh fields.

In the course of the fifth and fourth centuries B. C. the Samnites learnt much from their Greek neighbours; they improved their weapons, adopted Greek methods of warfare, put the organization of their clans and leagues on a firmer footing, and began to build cities of their own and fortify them. Thus they became able to seize one after another of the most defenceless Greek colonies. Trade with the Greeks enriched them and developed their tastes : in their graves of the fourth century we find excellent painting and many objects of gold, silver, and bronze, with vases manufactured by themselves after Greek models. The nearer they lived to Campania, the more they came under the influence of Greek civilization. They were able at last to drive the Etruscans out of Campania, to seize most of the Campanian cities, and to make Capua their capital in 438 B. C. Thus there grew up and flourished a new and vigorous offshoot of Hellenism, which may be called Graeco-Samnite or Campanian; and this culture is well known to us from the earliest monuments and graves found in many of their cities.

In this way the Samnites were the people who set a limit to the southern expansion of the Etruscans. But they were not sufficiently consolidated to substitute an expansion of their own. Their forces were divided, and each separate clan was entirely occupied in obstinate conflict with the Greek cities on the coast. The largest of these cities proved too tough for them to the end : Tarentum and Naples never ceased, until they were absorbed by Rome, to be strong and flourishing centres of Greek life and politics. The Samnites found another formidable obstacle in the Greek tyrants in Sicily, especially the rulers of Syracuse, who were always eager to extend their influence over the Greek settlements in Italy and to support them in their struggle against the Samnites.

The other battering-ram which smashed the might of Etruria was Latium. In this district alone the Italians still had access to the sea : Tarracina, Antium, and the Tiber mouth still belonged to the Latins. Their position there was not disputed either by Greeks or Etruscans : their only rivals were the Volscians, a mountain tribe occupying the spurs of the Apennines which divide Latium from Campania ; and the struggle between the two was fierce and continuous. Possession of the sea determined the future destiny of Latium, and the fact that the Latins were never cut off from the coast must be explained by the operation of two causes.

In the first place, Latium was not specially attractive to the Etruscans and Greeks from the commercial point of view. The plain that bounds the lower Tiber on the south was a marshy valley intersected by steep ravines which made communication difficult. South of this plain runs a rather narrow strip of hilly country, more suitable for corn, vines, and stock-raising, but very limited in extent. Above this strip rise forbidding mountains, inhabited by the Volscians, Aequi, and Sabines, who fed their flocks there and were little better than robbers. It cost the dwellers on the Alban and Sabine hills long and arduous efforts to conquer the Latian plain for the plough : we can still see the network of sub-terranean drains which made agriculture feasible there. It is very possible that these drainage-works were due to the influence of the Etruscans, who had learnt all about drainage and irrigation in their ancient home in Asia Minor. The second cause for the independence of Latium and its control of the coast must be found in the rivalry between Greeks and Etruscans, which turned Latium into something like a buffer-state between two contending spheres of influence.

This independence and this connexion with the sea, kept up for a number of centuries, were of immense importance for the development of Latium and the Latin race. The current of civilization, flowing in from Greece, Etruria, and Carthage, helped to raise the level of economic and social life. At the same time, the constant danger of attack from three

14

if not four quarters taught the people to regard themselves as a single unit, bound by ties of blood and religion. And lastly, their arduous struggle with the treacherous soil of the plain tempered the spirit of those early settlers and husband-men, and attached them strongly to the soil which had been mastered by their own unremitting efforts.

There is no doubt that the first settlements and first political associations were formed on the hills of Latium, not on the plains. The cities that rose there were rich and pros-perous, when life on the plains was only beginning its develop-ment. On the hills were laid the foundations of those institutions which we find later in Rome. It is highly probable that the site of Rome, defended by ravines and the river below, was occupied originally by shepherds, immigrants from Latium and from the Sabine hills. It is further quite credible that two such settlements were made—one by Latins on the Palatine hill, and the other by Sabines on the Quirinal. Both these heights were defended—the former on all four sides, the latter on three—by deep ravines with steep slopes. Local tradition preserved the belief that the Palatine, or, in other words, primitive Rome, was a colony from two Latin towns in the vicinity—Alba and Lavinium. This spot was chosen, we must suppose, because it commanded the only point on the lower Tiber that offered facilities for crossing from the left bank to the right, from Latin soil to Etruscan: opposite the Palatine there is a fairly large island in the Tiber, which made it easy to throw a wooden bridge across the stream.

We do not know when and how these Latin and Sabine colonies on the banks of the Tiber were converted into a strong and united community. The accounts which we find in the ancient historians were undoubtedly pieced together from various sources, all equally untrustworthy. Most of these accounts were borrowed from Greek historians, who endea-voured, as has been said already, to connect the history of Rome with that of Greece, and especially with the Trojan war. We cannot tell how far this literary material was supplemented by local half-mythical tradition, or to what extent these traditions embody actual fact. The main tradi-tion accepted by the Roman historians amounts to this—that Rome owed its origin to Aeneas, an immigrant from Troy, and that Romulus and Remus, his grandsons or remote descen-

15

dants, were the founders of the city. From the former of these brothers were descended, in one way or another, the seven kings of Rome, who ruled until the establishment of the Republic. Tradition assigned the origin of the Republic to 508 B. C. Tradition, it is instructive to note, insists also upon the fact that some kings of ancient Rome were of Sabine origin, and that the Sabine element was prominent in the life of the city. This view is confirmed by a number of Sabine ceremonies practised in Roman religion, and perhaps supports the belief that a new era in Roman history began when Latins and Sabines combined to form a single community on the banks of the Tiber. Various dates were assigned by later historians for the foundation of the city—814 B. C., 753, 751, 748, and 729. We do not know whether they relied upon any documentary evidence for fixing the date, or whether it was reached by artificial calculations and intended to create the impression that Rome was as ancient as her rival, Carthage, and the majority of Greek cities in Italy. It is, however, of interest to note that the eighth and seventh centuries B. C. were a time of great prosperity for many cities of Latium—Praeneste, for example.

Our knowledge is very imperfect concerning the history of Rome in the eighth and seventh centuries B. C., and even in the first half of the sixth. The whole period is a region of guess-work and is differently represented by different historians of our time. From the fragmentary and untrustworthy evidence at our disposal, we may suppose that during this period Rome not only became by degrees a powerful community in the Latian plains, but also increased her territory at the expense of her neighbours who lived on the hills. This collision of Rome with her neighbours assumed a legendary form, which described her warfare against Alba Longa—the principal city of Latium and perhaps the mother-city of Rome—and destruction of her rival. This victory in its turn helped to consolidate the union under Rome of the Latian plain, and to strengthen the military and religious position of the king who led the Roman forces to battle against their neighbours.

We know as little about the constitution of ancient Rome as about her political activities. But there is no doubt about one point—that she was ruled in early times by kings. For this there are two pieces of evidence. First, at Rome during the historical period, as at Athens, one of the priests bore the name of king (*rex sacrorum*) ; and secondly, whenever it happened that the city had no elective magistrates in office, an official called *interrex* had to hold elections of new magistrates and to carry on the government. Another fact is equally well established—that the city population was divided into religious and military groups called *curiae*, which included all the inhabitants with the exception of slaves. It is possible that this primitive classification was artificial, like the division into *phratriae* and *phylae* in Greece, and was intended mainly to meet military objects. It is also possible that the number of *curiae* increased in proportion to the growth of the Latin city on the Palatine. The division into *curiae* was preserved in later times, when they were thirty in number, each with a meeting-place, representative members, and religious rites of its own. The *curiae* retained also some political functions : it was their business, by means of a special law (*lex curiata de imperio*), to invest a magistrate with his executive power.

We must suppose that from time immemorial the Senate also existed at Rome, as a council of elders to advise the king. Its members were representatives of the richest and noblest families (*gentes*). It is probable that these persons were commonly called ' fathers' (*patres*), and their descendants ' patricians'. From a very early date the patricians enjoyed a number of privileges, among the most important being the right of acting as intermediaries between the king and the gods: the priestly colleges remained exclusively patrician till late times. The most prominent of the priests were the *flamines*, or ' burners of offerings', each of whom supervised the worship of a particular god ; the augurs, who foretold the future from the flight of birds ; the *salii*, or dancers, who propitiated the god Mars by sacred dances in armour ; and the *luperci*, or wolf-brotherhood, who ran round the *pomerium*, or sacred boundary of the city, and thus drove away evil spirits and assured fertility to the women and flocks of the community. But the *pontifices*—the origin of the term is unknown—were the highest of the king's coadjutors in religious affairs : they drew up the religious calendar of the community, advised the king on matters of ritual, and were the guardians of *fas* and *ius*, the religious and civil law.

The army consisted of the entire population, of the whole

I. ALTAR FROM OSTIA

1. One side of an altar found at Ostia. The bas-relief represents the twins, Romulus and Remus, with the she-wolf. To the right is a personification of the river Tiber, to the left the Palatine Hill with various animals; on the top is the God of the Hill. In the background are two shepherds running and looking toward the Tiber, where they have just discovered the twins. On the other side, not here reproduced, is the holy wedding of Mars and Venus. This altar, according to the inscription, was dedicated to the God Silvanus on the 1st of October, A.D. 124, by a freedman P. Aelius Syneros and his sons. Museo delle Terme, Rome.

PLATE II

2. CAILE VIPINAS FREED BY MACSTRNA

2, 3. Part of the mural decoration of a grave excavated in 1857 near Vulci in Etruria. The fresco represents an episode of the early half-mythical history of Vulci and Rome, according to Etruscan tradition which was not unknown to the later Roman historians (e.g. to the Emperor Claudius). The episode represented in the fresco deals with the exploits and misfortunes of Cneve Tarchu Rumach (Gn. Tarquinius Romanus, the names are written near the figures) and Caile Vipinas and his companions, among them Macstrna and Aule Vipinas. It appears that Tarchu had succeeded in capturing Caile Vipinas. When Tarchu and his companions were asleep, Macstrna and Aule Vipinas with their retinue broke into the camp of Tarchu, killed him and his companions, and freed Caile Vipinas. The first group to the left represents Caile Vipinas freed by Macstrna—the last (our fig. 3), Tarchu killed by Marce Camitlnas. The three other groups show the companions of Tarchu killed by those of Vipinas. There is no doubt that Gn. Tarquinius belongs to the family of the Tarquinii who ruled in the 6th cent. B.C. at Rome and in the Latin cities. He may be identical with the first Tarquinius—the so-called Tarquinius Priscus. Macstrna was identified by the Emperor Claudius with Servius Tullius, the successor of Tarquinius Priscus. The fresco shows that the Etruscans had an historical tradition which was formed and fully developed as early as the 5th cent. B.C. Late 5th cent. or early 4th cent. B.C. Etruria, Vulci.

3. TARCHU KILLED BY MARCE CAMITLNAS

PLATE II

Roman people (*populus Romanus et Quirites*—the meaning of the last word is disputed—or *populus Romanus Quiritium*). The patricians acted as cavalry (*celeres*) on a campaign, or perhaps drove in chariots. As a matter of course, the kings were commanders-in-chief, and also supreme as judges and priests. We do not know whether their power was hereditary or held for life. They communicated their decrees to the people at specially summoned meetings (*comitia*).

About social and economic institutions we know little. In later Rome the life of the community is based upon the family (*familia*), in which the power of the father is absolute, and which includes not only the wife and children but also dependants—the *clientes* or 'listeners' and the slaves. It must, however, be remembered that, together with the patriarchal system which prevailed at Rome in historical times, considerable traces survived of another system, called ' matriarchal ', in which the mother is regarded as more important than the father. The wealth of the family consisted mainly of cattle (*pecus*), and for this reason money was called *pecunia*. In Roman primitive religion, however, the gods who protect agriculture and the evil spirits who injure it are as important as the corresponding gods and spirits who control cattle-breeding ; and this shows that agriculture early became the mainstay of economic life at Rome.

The rapid growth of Rome was due to two causes—proximity to Etruria and access to the mouth of the Tiber. The second of these advantages soon made her a centre of exchange, where goods came down by water and came up in Greek and Phoenician ships. But thus she became a competitor of the adjacent Etruscan cities, and Etruria was forced to think seriously of conquering Latium. (It is worthy of remark that the Etruscans penetrated into Campania at the same time.) It is quite certain that a considerable part of Latium was occupied by the Etruscans in the sixth century. It is possible that they established themselves in some of the cities, such as Praeneste and Tusculum, even earlier. One centre of Etruscan predominance in Latium was certainly Rome, where the powerful half-Etruscan dynasty of the Tarquins ruled for some time. As elsewhere, so at Rome the Etruscans formed a dominating caste, from which the native population was excluded except the aristocracy who were rich in land

and flocks.] It is unlikely, however, that they were able to master the whole of Latium, and they were certainly unable to force their culture upon the Latin inhabitants of Rome. It may be inferred that the Latin nation had by this time a special culture of their own and, perhaps, a system of writing of their own—both borrowed from the Greeks. But Etruscan domination was beneficial to Rome : she ceased to be a settlement of armed herdsmen, husbandmen, and traders, and became a city like the Etruscan and Latin cities, her neighbours ; she surrounded herself with a rampart, and extended and consolidated her commercial relations, especially with Carthage. As the chief centre of Etruscan predominance in Latium, Rome now for the first time aspired to be the controlling power not only over the plain of Latium but over the whole country.

It must be supposed that some changes took place in the constitution during the period of Etruscan superiority : the aristocracy was strengthened and made more exclusive ; it became richer, and part of the population became economically dependent on the great families. To Etruria, apparently, was due the very name of the city—*Roma* being derived from the Etruscan *ruma*—and also the division of the community into three 'gentile' tribes with Etruscan names—Tities, Ramnes, and Luceres ; and the *curiae* became at the same time subdivisions of the tribes. Under Etruscan influence the king's power also was more precisely defined. It consisted of the *imperium*, or supreme civil and military authority, based on the king's right to ascertain by divination (*auspicium*) the will of the gods.] The symbol of this absolute authority, which gave the king power of life and death, was a two-headed axe enclosed in a bundle (*fascis*) of rods.] The king was always preceded by six or twelve of these axes, carried by special attendants called 'lictors'. This regal ceremonial was introduced by the Etruscans from Asia Minor, where the axe (*labrys*) had been from time immemorial the symbol of the supreme deity. To the same time, probably, must be referred the exclusive right of the aristocracy to serve in the army. It was their interest to admit to the army as few persons as possible who were not included in the aristocratic tribes.

It can hardly be said that Etruscan supremacy at Rome was put down by force, that they were expelled from Latium and that war followed. Even our tradition only speaks of an internal revolution at Rome, in which the local aristocracy overthrew the power of the kings. Our tradition reckons Tarquin as the last Etruscan king of Rome, and we have no reason for doubting the statement. The overthrow of Tarquin by the Etruscan and Latin nobles has nothing surprising in it ; such events were probably common enough in Etruscan cities. The statement that the nobles had afterwards to carry on war, and unsuccessful war, against one of their Etruscan neighbours is quite probable. It is quite credible that a second conquest of Latium was averted by the intervention of Cumae in Campania on the side of Latium.

Thus, from the end of the sixth century Rome lived under a constitution framed during the Etruscan supremacy, and the ruling class was the local aristocracy, Etruscans and Romans, some hundreds of families, consisting of large land-owners, traders, and stock-raisers. This aristocracy was neither purely Etruscan nor purely Roman. Whatever their origin, however, they spoke and wrote Latin and felt themselves more closely connected with the Latin cities than with the Etruscan. If this was the case with the nobles, there is no doubt that the general population was purely Latin, both in the territory of Rome and in the petty settlements and villages of the Latin plain, which Rome had swallowed up before, and still more after, the domination of the Etruscans.

The overthrow of the Etruscan dynasty made no radical change either in the constitution of Rome, or in her commercial relations, or in her influence upon the neighbouring tribes. Even under the last Etruscan kings, the power of the Tarquins might be regarded as the power of a single strong and wealthy Etruscan family, whose members ruled different Latin cities, while the eldest of the family ruled Rome. The constitution remained approximately the same after the expulsion of the dynasty, which was perhaps partly due to the unwillingness of the Latin section of the Roman nobility to give precedence to the Etruscan. We know at least that not long after the expulsion of the Tarquins another distinguished family, that of the Fabii, ruled continuously at Rome for seven years, from 485 to 479 B. C. ; and later the chief magistrates were chosen almost exclusively from a very limited group of great 'princely' families. With regard to the commercial connexions of Rome, it should be noted that immediately after the overthrow of the Tarquins Rome made a commercial treaty with Carthage, in which she stands forth as the most important city of Latium. The connexion with Carthage was inherited from the Etruscans. But the general drift of her foreign policy was now different : her relations with her Etruscan neighbours were strained, and she devoted herself to developing her influence in Latium. Tradition testifies to the formation of a league, political as well as religious, between seven Latin cities, as early as the time of Etruscan domination. Rome was not a member of that league ; and her subsequent adhesion to it is a clear proof of the steady consolidation of strength, to enable Latium to cope with her neighbours. The systematic colonization of lands taken from those neighbours served to spread the limits of the league.

This course of events in Latium finally arrested the south-ward movement of the Etruscans. They lost hold of Campania as soon as Latium started an independent foreign policy, and all its considerable cities, Rome included, ceased to be members of the Etruscan league. It is probable that what had happened at Rome was happening in other out-lying parts of the Etruscan nation. Connexion between the different parts of the league was relaxed, and in remote places the native inhabitants asserted themselves and ousted their Etruscan conquerors, as they had in Latium. Thus in the valley of the Po, for instance, at Bononia (the modern Bologna), and in Umbria, the local element now came to the front. This would account for the successful invasion of the north by the Celts or Gauls, the last immigrants of Indo-European stock. It is certain that the Celts appeared in Italy not later than the fifth century B. C. ; and they occupied by degrees almost all the Po valley, except the country of the Veneti and a considerable part of Umbria. Their appearance on the scene confined the political operations of Etruria in Italy to very modest dimensions : she was cut off from the south by the Latins and from the north by the Gauls ; and it was likely that both these nations would before long proceed to attack her.

III

ROME IN THE FIFTH AND EARLY FOURTH CENTURY B. C.

THE expulsion of the Etruscan dynasty, which our tradition refers to the very end of the sixth century, did not, as I have said already, produce any radical changes in the constitution of the city. Rome was still a strong, mainly military, power, with an aristocracy ruling over a population which was chiefly agricultural. Etruscan domination had done her service: she had become larger, stronger, and more civilized, and her life grew more varied. The city of Rome, the centre of the state, had gained great commercial importance. Hence there were greater changes in social and economic relations than in the constitution. The one important constitutional change was this—that the victorious aristocracy, instead of choosing a new king, put in his place two elected leaders—praetors or consuls—each of whom was elected to hold office for one year and exercised complete authority over civil, military, and religious affairs. Further, in case of necessity, the kingly power might be temporarily renewed in the person of a dictator, whose term of office, however, was limited to six months. In like manner the Senate and popular assembly acquired greater importance. The assembly, which used to meet merely to register the king's edicts, now voted ' Aye ' or ' No ' to questions submitted to them by the consuls: Should there be war or peace ? should one of the fully qualified citizens be punished with death ? should any new citizens be admitted ? should the persons recommended by the annual magistrates as their successors be accepted or rejected ?

In social life the chief novelty was the growth of the *plebs* or class of plebeians. The term is purely political ; but the political importance of the *plebs* was certainly a consequence of gradual changes in social and economic conditions. *Plebs* means ' multitude ' ; and the term denotes the multitude of citizens who did not belong to the group of patrician families — citizens, in fact, of Rome, but citizens of an inferior kind.

24

The *plebs* included the clients also, though the clients were by no means the whole of the *plebs*. The ranks of the *plebs* consisted from early times of those persons whom the Roman nobles could not convert into clients of their own; these belonged to the ancient free inhabitants of the city and were real Roman *Quirites*. We do not know whether many were able to escape social and economic dependence, especially during the period of Etruscan supremacy; but there is no ground at all for disputing the fact that even then there were free plebeians at Rome. By degrees the number of these free citizens, belonging neither to the nobility nor to the class of clients, became larger; and this increase was probably due to three main causes. The commercial importance of Rome attracted settlers from other parts of Italy, especially Latium, just as the class of *metoeci* was created by a similar development at Athens. Further, industry was stimulated by the political growth of Rome. The government needed skilled workmen for the manufacture of weapons, and therefore summoned good carpenters and blacksmiths to the city, forming them into three guilds (*collegia*) and conferring various privileges upon them. And lastly, as parts of Latium were steadily annexed either by conquest or agreement, the local aristocracy was either destroyed or admitted by the patricians to their own body; but the smallholders, clients of the local aristocracy, often became free peasants after the annexation. The *plebs*, composed of these elements, was uninfluenced by the half-Etruscan culture of the Roman nobles, and more sensitive to the Greek influences that came from south Italy.

Such was the constitution of Rome after the expulsion of the kings, at the beginning of the fifth century. The efforts of the ruling class were aimed at retaining for Rome her predominance over Latium. Her relations to her neighbours were full of peril. The Etruscan cities looked with displeasure on the growing commercial importance which had brought about a treaty of agreement with Carthage. Nearer home her prospects were brighter; for the Latins felt that, without the co-operation of Roman power, it would be difficult for them to meet either the constant pressure of the Volsci and Aequi from the mountains or the standing danger of a new Etruscan conquest. Hence, in view of their common interests, it was natural that the alliance of all Latin communities should be consolidated at this time; and Rome again began,

LATIN WARRIORS AND AN ETRUSCAN PEASANT

1. IVORY PLAQUES FROM PRAENESTE

1. Ivory plaques, found in a grave at Praeneste (Palestrina) in Latium. The plaques, which were originally painted, belonged to the adornment of a wooden box. I give a selection of six plaques. On the two larger two Latin warriors fully armed are represented. The arms and weapons are Greek but coincide almost in all details with the typical Roman military equipment. On the smaller plaques are seen from left to right: Hercules r. standing near a fountain with his left foot on an amphora, a warrior, a woman with a flower (Venus?), and another warrior. 3rd cent. B.C. Museo Papa Giulio, Rome.

2. Group of Etruscan votive bronze figurines, found near Arezzo in Etruria. The group (apart from the figure of Minerva behind the peasant, which is a modern addition, and not part of the original) represents an Etruscan peasant ploughing his own or his master's field. He wears a hat, a chiton, and a hide, perhaps also boots. The plough consists of a wooden share-beam of one piece of wood (*buris*), a metal share (*vomer*), and a wooden handle (*stiva*). A similar plough (4th–3rd cent. B.C.) has been found near Telamone. The same plough is still used by the peasants in many remote corners of Italy. 6th cent. B.C. Museo Papa Giulio, Rome.

PLATE III

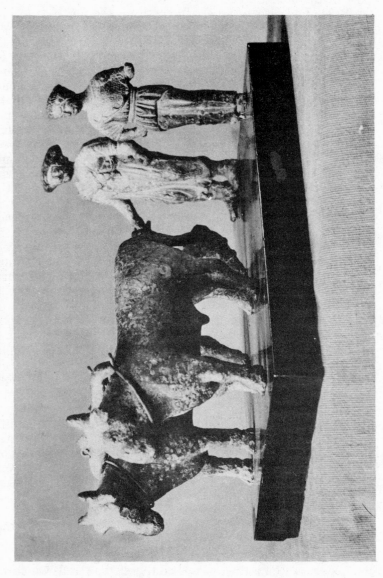

2. ETRUSCAN PEASANT PLOUGHING

PLATE III

as in the time of Etruscan predominance, to play a leading part in this federation.

Rome had also to repel attacks from the north, from the Sabine hills; and in this she was generally successful. We hear that in 449 B. C. the Sabines suffered a crushing defeat and a considerable part of their territory was annexed by Rome. At the same time or, perhaps, earlier, the rich and noble Sabine family of the Claudii together with their clients transferred themselves to Rome and were admitted into the patrician order. Similar migrations from many Latin cities were common enough and naturally increased the importance and power of the patricians at Rome. But the main business at this time was the struggle against more powerful neighbours —the Etruscan city of Veii, and the Volsci and Aequi, who attacked the Latin communities from the mountains. Of the two the Volsci were the more dangerous, as their object was to seize the coast and cut off Latium from the sea. Hence Rome fought fiercely against the Volsci for possession of the coast town of Antium. Her efforts and those of Latium were successful: the Aequi were driven back into the mountains, and a number of Roman colonies—military and agricultural settlements—were founded in the Volscian country. A notable Roman success was the victory over Veii, which was followed by the complete destruction of that city and the annexation of its territory. The question was, which of the two cities should control both banks of the Tiber and its mouth. Rome, if defeated, would have suffered the fate of Veii.

Almost immediately after this success a new and serious danger began to threaten Rome. The Gauls, as was said above, began in the fifth century to seize province after province in northern Italy and drive out the Etruscan occupants. About 400 B. C. they invaded Etruria and plundered the country; they attempted to take the cities but were powerless against fortified towns defended by stone walls. Nevertheless they carried their raids farther and farther south; and in the course of one such raid they reached the bank of the Tiber and the territory of Rome. The date is disputed, about 390 B. C.; and this is the first incident in the external history of Rome which was known to Greeks then living and can be assigned with probability to a definite year. It is unlikely that Rome then possessed those stone walls which are still partly visible and which bear the name of the legendary king, Servius Tullius; if they had existed, the Gauls would have failed in their assault. It is probable that all the city, except the Capitol which contained the chief temple, was defended merely by earthen ramparts. The Gauls defeated the Roman and Latin army on the banks of the Allia, took and burnt the city, and requisitioned a large sum of money.

The consequences of this disaster were of infinite importance to Rome. It revealed that an army, consisting almost entirely of patricians alone, could not cope with the military needs of the time, and that the city must be made into an armed fortress with strong walls of stone. Further, the Gallic peril forced Latium into closer union round Rome, since no other power was strong enough to check further raids. The Gallic wars had a notable influence, especially on the internal development of Rome in politics and economics. As Rome grew richer and more powerful in the course of the fifth century, her hereditary aristocratic constitution became more and more unstable. The plebeians, who were free from the burden of military service, rose in importance. In the constant wars of the fifth century, the nobles were forced more than once to seek assistance from the plebeians and supplement the ranks of their own army with these recruits. It is possible that the military system which bears the name of Servius Tullius, and was definitely introduced after the Gallic wars, came into existence as early as this time; more is said of it below. As the Roman territory expanded, the number of free non-patrician landowners increased; for plebeians who took part in successful campaigns received grants out of the conquered land; and many clients of the ruling families were perhaps rewarded in the same way for military service, and so became economically independent. There grew up by degrees among the plebeians a community of interest and a desire for organization. They found representatives, who were perhaps originally commanders of the plebeian troops, recruited according to territorial divisions, which were called ' tribes ', but must not be confused with the three ' gentile ' patrician tribes. Hence these representatives were called ' tribunes '; and they came to be champions of all plebeians. Four tribunes probably were originally elected annually; they represented the four tribes into which the city of Rome was divided; later their number was increased to ten. Their first victory in the struggle of classes was won when they forced the Senate and patricians to draw up and publish a code of civil law—the Twelve Tables—about 450 B. C. ; and next the law of Canuleius (about 445 B. C.) repealed the ban, half-political and half-religious, which forbade marriages between patricians and plebeians. And lastly the place of the two consuls was taken for a time by six military tribunes, some of whom were elected from among the plebeians.

The Gallic invasion made it clear that radical reforms must be made in military organization, and that a national army must be created to take the place, once for all, of the purely patrician force which had been sufficient for the kings and the infant republic. Tradition connects this creation of a citizen army, and also the erection of the first stone walls with the name of the king, Servius Tullius. According to this new system, the plebeians were included in the body of fully qualified Roman citizens, and ceased to be citizens of an inferior kind. On the other hand, all these new citizens, if they owned land within the limits of the Roman state, were bound, between the ages of seventeen and sixty-five, to answer the summons of the consul and join the ranks of the citizen army, which was generally divided into four regiments called *legiones.* The summons itself was originally called *classis* ; but the meaning of the word gradually changed, becoming equivalent to 'division', and then to 'class' in our sense of the word. The first 'summons' or class contained those citizens who were rich enough to buy a complete suit of metal armour ; and the richest among these appeared at the summons with two horses and formed divisions of heavy cavalry. The poorer citizens of the four remaining classes appeared in less complete and less costly accoutrements. Craftsmen formed separate divisions and were assigned to the second class. Others who possessed no land were excluded from the classes ; as *proletarii* these were distinguished from the *assidui* or 'settled men' ; but they also were obliged to serve in the train of the army.

The popular assembly consisted of all citizens who served in the army. It was divided into 193 centuries (*centuriae*) ; it elected the consuls, passed laws, decided questions of war or peace, and acquitted or condemned citizens tried on capital charges. The new constitution greatly increased the military strength of Rome ; but its introduction forced the old patrician families to resign their political supremacy, and thus opened up to the plebeians great opportunities for acquiring allotments of land, and so for extending and strengthening the basis of their new organization. It is therefore highly probable that tradition is correct in fixing the date of laws passed by Licinius and Sextius, tribunes of the *plebs*, at 367–366 B.C. After these laws newly conquered lands were distributed mainly among the plebeians, and the now restored consulship was thrown open to the same class: the community could elect to the consulship a plebeian as well as a patrician. At about the same time all Roman citizens gained the right, known as *ius provocationis*, to appeal to the popular assembly against a sentence of death pronounced by the consuls. The plebeian tribunes also began to take a higher position : their persons were recognized as inviolable, and they extended their right of defending plebeians against the arbitrary proceedings of the consuls ; the power of veto, which was their weapon in these contests, was recognized as a part of the Roman constitution, and the tribunes did not let it rust.

All these victories of the plebeians, though they led to the steady democratization of the Roman state, were not gained, as in most Greek states, by acute class-warfare accompanied by bloody but barren revolutions. At Rome, as at Athens in the sixth and fifth centuries, they were the result of a gradual process and of successive agreements between patricians and plebeians. Tradition tells of only one weapon regularly used by the plebeians : this was a kind of ' strike ', by which they refused to take their share in the defence of the country and threatened to secede from the community. But it is doubtful whether they had recourse even to this expedient before the beginning of the third century B.C.

It is certain that the new organization of the citizen-body infused fresh strength into the community. The common interest now came home to the heart of each citizen : he felt himself responsible for the state and its prosperity. At the same time the purely military organization of the state, together with the extensive and unlimited power of the consuls during a campaign and outside the bounds of the city, taught the people strict military discipline and obedience to the commands of their leaders. The functions of the tribunes were confined to the city : their veto was powerless against the magistrates during military operations, nor could the right of appeal be exercised at such times. The results of the new organization soon became apparent when Rome and Latium, after a victorious struggle with the Volsci and Aequi, were forced in the second half of the fourth century to face other and more formidable enemies.

Of Roman civilization from the beginning of the sixth century to the middle of the fourth we know very little. Excavation in Rome has been unproductive, much more so than in some Latin and Etrusco-Latin cities, such as Praeneste and Fidenae, where discoveries have enabled us to trace the growing influence of Greek culture upon the Latins. About religion we know more. The primitive religion of the Latins and of Rome in particular was very like the primitive religion of other Indo-European stocks which gave up the pastoral life for agriculture. An official calendar of festivals, which was drawn up about the time when Rome was founded, has been preserved and is the chief source of our knowledge concerning the subject. These festivals are either purely agricultural or military. Prominent in this calendar is the cult of Jupiter, the great god of the sky and also the guardian of civilization and the state, and of Mars, who personifies the hostile powers of the uncultivated country near Rome, the mountains and forests and their perils. After the union with the Sabines on the Quirinal hill some Sabine gods make their appearance, for instance, Quirinus, the Sabine Mars. Roman notions of the deity are in general of a primitive type, and do not show the rich creative fancy of the Greeks. Their gods were abstract personifications of the powers friendly or hostile to man, less human and more remote than the Greek gods. Even in primitive times the government prescribed the ritual for the chief of these divine powers ; and worship, so controlled, became a merely formal ceremony, strictly and precisely defined.

The religion of the family was less formal. It was addressed to the *Genius* of the master and head of the household, in which was personified the creative power of the householder and the continuous life of the family. The *Manes*, or spirits of ancestors, also survive in the household and family ; and rites are necessary to propitiate them. The genius (called *Iuno*) of the mistress of the house must be worshipped as well as that of the master. Then there are the *Penates*, the spirits who guard the wealth of the family, its store-closet and barns ; and the *Lares* who watch over the fields and paths ; and lastly, the domestic hearth is an object of worship. The state also has a hearth, and Vesta, the presiding genius of that hearth, has rites paid to her; and so has Janus, the two-faced god, who guards the gates which lead from the civilized life of the citizen to the region of foes.

This religion was modified, as time went on, by various causes—the development of the city-state, the formation of a powerful plebeian class consisting chiefly of Latin immigrants, and the strong influence of the Etruscans over the political and economic development of Rome. A twofold aspect is henceforth noticeable in Roman religion. The plebeian immigrants from the Hellenized cities of Latium develop trade and industry and bring with them a number of cults, some of them Greek but adopted by the Latins, and others Latin but modified by the Greeks. All the new gods have to do with trade and industry, and temples are built for them all either close to the Tiber or on the Aventine, the plebeian hill. The earliest of these deities is Hercules or Heracles, who watches over trade and business life; his altar is in the cattle-market (*forum boarium*); next comes Minerva, a Latin goddess, who borrows some traits from the ancient Athena of Greece, the protectress of craftsmen. But at the same time a religion grows up, peculiar to the patrician houses—the Etrusco-Latin families which predominated under the rule of the Etruscan kings. And so Rome, like other city-states of the ancient world, receives a religious centre and Acropolis of its own in the Capitol, which supports a temple sacred to the trinity of Jupiter Optimus Maximus, Juno, and Minerva. The temple was built in the Etruscan style, and the ritual was Etruscan in its external aspect; but the deities themselves were not Etruscan.

Jupiter Optimus Maximus was the Jupiter of all the Latins, while Juno and Minerva came to Rome from the Latin cities. The national character of this Capitoline trinity shows, in the first place, the predominantly Latin aspect of the aristocracy which ruled in Latin-Etruscan Rome, and also the ambition of this Rome to be the head of Latium, and to have within her walls the worship of the lord over all Latium, who became the supreme deity of Rome as a state. (It is not surprising that at the same time the cult of Diana, another deity connected with the Latin league, was established in the woods which cover the slopes of the Aventine.) This 'establishment' of a cult, under Etruscan influence but

33

in a purely Latin spirit, is highly characteristic. Still more so is the fact that the plebeian husbandmen, as a counterpoise to the trinity of the patricians, introduced a trinity of their own as early as the fifth century. In a temple on the Aventine they worshipped Ceres (the Greek Demeter) and the divine pair, Libera and Liber, and combined with these the cult of Dionysus or Iacchus, which carried all before it in southern Italy at that period. It is noticeable that the chief place in this plebeian trinity is occupied by a female deity ; and this may be due to that stratum of the indigenous population which blended with the Indo-European immigrants to form various branches of the Latin stock.

IV

ROME IN THE SECOND HALF OF THE FOURTH CENTURY AND BEGINNING OF THE THIRD

AFTER the first Gallic invasion Rome was able, thanks to the vigorous co-operation of the Latin communities, to check any further southward movement on the part of the Gauls. By degrees she extended her possessions in Etruria and settled accounts, as we have seen, with the Volsci and Aequi, her dangerous neighbours on the Latin hills. The Volscian country was finally annexed by Rome, and a number of military colonies were founded there, as also in Etruria. After these victories the territory of Rome and the Latin league extended to nearly 3,000 square miles of land which was mostly under cultivation. Within these limits Rome was the supreme and controlling power. From the fourth century B. c. her chief magistrates were the presidents of the Latin league. At the same time Rome came into direct political contact for the first time with the Samnites and Greeks, the two chief powers in the southern part of the peninsula. The Samnites were by this time masters of Campania, and formed the upper class of the population in the Campanian cities. Taking advantage of the weakness of the Greeks, who had refused to support the Syracusan Empire founded by Dionysius, they aimed at laying hands on those Greek seaports in the south, such as Naples and Tarentum, which still continued to play a conspicuous part. They strengthened their position also in Apulia. This being their object, their interest for a time coincided with the interest of Rome, for whom it was important to have peace beyond her southern frontier while she was fighting Gauls, Etruscans, and Volscians in the first half of the fourth century. This explains an alliance between Rome and a confederation of Samnite stocks ; but, unfortunately, we do not know exactly when this alliance was concluded or how long it lasted.

The alliance proved its importance at a crisis in Roman history, when Rome was forced to begin a contest against her neighbours and allies, the Latin cities. As has been pointed out already, the other members of the Latin league had been, from the fourth century, entirely dependent upon Rome in military and political affairs. So long as they were threatened by the Gauls on the north and the Volscians on the south, they submitted obediently to the military predominance of Rome ; but when both these dangers had passed away, they were anxious to secure larger rights and greater independence. This led to a serious war, in which the Latins were aided by the Volscians and Campanians, and which ended in the complete defeat of the Latins in 338 B. C. Most of the Latin cities were annexed to the Roman territory, and the Latin league ceased to exist. From this time onwards the chief Latin and Sabine cities, especially Praeneste and Tibur, were bound by separate agreements to Rome alone, and not to one another. Rome, however, showed great generosity in fixing her relations to her conquered allies. Latins at Rome enjoyed the same social and economic rights as Roman citizens and, in case they migrated and acquired a domicile within Roman territory, it was open to them to acquire even the citizenship itself.

After the Latin war Rome was the greatest military power in Italy, stronger and more consolidated than the moribund league of Etruscan cities, or the alliance of Samnite tribes, which was powerful enough but had no real political unity, not to speak of weaker combinations, such as independent Umbrian and Sabine tribes with their casual alliances. The Roman territory now amounted to 4,500 square miles with a population of at least half a million. Rome and Latium had long kept up relations with the Greek and half-Greek cities of Campania, especially with Capua and Naples. Tarentum, when pressed by the Samnites, had summoned to their aid Alexander, king of Epirus, and the king at one time had nearly succeeded in uniting south Italy under his banner ; but he was betrayed at a critical moment by Tarentum and defeated by the Samnites. This event and the Samnite conquest of Campania made the position of Naples very difficult : she also was threatened by the Samnite grip, and saw no means of deliverance except alliance with Rome. This alliance must involve Rome in war against the Samnites ; but on the other hand it held out a prospect of predominance over rich Campania and of establishing a solid and permanent connexion with the Greek world. She reckoned also on considerable help in the coming struggle from the cities of Hellenized Samnites in Campania ; and a majority of these, headed by the rich and powerful Capua, actually concluded an alliance with Rome in 334 B.C. The aristocracy in these cities, though Samnites, were Hellenized ; and they saw in the alliance with Rome a prop for their own privileged position, which they were likely to lose if the Campanian cities were seized by fresh immigrants from Samnium. The conquerors would undoubtedly usurp the position now held by their countrymen, the original conquerors of Campania. Lastly, Rome made sure of the neutrality of Carthage by renewing in 348 B.C. the commercial and military treaty formerly concluded between them.

The first Samnite war began in 325 B.C. and originally took the form of a contest for political predominance in Campania. It was a long and stubborn war. Taking advantage of Rome's difficult situation, the Etruscans strove to recover their political position in north Italy. This war on two fronts lasted more than twenty years—to 304 B.C. Though the Samnites again and again defeated strong Roman armies, yet at last, by the persistence of Rome and the solidity of her league with the Latin cities, they were forced to make peace on terms very favourable to Rome. They had to renounce their claims on Campania, and the Etruscans had to surrender some more cities on their southern frontier. But the peace of 304 B.C. could not last. The strength of the Samnites was still unbroken ; and also all the independent tribes and cities in Italy realized by this time that it was a question of their gradual absorption by the Roman alliance ; and they were prepared, all together and sword in hand, to defend their freedom. Rome had clearly unmasked her policy towards those of her neighbours who were still free, when she annexed the territory of the Aequi and a considerable part of the upper Tiber. In 298 B.C. a strong coalition of Italian peoples was formed against Rome, including not only the Samnites and Etruscans but also the Gauls of north Italy. To this coalition Rome offered decisive battle at Sentinum in Umbria (295 B.C.) and utterly defeated the Gauls. She then proceeded to deal methodically with the separate members of the coalition. In 280 B.C. she was able to force almost all the Samnite tribes and all the Etruscan cities to enter into an alliance with her and to forfeit considerable parts of their territory, which were declared to be the property of the Roman people. The Sabines were finally incorporated in the Roman state, and were made citizens, without the right of voting in the popular assembly. The Gauls were driven back into the Po valley after a series of bloody battles.

The conditions under which the Samnites and Etruscans were included in the Roman alliance were approximately the same as those under which the Latins had been incorporated. With each tribe and city Rome concluded a separate agreement, not permitting any of them to enter into other alliances or agreements of any kind. The tribes and cities of Samnium and Etruria kept their domestic self-government but were forced to submit to the political control of Rome. They still lived and governed themselves by their own laws and customs ; they had their own magistrates and priests, and their own territory ; but their troops were entirely at the disposition of the Roman magistrates and, in case of war, formed part of the Roman army under the supreme command of the Roman consuls or their substitutes, the praetors. These new allies were less favoured than the Latins had been. Though they did have the right of transacting business (*commercium*) in Rome, and these transactions were protected by law, they hardly possessed the right of acquiring landed property in Roman territory ; not all of them had the *conubium*, i.e. the right of intermarrying with Romans ; even by settling in Rome they could not acquire the citizenship without special permission from the popular assembly.

In order to secure her predominance in Italy, Rome made use of the lands ceded by her rivals which had become the property of the Roman people (*ager publicus* or *ager Romanus*). These lands were now planted with Roman citizens and made over to them in full possession. As forming part of the city's territory, they were incorporated in the tribes into which the original territory was divided. Different methods of colonization were adopted in different places. At the most important points, where there were good harbours on the coast and where military roads crossed inside the country, fortresses were built and garrisoned with Roman citizens, and a considerable extent of public land was assigned to them for cultivation. These fortified places were called Roman colonies. There were also many fortified settlements known as Latin colonies, where the settlers were partly citizens and partly Latins. Lastly, large portions of the newly acquired territories were either leased or given outright to citizens who settled down there on detached farms. These immigrants from Rome united in groups for common worship of the Roman gods and for exchange of the produce which they raised. Their meeting-places, called *conciliabula* or *fora* (markets), were soon built over, artisans and traders settled there, and what had once been a market became a settlement of an urban type.

When the political supremacy of Rome spread to south Italy, the Greek cities there had to face the problem whether they should or should not submit to her. Some of them, Naples, for example, had no other course open to them but to submit and enter the Roman alliance. The Sicilian Greeks were powerless to help them. At one moment, indeed, it seemed that Sicily had again a prospect of union and strength, as in the time of Dionysius. Agathocles, citizen of Syracuse and a man of high ability, made himself tyrant of the city and began a successful campaign against the Carthaginians, in which he almost conquered Carthage and at least established his own power in eastern Sicily. Like Dionysius, he turned at once to south Italy and endeavoured to extend his influence there. He was able to annex Bruttium and part of Apulia to his Sicilian Empire ; but his death in 289 B. C. set a limit to his achievements and untied the hands of the Romans.

Tarentum was the controlling power in south-east Italy. This rich trading community possessed an extensive territory and kept up constant commercial relations with Greece, whom she supplied with grain and other commodities necessary for the subsistence of her population. In her struggle against the Samnite tribes on her borders and the Messapians of Apulia, Tarentum had repeatedly received help from the kingdom of Epirus, from Sicily, and from Sparta, whose kings and tyrants had landed many times in Italy and fought for Tarentum against her chief enemy—the Samnite tribes of Lucania. Thus Archidamus, king of Sparta, was there in 338 B. C., Alexander, king of Epirus (as has been mentioned already), in 331, Cleonymus of Sparta in 303, and Agathocles in 300.

At the end of the second Samnite war, the territory of the

Roman alliance came right up to the territory of the Messapians in Apulia and of the Samnite tribes in Bruttium and
Lucania—up to the last refuge of freedom in Italy and the
immediate neighbours of the Greek cities. These tribes saw
as clearly as the Greeks that their turn had come now and
that they must either submit to Rome or fight her. The
former course was chosen by Thurii, the latter by Tarentum.
In 281 B. C., in alliance with the Lucanians, Bruttians, and
Messapians, Tarentum began war against Rome. But the
allies, conscious of their military weakness, in 280 summoned to their aid Pyrrhus, king of Epirus, a skilful commander and ambitious statesman who played a conspicuous
part in the history of the Greek world after the death of
Alexander. Like so many of his contemporaries, the successors
of Alexander the Great, he dreamed of restoring the mighty
monarchy of Alexander ; and, in order to realize this object,
his first task was to seize Macedonia, which had passed from
hand to hand after the death of the conqueror. But the
strength of Epirus proved insufficient for this ambitious
project, and Pyrrhus suffered failure after failure in his Greek
policy.

Hence the proposal of Tarentum that he should undertake
the supreme command in the contest with the Romans was
readily accepted by him. He hoped to rally the Italian and
Sicilian Greeks under his banner and so to do in the West
what Alexander had done in the East—to create a powerful
Greek Empire that could master Rome and Carthage and
lead all the armed forces of the West to conquer the East.
But it was fated that this dream should never be realized.
Tarentum and the Italian Greeks were not strong enough to
inflict a decisive blow upon Rome. In spite of two successful
battles in 280 and 279 B. C., Pyrrhus was unable to establish
himself in Italy. His attempt to secure a base in Sicily
ended in failure also : he won victories against Carthage, but
the separatism of the Greek cities proved fatal to his plans.
In the end, after fighting and losing a third battle against
the Romans in 275 B. C., he was forced to abandon Italy and
leave Tarentum to her fate. Thus Rome had completed her
task of uniting Italy. The Lucanians and Bruttians alone
kept their freedom for a time : the rest of Samnium finally
submitted to Rome and was deprived of the best part of its
territory. The submission of the Gauls in north Italy was

now merely a question of time, though it called for a great expenditure of treasure and effort.

Rome had now become the largest and most compact state in the western world. The Roman alliance occupied approximately 50,000 square miles of Italy, from the Rubicon in the north to the Straits of Messina in the south, with a population of at least four millions. Only a fifth part, or perhaps a quarter, of this territory was inhabited by Roman citizens; but in questions of politics and war, the whole alliance formed a single unit, controlled by the people, the Senate, and the magistrates of Rome.

Her success in the struggle for political control over Italy Rome owed undoubtedly to the conduct of her public affairs being completely organized upon a sound basis. The citizen-body, constantly increasing in number and at the same time becoming more consolidated, was the foundation of this system. Not a little labour and effort was expended by Rome in order to extend this foundation of her power. Within the actual territory of the city the land was generally owned by smallholders; large estates were exceptional. These yeomen tilled their land themselves with the help of their family and a few slaves. The same form of landowner-ship was introduced on territory taken from the allies. The colonies, Roman and Latin, consisted of groups of small-holders; and the allotments granted to old and new citizens in different parts of Italy were also of moderate size. And so a very large majority of Roman citizens were yeomen who tilled their land with their own hands.

Nevertheless, the form of government in the Roman state was not democratic. Just as before, in the fifth century and beginning of the fourth, the direction of public affairs was restricted to a group of wealthy and ancient families, belong-ing almost exclusively to the old patrician nobility. Since the Licinian laws of 367 B. C. any citizen was eligible for the consulship, and a succession of later laws had opened the other offices to patricians and plebeians alike; but still the people persisted in electing their leaders from among a small group of families. When their time of office had expired, the ex-magistrates became members of the Senate.

This practice of the electors was chiefly due to the force of habit, and also to a general feeling that government required special experience and knowledge, which the ordinary

AN ELEPHANT OF PYRRHUS AND
SAMNITIC GLADIATORS

I. AN ELEPHANT OF PYRRHUS

1. Painted clay dish of Italian workmanship, found in south Italy. The inside is decorated with a figure of a war-elephant driven by a 'cornac' and carrying on his back a tower containing two soldiers in Hellenistic armour. The elephant is a female; her baby elephant is tied to her tail. Since the dish belongs to the early 3rd cent. B.C. there is no doubt that the picture represents one of the elephants which Pyrrhus, the king of Epirus, brought with him to Italy. Early 3rd cent. B.C. Museo Papa Giulio, Rome.

2. Part of the mural decoration of a Samnite grave at Capua. Two men are fighting. They wear short *tunicae*, round helmets, and metal greaves. Both have been several times wounded but keep on fighting. They are armed with spears and round shields. Probably Samnite warriors fighting as gladiators at funeral games. 3rd cent. B.C. Museo Campano, Capua.

PLATE IV

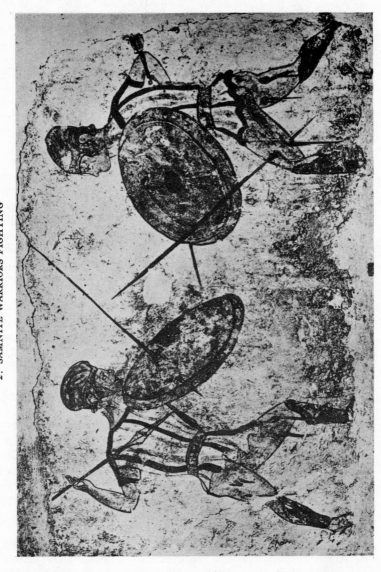

PLATE IV

citizen had not got, but which were the slow growth of centuries in the great families. Moreover, as in Greece, public service was not paid, so that only the wealthier citizens could undertake it. Lastly, it was of great importance that every influential family was surrounded by a group of persons connected with the family by traditional ties. Clients, when they became free citizens and owners of land, still kept up the religious and legal connexion with their former master. In the view of Roman religion this connexion was inviolable, whatever might be the economic relations between patron and client. The patron was bound as before to come forward in the law court and defend his client ; the client as before assisted his patron when the latter had to give his daughter in marriage, or to go forth on campaign, or on other occasions. The connexion was prized by both parties ; and in the popular assembly the client naturally voted for his patron or his patron's nominees and friends. As the great families grew in influence, so the number of their clients increased. The poorer citizens competed for the honour of being included among the clients of an influential and noble house ; for such a position assured them of support and assistance in the trials and troubles of life.

The same relationship existed among the plebeians also : they had their own aristocracy and their own patrons and clients. Influential plebeians who were elected tribunes kept up the connexion with their constituents, and continued to defend their interests even when they had gone out of office. When equal rights had been gained by the plebeians, this plebeian aristocracy exercised as much influence in the community as the patricians themselves, and, together with the patricians, formed the Roman aristocracy which governed the state. But particular families, which possessed a larger retinue of clients and whose connexion with other influential families was more extensive, towered above the rest. The more consuls, priests, and senators that this family produced, the more its clients increased in number and its political influence in extent. Hence we notice in the lists of Roman magistrates that the aristocracy in general is strongly represented, and a few influential families in particular recur again and again.

The number of these families was increased by degrees. The old nobility was not exclusive. While admitting to their ranks persons not of noble descent, the patricians, in order to preserve their influence, not only concluded political and family alliances with the most distinguished and richest plebeians, but also found room for illustrious citizens of Latin and Italian communities that had once been independent— the descendants of former kings and chief magistrates. Tusculum sent to Rome the famous families of the Fulvii, Mamilii, Coruncanii, and later the Porcii ; the Plautii came from Tibur and Praeneste, the Atilii from Campania, the Ogulnii from Etruria, and the Otacilii from Samnium. Together with the old princely houses of Rome—the Fabii, Aemilii, Cornelii, and Julii—and the most eminent plebeians, whose ranks they often joined, these formed the governing aristocracy.

Nor can the popular assembly be called a purely democratic institution. The supreme power in the state belonged to this body : they elected the magistrates and passed the laws ; they voted for war and peace, disposed of the revenue, and annulled or confirmed sentence of death against citizens. After the reform attributed to Servius (see p. 30) the method of voting was unlike the Athenian practice, by which each individual citizen recorded his vote and these votes were added up. The Roman citizens, as we have seen already, were divided into five classes according to the property they owned. Further, each class was divided into a fixed number of centuries. In voting, a majority of the votes in each separate century was reckoned as the vote of that century, and a majority of votes by centuries was decisive, not, as at Athens, a majority of votes recorded by individual members. But also the body of citizens was unevenly distributed among the centuries. The richest citizens, who formed the first class and were generally patricians, were divided into eighty centuries ; and there voted along with them eighteen centuries of horsemen, who also belonged to the first class. Since all the remaining classes were divided into ninety-five centuries, it follows that a majority of votes in the popular assembly belonged to the citizens of the first class, irrespective of their number. Again the centuries of the first class voted first, and in case they were unanimous, no further votes were taken. Lastly, the popular assembly could only meet when summoned by the magistrate ; there was no debate at the meeting, and the citizen had no right to put to the vote any proposal that had not the sanction of the magistrates and the Senate.

On the other hand the Roman constitution cannot be regarded as purely aristocratic. I have said already that the rank and file of the citizens, now divided into thirty-five tribes according to their place of domicile, had gained in the fifth and fourth centuries the right to elect tribunes as their representatives and to hold assemblies of their own, from which the patricians were excluded. The tribunes were the people's champions, were inviolable, and could use their veto to annul the decree of a magistrate. They had also power to convene an assembly of plebeians, to put before them for debate and decision measures concerning the whole state and not the plebeians alone, and to communicate these decisions (*plebiscita*) to the magistrates. By means of a political ' strike' in 287 B. C. the plebeians gained this further concession—that their decisions, like the decisions of the popular assembly voting by centuries, should have the force of law. Certain questions, such as declarations of war and peace, and the election of magistrates other than tribunes, were excluded from their competence ; but with these exceptions their legislative power was unlimited.

But the people did not wish to take advantage of the facilities thus opened up to them for democratizing the constitution. Content with the victory of 287 B. C. which secured to them equal rights with the patricians, they ceased to be an aggressive force in politics and left the government of the state to the new aristocracy of patricians and plebeians. They did this because the struggle between the orders was not a struggle to democratize the constitution but a struggle for definite social and economic rights. Two influential groups of families, one patrician and the other plebeian, carried on the struggle, each backed by its clients. When the plebeians were victorious, their leaders were not at all anxious to continue the fight ; and the rank and file, having gained a tolerable economic and social status, did not proceed to radical changes in the constitution by increasing the powers of the popular assembly at the expense of the Senate and the magistrates. Ideas of this kind had never entered their heads : they had fought only for equal rights with the patricians in social, economic, and political affairs.

The magistrates—whether as commanders of the army, presidents of the popular assembly and the Senate, judges, treasurers, or intermediaries between the state and the gods—

were the real rulers of the state. They were elected for one year by the citizen army voting by centuries. The two consuls were the chief magistrates. To each of them the people gave the *imperium*—full civil and military command. In case of disagreement between them, the decree of one consul could not be executed : the negative power of one colleague overruled the command of the other. As public affairs became more complex, the people elected ' minor ' magistrates, ranking below the consuls. These were—the praetors, to command the army and to act as judges ; the quaestors, to manage the finances ; and the aediles, to supervise the streets and buildings of the city. Of great importance in public life were special magistrates, who were elected, at irregular intervals but generally once in five years, to hold office for eighteen months ; they were called ' censors ' ; and their duty was to take a census of the citizens and distribute them in centuries and classes, according to property qualification, and in tribes, according to domicile. Other duties were transferred to them by degrees : they filled up vacancies in the Senate ; they controlled the revenue and fixed the expenditure for five years ahead ; and they acted as supervisors of private morals, with the right to expel from the Senate and body of knights all persons who were in any way compromised. Each group of magistrates, the consuls included, consisted of two or more persons and formed a *collegium*.

The Senate was the body which advised the consuls. In the early history of the Roman state it represented, as I have said above, a group of ruling families, and its character was unchanged in the fourth century B. C. The normal number of the members was regarded as three hundred. Its ranks were filled up by the consuls and later by the censors. Each senator held office for life. The magistrates had no rules or laws to guide them in appointing senators, but it gradually became a fixed custom that all ex-magistrates, unless there were some special reason for their exclusion, should take their seats in the Senate-house. In this way the Senate came to represent the whole body of citizens. We have seen, however, that the people preferred to choose as magistrates, and therefore as senators, members of the noble Roman families.

All that immense importance which the Senate acquired in the public life of Rome was based not so much on constitutional rights as on custom. The unwritten constitution merely secured the existence of the Senate as the source and guardian of the power exercised by the magistrates. In case both consuls died or were taken prisoners, their *imperium* ' reverted to the Fathers ', or Senate, to quote an ancient rule of Roman political practice. The Senate then chose from their own body an *interrex*, to summon a popular assembly for the election of new consuls. Unless summoned by a consul the Senate could not meet ; discussion and voting were restricted to measures proposed by the consul, and its decisions, called *senatus consulta*, or ' advice of the Senate ', were not binding upon the president. For all this, the importance and influence of that body were such that the consuls constantly consulted it, nearly always followed its ' advice ', and seldom brought before the assembly any proposal which the Senate had not previously approved. Thus the Senate was the real ruler of Rome, while the consuls and other magistrates were its executive organs. This was partly due to the profound respect in which the Senate was held by the people, and partly to the continuous existence of the Senate, while the consuls held office only for twelve months ; and further, consuls and senators belonged to the same class. For an individual consul to oppose the Senate was neither feasible nor profitable.

The priestly colleges also played an important part in public affairs. Admission to these bodies, or to most of them, was thrown open to the whole body of citizens, by the same concession which the patricians had made in the case of secular magistracies. More and more the state concentrated in its own hands the religious life of the community as well as political affairs and economics. The relation of the citizens to the gods was precisely defined, and exact rules were established for communicating with heaven by the mediation of special priestly colleges, which guarded the divine law (*ius divinum*) and assisted and advised the magistrates in religious affairs. I have spoken already (see p. 17) of the different colleges. The chief of these still was, as it had been in the primitive days of Rome, the college of pontiffs—a body of men who knew exactly all the refinements of religious law and of the closely allied secular code. They determined the time and manner of the chief acts of public worship ; they were the guardians of ancient historical tradition. The public life of Rome was inseparable from religion : every action of the state began and ended with a religious ceremony, and the religious part of the proceedings was just as important as the secular part. The *imperium* or executive power of the magistrate was closely connected with his exclusive right of ascertaining the will of the gods by auspices, of soliciting, in the name of the community, their protection, and lastly of propitiating them, when their dissatisfaction or anger was made manifest by signs and wonders (*prodigia*). Under these conditions it was important to the state to know the history of its relations with its gods. The duty of keeping these records was laid upon the pontiffs ; and the records, as far as they were preserved, were the earliest annals of religious and political life at Rome.

We have already spoken of the part played by the citizens as a whole. As well as political rights, each citizen had a number of political duties. He was bound to defend the state by serving in the army, to contribute a part of his income to the needs of the state, and to give his labour to the state when the public safety required it, as, for example, in the building of walls.

Thus, at the end of the fourth century and beginning of the third, Rome becomes a powerful state and enters the arena of international politics over the civilized world. She was now not merely a strong city-state with a large and wealthy population : she was also the centre of a great confederacy between Italian tribes and cities. In international affairs she speaks henceforth not only in the name of her own citizens but also in the name of a powerful confederation, all of whose members had, in a greater or less degree, assimilated the results of the culture generally diffused in that age.

V

ROME AND CARTHAGE

AFTER the long and arduous wars which led to the creation of the Italian confederacy, Rome became one of the strongest powers in the civilized world. Her military strength was more considerable than that of any one of the empires which then maintained a balance of power in the East —more considerable not so much in point of numbers as in the solidarity, organization, and intelligence of her soldiers. To the troops of the other empires, serving for pay and enlisted by force from the native populations, she could oppose an army as well trained and as numerous, and manned by citizens and allies, who fought, not for money nor by compulsion, but by the voluntary decision of the whole body of Roman citizens.

When Rome defeated Pyrrhus, one of the most gifted Hellenistic kings, and thus claimed a place in the family of empires in the third century B. C., this apparition was noted and studied by the Hellenistic statesmen of the time. Macedonia, Italy's nearest neighbour, began to attend to the course of events in Italy ; Egypt was the first to enter into diplomatic relations with Rome, in 273 B. C. ; and in Greece the Leagues and free communities began to take account of this new power as a possible ally both in their mutual strifes and in the contest carried on by the western Greeks against the growing insolence of the Illyrian pirates. But more than any of these, Carthage, with her commercial and political interests in the western Mediterranean, was affected by the foreign policy of Rome. To her Rome and the political successes of Rome were no novelty. At first she looked on Rome as the successor of Etruria in Italy and hoped that her own trade would not be damaged. For Rome was not a great maritime empire in the fifth and fourth centuries B. C., and owned no fleet either for war or commerce. The trade of the Latin and surviving Etruscan ports kept up its semi-piratical character and could not compete with the trade of Carthage.

For this reason Carthage renewed in 348 B. C. the commercial treaty concluded with Rome at the end of the sixth century ; and for this reason the commercial treaty was converted in 279 during the war with Pyrrhus into a military alliance against the common enemy. It is clear that Carthage still regarded Rome as a counterpoise to the Greek cities, just as she had regarded Etruria at an earlier date.

But the position was altered when all the harbours of south Italy were annexed to the empire of Rome, and when the interests of Naples and Tarentum, those ancient rivals of Carthage, became the interests of Rome also. It became clear to Carthage that Rome, as the leader of the western Greeks, was bound in the near future to take a hand in Sicilian affairs and to support the Sicilian Greeks in their secular struggle with the Carthaginians. It was significant that Rome had long been the ally of Massilia, the other Greek rival that Carthage feared. It must also be observed that relations between the Sicilian Greeks and the native Italian tribes, always frequent and uninterrupted, were especially active in the fourth century B. C. Detachments of Samnites were frequently hired for military service in Sicily, and many of them, after a period of service, were rewarded by their employers with allotments of land. A striking instance of the Samnite desire to establish themselves in Sicily is afforded by the history of the Greek city of Messana. It was seized by Samnite mercenaries in the pay of Agathocles and converted into a Samnite city—a fate which had long before befallen Rhegium, a Greek city on the eastern side of the Straits.

Thus the collision between Rome and Carthage was inevitable ; and the sooner it came, the better for Carthage. The strength of the rivals was nearly equal. Both powers were based on a community of citizens and originally relied on a citizen army, numerous and well trained. Both powers had allies, who were bound to contribute their forces in case their principal was involved in war against any enemy whatever. On one side were Etruscans, Samnites, Umbrians, and Italian Greeks, while the African Empire of Carthage could count on the Berbers or Libyans who inhabited her territory, and on the Numidians who were neighbours and tributaries ; and both these were warlike nations and by no means uncivilized. In neither case was there any strong feeling of attachment on the part of the allies to their principal ; still, under ordinary circumstances, both Rome and Carthage could reckon on their support. Carthage had better cavalry than Rome and more of it, and her infantry was armed as efficiently. She had also a large body of excellently trained mercenaries, who had passed through the severe school of Hellenistic warfare, and a considerable number of armed elephants—a recent addition to the fighting power of Hellenistic armies. Indeed, in every branch of tactics studied by the Hellenistic generals, and especially in engineering, the Carthaginians were even superior to the Romans. Lastly, they had a powerful fleet and great wealth. Nevertheless, when it came to fighting on land, the Romans had considerable advantages. For at this time the citizens of Carthage hardly ever served in the ranks, and their places were filled by mercenaries and allies who were liable to fail at the critical moment ; whereas the Roman army contained no mercenaries and consisted entirely of citizens and allies ; and some of the latter, for instance, the Latins, were no less to be trusted than Roman citizens themselves.

This equality of strength made it impossible to foresee which antagonist would prove victorious. The contest was bound to begin in Sicily, and the attitude of the Sicilian Greeks was of great importance. It so happened that just at this time they had found once again an able and prudent leader in Hiero II, tyrant of Syracuse, who had seized control of the city in 269 B. C. He had then, following the example of Agathocles and Pyrrhus, declared himself king of Sicily and had subdued several of the neighbouring cities.

The war began in 264 B. C. and, as always happens in similar cases, on a comparatively trifling pretext. The Samnites, who had taken Messana in 289 B. C. and now called themselves Mamertini, lived by plundering the Greek cities in their neighbourhood. When Hiero, wishing to stop their depredations, laid siege to Messana, a section of the inhabitants appealed to Carthage for help. This opportunity of occupying the city was welcomed, and a Carthaginian garrison was sent : it was important for Carthage to establish herself on the Straits of Messina in close proximity to her ancient enemy, Syracuse. But a majority of the Mamertines sought aid from Rome. The Romans understood that to help the Mamertines meant war with Carthage. But on the other hand, if Carthage controlled the Straits, the vital interests of Rome were affected : not only would her shipping be subject to interference in the straits, but also it would be possible, in case of need, to land a foreign army in Italy. After some hesitation Rome determined on war and sent a strong army into Sicily. The Mamertines then obliged the Carthaginian garrison to decamp and surrendered their city to the Romans.

Confronted by a common danger, Hiero and the Carthaginians made an alliance ; but their armies failed to take Messana. After this failure, Hiero abandoned his ally and took sides with the Romans : they seemed to him more powerful, and they promised, if victorious, not only to recognize his rule over Syracuse and his independence, but also to extend his kingdom at the cost of the Carthaginian dominions in Sicily. When this treaty was once made, the king remained faithful to it throughout the war ; and the Romans were greatly indebted to him for their final victory. Without his aid Rome could hardly have solved the problem of feeding her army, and Syracuse was essential as a station for the Roman fleet. We shall see later how the struggle with Carthage forced the Romans to create a powerful navy.

The war for Sicily dragged on for twenty-three years, from 264 to 241 B. C., with hardly a break. The antagonists put forth every effort, and both sides revealed a remarkable genius for war and sent out great generals to command their armies. Neither the Graeco-Oriental monarchies nor Macedonia and Greece took any part in the conflict. The feeling of the Hellenistic world was neutral, and not one of the Hellenistic monarchies was directly interested in the result. Ptolemy Philadelphus, king of Egypt, was the nearest neighbour of Carthage ; and it is an interesting fact that he kept up friendly relations with both the combatants.

The victory of Rome in the first Punic war—this name was used by the Romans who called the Carthaginians *Poeni* or Phoenicians—was due chiefly to a number of mistakes made by the Carthaginians at the very beginning. In spite of their original superiority at sea, they suffered the Roman armies to cross from Italy into Sicily ; they were unable to retain Hiero's support ; and they failed to send a force sufficient to destroy the first Roman detachments that landed in the island. The Romans, on their side, surprised Carthage by their activity at sea. Helped by Sicilian and Italian Greeks they built a large fleet, and equipped their ships with

I. FUNERAL MONUMENT
NEAR THUGGA

2. CEMETERY AT CARTHAGE

1. A funeral monument near Thugga in Northern Africa (Tunisia). Thugga was a Berbero-Punic city ruled by a Berbero-Punic aristocracy. The inscription in the Libyan and the neo-Punic languages gives the name of the local aristocrats who were buried under this monument. The style of architecture is Graeco-Phoenician. 2nd cent. B.C.

2. A cemetery discovered at Carthage, in the sacred precinct dedicated to the great goddess Tanit. Scores of dedicatory monuments of various forms were discovered, all bearing dedicatory inscriptions both incised and painted on a surface of stucco (those last are not preserved). The

PLATE V

dedicants are members of the Punic aristocracy of Carthage. The gods to whom the stones were dedicated: Tanit Face of Baal and Baal-Hammon, the Lord. Under the stones were cinerary urns containing charred bones of young children, kids, lambs, and little birds, and children's toys. It is evident that the area contained the remains of infants who were either buried here after they died a natural death or were sacrificed (burned alive?) to the great goddess Tanit. Three strata of urns have been discovered. The earliest may be dated in the 8th–7th cent. B.C., the next before the 4th cent. B.C., and the last after 300 B.C., i.e. shortly before the destruction of Carthage. From a photograph with the kind permission of Mr. Byron Khun de Prorok.

3. Clay statuettes of the great goddess Tanit, found at Carthage. The goddess Tanit was with Baal-Hammon the greatest deity of Carthage, the 'Celestial Juno' as the Romans later called her. 3rd cent. B.C. Bardo Museum, Tunis.

4. Two sacrificial knives or 'razors,' which are commonly found in the Punic graves of Carthage. The shape recalls Egyptian originals. The engraved figures which adorn the blades are Hellenistic-Egyptian. 4th–3rd cent. B.C. Bardo Museum, Tunis.

3. THE GREAT GODDESS TANIT   4. SACRIFICIAL KNIVES

PLATE V

a contrivance unknown to the Carthaginians, which they probably owed to Greek engineers—bridges for boarding the enemy ships, which enabled the heavy-armed Roman infantry to fight just as they were accustomed to fight on dry land.

Thanks to these mistakes on the part of Carthage and the strength of their own fleet, the Romans were able to drive the enemy out of many Sicilian cities and to win a series of decisive victories by sea. Encouraged by these successes, Rome hoped to end the war with one blow, and sent a fairly strong army to Africa in 256 B.C. The plan was to come upon the Carthaginians by surprise, to take Carthage as soon as possible after landing, and to force the government to accept the conditions dictated by Rome. The attempt nearly succeeded. The army, commanded by M. Atilius Regulus, disembarked safely, ravaged a large part of the Carthaginian territory, and advanced right up to the city. But the city held out against Regulus. His army was too small to take it; and the Romans, occupied with the fighting in Sicily and aware that Carthage still possessed a strong fleet, were afraid that, if they sent reinforcements, their whole enterprise might be ruined. With the aid of Xanthippus, an experienced Spartan general whom they invited to Africa with a body of mercenaries, the Carthaginians defeated the army of Regulus, and only a few survivors were able to sail back to Sicily.

Sicily now became once more the sole theatre of war. Here, too, Rome displayed the same stubbornness and persistence as in her Italian campaigns. Towards the end of this war there were times when she suffered defeat after defeat. At one time she had hardly any fleet left: several squadrons, one after another, were driven by storms to destruction on the coast of Sicily. But no disaster could weaken the resolution of Rome; and she was encouraged by the failure of Carthage to take advantage of these disasters. At last this stubbornness, together with the excellent quality of the Roman infantry, proved victorious. By degrees the Carthaginian armies were forced back into the south-west corner of Sicily, in spite of stubborn resistance, which was led, towards the end of the war, by Hamilcar Barca, a young Carthaginian general. The last phase of the war exhausted the strength of both combatants so completely that Rome consented to conditions of peace which were comparatively lenient to her rival. Carthage was forced to pay a moderate sum of money and to forfeit to Rome her Sicilian possessions. The first Roman 'province' (see Chapter VII) was thus acquired.

After the conclusion of peace, Carthage had to undergo further trials and dangers. A body of mercenaries who had served in Sicily, enraged by the retention of their pay, mutinied on their return to Africa. Ruined by taxes and exhausted by drafts, the Berbers, some Numidians, and even some Phoenician cities on the coast, joined the mutineers. The position was critical. But Carthage showed in the hour of danger how much vital power she still possessed. Hamilcar Barca, the able young general mentioned above, to whom Carthage owed the favourable conditions of peace, crushed the revolt and restored order in the Carthaginian Empire ; indeed, by a series of successful campaigns he extended the Carthaginian sphere of influence in Numidia.

After the war with the mercenaries the next task of Carthage was to restore the shattered resources of the state. Her markets in Italy and Gaul, her provinces of Sicily, Sardinia, and Corsica, were lost beyond recall ; the two last were annexed by Rome after the conclusion of peace, and their loss was especially grievous, as these islands were not only the granaries of Carthage but also furnished copper and iron with other metals. The necessity of repairing this twofold loss explains the efforts of Carthage to extend her possessions in Spain, a land fabulously rich, according to ancient standards, in minerals. Spain might also, if properly cultivated, take the place of Sardinia and Sicily as a producer of grain. Operations in Spain were not hindered by the Romans, whose present object was to force the Carthaginians to pay up the whole sum of money required of them.

The task of creating a Spanish province, entrusted to Hamilcar Barca, was bequeathed by him to his son-in-law Hasdrubal, and later to his son Hannibal. There is no doubt that Hamilcar and his successors were led on by the hope of revenge as well as by economic considerations. They reckoned on turning Spain not only to a source of wealth but also to a weapon of war. The people had long been famous for their warlike spirit ; and the country, by reason of its mineral wealth, was eminently suitable for the creation of extensive arsenals, and might prove an excellent base for a campaign against Rome. By degrees what had been small trading factories were converted into large seaport towns with considerable territories ; one such town was Gades, the modern Cadiz. The Spanish tribes, one after another, some by force of arms and others by diplomatic means, became allies and tributaries of Carthage ; and thus the Carthaginian base in Spain became steadily stronger and more extensive.

Rome now began to look with some anxiety at this activity in Spain, but she was powerless to prevent or check it. This would have meant a second war against Carthage under unfavourable conditions. Her most pressing task was to secure her rear in north Italy, which sent forth independent Gallic tribes in 225–222 B. C., eager to invade once more the centre of the peninsula. With a great effort the Romans were able to beat back this incursion and to drive the invaders to the upper course of the Po. Somewhat earlier, in 229 B. C., Rome was drawn into a war against the pirates of the Illyrian coast, who had gained full control of the Adriatic and repeatedly plundered Italian merchants and Italian cities along the coast. This campaign brought Rome for the first time into contact with the ruling powers of Greece : Macedonia, the Aetolian League, and the Achaean League, all tried to turn it to their own advantage. For the first time Rome made an alliance with Greek communities—Epidamnus and Apollonia, the chief harbours on the west coast of Greece and the chief victims of the pirates. These wars made it plain that a collision between Rome and Macedonia was inevitable in the near future ; for the annexation of Illyria, so close to Macedonia, and the interference of Rome in Greek affairs, could not but be offensive to the Macedonians. But the Romans themselves were careful to avoid this collision, both in 229 B. C. and ten years later, when they had to fight again on the Illyrian coast in order to deprive the pirates of their naval bases.

Yet, in spite of these wars and the complicated situation both in north Italy and on the east coast, it was nevertheless necessary for Rome to stop the progress of Carthaginian ambition in Spain. The expansion towards the East was especially dangerous. Carthage was approaching the Pyrenees, so that Rome might eventually be confronted by a coalition of Carthaginians and Gauls from what is now France and from Italy. An attempt was first made to arrest the expansion of Carthage by peaceful means. For this purpose Rome made use of her ancient connexion with the Graeco-Iberian community of Saguntum, which now became her ally. Saguntum might be useful in case of need, as a military base against Carthage. Rather earlier, in 226 B. C., Rome made an agreement with Hasdrubal, the Carthaginian general in Spain, by which the river Ebro was fixed as a limit between the spheres of influence of the two rivals.

From 236 B. C. to 228 Hamilcar commanded the Carthaginian army in Spain; when his son-in-law and successor Hasdrubal died in 221, Hannibal, the son of Hamilcar, was chosen by the army to be their leader. The new general began at once to prepare for war with Rome and to work out a plan for invading Italy. By 219 B. C. his preparations were complete. But before marching against Italy, it was necessary to make his rear secure and to deprive the Romans of a possible base for military operations in Spain. Saguntum, which was in alliance with Rome and might well be used for such operations, was taken after a siege of eight months. Rome promptly declared war against Carthage. In order to anticipate the Roman plan of sending one force to Africa to take Carthage, and another to Spain to destroy the Carthaginian army, Hannibal marched with extraordinary speed over the Pyrenees, through southern Gaul, and across the Alps into Italy. Here he counted on the support promised him by the Gauls of north Italy; he also believed that a series of victories would enable him to break the alliance that bound the Italian clans and communities to Rome, and that thus he could force her to make peace on terms favourable to Carthage. To take Rome itself, surrounded as it was with a ring of fortified colonies and Latin fortresses, seemed to him impossible, and formed no part of his plan.

The approach of Hannibal was so speedy and sudden that the Romans had no time to organize an army in Sicily and dispatch it to Africa; they could not even muster sufficient forces to defend the passes of the Alps and keep the invader out of Italy. When Hannibal's army had reached Italy and was joined by the Gauls in 217 B. C., it was too late to think of invading Africa: Rome had to hurl her last man into north Italy. The arduous passage of the Alps

THE FIRST ORIENTAL CULT AT ROME—
MAGNA MATER

I. MAGNA MATER OR CYBELE IN HER CHARIOT

I. Bronze statuette of *Magna Mater* or Cybele in her chariot drawn by two tamed lions. The group represents no doubt a religious procession in which the statue of the goddess was put on a chariot (*tensa*) and driven by a team of tamed lions. The earliest and chief temple of *Magna Mater* was dedicated to her after the second Punic war (191 B.C.) on the Palatine; the black stone, the sacred symbol of the goddess, was sent to Rome from Pessinus by the King of Pergamum. 1st–2nd cent. A.D. Metropolitan Museum of Art, New York.

2, 3. Bas-relief of an altar dedicated, according to the inscription, TO *MAGNA MATER* AND ATTIS BY AN AUGUR L. CORNELIUS SCIPIO ORFITUS in A.D. 295 in memory of a *taurobolium* and *criobolium* performed by him (these were ceremonies of initiation into the mysteries of Cybele by the sacrifice of a bull and a ram). The front of the altar was adorned by a bas-relief which represents the goddess Cybele in her chariot roaming in a forest in search of her beloved Attis, who stands hidden behind his sacred tree, the pine. The same tree with the sacred attributes of Cybele and Attis was represented on the other side of the altar between two sacrificial animals, the ram and the bull (fig. 3). A.D. 295. Villa Albani, Rome.

PLATE VI

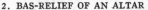

2. BAS-RELIEF OF AN ALTAR   3. BAS-RELIEF OF AN ALTAR

4. SCULPTURED BASE FROM ROME

4. Sculptured base found at Rome and dedicated to *Magna Mater* and to the *Navis Salvia* by Claudia Syntyche. The bas-relief represents the legend connected with the introduction of the cult of *Magna Mater* at Rome. The sacred black stone arrived at Rome from Pergamum in a ship (*Navis Salvia*). The ship entered the Tiber, but stuck in the sand and could not be moved by the efforts of men. A Vestal Virgin, Claudia Quinta, then fastened her belt to the ship and drew it without effort to the Palatine, where a temple had been prepared for the divine foreigner (imposing ruins are still in existence). To make the subject clear, the black stone is replaced on our bas-relief by a statue of Cybele. 2nd–3rd cent. A.D. Capitoline Museum, Rome.

PLATE VI

had caused heavy losses to Hannibal's army, especially to what may be called his ' tanks '—the armed elephants. But his missing men and horses were replaced by the Gauls ; and he hoped in future to detach her Italian allies from Rome. The Samnites were the most doubtful in their allegiance ; and therefore Hannibal's immediate object was to penetrate to south Italy, where it would not be difficult for him to receive reinforcements from Carthage also. This plan of campaign was brilliantly carried out. One great Roman army after another was defeated—on the Ticinus and on the Trebia in the north, and at Lake Trasimene in central Italy. In the south decisive battle was offered by the Romans at Cannae in Apulia in 216 B.C.; and this also ended in the utter defeat of the Roman army and the destruction of Roman citizens and allies by tens of thousands. By this victory Hannibal became master of south Italy : he could communicate freely with Carthage and Spain and form a direct connexion with Macedonia, whose eyes had been opened by the Roman victories in Illyria to the fact that the Eastern interests of the two powers were diametrically opposed to one another.

But even when a multitude of Roman citizens and allies lay dead on the battle-fields of Italy, the Roman cause was by no means lost and the task of Hannibal by no means at an end. This was the crisis of the war. Hannibal reckoned that Rome would be forced to conclude peace by defeat, defection of allies, and the menacing attitude of Macedonia. When the Carthaginians had moved from Apulia into Campania, when Capua, Rome's ancient ally, had opened her gates to Hannibal, and especially when Syracuse, after Hiero's death, proved an unfaithful friend, and Macedonia formed an alliance with Carthage, the feeling of depression was general at Rome. But in that dark hour the rulers of the state rose to the height of the situation. They brought into the field the whole free population of the country ; they even included a part of the slaves, to whom they promised freedom. The allies of Rome increased their efforts. Hannibal's hope that Rome would be stripped of her allies was not realized : the Latins remained loyal, and most other Italian cities preferred Roman rule to that of Semitic foreigners. The position of Hannibal was therefore embarrassing. His force was not sufficient to advance into Latium and there to take one fortress after another, and finally Rome itself. It is probable that the utmost effort of Carthage could not have supplied an army large enough for such a task. Therefore, while awaiting reinforcements from Carthage and Spain and from Philip of Macedonia, Hannibal continued to subdue those allies of Rome who still held out against him in southern and central Italy, especially in Campania ; and he manœuvred in such a way as to force the Romans to fight one more battle which would certainly end in the defeat of the Roman commanders.

But the Romans were determined to reverse their plan of campaign and to fight no more battles. The war had now become a war of exhaustion. The Roman army, skilfully led by Quintus Fabius, surnamed *Cunctator*, ' The Delayer ', by Marcellus in Sicily, and by Tiberius Gracchus, dogged the steps of the invader, trying to seize his baggage and to save the cities in Campania and south Italy which still held out against him, and, as far as possible, to drive him out from the cities he had already taken. Outside Italy the struggle was carried on with all the more activity, in order to isolate Hannibal entirely and prevent him from getting reinforcements from any source whatever. The most considerable operations were begun in Spain even before the battle of Cannae. Active steps were taken against Philip V, king of Macedonia and an ally of Hannibal. Fearing that he might invade Italy the Romans sent a powerful fleet to keep a sharp eye on the Adriatic and hinder descents upon the coast. When Philip tried to seize the Greek city of Apollonia, in order to use its harbour as a base for his contemplated invasion of Italy, the Adriatic fleet sailed to the rescue and delivered the city from the Macedonians. Finally, in 212 B.C., when Philip's victories in Illyria and conquest of the excellent harbour at Lissus, together with Hannibal's capture of Tarentum, made a Macedonian invasion seem almost inevitable, Rome raised up against Philip a strong coalition in Greece, headed by the Aetolians, and promised them money and military support. And Philip was actually prevented by the war in Greece from taking an active part with Hannibal against the Romans in Italy. And lastly, Rome endeavoured to weaken Carthaginian influence in Sicily, where Syracuse, influenced by the death of Hiero II and Hannibal's victorious career, had renounced her alliance with Rome and taken up a hostile attitude.

63

All these activities needed time and were not, at first, very fruitful in results. But here, too, Rome displayed her customary stubbornness ; and victory began slowly but steadily to smile upon her. In 212 B. C. the consul Marcellus took Syracuse after a long and arduous siege, in which the Roman army had to cope with the most recent discoveries of Greek genius ; for the defence was directed by Archimedes, the greatest mathematician and engineer of antiquity. When the city was taken, Archimedes was killed by a Roman soldier. A year later the Carthaginians were expelled from Campania, and Capua was recovered by the Romans. Success followed failure in Spain also, when the youthful genius of Publius Cornelius Scipio was raised to the command of the Spanish army. Under these conditions it became clear to Hannibal that nothing could save the situation but new and decisive victories. But his force was insufficient for the purpose. Carthage, expecting every moment a Roman invasion from Sicily, could not help him ; Spain alone was left. He summoned thence in haste his brother Hasdrubal with the larger part of the army in Spain. Hasdrubal succeeded in reaching Italy but failed to effect a junction with his brother : he was met at the Metaurus by a Roman army and utterly defeated in a decisive battle (207 B. C.).

This defeat settled the result of the campaign. The military genius of Hannibal was such that the Romans were never able to beat him in Italy. All they could do was to push him by degrees farther and farther to the south. But his growing weakness made it possible for Rome to transfer the war to Africa by sending an expedition against Carthage ; and thus Hannibal was forced to sail away from Italy with his army to the defence of his country. The war in Africa, in which Scipio was the Roman general, began in 204 B. C. and ended after a series of operations with the battle of Zama two years later ; and Hannibal was there defeated for the first time. Masinissa, a Numidian king who had made an alliance with the Romans, gave them valuable assistance in this campaign. Peace was concluded in 201 B. C. Carthage was forced to pay a large sum of money, to destroy all her ships of war, and to accept a limitation of her independence in foreign relations. The prestige which she had hitherto enjoyed in the West was thus swept away. Her commercial supremacy was at an end, and she became only one of a number of existing states which depended on agriculture and combined with it a limited amount of foreign trade. Her political activity shrank more and more, till it was confined to perpetual wrangles with Masinissa, the Numidian king who enjoyed the protection of Rome. Her possessions in Spain became one Roman province, and the whole of Sicily was formed into another. She was now surrounded on all sides by Roman possessions and Roman dependants.

VI

ROME, THE HELLENISTIC EAST, AND CARTHAGE
IN THE SECOND CENTURY B. C.

WHEN she had conquered Carthage and converted her rival into a dependent ally and vassal, Rome entered the family of Hellenistic Empires, which followed Alexander and maintained a balance of power in the East from about the middle of the third century B. C. In this sphere Rome was called upon by the force of circumstances to play a great, and eventually a decisive, part. She had no direct interests of great moment in the East : she needed no support from any Hellenistic state, in order to consolidate her empire in Italy and in the West. Her actions betray no imperialistic tendency, that is, no definite ambition to found a world-wide power, such as the empire of Alexander the Great had once been. Such an idea can hardly be attributed even to individual statesmen ; still less likely is it that the policy of the Senate and national assembly was dictated by motives of deliberate imperialism.

To the Hellenistic East the rise of Rome as a powerful empire was a portent in political history with which each of the existing powers was bound to reckon. Most of them tried to use her as a cat's-paw ; certainly no one believed that her interference was destined before long to put an end for ever to the Hellenistic balance of power. It must be remembered that to many Hellenistic states this equilibrium was no ideal but a disagreeable state of things which they had to put up with. In fact, only those states which could not exist without it gave it their deliberate support : such were the great commercial republics of Rhodes, Cyzicus, and Byzantium, and the petty Hellenistic monarchies, especially Pergamum. All these regarded their own freedom as lost if any one of the great monarchies became more powerful. The two strongest Eastern empires, Macedonia and Syria, were definitely hostile to the balance of power. Egypt, at the beginning of the second century B. C., had lost most of her foreign possessions and was ruled by weak and incapable kings ; she was therefore more inclined to support existing conditions than to dream of world-wide dominion. But both Macedonia and Syria had visions of restoring the empire of Alexander and combining the Hellenistic world into a single political unit. These aspirations were stubbornly disputed, not only by the states mentioned above, but also by all Greece, in which, however, two currents of opinion were plainly visible. All Greeks were opposed to foreign rule and Macedonian ' tyranny'. But a majority of city-states, including Sparta and Athens, still clung to the old ideal of freedom for each city, except, of course, cities in subjection to themselves ; whereas the two confederations of cities and peoples—the civilized Achaean League and the semi-barbaric Aetolian League—both endeavoured to unite Greece into one federated state, mainly with the object of fighting Macedonia.

As the result of these conditions diplomatic intrigues were rife in the East, and to each player in the game the possibility of throwing the Roman legions into the scales was tempting and apparently free from danger. This new weapon in the fight against Macedonia and Syria was specially welcome to Pergamum and Egypt, as well as to Rhodes and the Greek cities in her alliance ; and they all made haste to begin friendly relations with Rome. It cannot be said of Rome that she was entirely without interest in the affairs of Greece. Macedonia might be called a near neighbour of Italy, divided from it only by the buffer-states of Illyricum and the Greek cities on the Adriatic coast and the Ionian islands. Moreover, Rome remembered that Philip V, king of Macedonia, had tried to use for his own ends the failure of Rome at the beginning of the struggle against Hannibal, so that she had been forced, in 205 B.C., to make an unfavourable peace with Philip, that she might be free to send an expedition to Africa. Even though Italy was in no immediate danger from Philip, it would do no harm to check by every means the rise of a single dictator in the East. For the present, Philip was restrained by an alliance with Antiochus III, king of Syria, who was as ambitious as himself ; but that he aimed at such a position was certain. Greece and Asia Minor, and Egypt as well, were in no little danger just at this time ; and the less important members of the Hellenistic family were well aware of this. The temporary alliance between Philip and

Antiochus might have serious consequences, though Philip had not gained much so far. It was therefore natural that petitions for support and alliance should pour into Rome from all the petty Hellenistic states.

The position was flattering to Roman feeling. Life at Rome had long ago acquired an external resemblance to the life of Greece ; and the influence of Greek civilization was much increased by the annexation of the Greek cities in Italy, the conquest of Syracuse and other cities in Sicily, and the formation of that island into the first Roman province. Every Roman of that age felt the fascination of Greek genius and Greek culture, and realized the beauty and brilliance of the Hellenistic period. The legend which connected the origin of Rome with the Trojan war and thus with the earliest Greek history—a legend which passed for history with every Roman—took definite shape at this time for good reasons. Besides, Rome herself was a free city-state, and the Italian confederacy was an alliance of similar city-states. The word ' king ' was a bogy to Roman ears : there was something American in their aversion to kings and kingly government. And now, victorious over a most dangerous enemy, conscious of her own strength and solidarity, and fully convinced that no shock could hurl her from her place, Rome was appealed to by city-states like herself—the states which had created the marvellous civilization of Greece—to aid them in the struggle against ' kings ' and tyrants. The policy of Rome was never sentimental ; but when feeling was not at variance with interest, it was possible for once to let feeling assert itself. If the Greeks could be helped and Philip at the same time hindered from repeating his former successes in Illyria, that was sufficient reason for active interference in the tangled international politics of the Hellenistic powers.

Therefore, when soon after the second Punic war an alliance was formed in the East to thwart Philip's schemes of aggrandizement, it was quite natural that Rome should not refuse her support to the alliance. War was declared against Philip, and troops were sent to Greece and Macedonia. The war turned out a less serious affair than was at first expected. Though Rome had eventually to bear the main burden of the campaign, and though the battle of Cynoscephalae, fought in 197 B. C., was won by the Roman armies alone, yet their task was appreciably lightened by the active support of the Aetolian League, which provided a land army, while Rhodes and Attalus I, king of Pergamum, provided ships. Philip's defeat was not decisive. He was obliged merely to pay a sum of money, to resign the cities and territory which he had taken in Asia, and to recognize the freedom of the Greek cities and leagues. When Titus Quinctius Flamininus in the name of the Roman people solemnly proclaimed the liberation of Greece from Macedonian rule, the announcement was hailed with enthusiasm in Greece and at Rome. Yet this same policy of proclaiming the freedom of Greece was a regular device in the Hellenistic East, in the strife of one empire against another : the Ptolemies and Seleucids used it as a war-cry in their contests with Macedonia, though that did not prevent them from very arbitrary treatment of those Greek cities which happened to lie within their own dominions. But on this occasion the Greeks believed that they had at last found a genuine and disinterested champion of their freedom. For Rome was a free city, though the Greek cities in Italy and Sicily received only a moderate allowance of freedom from her. The leading Roman statesmen also regarded the freedom of Greece as something more than a mere phrase : even to the injury of their own interests, they withdrew their armies from Greece at the first opportunity, and left the Hellenistic world to follow its own devices.

But this abstinence from interference in Greek affairs did not last long. Soon after the end of the Macedonian war, Antiochus III, first the ally and then the enemy of Philip, was tempted to avail himself of a convenient opportunity, in order to restore the rights of the Seleucid house over Asia Minor—rights which had been upset by the formation of the kingdom at Pergamum, the aggressions of Egypt, and the declaration of independence proclaimed by many Greek cities. Antiochus had recently been able, by a succession of brilliant victories in the East, to enlarge the Seleucid Empire almost to its former extent. For this he received the title of ' The Great'. With Egypt he concluded an agreement, and it seemed that Rome had no ground for interfering in the internal affairs of the Hellenistic states in Asia. For a time she stuck to the policy of non-interference : she was glad to leave Asia to Antiochus and only insisted that he should not advance farther west. But this moderate attitude of Rome and his conviction of his own power drove Antiochus into adopting bolder measures. Hannibal was now at his elbow, promising the support of Carthage, in case of a war with Rome and an invasion of Italy. In Greece the Aetolian League was dissatisfied with the situation of affairs : they considered themselves wronged, because they had never received what they hoped for on the successful conclusion of the Macedonian war. Eventually the Aetolians began war against Rome and proposed to Antiochus that he should take command of their army.

Antiochus now determined upon war : by sending an army into Greece he forced the Romans to declare war against him. The campaign was soon over and ended in the utter defeat of his semi-Asiatic army, first in Europe and then in Asia near the city of Magnesia in 190 B. C. He received no material support from the Aetolians, and all the rest of Greece remained neutral. Egypt, Rhodes, Pergamum, and even Macedonia, sided with Rome. The conditions of the peace concluded with Antiochus showed once more that Rome had no wish to extend her territory by including in it part of the East. Her object was clear—to prevent the rise of any Eastern power that might prove dangerous to herself. Hence Antiochus was forced to pay a sum of money, to withdraw his armies from Asia Minor, and to destroy that powerful fleet which made it possible at any moment to transport soldiers to Asia Minor, Egypt, or Greece.

The general situation in the Hellenistic world was not affected by this war. The balance of power, of which Rome had become the recognized guardian, continued to exist, but in a peculiar form : Rome now settled all the internal disputes of Greece but never consulted Greek opinion even in Greek concerns. All the Hellenistic kingdoms were independent, but not one of them was powerful. To all of them, and especially to the Greek cities, Rome guaranteed ' freedom ' ; but the moment that any one of them showed a tendency to carry on an independent policy, she promptly put her foot down. As a matter of course, the real position of Greece and the Hellenistic powers was no secret to the most clear-sighted among the Greeks. Eumenes II, king of Pergamum, felt that he was not an ally of Rome, but a vassal and a servant ; and the other Asiatic states and Greek cities were no better off. Though Rome had no wish at first to use too plain language, yet the taste grew upon her by degrees, until her advice to her friends, which even earlier had been very like commands, became orders pure and simple, which the allies were forced to accept and obey without making excuses.

The Greeks especially resented the frequent interference of Rome in the local affairs of their communities, though this interference was often invited by the complaints of one political party against another. As a rule the well-to-do class was in favour of Rome and was consistently supported by Rome against the agitation of the lower class. An aristocratic government was more akin to the Roman constitution and had the sincere sympathy of the Senate. Hence Greece would have been very ready to free herself from Roman guardianship and revert to earlier political conditions. Macedonia resented even more strongly the pressure of Rome; and after the Syrian war Philip V began to work hard at the restoration of his country. War with Rome was not his object; but he strove to create conditions by which Macedonia might continue to exist as an independent kingdom. He did not wish to fight, but to prepare for a struggle, in case Rome should wish to deprive Macedonia of freedom. For this purpose he sought to extend his possessions in the Balkan peninsula, to strengthen himself by alliances with the independent tribes of Thrace and Illyria, and to enlist the sympathies of Greece under his banner. All these projects were carried out successfully, and Perseus, his successor, inherited from him in 179 B.C. a kingdom stronger and richer than it had been at the accession of Philip.

The Romans had no serious pretext for renewing war against Macedonia. They were threatened by no danger from the East; and the Senate was quite aware of this. None of the Hellenistic states could dream of defying the arm which had inflicted such blows upon Syria and Macedonia. A large hostile coalition of Greek states was inconceivable: the political objects of each were so limited and so readily sacrificed to immediate interests that a bolder plan was excluded; and moreover each contained a considerable number of Roman partisans who would oppose any policy likely to end in war against her. But thirty years of activity in the East had taught the Romans to treat her 'allies' as subjects who were bound to obey, and to regard any independent action on their part as treason. Meanwhile the East grew more and more discontented, in consequence of this policy. Macedonia became an object of sympathy ; and the Greeks began to consider her as a possible deliverer from the grievous yoke of Rome.

It is no wonder that under these conditions Rome was alarmed by the growing strength of Macedonia. It was bound, sooner or later, to result in the complete severance of Rome from Greek affairs ; and this might, in the opinion of the Senate, create a position in which it might be possible for the East to attempt an attack upon Rome. Considering this risk of possible future complications, Rome decided in 171 B. C. to make war against Macedonia. Perseus sent an embassy to Rome, in the endeavour to preserve peace ; but the conditions brought back by his ambassadors were tantamount to the loss of Macedonian freedom. Perseus preferred war. Though Greek sympathy was mainly on his side, no part of Greece except Epirus was able to give him military support, and the Achaean League, now the strongest power in Greece, observed a strict neutrality in spite of the increasing dislike felt for Rome by the democratic party in the Achaean cities. Rhodes and Pergamum remained neutral. The first two years of the war were, on the whole, favourable to Perseus. Influenced by this success and fearing that a Roman victory would reduce them to complete slavery, even Eumenes, the king of Pergamum, and the Rhodians, though bitter enemies of Macedonia, made an attempt at diplomatic intervention, and urged Rome to make peace with Perseus and to restore in the East the state of things which had existed before the war. Rhodes even sent a special embassy with this object, but Perseus had fallen before the embassy reached its destination. Though the war had lasted two years, the Senate had no thoughts of peace. They sent out Aemilius Paullus, an abler and bolder commander than his predecessors. He carried on a vigorous attack and forced Perseus to fight a decisive battle near the Macedonian port of Pydna. In this battle, which took place in 168 B. C., Perseus was utterly defeated.

It is a notable fact that, even after her latest victory over her last rival in the East, Rome did not think it necessary to annex any portion of Eastern territory, though she had acted differently in Sicily after the first and second Punic wars and in Spain after the defeat of Hannibal. In theory, the East remained free and independent even after the battle of

Pydna; but its political destiny was now settled arbitrarily by the conqueror, with no regard to the interests or wishes of the peoples concerned. The Macedonian monarchy had always been distasteful to the Romans; and they now suppressed it by conferring on Macedonia a ' freedom ' which it had never possessed and never desired. The country was split up into four separate states, formed by a union of tribes and cities, and governed in the same way as the Leagues in Greece. Each state was ruled by magistrates responsible to a standing council which consisted of representatives from the different communities. Both magistrates and council were elected from the well-to-do class which alone had political rights. Rhodes and Pergamum had to pay dear for their sympathy with Perseus. The former lost much of her commercial importance by the formation of a free port at Delos, which was assigned to Athens and controlled by Athenian governors. With a weakened fleet she was unable to continue her task of policing the seas, so that piracy flourished and the trade in slaves grew apace. Delos became the chief slave market, and the supply came mainly from the Anatolian and Cretan pirates. Pergamum was punished by the loss of part of her territory which was made over to her neighbours, the Galatians and the King of Bithynia.

Severe punishment was dealt out to all Greeks who had not sided with Rome, and especially to the Achaean League. Though there was no proof of their complicity with Perseus, the Senate demanded that the most conspicuous and independent members of the League, to the number of a thousand, should be transported to Rome. When they reached Italy, they were not put on their trial but detained and distributed among the Italian towns.

Such arbitrary and unfeeling action aroused intense hatred in Greece, which Rome met with something like contempt. Enthusiasm for Greece was no longer in fashion; and a national party at Rome, of whom M. Porcius Cato was the most striking representative, spoke always of the Greeks as *Graeculi*, and openly preached the doctrine that Greek civilization was ruinous to Roman life. The treatment of the East by Rome was now purely arbitrary; and the position would perhaps have been less harmful, if she had governed it herself without disguise. She kept no army in the East, and the separate Hellenistic states had no military force worth speaking of.

Hence anarchy reigned in the Greek cities, and the strife of parties was even fiercer than in earlier times. As Rome kept no standing fleet in Greek waters, the pirates who were masters of the sea made it almost impossible to import foodstuffs regularly into Greece from the Black Sea, Egypt, and Asia Minor ; and the war of classes in the Greek cities was made fiercer by repeated periods of dearth. The Hellenistic monarchies were constantly at war with one another— Pergamum with Galatia, Bithynia, and Pontus, Syria with Egypt ; and these wars were complicated by the frequent interference of Rome, exercised by means of embassies, which were open to bribery and contributed nothing to the triumph of right and justice in the Hellenistic world. Macedonia suffered constant inroads from the north and was too weak to repel Thracians, Celts, and Illyrians.

The conditions of life thus created were intolerable ; and discontent, irresistible and universal throughout Greece and the East, brought on the final act of the drama. In 149 B.C. a certain Andriscus, who professed to be the son of Perseus, raised the standard of revolt in Macedonia : the unity of the country and the restoration of the dynasty were the war-cries of the rebels. The revolt was quickly suppressed. At the same time the Achaean League, especially the democratic section of it, rose against Rome, demanding that she should not interfere in their internal affairs and local differences with Sparta and other neighbours. The Romans declared their protests to be a revolt and suppressed it with extreme severity. The consul Lucius Mummius finally defeated the Achaeans in a battle fought at Leucopetra on the Isthmus in 146 B.C. After these blows inflicted on the Greeks and Macedonians for their final attempt to regain their liberty, Rome had no resource except to convert Macedonia into a province, with a military governor and a standing army, whose business it was to keep order in Macedonia and Greece, and defend them from attack on the north and west. A shadow of independence was left to Greece ; but she paid heavily for her love of freedom. The Achaean League was suppressed ; and the rich commercial city of Corinth, one of its chief strongholds, was destroyed by Mummius, and its territory declared to be the property of the Roman people. The whole of Greece was placed under the supervision of the governor of Macedonia, but the country was not converted into a

Roman province: some of the cities continued to be in alliance with Rome and were not forced, like the people of Macedonia, to pay tribute.

In the West meanwhile the foreign policy of Rome was shaped by the conditions which resulted from the second Punic war. The Gallic tribes in the valley of the Po were finally subdued, and north Italy was planted with colonies of Roman citizens and speedily became Romanized. The whole of Sicily was made into a province. In Spain the position was more complicated. The southern part of the country, once a province of Carthage, now became a province of Rome. But this narrow strip of Roman territory, being conterminous with a number of independent and warlike tribes, such as the Celtiberians and Lusitanians, was always in a state of war. To defend it, and to protect the rich silver and copper mines from the depredations of the neighbouring natives, the Romans were forced to maintain a strong standing army which carried on continuous fighting against the independent tribes inhabiting the central tableland of Spain. In this war they suffered more than one serious defeat. The cruel methods of repression adopted by their generals made peace impossible. The contest with the Lusitanians in what is now Portugal was exceptionally stubborn. These tribesmen, under an able leader named Viriathus, struggled against their enemies with success for eight years, from 147 to 139 B.C.; and the Celtiberians, whose chief centre was the city of Numantia, prolonged their resistance for even longer, from 143 to 133 B.C., and inflicted a number of severe reverses on the Roman arms. The Senate refused to recognize agreements which her defeated generals had made with the Celtiberians. The Roman governors pillaged and murdered without mercy the native population of the conquered territories. At last Scipio Aemilianus, son of Aemilius Paullus and adopted son of Scipio Africanus, the conqueror of Hannibal, took Numantia after a long siege.

The main point in the West, however, on which the eyes of Roman statesmen were fixed, was Carthage. Though constantly at feud with Masinissa, the Numidian king, and repeatedly robbed by him of territory—though the loss of her fleet and trading factories on the Mediterranean had greatly restricted her commerce—nevertheless Carthage was rapidly recovering from her fall. Her main efforts were concentrated on increasing the productive power of her African possessions by scientific agricultural methods backed by capital ; similar methods were applied to the breeding of stock and the cultivation of fruit and vegetables. She was still the chief source of export for the produce of central Africa—dates from the oases of the Sahara, ivory, gold, and slaves. African corn was coming to be an important item in the world markets. The rising prosperity of Carthage was no secret to the Romans. The story told of Cato, chief of the nationalist and landowning party, is well known : returning from an embassy to Carthage, he rose in the Senate and held out a splendid bunch of figs, as a proof that the new birth of Carthage was dangerous to Rome, and that Carthage must be destroyed.

It must be admitted that the proofs of this danger, urged by Cato and his partisans, were uncommonly weak. Carthage had no fleet and no powerful army ; her whole attention was taken up by the greed and restless activity of Masinissa, and war with Rome never entered her head. For all that, there was a party at Rome whose personal interests made them desire the disappearance of Carthage as an independent kingdom. This party did not consist of persons engaged in trade and industry : such persons had as yet no political influence, and indeed the part which Carthage took at that time in international trade was inconsiderable. The real enemies of Carthage were the large landowners in Italy, who viewed with great displeasure the export of wine and oil from Africa to the West. The whole of the West, as we shall see later, from this date onward drew their supply of these commodities mainly from Italy. These men wished to restrict the production of Africa to corn, for which there was an increasing demand in Italy, and also to add to their own acres by robbing the Carthaginian landowners of their estates. It was just this class of wealthy landowners who then directed the policy of Rome.

All this explains why the Romans, without any provocation, challenged Carthage again to war, ruthlessly and needlessly destroyed that flourishing city, and put to death most of the population. The third Punic war lasted from 149 to 146 B.C. Carthage made a heroic but hopeless resistance. Her executioner was the same Scipio Aemilianus who had destroyed Numantia ; politically he was sharply opposed to

Cato and the landowning party. The territory of Carthage was annexed and named the province of Africa. Most of the land was bought up and leased out by wealthy Roman landlords. Most of the other cities of the Carthaginian Empire were not destroyed, and some even kept their local self-government.

Once launched on the path of annexation, it was difficult for Rome to stop, especially as the Hellenistic states were ready to meet her halfway. From Greece she passed on to Asia Minor. The kingdom of Pergamum had long been no more than an obedient vassal of Rome ; and that the kings were well aware of this was shown by the action of Attalus III, the last of his line. He bequeathed his kingdom to Rome, and when he died in 133 B. C., the heir stepped in and named the inheritance the province of Asia. This transference to Rome of part of Asia was not, indeed, carried through without bloodshed. As in Macedonia, so here there was some opposition. A party, led by Aristonicus, who claimed kinship with the dynasty of Pergamum, and recruited mainly from the slaves and serfs of the late king and the rich men and from the mountain tribes of Mysia, carried on a fight for freedom for several years. But in the end this revolt also was crushed.

Thus in the course of little more than half a century the Roman state ceased to be a federation of Italian cities and clans, and became a great empire without a single rival either in the West or in the East. The Romans did not work for this position, or prepare for it, or desire it : it was the natural result of a series of incidents, whose consequences no one at Rome foresaw or could foresee. Yet this growth of Rome into a world-wide empire is one of the main events in the history of the world and has changed the course of that history. It also imported many new elements into the life of Rome, political, social, and economic—elements which worked a radical change in the whole aspect of the Roman state.

VII

THE ROMAN PROVINCES

TOWARDS the end of the second century B. C. the Roman state was a much more complex organization than it had been at the time of the Punic wars. The city of Rome was still the centre of it, with the normal constitution of a city-state (see Chapter IV), an extensive territory scattered all over Italy, and a body of citizens distributed throughout this territory. Round Rome were united other city-states bound to it by treaties varying in different cases : first and nearest came the Latin cities, followed by the Latin colonies scattered over the peninsula, and the more distant Italian cities—Etruscan, Greek, Umbrian, and Samnite. All these were grouped round Rome as her allies and formed an Italian confederation. While representing a single unit in all matters of foreign policy, yet the component parts of the league were united by no common tie of blood ; and the individual constitutions of the communities allied to Rome were surprisingly various. Such was the organization of the Roman-Italian state. A single principle, consistently carried out, was the foundation on which it stood—that no one formed part of the state except Roman citizens and Roman allies.

But even after the first Punic war Rome had to face a new and difficult problem of government. The south-west half of Sicily, and then Corsica and Sardinia, had been foreign possessions of Carthage, and the population were Carthaginian subjects or vassals ; the islands also contained a few Carthaginian cities, which served as trading factories, fortresses, and centres of administration ; but of local government there was no trace. The general population were obliged to pay over to Carthage a fixed part of their gains, this tribute being a sign and symbol of their subordinate position. When a treaty was made with Carthage, but not with the cities and tribes of the conquered territory, these islands became a part of the Roman state. Thus arose the question—what place in the constitution of the Italian confederation should be assigned to these new dominions ?

So long as war lasted, all was plain enough. The Roman military authority, the consul or praetor, settled all matters autocratically. But when war was over, it became necessary to define the future position of these countries. It was unlikely that Rome should wish to include them in the Italian confederation : the native population were too primitive in their political and social ideas, their level of culture too low ; it was impossible to regard them as conceivable allies. Besides, before they were incorporated into the Roman state, these peoples had no independent political existence, which made it impossible to make a treaty on equal terms (*foedus aequum*) with them. The simplest solution of the difficulty was for Rome to accept the situation as it stood, without making any changes ; thus the countries were regarded as still subject to military law, and military magistrates were sent there yearly from Rome.

From this point of view, the territory was, in accordance with Roman public law, the *provincia*, or ' sphere of activity ', of the Roman magistrate, whose edicts defined the relation of the inhabitants to the central power at Rome. Rome simply took the place of Carthage : the governor and the army were now Roman, while the natives tilled their land and fed their flocks as before, and paid a part of their gains to the sovereign power, represented by the praetor and his financial assistant, the quaestor. Of this tribute part was spent locally, and part was sent to the treasury at Rome. In this way the overseas dominions belonged to Rome herself, and not to the confederation ; and the Roman state consisted not only of citizens and allies, but also of subjects—a conception foreign to Graeco-Italian ideas of government and borrowed from the repertory of the Eastern monarchies. According to Roman terminology, these subjects were *dediticii*, i. e. they had surrendered at discretion to a conqueror ; they were neither citizens (*cives*) nor allies (*socii*), but foreigners (*peregrini*). In Italy after the conquest of different communities and peoples, this status had given place at once to a compact between the conqueror and the conquered ; but in the provinces it remained unaltered. The application of the same principle to Spain was natural, because Spain also had been transferred to Rome from Carthage.

But the problem was less simple when the rest of Sicily, the part owned by Greeks, also became part of the Roman state after the second Punic war and the capture of Syracuse. Here, just as in Italy, there were ancient Greek cities, and the population stood on a far higher level of culture than in western Sicily. Yet the Romans were unwilling to depart from the lines they had once laid down. Those Greek cities which had been in alliance with Rome before, continued to be allies, and were in the same position as, for instance, Massilia and Saguntum ; but all the rest of the island became a Roman province. Such a settlement was suggested by the fact that for nearly half a century this part had not been governed as a group of independent city-states, but like the territory of a Hellenistic monarchy, with Syracuse for a capital. The tyrant of Syracuse regarded the inhabitants as his subjects, and bound to pay him a tithe on the produce of their land, a tax on their cattle, and profits from trade and industry. Yet, when these subjects lived in cities, or on land which formed the appanage of individual cities, they were permitted to have local government with magistrates, councils, and popular assemblies of their own. The tyrant used these local authorities for the collection of the taxes due to him from the inhabitants of the city and land belonging to it. Hiero kept under his own immediate authority lands not belonging to particular cities but with a native population engaged in agriculture and cattle-breeding. The taxes due from these were collected by his own officials.

These relations between government and the people remained unchanged. The Roman people took Hiero's place, and the Sicilians, except the inhabitants of allied cities, became its subjects. The praetor and his financial assistant, the quaestor, acting in the name of the Roman people, exercised full power, military, administrative, and judicial, in the province. The western part of the island, which had become a Roman province after the first Punic war, was now united to the other half ; and the laws which had been promulgated by Hiero at Syracuse and subsequently confirmed by the Senate and the governors of Sicily were extended to it also.

From the lines thus laid down Rome never departed : the other overseas dominions were treated in the same way as Sicily. Up to the time of their annexation Macedonia and Asia (formerly the kingdom of Pergamum) had been monarchies with much the same constitution as Hiero's kingdom in

Sicily; and all the framework of government employed by the Hellenistic kings was retained by the Romans. Here too the praetor took the place of the king; here too the royal decrees and laws were included by the praetor in his ' edict ', which had the force of law, and in which he laid down the rules by which he would govern the people. Here too the praetor was the supreme judge and gave sentence in cases where the provincials were dissatisfied with the decrees of their own local courts. And here too certain cities, which had formerly been allied with Rome, still retained their status as allies and were not formally included in the province. The same line of action was followed exactly, when the territory of Carthage was converted into a province : certain Phoenician cities on the coast, which had betrayed Carthage and formed an alliance with Rome during the third Punic war, continued to be Roman allies even after the province of Africa came into existence.

Thus from the end of the second century B. C. we find a complex scheme of government which may be described as follows. Rome and the Italian allies formed as before the nucleus of the state. But the Roman alliance had been extended. There were new allies, and a considerable number of them, outside the boundaries of Italy. Many of these were domiciled in countries which were reckoned as Roman provinces, and in which the military and civil authority of the Roman praetor was absolute. It is therefore not surprising that these allies were hardly distinguishable from subjects, and that the Roman tendency was to degrade them to that rank rather than to raise the subjects to the rank of allies. The same tendency governed the relation of Rome towards those friends and allies who were still reckoned as independent political units—for instance, the cities in Greece and some of the Greek islands, and in some parts of Asia Minor which had never been included either in the Roman province of Asia or in any of the still surviving Hellenistic kingdoms. In name these cities were independent states, but in reality their position differed little from that of allied cities whose territory formed part of a Roman province. To both alike Rome issued her commands ; and she generally did so not directly but through the governor of the nearest province : thus the praetor of Macedonia dealt with Greece, and the praetor at Pergamum with Asia Minor.

The Hellenistic monarchs of the East and the native kings of Numidia and Mauretania were no better off : they, too, were mere vassals of Rome, and their foreign policy depended entirely upon her. The most prudent of them made no attempt to assert independence in their foreign relations, and sought to discover the wishes of Rome before they took any step in such matters.

The formation of the provinces as part of the Roman state was of capital importance in the political development of Rome and Italy. For her revenues Rome could rely chiefly on her new possessions, but her own citizens were reluctant to serve in distant wars. Thus Rome exacted more strictly than ever before the military service due her from her Italian allies, and began not unnaturally to treat them like her allies overseas, interfering in their local affairs and demanding implicit obedience to her edicts. Nor was it less natural that the Italian allies should claim a share in the advantages reaped from foreign dominions which they had helped to conquer. But the citizens were not inclined to share their possessions and revenues with the allies, and their unwillingness to grant an extension of the franchise became more marked. A collision between citizens and allies was plainly inevitable.

It is doubtful whether the Roman system of provincial government was capable of becoming popular among the subjects thus ruled, especially in the East and among the Greeks, who set so high a value upon the mere external forms of self-government and political independence. But, apart from this, the actual form of government was such that it did not secure right and justice to the provincials. The Hellenistic kings after all took account of their subjects' feelings, if only with a view to their personal wellbeing. But the Senate and Roman magistrates looked on the provinces as the ' estates of the Roman people' (*praedia populi Romani*), in whose prosperity they took but little interest. There were, indeed, not a few governors who were honest men and wished well to the provinces. But the mere fact that one man was absolute ruler over a vast country and then left it at the end of a year was bound to have a corrupting effect upon the governors. Thus it became more and more the fashion for the ruler to plunder the provincials and allies for his own benefit, and to treat his office as a gold mine for himself and a means to smooth the path of political advancement. It was not, indeed, forbidden to complain of dishonest governors before the Senate and Roman people ; but it was not easy for provincials to secure a just investigation of their grievances. For Greek cities, which possessed organization and money, this procedure was possible ; but for the general population who lived outside the cities such an attempt was hopeless.

This system of provincial government contributed in a marked degree to those new, social, and economic conditions at Rome which will form the subject of the following chapter, and also to the change, noticeable in the second century B. C., in the mentality of the ruling class. Patriotism now retreats to the background, and personal motives, often merely selfish motives, step to the front.

VIII

ROME AND ITALY AFTER THE PUNIC AND EASTERN WARS

THOUGH the wars in Africa and the East brought about a radical change in the social and financial arrangements of Rome and Italy, yet the political constitution of Rome remained unshaken. Rome was still a city-state governed by an aristocracy. As in the fourth century B. C. and at the beginning of the third, the chief political agent was the Senate, a body whose ranks were filled mainly by persons belonging to the Roman aristocracy of which the nucleus was formed by the patricians, who had long been large landowners and possessed the time and the means to devote their whole life to the business of government. This ancient aristocracy gradually co-opted the richest and ablest representatives and leaders of the plebeians, and also the richest and most influential citizens of the Latin and allied cities who had been admitted to the Roman franchise. There was formed in this way a special class representing wealth and distinction, and from it the magistrates were elected by the people and vacancies in the Senate were filled up. The past history of his family determined the eligibility of any man to this senatorial class, to the nobility (*nobilitas*) : the question was, whether he could point to kinsmen who had been magistrates of the Roman people and senators. If any one, by dint of personal ability and good service, found his way into the Senate or was elected to a magistracy—and this seldom happened—he was called a ' new man ', and the old aristocratic families treated him with some contempt and suspicion.

The tendency towards democracy, of which there had been indications in the fourth century B. C., stopped short in the third century and at the beginning of the second. Meetings of the plebeians were hardly ever held without the presence of patricians. Indeed, the social position of a citizen was not defined by the mere fact that he belonged to a plebeian family, because many plebeian families had been incorporated with the ruling nobility. At the end of the third century B. C.

the assembly of the plebeians by tribes was combined with the assembly of the people by centuries, and a mixed form of popular assembly was created out of the two earlier bodies. The tribunes, once the leaders of the plebs, though still elected by the plebeians, no longer played an important part in public life : they belonged themselves to the senatorial nobility, were generally senators themselves, and lost touch more and more with the masses. The actual control of domestic and foreign affairs belonged to the Senate. The magistrates were nearly always subservient to it. Its decrees in matters not covered by laws passed by the assembly had equal force with the laws. The Senate guided the foreign policy of Rome, managed the public finances, controlled the generals in the field, and directed usually the legislative activities of the popular assembly. Moreover, the senators as a class had vast judicial authority, since in the courts presided over by the praetors sentence was pronounced by jurymen chosen exclusively from among members of the Senate. The Senate was almost omnipotent.

The explanation is simple. In those difficult times when foreign wars went on almost continuously, the citizens realized instinctively the necessity of a single strong government. Such a government could not be supplied either by the magistrates or by the tribunes of the people. The former were elected annually and were too fully occupied with the current business, civil and military, to direct the state firmly and systematically. Nor was the popular assembly more competent for the task. The best citizens, the ripest and most experienced, were fighting in the ranks year after year. This being so, government by the popular assembly would have meant handing over the destinies of Rome to a chance group of citizens—a miserable minority of the whole body. On the other hand there was the Senate, the only body which was always in session and which enjoyed universal respect, a body long familiar with public affairs and consisting of men who had gone through a long and varied training in the business of government. The Senate proved its excellence in its conduct of the state's business. We have no reason to suppose that the senators possessed exceptional perspicacity or followed an infallible system in their management of affairs : they made frequent mistakes, were often vacillating and far from consistent in their foreign policy. But credit must at least be allowed them for intense patriotism and for an unexampled firmness and strength of mind, which was proof against all defeat and disaster. Aware of this, the citizens left to the Senate almost absolute control of public affairs.

To the Senate also belonged in general the control over the army. The Roman legions, i. e. the militia of Roman citizens, well to do and in most cases landowners, together with the infantry and cavalry (*cohortes et alae*) which formed the militia of the allies—the legions so composed were the weapon which enabled Rome not only to unite Italy but to construct the Roman Empire, the world-wide state of Rome. These same men fought on board the ships of the Roman people, when it was necessary to wage war by sea, as, for example, in the contest with Carthage and later in the East. This militia was commanded by consuls and praetors, the magistrates elected annually at Rome, and by military tribunes, who held office for a year if elected by the people, or to the end of the campaign if nominated by the commander-in-chief. But the real strength of the army was not derived from these well-born officers who came and went : it was due to the centurions of different ranks, who commanded the centuries and maniples—the separate mobile units into which the legion was divided. These men understood the fighting art to a nicety ; they kept up Roman discipline and Roman military traditions ; and they were past masters in the science of constructing those fortified camps on which a Roman army in the field always relied. Thanks to them, and also to great individual commanders, and lastly to the Senate which strictly maintained the stability of the army and welcomed technical improvements, a peasant militia was quickly converted in the stress of war into an efficient force of citizens in arms, that proved more than a match for the armies of Carthage and the mercenary soldiers of the Hellenistic kings.

But the fearful struggle of the Punic wars passed by, and was followed by years of victory in the East—victory enough to intoxicate men and turn their heads. The effect of both these periods was visible first of all in the economic and social life of Rome. The enormous losses suffered by citizens and allies during the great wars stopped the increase of population : before the second Punic war there were 270,000 male citizens of full age ; this number was reduced to 137,000 in

209 B. C.   This immense fall must be ascribed partly to the casualties of war and partly to the secession of Capua.   In 203 B. C. the number of adult male citizens was 214,000.   But even when peace was restored, the increase in the number of citizens was slow and irregular.   The highest point was reached in 163 B. C. with 337,000, after which there was a gradual fall to 317,000 in 130 B. C.   We have no statistics for the rest of Italy, but it is possible that the same process went on there. There was a change also in the distribution of the citizens. Latium ceased to be their chief centre, and the smallholdings in Latium gradually gave place to large estates.   A great number of citizens were now scattered over the whole of Italy as smallholders in colonies or with separate farms ; and the north of Italy, the fertile valley of the Po, was densely populated with these citizens, much more so than the south. There was more than enough land in Italy for citizens who wished to become settlers : vast spaces had been cleared in the south by the repeated slaughter of the Samnites in the Samnite and Punic wars, and in the north by the extermination of the Gauls during the second Punic war.   But those who were willing to accept and cultivate this land were comparatively few.

During this period the Roman peasantry, with the other smallholders who belonged to the allied Italian communities, still formed the military and social basis of the state.   These formed a large class, but other classes now took a place beside them, who increased more rapidly and whose development was furthered by new economic conditions.   The burden of the Punic wars fell mainly upon the class of yeomen. More than others they had to bear the weight of the *tributum*, or war-tax, which was levied again and again ; their losses in men were the largest, and swept away the strongest and soundest members of the community.   The large landowners suffered less ; but even they suffered more than the rising class of business men, who grew rich by contracting for supplies, building ships, making roads, and other services.

The Punic wars were followed by a series of victorious campaigns in the East, in the wealthy countries of the Hellenistic world.   War in the ancient world was not merely a political enterprise : it was commercial as well.   A war contribution levied by the conqueror might reach the Roman treasury intact ; but a considerable part of the spoils of war, legally or illegally, stuck to the fingers of the generals, officers, and soldiers, in the shape of gold and silver, cattle and slaves. Hence there appears at Rome in this period a large amount of capital in the form of coin, some of it held by generals and officers, i. e. by members of the senatorial class, and some of it by army contractors and brokers of military spoil. This capital was in search of investment. On the other hand, the state, whose standing source of revenue was the public land, was in search of capital to develop these lands. The safest investment of capital was in land ; and the slaves, who poured unceasingly into Italy from East and West, supplied abundance of labour. During the Punic wars much of south Italy and Apulia, belonging to communities that had sided with Hannibal, had passed into the hands of the state. In its devastated condition it was unattractive to the smallholder, and was now gradually taken up by capitalists chiefly of the senatorial class, who found it easy to get leases of public land from the Senate, or to occupy it without any legal title, and to buy up at low prices the estates of private owners whom war had ruined.

But war also created a new class of wealthy citizens who did not belong to the class of senators. I have spoken already of army contractors, commissaries, and sutlers. Business of this kind was improper for a senator and contrary to the traditions of the aristocracy ; nor was it approved by the state, which eventually, by a Claudian law passed in 220 B. C., forbade senators to engage in commerce or take contracts. But the state, as it grew richer, felt a greater need of persons experienced in business affairs. After the Punic and Eastern wars Rome had accumulated an immense amount of real property, both inside and outside Italy—forests, mines, stone quarries, fisheries, salt pits and salt works, pastures. These assets must be used, and the only method was to let them out on lease or by contract. The city-state, with its system of annual magistracies, had not the means of developing its resources except indirectly. Therefore such leases and contracts naturally fell into the hands of men who did not belong to the senatorial class, and who, having been attracted to business by the needs of war, had brought some capital out of it. They worked separately and in groups, forming societies and companies in order to exploit in common the various kinds of government property. Since the amount of their private wealth qualified them for military service as cavalry, therefore the class of rich business men became by degrees identical with that part of the citizen body who answered the call to arms on horseback—in other words, with the *equites*, who had once formed the first eighteen centuries of the first ' class '.

The rise of a large class of capitalists desirous to invest their capital in land resulted in a treatment of the soil which was new in Italy, though it had long been practised in the Hellenistic East and at Carthage. Under the old system the citizen farmer lived on his land and tilled it with the help of his family, or perhaps with a few slaves who formed part of the family from the economic point of view : the *familia* or family, according to Roman ideas, included not only the members of the family but also all the clients and slaves who took an active part in the business of husbandry. This system was still in force in Italy ; but another system now appears beside it—a system based on capital and servile labour, and directed by an absentee landlord, who lived at Rome or some other Italian town and gave up his time to other business. These landlords regarded the land merely as an investment, and therefore were eager to discover the most profitable methods of cultivation.

Such methods had been discovered long before by the Greeks. Aristotle and his pupils, in their study of botany, had always given their chief attention to the plants valuable to man ; and the domestic animals were the chief objects of their zoological researches. The observations of botanists and zoologists were utilized on the land by a succession of practical farmers. Combining scientific theory with the results of experiment, they composed text-books on agriculture, indicating precisely the most profitable methods of treating the soil, and the most suitable methods for different localities. These text-books were not intended for the smallholder but only for the wealthy landlord, who had capital at his disposal and abundant labour of slaves and serfs ; the object they had in view was not the maintenance of a family but the disposal of produce in the market. From this point of view a crop of cereals was the least profitable of all crops. The Greeks from time immemorial had got their grain from abroad —from Italy, Sicily, Egypt, the north of the Balkan peninsula, and the vast steppes of south Russia, and had paid for this imported corn by exporting wine, oil, fruit, woollen and linen stuffs, metal manufactures, and objects of luxury. It was natural, therefore, that cultivators working for export should give their chief attention to vineyards and olive groves, fruit-growing and cattle-breeding, and especially to the raising of fine-woolled sheep. These were the branches of agriculture which received special attention in the scientific text-books. The production of corn was left either to small farmers who had not the capital for more profitable enterprises, or to tillers in the remote quarters of the world who relied mainly on the labour of serfs.

These conditions repeated themselves in Italy during this period. The south of the peninsula had long produced not corn only but also wine, oil, and a fine quality of wool ; and, with the land, the Romans inherited from the Greeks their methods of producing these commodities. The growing accumulation of capital in the hands of Roman citizens turned their attention more and more to these special branches of farming. From the Greeks of south Italy Rome inherited not only agricultural methods but commercial relations as well ; and the result of the Punic wars was to extend these relations. Spain and Gaul, the chief markets for Carthage, now became Italian markets. It was natural for the Roman capitalists to increase the scientific culture of vines and fruit on their lands, to plant large tracts with olive trees, and to use the excellent pastures of central and south Italy for scientific stock-raising. All that they thus produced was exported by the Greeks of south Italy to the West, and then to the East as well, when the wine, oil, and fabrics of Italy could compete in quality with the produce of Greece.

As this capitalistic system of agriculture extended, and as more and more capital was invested in plantations and flocks, the disposal of her produce became a more urgent question for Italy. We have seen already how foreign policy was affected by the agricultural interests of Roman statesmen : it was Cato, the author of the first Latin treatise on agriculture, who insisted on the destruction of Carthage—a measure which can only be explained as the suppression of a rival in the production of wine and oil for the western market. Rome intended that the Carthaginian territory, like Sicily and Sardinia, should feed her and grow corn for a main crop. The same policy was carried out in Gaul and in Spain.

The economic changes described above were of great

importance socially and politically. The inhabitants of south Italy, whose lands were bought up by speculators, emigrated in increasing numbers to the East and West. The peasant population of Italy ceased to grow. The most active of the peasant class became landlords themselves ; the less capable, working on in the old fashion, divided up their land among their children in ever-dwindling portions, got into debt, and ended by going off to the towns ; or else they stayed on the land and became an agricultural proletariate, as hired labourers or tenants on the large estates. Hence the policy of Rome was less and less influenced by the smallholder, and more and more by the big landlords. The latter lived at Rome, where their wealth gave them great influence over the city population. The idle proletariate, flowing thither from every part of Italy, was now becoming prominent, and had no means of support but what they could get from their franchise. Every famous family in Rome and Italy maintained a number of clients, socially and economically dependent ; and the number of these retainers grew irresistibly.

These economic and social changes were accompanied by a remarkable transformation in the whole civilized life of Rome. The Romans wished to be recognized by the Greeks, not merely as a supreme political force but also as a civilized state and a part of the Greek civilized world. Many of the important public men learned Greek, guided at first by purely practical aims. Knowledge of Greek was a key to Greek literature ; and this literature, especially the historical and mythological parts of it, suggested to Roman patricians to supplement it by historical narratives, which should throw light upon the part played by Rome in the world's history. We have seen already that the first attempts to write a complete history of Rome from primitive times and connect it with that of Greece were made by members of noble Roman families, and were written in Greek for Greek readers.

Yet we find at the same time another tendency—to create a national literature after Greek models. The period of the Punic wars saw the first translations of Homer by Livius Andronicus, the first Latin comedies and tragedies, and the first attempts at a national epic—Naevius's history in verse of the first Punic war, and the history of Rome from the beginning by Ennius, in hexameter verse. About the same time Graeco-Roman comedies were written by Plautus, and Graeco-

Roman tragedies by Pacuvius and Accius. Stage plays became a favourite entertainment at Rome. In aristocratic families the children were educated by Greek tutors and masters. A knowledge of Greek and of Greek literature became almost indispensable to all who laid claim to higher education. The multitude of Greek slaves who gained their freedom and the citizenship imported a new element of culture into the middle and lower middle classes as well. It must be remembered also that there were constantly Greek embassies in Rome, staying there long and warmly welcomed in the great houses where Greek was patronized.

Both Rome and Italy were considerably affected by the presence of the Achaean hostages already mentioned—a thousand of the most enlightened and highly educated men from the cities of the League. The most conspicuous was Polybius of Megalopolis, a man of high culture, distinguished in political life, and famous as an historian. Chance brought him into contact with the younger Scipio, the conqueror of Numantia and Carthage and one of the greatest Romans of his time. Scipio, highly educated himself, was among those who opened their arms to Greek letters. He made Polybius an inmate of his house and constantly consulted him. Polybius was present at the siege and capture of Carthage. During his long residence at Rome he learnt Latin and became familiar with Latin historical writing and the Roman constitution. The fruit of this knowledge was his Roman History, which began with the second Punic war, after a short introduction devoted to the early history of Rome. This work was the first scientific book on the subject : it was written in the spirit of Thucydides and according to his method ; he used all the available material with good judgement. He was also the first to give a brief but scientific sketch of the Roman constitution, in its civil and military organization, and explained its points of resemblance and points of superiority to the constitutions of the Greek city-states. The greatness of Rome he attributed to the perfection of her constitution— to the fact that she realized that ideal state which Greek thinkers from Plato downward had so often discussed. He saw Rome as a state in whose constitution the monarchical, democratic, and aristocratic elements were blended into one harmonious whole—in fact as the very state which Plato and Aristotle had believed to be ideal.

Protests were not, indeed, wanting against the tendency to welcome Greek influences. Such statesmen as Cato saw terrible danger to Roman society in the victorious march of Greek culture, and the only language they used of Greeks was language of contempt. Yet even they could not escape its influence. Though Cato boasted that he was ignorant of Greek, yet his works—*On Agriculture, On the Latin Language,* and *On Italian and Roman Antiquities (Origines)*—prove that the writer, or at least his secretaries, had some acquaintance with what the Greeks had written on similar subjects.

In the domain of religion also Greek influence was strong. The horrors of the second Punic war caused a great religious upheaval in society. The strictly ceremonial character of the state religion gave no outlet to the religious feeling of the population, especially of the women, stimulated by the awful blows inflicted by Hannibal. The forms of Greek ritual and the images of Greek gods, less rigid, less gloomy, less remote, did more to satisfy the requirements of the people. Two facts contributed to spread the knowledge of Greek religion. First, the number of Greeks at Rome, coming especially from south Italy, was constantly increasing ; and secondly the national literature of Rome, whether tragedy, epic, or even comedy, was chiefly translated from Greek and thus familiarized every Roman with the images of Greek gods and heroes and also with the ritual of their worship. The Greek gods, indeed, received Latin names from the Roman poets, but no one could fail to recognize Zeus in the Jupiter of the Latin tragedies, or Hera in Juno, Athena in Minerva, and Dionysus in Bacchus. Some Greek gods, Apollo, for instance, had long been worshipped at Rome under their Greek names, and possessed temples and priests of their own. The Senate did not oppose the extension of Greek cults : on the contrary, during the second Punic war they took decided steps in the direction of combining the two religions and cults in the official religion of the state. Temples were raised to Greek deities within the walls of Rome ; and many Greek rites were included within the practice of the state. Such was the *lectisternium* now introduced in honour of Jupiter and often repeated : this meant that at Jupiter's festival couches were erected for him and other gods ; and the deities, reclining upon these, were supposed to take an interest in the sacred meal supplied in their honour.

Rome was now invaded also by the orgiastic religions of Greece and the East. The cult of Dionysus or Bacchus, long familiar to south Italy, made such enthusiastic converts in the city that the Senate was forced to take measures (186 B. C.), in order to restrain within the bounds of decency the unbridled licence of their nocturnal festivals. It is a notable fact that the Senate itself, during the second Punic war, entered into diplomatic negotiations with the kingdom of Pergamum, in order to have the black stone of the Great Mother of the gods conveyed from Asia to Rome. In honour of this fetish a temple was built to the goddess on the Palatine, on the advice of the Sibylline books—a collection of prophecies uttered by the Sibyl of Cumae. The collection had long before been transferred to Rome and figured largely in the worship of Apollo, whose temple was always associated with an oracular seat. In order to explain these books and to watch over Greek cults in general, the Senate created a special priestly college, consisting of two, later ten members who were called *decemviri sacris faciundis*.

The influence of Greece naturally showed itself in other ways and worked changes in private life and popular taste. Greek art and artistic production became more and more fashionable. Statues of Roman gods were often made by Greek sculptors after Greek models ; the aspect of the temples even was modified. The furniture of private houses began to take on Greek fashions, and much of it was imported from Greece. The city itself became more and more Greek in appearance. The practical skill of the Greeks made it possible to introduce more comfort into the conditions of life at Rome. As early as the end of the fourth century B. C. the first aqueduct was brought to the city by Appius Claudius, and the first stone bridge across the Tiber was built about the same time. Lastly, Appius Claudius also connected Rome with Capua by the first paved highway.

IX

THE GRACCHI, AND THE BEGINNING OF POLITICAL AND SOCIAL REVOLUTION AT ROME

THE peculiar conditions which had come to a head at Rome in the second century B. C. were no secret to reflecting men of all parties and ways of thinking, whether nationalists, or lovers of Greece, or radical reformers. The objectionable features of the existing system and the dangers to the healthy development of the state were clear enough. It was clear that the power of a single class, of a small group of noble families who used that power to promote their own interests, was a great evil. For the existence of such a power led inevitably to the growing demoralization of the ruling class : it became venal, accepted bribes, and itself bought votes at elections. The different parties prescribed different cures for the malady. Cato tried to conquer it by removing what seemed to him the root of the evil, that is, the influence of Greece, and by prosecuting in the courts individual representatives of the ruling aristocracy. Scipio and his friends proposed a number of moderate reforms in the social and economic system. The radical reformers saw no way to recovery except a renewal of the warfare between classes, in which the popular party were to be led, as of old, by the tribunes of the people ; their aim was to restore complete popular control after the Athenian model, and to destroy the predominant influence of the Senate in state affairs.

But all parties also saw clearly that the problem of altering the constitution could not be solved without reforms in social life and especially in economics. Here the chief evil was the rampant growth of large estates and a simultaneous fall in the number of those who owned small or moderate holdings. The result was an increase in the slave population of Italy which worked on the large estates of the nobles, and a diminution in the number of those who formed the nucleus of the army ; and thus the military power of the state was lessened. How dangerous the system of slave labour could be, was forced upon the Romans especially during the tribunate of Tiberius Gracchus (133 B.C.), when the slaves rose in fierce and stubborn rebellion both in Sicily and Asia Minor. The past history of Rome and the example of the Greek city-state proved that it was possible to fight against the growth of large estates. The law of Licinius, limiting the area of public land which any citizen might occupy and use, was passed in the fourth century B.C.; but this, though renewed at the beginning of the second century, remained a dead letter. In Greece also it had long been the practice to confiscate large estates and divide them up among the needy. All students of Greek history were familiar with the redivision carried through at Sparta in the third century B.C. by the Kings Agis and Cleomenes. And a sweeping measure of the kind seemed specially feasible at Rome, where the large estates of the nobles were situated on land belonging to the state. The land had been granted to nobles, either of Rome or of allied cities, not in absolute possession but on lease, either for many years or for an unfixed term. In the eye of the law, this land belonged to the state.

The question of the allies was also highly important in Italian politics. The allies fought stubbornly to acquire the Roman franchise, since this was their only means of getting a share in the government of the state. But as time went on, it became more and more difficult, even for individual citizens of the allied cities, to acquire that franchise. While freely admitting former slaves to the citizen body, the Senate and the magistrates hedged round the access to this privilege with such obstacles in the case of the allies, that hardly any of them were granted it during the second century B.C. The allies of course did their utmost to get the obstacles removed; and the obstinacy of the Senate and popular assembly was answered by growing discontent, which even led to attempts at armed rebellion. Thus in 125 B.C., even after the death of Tiberius Gracchus, Fregellae and Asculum actually started a revolt which was ruthlessly repressed.

Most of the ruling nobility, in other words, of the senators, while well aware of the obstacles which blocked the path of sound progress for the state, were nevertheless not inclined to take the line of serious reform in any direction. Any possible reform touched in one way or another their pride or their pockets. But there were also senators who were ready for reforms, even radical reforms. Most of the latter group were comparatively young and had been brought up with Greek democratic ideas ; they were ambitious but inspired by the sincerest patriotism. One of these was Tiberius Sempronius Gracchus, highly educated, absolutely honest, and remarkably able. Though his family belonged to a plebeian *gens*, it had long been prominent in public life and was reckoned among the families which constituted the high aristocracy. His father's career had been conspicuous and even glorious ; his mother belonged to the house of the Cornelii Scipiones. Tiberius himself began his career in the customary fashion. When fifteen years old he fought at Carthage under the command of his cousin, Scipio Aemilianus, and won much distinction. In 137 B.C. he was elected quaestor at the age of twenty-five and sent to Spain with the consul, Gaius Hostilius Mancinus. As quaestor he was forced to sign the ignominious compact by which Mancinus saved his army at the price of surrender. The Senate refused to ratify the compact. To Gracchus this was a great blow : his share in the shameful transaction was no augury of a brilliant future.

On his return to Rome he allied himself closely to the group of reformers in the Senate, who were led by Appius Claudius and Publius Licinius Crassus Mucianus. He married a daughter of Appius, and his younger brother, Gaius, married a daughter of the other leader. In agreement with them, and under the influence of his own experience, Tiberius worked out an extensive project, intended mainly to improve the fighting quality of the army, which had disgraced itself by surrender at Numantia. He considered that there was only one means of attaining this end—to improve the condition of the Roman peasantry and to increase their number by grants of land to those Roman citizens who had little or none. So radical a reform could not be carried except through the popular assembly ; and since, by Roman custom, the tribunes had the right to initiate legislation, Tiberius came forward as a candidate for the tribuneship of 133 B.C., and developed his programme in his election speeches. When elected he at once introduced his agrarian proposals in the popular assembly ; they were, he said, no more than a repetition of the existing law. He allowed no citizen to hold more than 500 *iugera* of public land ; but this maximum was doubled if a man had two grown-up sons. All other public land, at present enjoyed by great landlords, was to be taken from them and allotted to landless Roman citizens. On the other hand, the permitted amount of land, whether 500 or 1,000 *iugera*, was to become the property of the present holder, the state resigning its right of ownership. But the land allotted to the needy did not become their private property : the new owners could not sell it and had to pay a special tax or rent (*vectigal*) to the treasury. To put the law into execution, it was provided that a commission of three members should be appointed, with power to take away the lands and pronounce sentence in doubtful cases, and charged to allot land to those who had little or none at all.

When this proposal was brought before the popular assembly, it split up the Roman citizens into two camps—the rich and the poor ; and it had the same effect among the allies, among whom agrarian conditions were not very different, and where the local aristocracy occupied a good deal of land which belonged either to Rome or to the particular community. The rich rallied round the majority of the Senate, while the poor supported Gracchus in every way. When the day for voting came, a multitude of peasants collected at Rome, some of them from distant communities of citizens and allies. It was clear that the law, if once introduced, would be carried by an immense majority. The Senate resolved to resort to an ancient constitutional device. Some of the tribunes sided with the Senate ; and Octavius, one of the body, pronounced his veto against the voting. This was a sentence of death against the law. Tiberius urged the Senate not to oppose the law, but in vain. Now he had either to accept defeat or to resort to unconstitutional measures. After much hesitation he adopted the latter course. He proposed in the popular assembly an unprecedented step—that the tribune should be removed from office for betraying the popular cause, which he was bound by the original purpose of the tribunate to defend. The people then voted that Octavius should be removed from his office and a successor appointed in his room ; and next they passed the agrarian law. In accordance with the law, the commission also was appointed. It consisted of three members—Tiberius Gracchus, Appius Claudius, his father-in-law, and his brother, Gaius Gracchus, a youth of twenty. The commission began work at once.

Without support from the tribunes the commission was

powerless, and its successful activity depended entirely upon the composition of that body for the following year. Moreover, Gracchus did not intend to stop short with the passing of his agrarian law. When Attalus bequeathed his kingdom of Pergamum to the Roman people, Gracchus broke through established custom, and without consulting the Senate carried a law in the popular assembly, providing for the organization of a new Roman province, and using the inheritance to swell the funds of the land commission. It was clearly his object to remove from the competence of the Senate to the direct decision of the national assembly as much public business as possible. And for this purpose it was absolutely necessary that the body of tribunes for the coming year should be in sympathy with the policy of Tiberius, and that he himself should be one of the body.

Hence he stood again as a candidate for the year 132 B. C., and also endeavoured to fill the other places with his candidates. Though there was no definite law against the re-election of a tribune, yet it was contrary to established custom, which was often more powerful at Rome than the written law ; and his intention to stand was fiercely attacked by his opponents. His electoral address was also the subject of severe criticism. He included in it proposals to shorten the period of military service, to change the composition of the jury courts, and to make the franchise more accessible to the allies. The Senate believed, or pretended to believe, that Tiberius was aiming at monarchy, at a tyranny of the Greek type. On the day of election a number of his partisans, being busy with their farm-work, were unable to attend, and the senatorial party took advantage of this weakness to attack him in earnest. Finally there was an armed conflict in the open space before the Capitoline temple : the partisans of the Senate prevailed, Tiberius was slain, many of his supporters were killed in the tussle, and still more were sentenced to death afterwards. The murder of Tiberius was undoubtedly a revolutionary and illegal act ; but the Senate justified it as the suppression of a rebellion started by the tribune.

Yet the radical reformers did not consider themselves a beaten party. Their activity was renewed when Gaius Gracchus, the younger brother of Tiberius, after spending two years in Sardinia as quaestor, reached the age which qualified him to be a candidate for the tribune's office. In

124 B.C. he was elected to hold office in the following year, and at once brought forward a comprehensive programme of reforms, more precisely worked out than his brother's had been. The order in which Gaius Gracchus carried his various laws is not exactly known ; but we have more or less detailed information about each of them. It is probable that most of them were carried in his first year of office. These laws formed the programme of the so-called democratic party, which came into existence at Rome after the death of the Gracchi and waged unceasing war against the Senate. His chief objects may be summed up as follows.

First, he sought to transfer from the Senate to the popular assembly the decision of all important business, or, in other words, to set up at Rome a democracy after the Athenian model. To secure this point no special law was required : according to the constitution all important business was, in theory, settled by the popular assembly ; the innovation was this, that business which by custom had hitherto been decided by the Senate was now laid by Gracchus, as tribune, before the popular assembly, for their consideration and decision. Secondly, in order to carry out the forfeiture of public land on a wider scale, and to revive the system of allotting land to citizens, he carried a new agrarian law. According to his plan, the allotments were not to be limited to Italy, but the public land in the provinces was to be used for the same purpose. He passed a number of laws for the foundation of Roman colonies in south Italy and the provinces ; one of these was to occupy the site covered by the ruins of Carthage. Thirdly, he designed to extend the Roman franchise to the Latins and probably to the Italian allies as well. He brought forward a law to this effect in his first year of office, but failed to pass it through the popular assembly even in the following year. This was closely connected with his agrarian law ; for some of the public land was occupied by Latin and allied communities, and by large landlords who were citizens of these communities. Fourthly and lastly, there was a further law, probably connected with the last, which changed the conditions of service in the army both for citizens and allies.

Together with these four fundamental laws Gracchus brought forward other equally subversive measures, not perhaps intending them to be permanent, but using them as weapons against his opponents. The chief of these affected the jury courts, which were no longer to consist of senators only; but knights (*equites*), probably in equal number, were now included in them. This class of business men and capitalists, which, but for military service, took no active part in public affairs, was powerful already and now acquired great political influence, since not only civil suits but also the cases of Roman magistrates who had misused their power were tried by these courts. At the same time a law to regulate the province of Asia extended the operations of the knights in the sphere of public finance. Formerly the dues and taxes levied on Asia Minor were paid by the governments of the different cities to the Roman governor and by him to the treasury at Rome; but now these were farmed out by companies of Roman capitalists who proceeded to collect the money due by means of their agents. For a time, until the senators became reconciled to the change, these measures made a split between the Senate and the knights, which was the main object of Gracchus. Their temporary effect was to improve the administration of justice and to increase the public revenue; but in the sequel they only complicated the position and made it worse, by increasing the number of persons who could enrich themselves at the expense of the provinces, without giving to the inhabitants any new security for just and honest government.

Of not less importance in the future history of Rome was the so-called 'corn law' of Gracchus, by which the state was bound to sell corn to the citizens of the capital below the market price. Such a measure was quite in the spirit of Greek democracy, which held that the citizens had the right to dispose at will of the state revenue, or in other words, to spend the public money upon the maintenance and comfort of private citizens. The Roman populace welcomed the law with enthusiasm. This custom of feeding the Roman mob at the cost of the provinces survived not only Gracchus but the Republic itself, though perhaps Gracchus himself looked upon the law as a temporary weapon in the strife, which would secure him the support of the lower classes, his main source of strength. With the same object, and also to facilitate the redistribution of land and provide a market for the new settlers, he began to construct a number of new roads in Italy for economic as well as military purposes.

Probably shortly before the tribunate of Gracchus a law

was carried to permit the re-election of a tribune; and therefore his candidature for 122 B.C. escaped the opposition which had ended in his brother's death. But the Senate contrived to secure the election of another candidate, M. Livius Drusus, an able and influential adherent of their own, an eloquent speaker and skilful demagogue. When Gracchus travelled to Carthage to organize the colony of Roman citizens there, and was absent seventy days, Drusus began a violent agitation against his colleague. He stirred up the superstition of the mob against him, by pointing out that the soil of Carthage had been cursed after the destruction of the city. He also attacked the whole scheme of transmarine colonization, and offered in the Senate's name to found twelve colonies in Italy with 3,000 citizens in each. These attacks and counter-proposals did much to undermine the influence of Gracchus. His position grew still more difficult when on his return to Rome he tried to carry through the popular assembly bills for granting full Roman citizenship to the Latins and Latin rights to the Italian cities. The Senate replied to these proposals by expelling from the city all who were not Roman citizens, and by carrying on a fierce campaign against the new legislation. Even the consul Fannius, whose election Gracchus had supported, took part in this agitation. The bills were rejected, and Gracchus, when he stood for the office of tribune for the following year (122 B.C.), was defeated.

This defeat was followed by a struggle between his partisans and those of the Senate. Personally he was still one of the three commissioners appointed to conduct the settlers to Carthage, and therefore protected from prosecution by his official position. But the augurs were disquieted by portents at Carthage, where hyenas had dug up the boundary stones by night; and the Senate, acting on their representations, proposed to the popular assembly to repeal the law for founding the colony. The repeal was proposed in the assembly by one of the tribunes. On the voting day the people collected on the Capitol. Gracchus was surrounded by his armed supporters. Before the vote was taken, a certain Quintus Antullius was mysteriously slain by one of the crowd round Gracchus and in his presence. The Senate used this pretext to declare that Gracchus and his supporters were rioters, to mobilize the knights who had withdrawn their support from the tribune, and to summon to their aid a detachment of Cretan archers who happened to be at Rome. The other side also took up arms. They occupied the Aventine, where most of the residents belonged to the proletariate, and entrenched themselves in the temple of Diana. The Aventine was stormed by the forces of the Senate. Gracchus fled ; and when he was overtaken by his enemies he put an end to himself in the grove of Furrina on the right bank of the Tiber. About 250 of his supporters fell with him in the fight, and nearly 3,000 were put to death later without trial—a proceeding which was justified by the *senatus-consultum ultimum* or declaration of a state of war.

The death of Gaius Gracchus was followed by a conservative reaction. Some of his laws, however, the corn law for instance, his enemies shrank from repealing. The law which admitted knights to the juries and gave over the taxes of Asia to companies of contractors was also retained for a time. Nor was the agrarian law repealed. The commission, which Tiberius had created and Gaius had renewed, continued to act for some time. But it first lost the right to settle disputes between the old and the new occupiers ; and then the prohibition against the sale of allotments was withdrawn ; till at last the commission ceased to work and the allotments began to pass back into the hands of the capitalists. Yet the ideas which had inspired the Gracchi were not destroyed by this reaction. Their work was carried on after their death by a group of their supporters who took the name of *populares*, champions of the people. Their efforts were aimed chiefly at the Senate, and their weapons were the measures proposed by Gaius Gracchus, which now became the programme of the popular party. In opposition to the *populares*, the senatorial party came to be called *optimates*, ' the best men '. The struggle between these two parties did not turn so much on the main items of Gracchus' programme—complete control by the popular assembly, allotments of land to the needy, the colonization of the provinces by Roman citizens—the real object of contention was the helm of government. The democrats strove to wrest this from the hands of the Senate, while the *optimates* struggled to retain their old unquestioned control of public affairs. The contest dragged on for a long time and led to civil wars exceptional in their duration and ferocity.

The activity of the Gracchi was the subject of passionate debate and was diversely estimated both while the brothers lived and after their death. Roman politicians were sharply divided into two groups or parties, by which the Gracchi were regarded either as heroes or as criminals. A moderate and unprejudiced judgement was impossible in the disturbed political conditions of the time. Nor is the task much easier to the modern historian. Our own age is full of the same violent political contrasts that are presented by the time of the Gracchi and the age that immediately followed their deaths ; and modern thinkers also are divided in their opinions. It is certain that the Gracchi were inspired by the noblest intentions and fully convinced that they were doing right. But it is also certain that they did not realize the difficulty and complexity of the situation ; and it is unlikely that they foresaw the ultimate result of their revolutionary policy. Even if the programme of the brothers had been completely carried out, it could hardly have sufficed to make a radical change in the position. To set up at Rome a demo-cracy of the Greek type was a dream or a farce ; and to allot land even to every member of the proletariate could never bring back the time when the state rested securely upon a strong peasant population. They should have taken into account the power and influence of the highest classes, and recognized the fact that Rome was a world-wide power. The right course was to soften, not to exasperate, the feelings of classes, to devise new forms of government for the Roman Empire, and not to galvanize into life the ancient democratic institutions of Greece. But this the Gracchi neither did nor even tried to do ; and therefore action led to nothing but a prolonged and bloody conflict.

X

BEGINNING OF CIVIL WAR. THE ALLIES. MARIUS AND SULLA

HOW far the state had been crippled by the first manifestations of acute party strife begun by the Gracchi was shown by the events which followed the death of the younger brother. Hoping, probably, to divert popular attention from the critical issues raised by the Gracchi, the Senate, immediately after their victory at home, began a succession of foreign wars. These wars resembled the final campaign against Carthage. Their object was to promote the financial interests of the large landowners who formed the ruling class, and to increase the territory of the Roman state in Gaul and Africa, as well as to draw away the attention of the people from domestic affairs. It was intended to send thither as colonists the unruly section of the proletariate. The senators also hoped to find a good investment for their capital by buying up the land taken from the native inhabitants.

The first attack was made without any reasonable pretext upon the independent tribes of Gaul in the neighbourhood of Massilia. Between 125 and 121 B.C. a considerable part of the Rhone valley was occupied by Roman armies and converted into a Roman province. In 118 B.C. Narbo, the first Roman colony outside Italy, was founded, and the province was called after it *Gallia Narbonensis*. About the same time operations were begun in Africa against the heirs of Masinissa. Jugurtha, one of Masinissa's grandsons, sought to deprive his cousins of their shares in the kingdom of Numidia. The Romans then interfered, and when Jugurtha refused to submit to their demands, war followed. The story of the war was related by Sallust, a partisan of Caesar's, with the object of painting in dark colours the defective foreign policy of the Senate, and of showing up the corruption and venality of the senators as a class. In itself the war was not specially important ; but it gave a handle to the enemies of the Senate, and they used it to accuse the Senate's generals of many heinous crimes. Having little but Sallust's narrative to guide us we do not know the exact truth of these charges ; but it is certain that many of the generals sent by the Senate to Africa were guilty of dishonesty and incompetent, and that Jugurtha was able by means of bribery to put off the war for a time. It is certain also that the war was quite unnecessary, and that the destruction of thousands of Roman soldiers was due not only to the senatorial party but also to their opponents who insisted that the war, once begun, should be prosecuted with vigour. It brought to the front an able commander in Gaius Marius, a native of Arpinum in the Sabine country and a member of the equestrian class. He was held up by the popular party as a contrast to the generals appointed by the Senate. Supported by this party, he was elected consul for 107 B.C. and sent to Numidia, where in two years he actually ended a war that had dragged on for twice as long before his appointment. It should, however, be noted that his predecessor and former commander, Metellus, had paved the way for his success.

Other wars were fought at this time in Macedonia and Spain. For all this fighting constant drafts of recruits were needed; but the purpose and meaning of it all was hidden from the combatants. The smallholders and allies naturally became less and less willing to answer to the consul's summons, desertion became rife, and it was difficult to force the soldiers to fight. Still more difficult was it to maintain the internal discipline of the army.

With an army in this condition, and at a time when part of it was away in Africa, the Romans were compelled to meet a formidable and powerful foe. In 113 B.C. the Cimbri and Teutones, a number of German and Celtic tribes, came close to the Roman frontier, and two years later inundated the new Roman province of Narbonese Gaul. One Roman army after another was defeated; and two combined armies suffered a frightful reverse at Arausio (now Orange) in southern Gaul. Italy was in imminent danger. Fortunately for Rome, the Teutones stayed in Gaul, and the Cimbri, instead of invading Italy, went off to conquer Spain. Yet Rome foresaw the possibility that Germans and Celts would yet appear in Italy; and the citizens, who could never forget how Rome was taken and burnt by the Gauls in about 390 B.C., were filled with dreadful forebodings.

So imminent was the danger that the Senate made no protest when Marius, the conqueror of Jugurtha and leader of the popular party, was elected consul; they even suffered him subsequently to be re-elected for three years in succession, from 104 to 102 B. C., though this was contrary to all Roman political traditions. The first business of Marius was to reform the army. Owing to the force of circumstances, that army had ceased in practice to be a militia of citizens owning land and answering to an annual summons. The militia had been transformed by degrees into a standing army, because the provinces required the presence of such a force. The custom, by which the army was recruited solely from Roman citizens in possession of land, made it almost impossible to enrol men fast enough. It has been said already that men were unwilling to serve for years in the army, knowing all the time that their land at home was going to ruin. Meanwhile, as the number of landholders decreased, the same families were again and again called upon for recruits, while the landless population of the towns and villages, which was constantly increasing, escaped almost altogether. Marius carried through his reforms in the dark days of the Cimbrian war, and put an end for ever to the conception of a militia consisting of landholders. He summoned the proletariate to the colours, attracting them by pay and a promise of allotments of land when their time of service had expired. Thus what had been a militia became a professional army of long-service volunteers. With this new force Marius was able to defend Italy against the invasion of the Cimbri and Teutones in 102 B. C.; some of them were defeated and destroyed at Aquae Sextiae (now Aix) in southern Gaul, and the rest at Vercellae in north Italy.

The difficulties of Rome during these anxious years were increased by a fresh revolt of slaves in Sicily, which went on for three years from 104 to 101 B. C. At sea, too, the activity of the pirates made all trade impossible, and it was necessary to send a powerful fleet against them in 102 B. C. commanded by the praetor Antonius. But the relief gained by this expedition was only temporary. All these misfortunes, humiliating to the pride of the citizens and affecting their material well-being, lowered the Senate greatly in the opinion of the population and forced again to the front the leaders of the popular party which had never given up their violent attacks upon the Senate. Marius was one of these leaders and Apuleius Saturninus the other.

In 100 B. C. Marius was elected consul for the sixth time and endeavoured with the help of Saturninus to carry an agrarian law for awarding land in the newly conquered part of southern Gaul to his veterans and members of the proletariate ; and he demanded at the same time that a number of colonies, consisting of Roman citizens and allies, should be sent out to the western provinces. The system of Romanizing the West by finding land for allotments in the provinces and not in Italy carried on the work begun by Gaius Gracchus ; the novel feature was the privilege awarded to those members of the proletariate who had served in the army. But the law of Saturninus was injurious to the interests of the great capitalists who owned land in the provinces and hoped to acquire more in Gaul. These proposals, therefore, led to another armed contest between the Senate and the popular party—a contest so serious that Marius himself, the author of the proposals, was forced to assist the Senate in suppressing the rebellion and the street fighting begun by Apuleius and his partisans.

Still more serious were the consequences which followed the attempt of Livius Drusus in 91 B. C. to carry a number of measures taken in part from the programme of Gaius Gracchus and unacceptable, in general, to the Senate. The chief of these measures gave the Roman franchise to all Italians, as compensation for the land on which twelve new colonies, to be taken from the proletariate of Rome and perhaps of Italy, were to be settled. In his anxiety to pass this law Drusus concluded a secret agreement with the Italian leaders, and they swore loyalty to him personally. The extension of the franchise met with bitter opposition. Nevertheless Drusus persisted and intended to put it to the vote, but he was mysteriously murdered the night before the adjourned meeting. His death did not stop the Italians. They were ready to support their demands sword in hand, and at once began a grievous and bloody war against Rome. At first they demanded only admission to the Roman franchise, but in the heat of the contest they proclaimed as their object the utter destruction of Roman supremacy and the formation of a new Italian confederation, in which Rome should rank on a level with the other allies.

The Italian or Social war dragged on for more than three years, from 91 to 88 B. C. The antagonists were equally prepared, equally armed, and equally brave; they had lately marched, hand in hand, to victory through the whole civilized world; and the contest between them was extraordinarily fierce and destructive of life. Both sides were inspired by the conviction of a good cause. Hence in the number of victims sacrificed on both sides the Punic wars alone are comparable to this. It ended only when both antagonists recognized that it was useless to go on. The Italians realized that they were no match for Rome, who could draw for men and money not only on the whole body of citizens but on all the provinces as well: the support of the detachments recruited in Spain was especially valuable. On the other hand, Rome was ready to make terms, because the war was undermining her world-wide supremacy.

The disorders in Italy had weakened the belief in the East of the invincibility of Rome. The East looked hopefully at the growing influence and military power of Mithradates VI, king of Pontus, who had contrived from 125 B. C. to annex the Greek colonies on the northern and Caucasian shores of the Black Sea, and had skilfully extended the limit of his dominions in Asia Minor. At the same time he prepared a strong army and fleet, on the chance of an armed conflict with Rome. To this conflict he made up his mind under the impression of the Social war. In 89 B. C. Rome had to reckon with the facts, that a large part of the Hellenized East had taken sides with Mithradates; that all the Latin-speaking population of Asia Minor, all the Roman officials and traders resident in the East, had been massacred; and that Delos, the chief commercial centre in the Aegean and the Roman slave market, had been taken and plundered by Mithradates, and its Italian inhabitants wiped out.

The Greeks who had joined Mithradates and helped him to extirpate Roman citizens and natives of Italy were doomed to suffer a rude awakening: the King of Pontus was half civilized, cruel, and arbitrary, and his rule was a bitterer pill than the interference of Roman magistrates. But in the meantime the danger that threatened Rome was serious. The loss of prestige in the East at the crisis of a furious war in Italy was a danger; but still more dangerous was the loss of the revenue from her richest provinces, just when the need of money was greatest, and assurance of victory in the Social war depended on money. It was therefore indispensable that a Roman army should show itself in the East. But to secure that object concessions must be made in Italy : the allies must be compelled to stop, or at least to relax, their efforts against Rome.

Terms were therefore offered to the Italians. The Roman franchise was promised to all who would lay down their arms ; and the new citizens were to be enrolled in a small number of tribes—our authorities are not agreed whether these tribes were newly created or not. This settlement of the question in some degree satisfied the Italians and was acceptable also to the existing citizens. The system of voting in the popular assembly must be remembered : each tribe voted separately, and measures were carried not by a majority of the voters present, but by a majority of the votes given by the tribes. Therefore, if the allies were once included in eight tribes, whether newly formed tribes or not, they received only eight votes, whatever their actual number might be ; and the former Roman citizens had matters their own way, just as before. Exhausted by war, a majority of the Italians accepted these conditions. It so happened also that the expulsion of Mithradates from Greece and Asia Minor was especially important to the Italians ; because most of the business men in the East were Italians and not Roman citizens. The Samnites alone refused to accept the Roman proposals. But the Italian war, when restricted to a fresh conflict with the Samnites, began to die out, leaving Rome free to begin systematic operations against Mithradates.

Such were the conditions at Rome when a dispute arose, not in itself of the first importance, but so hotly contested that it resulted in a furious civil war. The question in dispute was, what general and what army should be dispatched to the East. The constitutional answer was plain enough : one of the two consuls for 88 B. C. should be chosen by lot to lead the expedition. The lot fell on Lucius Cornelius Sulla, the hero of the last phase of the Italian war, whose victorious army was quartered in Campania. This was a fortunate result, for Sulla was an able general and a favourite with the soldiers. On the other hand, he was a foe of the democratic party and opposed further concessions to the Italians. This was enough to light the flame of faction. Contrary to all traditions, the democratic party put forward a candidate of their own : this was Marius, the great popular hero, the deliverer of Rome from the Cimbri and Teutones. Relying on the doctrine of Gracchus, that the sovereignty of the people extended to foreign affairs, the democrats, with the aid of Sulpicius Rufus, a skilful politician, carried through the popular assembly a proposal that the command should be transferred to Marius ; they tried at the same time to secure the support of the Italians, who hated Sulla, by giving them the full rights of Roman citizens.

Threatened with death Sulla was forced to yield : he fled from Rome to his army in Campania. His cause seemed utterly hopeless. But the legions in Campania supported him. They had been sure that he would lead them to a profitable and bloodless campaign in the East, whence they would soon return to Italy, to settle on rich land taken from the Italians. But now all these hopes were dashed. If Marius went to the East, he would not take them with him. Only one course lay open : they could compel Rome by force to submit to the will of the legions, they could start the first military revolution. Haste was necessary, for every day of delay made success more doubtful. Considerations of duty were suppressed ; the Italian war had already accustomed the Roman soldier to fight against his brothers. The general and the army quickly decided to march against Rome. The officers alone were left behind. The city was taken by assault ; though Marius managed to escape, the chiefs of the opposite party were destroyed ; and the new democratic laws were repealed.

After this easy victory over his rival two possible paths lay open before Sulla. He might either stay in Italy and prepare for the inevitable continuation of civil war, or leave Italy to itself and proceed to the East, in order to return victorious with increased resources and a devoted army prepared to execute all his commands. He decided on the latter course. Had he stayed in Italy, it is doubtful whether his troops would have continued to support him. Before his departure to Greece and Asia he hastily carried some measures of reform—a foretaste of the complete programme which was in future to restore and confirm the rule of the Senate.

Immediately after his departure power passed into the hands of his rivals. The management of affairs was concentrated in the hands of the democrats, led by Marius and Cinna ; the former crushed the resistance of the Senate with the aid of the forces left in Italy and the inhabitants of the Italian towns. Then began the first long reign of terror, so often to be repeated in later times. The enemies of democracy were slain by hundreds, on information and on suspicion, without trial and without investigation. The victims were all senators or knights. The massacre was carried out in part by bands of slaves who had been set free by Cinna, the second in command of the democratic party ; and these executioners Cinna himself was eventually forced to destroy by the hands of a detachment of Gallic soldiers. The years 88 and 87 B. C. were devoted to this massacre of their opponents. Marius and Cinna were elected consuls for the following year. In the first month of his consulship Marius died.

Sulla meanwhile had driven Mithradates out of Greece and also defended himself against L. Valerius Flaccus, the successor of Marius in the consulship, who had been sent out with an army to the East to fight both Mithradates and Sulla. Though the war with the king was not finished, affairs in Italy forced Sulla, after restoring Roman rule in Greece and Asia Minor, to make peace on terms which were acceptable to Mithradates and not very flattering to Rome. Next he forced the rival Roman army to surrender ; it had mutinied against Flaccus and killed him, and was commanded by Fimbria, the quaestor who had stirred up the mutiny. Sulla's object in the East was now attained. He had crippled Mithradates for a time at least ; his army had taken rich booty and looked forward to gifts of land in Italy which he alone could award them ; the plunder of the East had put immense sums of money in his hands ; and his mastery of the East secured to him a steady supply of fresh resources. In spite of certain overtures on the part of the Senate, a renewal of civil war was inevitable ; and Sulla was prepared for it.

The democrats also were prepared. They relied chiefly on the support of the Italians, especially the Samnites. The clash of arms began as early as 85 B. C. During the whole of the following year attempts were made to prevent Sulla from landing in Italy. The attempts failed, and Italy once more became the scene of a ruthless civil war, which went on for two full years. In the end the democrats were utterly defeated : they had failed to put their forces under a single command or to retain the loyalty of the citizen army. Though the Italians remained faithful, the legions formed of citizens were constantly deserting to Sulla's banner. The war ended with fierce battles at Praeneste in Latium and under the walls of Rome, in which Roman citizens and allies, especially Samnites, were slain by tens of thousands. To show the cold cruelty with which Sulla disposed of his enemies, I shall quote a single anecdote. After Rome was taken, a meeting of the Senate was held on 3 November 82 B. C. When the senators were horrified by cries that came from a neighbouring building, Sulla interrupted his speech to remark : ' Let us go on with the business, senators ; it is only a small number of rebels who are being executed by my orders.' The truth was that 8,000 Samnites, who had been promised pardon by Sulla, were being massacred in that building.

The conqueror followed the recent example of the democrats both in the savage extermination of his political opponents and in the means by which it was carried out. But a certain degree of method was added to this blind destruction by a device whose infamy was marked by a pretence of legality. It was called ' proscription '. Without trial or inquiry or proof of guilt list after list of victims was posted ; rewards were offered to their murderers, whether slaves or freedmen. The example thus set by Sulla was followed by not a few imitators in later times.

Sulla's motives, however, for all this were not merely cruelty and the desire to consolidate his personal authority. In exterminating the Samnites his intention was to put an end to the Italian war, and he believed that the reign of terror was inevitable, if Italy was to be thoroughly unified and Latinized. His measures were effective : there is no doubt that the almost complete extermination of the Samnites hastened the process of Latinization in south Italy. But was there no other possible method ? To Latinize the desert into which a large part of the Samnite country had been converted was no difficult task.

Sulla had a further motive for his atrocities : he wished to remove all obstacles to the introduction of his intended reforms. The essential part of his programme was to restore and increase the power of the Senate, and also to improve the system of government in the provinces. Since the tribunes were the sole opponents of the Senate, Sulla's blows were aimed principally at them and at their instrument—the assemblies of the proletariate of Rome which passed for assemblies of the Roman people. He struck at the proletariate by depriving them of the right to cheap corn, hoping in this way to stop them from flocking to Rome. Also, though decrees of the *plebs* were still regarded as having the force of law, he passed a law by which all Bills proposed by the tribunes must first be placed before the Senate and sanctioned by it before they were submitted to the popular assembly. At the same time the right of veto possessed by the tribunes was limited. Thus the office lost almost all its importance in political affairs, retaining only the right of giving individual assistance to plebeians. Even the right of sitting in judgement was virtually lost by the plebeian assemblies : most political and criminal trials were now, in accordance with new laws, referred to special permanent courts, in which a praetor presided and senators composed the jury. The title of tribune became not merely unattractive but positively injurious, because ex-tribunes were deprived of the right to compete for the higher magistracies, so that it was impossible for them to enter the Senate or command an army or govern a province.

The authority and power of the Senate were increased at the cost of the tribunes and the popular assembly. All the rights it had enjoyed before the legislation of the Gracchi were now restored to it. To Sulla it was obvious that the Senate could, and the rabble of Rome could not, govern a world-wide state. By a whole series of laws, on which thereafter the activity of the body was based, the Senate was made the actual head of the state, and the magistrates were made subservient to it. These laws strictly defined the magistrates' official career and limited their power. An obsolete law of 342 B. C., which required that an interval of ten years should elapse before the same office could be held a second time, was now re-enacted ; and a law was passed, based on one of 180 B. C., which fixed the age of candidates and the order in which offices must be held : no one could be quaestor before the age of thirty, nor praetor before he was forty ; it was expressly provided that two years must elapse between the tenure of one magistracy and the tenure of another. Of even greater importance was the regulation that the magistrates should remain at Rome during their whole year of office. Only in exceptional cases and by the express appointment of the Senate could the consuls carry on war in provinces assigned to them by the same authority. Each consul and praetor during his year of office was nominated by the Senate to a further post, generally the governorship of a province. When they ceased to be consuls and praetors, they departed to their provinces as proconsuls and propraetors, and there they remained until the successor appointed by the Senate came to take their place. Thus the supreme control of the whole state belonged to the Senate. Consuls and praetors were its obedient servants, since it alone could appoint them to a province, and no magistrate, until he was governor of a province, possessed military power. And even in his province the governor was in the same subordinate position : the Senate could at pleasure grant or refuse a prolongation of his tenure ; they could award or withhold a triumph ; and they could summon him to account for his conduct, when his term of office expired.

Further, the laws of Sulla restored to the senators their full judicial powers. The juries in the highest courts were chosen from among the senators, the knights being absolutely excluded from this function. The danger that proconsuls and propraetors might, like Sulla himself, overpower the Senate by means of an armed force was lessened by a law that there should be no army in Italy, and that soldiers, on their return from the provinces, should lay down their arms and become civilians. Also, the proconsuls themselves by crossing the boundary of the capital lost their military power and became ordinary citizens like their soldiers. Thus the policy of Sulla was not merely to restore the power of the Senate : it was the first attempt to place that power under the protection of law, to substitute legislation for tradition, to legalize the authority of the oligarchy of Rome, and to make a clean sweep of all attempts to place the power of the tribunes and the popular assembly in opposition to the power of the Senate.

Sulla carried out his reforms with the title of dictator ' for the regulation of the commonwealth ' (*rei publicae constituendae*), chosen by the people for an unlimited period. He exercised in this way autocratic power. For support he relied upon 120.000 veteran soldiers distributed by him throughout Italy in those towns whose population had been almost annihilated during the Social war, and on lands forfeited by persons suspected of democratic sympathies. These veterans received large allotments of land and formed a superior and ruling class in the Italian towns. They were not permitted to sell their allotments. In this respect Sulla was, to some extent, carrying on the work of the Gracchi. But his object was not to restore the old Italian peasantry : it was to create, or rather to strengthen, a class of smallholders. At Rome he was supported by 40,000 liberated slaves who all took his gentile name and were called *Cornelii* ; they had probably belonged to the democrats whom he had put to death. Their number is an indication of the immense wealth accumulated by Sulla ; and his partisans also made huge fortunes. All this wealth, the result of legalized robbery, was squandered as quickly as it was acquired. Its possessors were, of course, together with the veterans and the freedmen, fierce in their zeal for Sulla.

The dictator himself, however, considered his autocratic power as a temporary expedient, and never entertained the idea of retaining it for life. He was not ambitious, and he believed that the oligarchical constitution to which he had given legal form might last long. Thus, when he had completed his reforms, he laid down his authority and left Rome for south Italy in 78 B. C. There he lived as a private man, but not for long : within a year of his retirement he died.

XI

POMPEY AND CAESAR : THE SECOND STAGE OF CIVIL WAR

T HE sufferings of Italy in the first ten years of civil war, however dreadful, were but the beginning of a yet longer and more bloody conflict ; they served rather to inflame than to allay the rage of faction in Rome and Italy. Though the popular party was defeated and almost all its leaders were destroyed, it retained the power of recovery. Some aristocrats, leaders of the party, had somehow survived ; and these men hated the Senate more than ever and were ready to use any weapon in order to hurl it from power. Essential differences of opinion were ignored ; the endeavour to improve the social and economic condition of the citizens was shelved ; and all that remained was the personal hatred between the leaders of two sections of the community. Neither party was ill-provided with supporters ; but the discontented far out-numbered the contented. The Senate and Sulla's constitution had many enemies—the children of the democratic leaders who had been put to death ; the landowners whose land had been taken from them to provide for Sulla's veterans ; and the soldiers of the democratic armies who had never received the allotments which they counted upon. Even Sulla's veterans were not partisans of the Senate : they had fought for Sulla alone and were ready, after his death, to serve under any one who would enable them and their children to gain wealth again with little danger. Many of them had already squandered their ill-gotten riches ; and their allotments were gradually passing out of their possession. Thus there was no tranquillity in Italy after Sulla's death, and little hope of a lasting peace.

Disturbance was especially rife among the multitude of slaves in Italy and the East : their eyes had been opened to the weakness of their masters by the troubles of the civil war. Some slaves ran away and swelled the ranks of those bold pirates who had once more gained mastery over the Mediterranean, and had formed something like a regular league, with Cilicia and Crete for their chief centres ; others formed bands of robbers, which plundered the estates of the nobility and waylaid travellers on the roads of Italy and Asia Minor. Upon the frontiers also the state of things was unsatisfactory. In Spain the relics of the democratic party and of its armies had rallied round Sertorius, who ruled Spain in the interests of the party ; and he was strengthened by the warlike tribes of Portugal who were irritated by the oppression of Roman provincial government. In the East Mithradates was restoring and extending his kingdom, enrolling a new army, and building a strong fleet. In alliance with the Anatolian and Cretan pirates and Sertorius in Spain, Mithradates again hoped to realize his ambition of creating a Graeco-Oriental Empire which should be independent of Rome. There were disturbances in Rome itself. The democrats, headed by Lepidus, hoped that Sulla's death would bring them back to power ; but the attempt to restore the tribunate, and thus to renew in the forum the conflict with the Senate, ended in failure. Lepidus next tried to rekindle the flame of civil war : when his year of consulship was over, he brought an armed force from his province of Cisalpine Gaul, or north Italy, on purpose to seize the capital. But he failed once more : his army was defeated by the forces of the Senate, and the survivors sailed first to Sardinia and then to Sertorius in Spain.

The Senate was unable to cope with all these complications and dangers by ordinary expedients, that is, by sending one of the annual magistrates at the head of a militia enrolled in Italy. The time for such measures had gone by ; and Sulla realized this when he placed the military power of the state in the hands of extraordinary magistrates—the proconsuls and propraetors nominated by the Senate. But even this device broke down in the most serious emergencies. The soldiers would not fight for any commander unless they knew him well and had served under him long, and unless they could expect from him the same rewards that Sulla had given to his veterans. Thus the Senate, after vain attempts to solve their difficulties by ordinary means, were forced, whether they liked it or not, to create extraordinary commands, to be held, in violation of the constitution, by special persons for a long period. These commands were eagerly competed for in the time that followed Sulla's death, because any victorious general might thus make himself the master of Rome and fill the place of Marius or Sulla. The problem of the Senate was to find out among the aspirants to such commands the men who were least likely to overthrow the senatorial ascendancy. It was a problem which hardly admitted of a solution.

Among those who claimed to fill the place of Sulla there was one who had come to the front in Sulla's lifetime. This was Gnaeus Pompeius, young and able, very rich and inordinately ambitious. He owed his position entirely to the part he had played in revolutionary times. At the head of an army recruited by himself from among his own clients and tenants he had exerted himself greatly on Sulla's side in the civil war, though he derived no authority from the state. Brilliantly victorious in Italy, he was then sent to Sicily and Africa to fight what remained of the democratic armies. On his return he received the surname of ' The Great ' (*Magnus*) and the honour of a triumph. The latter distinction was illegal on two grounds : he was not a Roman magistrate and was therefore disqualified to celebrate a triumph ; and further, a triumph was granted only to a general who had conquered a foreign foe in a ' lawful war ' (*bellum iustum*), but the mutual extermination of citizens was not such a war and was not recognized as such by the law. When Sulla died; Pompey was in Italy, in command of an army. The Senate made use of him to crush the revolutionary attempt of Lepidus. But they had to pay a high price for his services : he demanded an extraordinary command in Spain, in order to fight Sertorius, and it was impossible to refuse his demand. The war in Spain dragged on for seven years, from 78 to 72 B.C. Pompey succeeded in ending it ; but his success was mainly due to the internal dissensions among his opponents, which followed upon a succession of defeats : the Roman generals, Sertorius and Perperna, quarrelled with one another, and the Spaniards quarrelled with the Romans. These dissensions ended in the treacherous murder of Sertorius, who had been the soul of the war from first to last.

Meanwhile matters in the East were coming to a head. The Senate was unable to check the growing power of Mithradates by any ordinary means. When Nicomedes III died and bequeathed to Rome his kingdom of Bithynia, Mithradates boldly ignored the bequest and seized the kingdom. The Senate was forced once more to create an extraordinary command : they sent L. Lucullus and Aurelius Cotta, the consuls of 74 B. C., to Asia Minor with a strong army and fleet, while M. Antonius, with very extensive powers over the whole Mediterranean coast, was to fight the pirates who were in alliance with Mithradates. The war went slowly on. Antonius was unsuccessful ; Lucullus did better, driving Mithradates out of Asia Minor back to Armenia, and inflicting a severe defeat on Tigranes, king of Armenia and allied with Mithradates.

War was only beginning in the East and still far from an end in Spain, when Capua in Italy became a centre of union for all the bands of runaway slaves wandering about the country, and for other discontented sections of the population. A band of gladiators, led by Spartacus, a Thracian, broke out of their barracks at Capua, and settled on the slopes of Vesuvius, where they soon grew into an organized and well-armed force. Celts and Thracians, excellent natural fighters, formed the backbone of this army ; and these men were not mere barbarians : they knew very well that their kinsmen in the far North were not only free but strong also, and they had grounds for hoping that they could fight their way back to their own country. If they lost the game, it was not because the Senate showed itself able to cope with the revolt. Spartacus, by winning victory after victory, actually opened the way to the North ; but a large part of his army preferred to remain in Italy, robbing and killing their former masters ; and thus the power of the revolted slaves gradually melted away. Even so, the Senate could only deal with these diminishing hordes of banditti by creating yet another extra-ordinary command : in 71 B. C. they commissioned M. Licinius Crassus, a praetor and one of Sulla's officers, to carry the war to a conclusion.

By 70 B. C. the crisis in foreign affairs was over : peace was restored in Spain, the claws of Mithradates were pared, in Italy the slaves were ruthlessly slaughtered, and only the pirates still mocked the power of Rome. But there was profound dissatisfaction at home, especially among the knights, the business men, and the capitalists. The destruction wrought by the slaves in Italy was felt by them as much as by the senators ; but the success of the pirates and the prolongation of war in the East were even more detrimental to their interests. And they had another grievance—that Sulla had deprived them of all share in public life by giving back the jury courts to the Senate. The democratic party also was raising its head again. Pompey and Crassus, each at the head of a victorious army, were encamped under the walls of Rome ; and each required that the laws of Sulla should be broken in his favour : they demanded a triumph and the right to stand at the consular elections for 70 B. C., without entering the city and thus laying down their executive powers.

These demands were opposed by the Senate, not because they were illegal but because the Senate feared to become once more a tool in the hands of ambitious soldiers. Pompey and Crassus, in spite of their rivalry and mutual distrust, saw that neither of them could fight the Senate single-handed ; but they believed that they might force it into compliance, if they joined forces and attracted the knights and the democrats to side with them. But the only way of attracting these allies was to sacrifice Sulla's constitution. That these two partisans of Sulla should ally themselves with the very men to whose destruction they had hitherto devoted all their energies, is a most instructive fact : it shows so clearly how political programmes and the idea of the common weal had been ousted by the personal ambition of military leaders. The Senate was forced to give way. Pompey and Crassus were consuls in 70 B. C. ; the constitution of Sulla was almost entirely repealed, and the political anarchy which he had brought to an end reigned once more at Rome.

Pompey and Crassus refused the ordinary proconsular commands : they preferred to wait for other possibilities ; they required something greater, some new and extraordinary commission. Pompey was the first to come forward. Supported by the tribunes and the knights, he received in 67 B. C. extraordinary powers in order to suppress the pirates in the Mediterranean. He performed the task successfully, and the tribunes brought forward a new law in the following year, that Pompey should supersede Lucullus in the command against Mithradates. The knights were discontented with Lucullus : they resented his leisurely method of campaigning and also the exceptional honesty with which he governed the East. His soldiers also objected to being detained in the East so long. After some opposition Pompey was given entire and absolute control over all the East for an unlimited period. He disposed of Mithradates and Tigranes without much difficulty. He satisfied the knights by adding to the eastern provinces of Rome not only the dominions of Mithradates but also fractions of the Syrian kingdom, including Judaea and Jerusalem. The army, too, was satisfied : Syria, hitherto untouched by Roman plunderers, gave them ample opportunities to enrich themselves ; and Pompey promised them allotments of Italian land in the near future.

At Rome, meantime, there was intense agitation. The democrats had made use of Pompey to repeal the constitution of Sulla. But now the menace of a second dictatorship hung over their heads, and who could foretell the course that Pompey would follow when he returned from the East ? They could not forget that he had destroyed their hopes of victory in Spain, and that he had spent his youth as the obedient coadjutor of Sulla. The Senate also distrusted Pompey : he had betrayed them once already, and it was not likely that he would consent now to be a mere instrument in their hands.

The democrats made feverish preparations for the conqueror's return. Their political leader was Gaius Julius Caesar, related to Marius and son-in-law of Cinna. Thanks to his youth and doubtful reputation he had survived by a miracle Sulla's proscription, though Sulla himself admitted the dangerous character of the young man. Money for political intrigues was supplied to Caesar by Crassus, one of the richest of all Romans; Crassus was intensely envious of Pompey, his former ally, and felt that Pompey's glory might have been his glory. But the democrats were in a difficult position. The optimates kept a sharp eye on them and prevented them from securing military commands and magistracies for their leaders ; and the thundercloud of Pompey's army lowered in the East. Hence the years of Pompey's absence were years of feverish attempts on the part of the democrats to make themselves by hook or by crook masters of the situation at Rome. They had once before made use of an aristocrat to gain their own ends, and they were prepared to repeat the same trick. They found a suitable tool in L. Sergius Catilina, a ruined aristocrat, a man of great ambition, who possessed no small influence upon the impoverished young nobles and also upon the dregs of society at Rome. He had quarrelled with the Senate and was ready to serve Caesar and his party, if they would smooth his way to the consulship.

The plot failed. This move on the part of the democrats was detected by the Senate ; and the knights had no wish for a fresh revolution just after Pompey had opened up such a promising field for them in the East. The mediator between the Senate and the knights was M. Tullius Cicero, a fellow townsman of Marius, and a brilliant and ambitious advocate, who had just started his political career on the democratic side by attacking the senatorial juries and the senatorial misgovernment of the provinces. His skilful conduct of the prosecution against Verres, who had plundered Sicily just as other senators plundered their provinces, had proved to the Senate that this ' new man ' might turn out to be dangerous. Cicero was ambitious : like every Roman, he wished to reach the highest position in the state ; he wished to found a new noble family, to be the first consul and the first consular—these ex-consuls formed the highest class of the Roman nobility—of a family hitherto undistinguished. His intelligence and patriotism made him dread revolution with all its horrors. As a professional man and member of the equestrian order, he dreamed of a reconciliation between the two highest classes of Roman society. Thus he was ready for a compact with the Senate ; and against Catiline, a deserter from the aristocrats, the Senate put forward Cicero, a deserter from the democrats.

Catiline made several attempts to win the consulship with the support of Caesar and Crassus, the democratic leaders, but was always unsuccessful. In 64 B. C. he tried again, relying on the same supporters. They had need of him, because they hoped to carry by his means a Bill proposed by the tribune, Servilius Rullus, which reaffirmed, on a much wider scale, the agrarian law of Gaius Gracchus. This Bill provided, first of all, for the establishment of an immense fund, with which land was to be bought in Italy ; and this land, together with the considerable territory in Campania which still belonged to the state, was to be distributed as allotments among veteran soldiers and the proletariate of the capital. A commission of ten members was to carry out this plan with unlimited powers for five years ; and the first duty of the commissioners was to collect this fund, which they might dispose of at pleasure. The money was to be realized by the sale of state property in Italy and the provinces, especially property acquired since the year 88 B. C.

The commissioners were granted full powers to confiscate and sell all that was considered to be state property. Under this clause they might take over all the districts of Greece and Asia Minor which had been restored to Rome by Sulla when he defeated Mithradates ; and eventually the territory and other possessions gained for Rome by Pompey in the East were to come under their control. Since the democrats insisted that Egypt also had passed to Rome by bequest, although a lawful king was then upon the throne, it is clear that they intended Egypt also to be taken and used by the commissioners, which could not be done without a military force. In the other provinces the commissioners were in the same spirit to re-examine the title of all landowners, and to lay a tax, at their own discretion, on land retained by the holders, in order to secure a constant supply of funds to the commission.

When this operation was completed, the commissioners were to begin buying land in Italy, chiefly from holders whose title was doubtful, that is, from those who had acquired estates at the time of Sulla's proscription. It is probable that this step would have been preceded by a distribution of land in Campania, where colonies of Roman citizens would have been formed out of persons favoured by the commissioners. It is clear that this law had a political object. In order to outweigh Pompey, Caesar was trying to create a great political force with a revenue and an army. The allotment of land to Pompey's veterans would rest with this force ; it would have absolute control of the provinces ; it would be supported by colonies of its own partisans in Italy, just as Sulla had been supported by his freedmen and his colonies of veterans. It is true that the proceedings of this commission could not enrich the state : they could only ruin it. It was proposed to sacrifice the provinces for the sake of a doubtful benefit to the Roman rabble ; and the smallholders of Campania, an excellent class of farmers, were to be sacrificed for the same object.

In order that they might fight against this proposal, the Senate put forward Cicero as a candidate for the consulship against Catiline. Cicero was elected, and the first business of his consulship in 63 B. C. was to defeat the Bill of Rullus. Thereupon Caesar and Crassus, realizing that their gamble had failed for the present, and doubting whether Catiline would ever prove a useful instrument, withdrew their support from him. But Catiline refused to give in, and resolved to proceed at his own risk. Defeated once more at the consular election in 63 B. C., he appealed to a band of political adventurers like himself, and began a vigorous propaganda at Rome in favour of anarchy. At the same time he enrolled supporters in Etruria among Sulla's veterans, some of whom had already lost their allotments by extravagance, while others welcomed any adventure that promised them gain.

Catiline's plan was to raise the standard of revolt simultaneously at Rome and in Etruria. His partisans in Rome were to begin a massacre of magistrates and senators, to set fire to the city, and to seize control, while Sulla's veterans were to march from Etruria, take the city, and organize the new government. The discovery of the conspiracy was due to the vigorous action of Cicero. Catiline was forced to leave Rome prematurely, in order to form his army. The other ringleaders were arrested at Rome and executed without trial, on the proposal of Cato the younger, supported by Cicero and approved by the Senate. Catiline's small army was defeated, and he himself fell in the battle.

Thus the schemes of the democrats had miscarried. Pompey's return was imminent, and it was generally believed that he would return as dictator. To the great surprise of Rome, however, he entered the city at the end of 62 B. C. as a private citizen and without an army. What motives induced him to disband his soldiers is uncertain. He was excessively ambitious ; he was bound by the promises he had given to the soldiers ; he was anxious to get legal sanction for his settlement of the East, where he had formed two new provinces, Syria and Bithynia with Pontus, and also a number of new tributary kingdoms. He could easily have gained all his objects, by doing what he had done more than once already, and appearing in Italy at the head of an army. But for once he preferred to set an example of strict conformity to the law. Possibly he was convinced of his own irresistible authority and of the support which his disbanded men would give him. Possibly he compared his own position favourably with that of Sulla, when the proscription was over and the dictator had laid down his office. At any rate he was grievously disappointed. Both parties at Rome were his enemies, senators and democrats alike. He did, indeed, celebrate a triumph of unexampled magnificence ; but that was the limit of his success. His veterans received no land ; his temporary settlement of the East was not regularized. He found out that he could not avoid new political alliances and fresh concessions to the democrats and to his chief rivals, Crassus and Caesar.

Caesar, whose connexion with Catiline was no secret, found it convenient to disappear from Rome for a time after the failure of the conspiracy. Having held the office of praetor in 62 B. C., he spent the following year as propraetor in Spain, carrying on war against some tribes who had never settled down since the time of Sertorius, and satisfying the demands of his hosts of creditors at Rome. Returning in 60 B. C., he soon formed the compact with Pompey and Crassus which is known as the First Triumvirate. He himself, elected as consul for 59 B. C., was to be the active member of the coalition. Against the opposition of the Senate and his colleague Bibulus, he carried all the measures previously determined upon by the Three. Pompey's veterans were settled either on the state domain in Campania or on Italian land bought with the money which Pompey had brought back from the East ; Pompey's settlement of the East was confirmed by the assembly ; by way of a sop to the knights, a third of the amount due from the tax-farmers was remitted ; and Clodius, the leader of the Roman rabble and a steady supporter of Crassus, was permitted to prosecute Cicero and drive him into exile.

For himself Caesar took nothing but the governorship of Cisalpine and Transalpine Gaul for five years. This seemed a harmless, if unusual, distinction ; but to him it was of vital importance. It enabled him to gain a military reputation, an army devoted to his person, and unlimited material re-sources ; and it threw a halo round him as the successor of Marius in the great task of destroying the Western barbarians who menaced Rome. Caesar's plan of action was settled when he took over his province. Against the new provinces acquired by Pompey in the East he intended to set new provinces conquered in the West. The 'new Dionysus' and 'new Alexander' had travelled far into the East and had been glorified by the chief Greek historians of the time ; Caesar had his own hard work to do—to end the conflict with those Celts who had taken Rome in the past and who not long ago had been, together with the Germans, driven out of Italy with such difficulty. Caesar himself undertook to explain to the Roman people the significance of his task in Gaul. He was an excellent writer, and knew how to address himself directly to his readers. His *Commentarii*, or Military Report, always terse and precise, never vague or exaggerated, and written in masterly style, told from year to year the story of his operations in Gaul, Germany, and Britain.

The annexation of Gaul required from Caesar nine years of difficult and dangerous warfare. He drew the sword first against the Helvetii or natives of Switzerland and the Germans near the Rhine; the latter were repeating their attempt made in the time of Marius to seize land in Gaul and settle down there. In this contest he was supported by the tribes of central Gaul, and came out of it their patron, if not their master. This relation was resented by the half-savage tribes of the north and west, the Belgae, Armoricans, and Aquitanians; and when he had subdued these with difficulty, a national movement began among the peoples of central Gaul, who now saw that the friendship of Rome meant slavery to Gaul and sounded the knell of their freedom. Led by Vercingetorix they collected all their forces and tried to expel the foreigner from central Gaul. By the utmost exertion of his activity and by a series of well-planned manœuvres, Caesar succeeded in surrounding the Gauls at Alesia and inflicting upon them a decisive defeat. His business in Gaul was finished, and all that Gaul could give him he had got— military reputation, an army, and money.

The years when Caesar was in Gaul were years of violent political disturbance at Rome. His victories were equally disquieting to his old enemies, the Senate and the constitutional party, and to his new friends, Pompey and Crassus. If his enemies and his friends combined, he was in great danger; or Pompey and Crassus might quarrel and so dissolve the triumvirate. When Pompey received extraordinary powers in 57 B. C., nominally to provide Rome with corn but really to suppress the rioting in the streets, the triumvirate was on the verge of dissolution. Crassus was willing to come to terms with the Senate. But in 56 B. C. Caesar contrived by a great effort to summon a conference at Luca in north Italy, where he made a reconciliation between the two rivals and renewed the compact.

It was arranged at Luca that Pompey and Crassus, who both desired high military commands, should be consuls for 55 B. C., and, after holding office, should govern the provinces of Spain and Syria respectively for a period of five years ; and that Caesar should retain the province of Gaul for five years longer. But the performance of this bargain did nothing to relieve the political situation. Crassus, indeed, vanished for ever from the political stage. A great campaign which he organized in Syria against the Parthians ended in disaster : he was defeated at the battle of Carrhae, his soldiers were killed or taken prisoners, and he himself was treacherously slain. But this event only complicated the relations of Pompey and Caesar. In 54 B. C. Julia, the daughter of Caesar and wife of Pompey, died ; she had exercised a strong influence over her father and her husband, and her death made it easier for Caesar's enemies to work upon the widower. Instead of proceeding to his province, Pompey remained at Rome, doing nothing to suppress the persistent rioting till the Senate should authorize him to act. Finally, in 52 B.C., when the state of things had become intolerable, and the actual government of the city was in the hands of armed ruffians who usurped the labels of political parties, the Senate was forced to sanction his election as sole consul with the powers of a dictator. He then brought his troops into the city and promptly restored order.

It was now clear that Pompey's methods could never restore order in Rome and Italy. It was impossible to reconcile the military power of one or more individuals with the existing constitution. If military power kept within constitutional limits—and this is what Pompey aimed at—the struggle of parties and personal ambitions at Rome must lead to anarchy. But if that power tried to restore order, it was bound inevitably to come into collision with the governing oligarchy, and a struggle in arms must follow. There was no escape from this dilemma, if the constitution were respected and the traditional influence of the Senate preserved. Pompey's chief mistake was his attempt to reconcile what could not be reconciled. To be the first man at Rome and to rule it, and yet not to destroy the very framework of the ancient constitution, was simply impossible. Pompey's position was made still more difficult by the necessity of sharing his power with Caesar, with a constant apprehension that Caesar would some day wrest from his grasp the first place in the state.

When Caesar's task in Gaul was ended, the question of future relations between the two rivals became acute. Caesar did not desire a rupture : he was willing to return to Rome and continue his political manœuvres there without drawing the sword. But wishing to insure safety for himself, he insisted that he should be allowed to stand at the consular elections without appearing in person at Rome and without laying down his proconsular powers. This obviously meant a continuance of military power for Caesar ; for his first business as consul would be to secure a fresh command with exceptional conditions. But if Caesar were to keep his army and yet be elected consul, Pompey would no longer be the first man in the state. He was conscious of his own inferiority, under such circumstances ; for Caesar's laurels were fresh and his own were withered by time, and Caesar's army was in north Italy and his own far away in Spain.

The Senate looked forward with no less alarm to Caesar's return. They knew that Caesar in power meant ruin to themselves. In his first consulship he had openly declared himself their enemy and had refused to recognize constitutional restraints ; there was no hope that his second consulship would prove less dangerous. But without allies they were helpless. Yet not one of their number was really popular with the soldiers, and no new Sulla could be found in their ranks. They were forced to appeal to Pompey. He had tried to avoid flagrant outrages against the constitution ; and it was possible to hope that it would be easier to make terms with him if he defeated his rival. Every effort was therefore made to detach Pompey from Caesar. For long Pompey hesitated. When at last, in January 49 B.C., he decided on a rupture, the military advantage was all on Caesar's side. Pompey had hardly any troops in Italy ; and therefore, when Caesar crossed the Rubicon, the boundary of his province, with a small force and marched on Rome, to leave Italy became inevitable.

Pompey had two possible courses before him—either to join his army in Spain, or to enlist a new army, take it to the East, train it, and bring it back to Italy. The objection to the former course was that in Spain he would be cut off from the abundant resources of the East. If he went east-wards, he would place Caesar between two strong armies, and might hope to cut off the supply of food to Italy and starve Caesar out, by means of the great fleet which the Senate controlled in Italy and the East. But Pompey's plan of campaign, though excellent, was unsuccessful. His failure was mainly due to the astonishing activity, speed, and resoluteness of his rival. His own movements were slow and hampered by the presence of a great number of senators at his headquarters. These men constantly criticized and interfered with the general's dispositions, and constantly demanded meetings to discuss the situation. The coadjutors whom they supplied to Pompey failed altogether to rise to the height of the occasion. Caesar, on the other hand, had absolute power within his own party ; he took little account of the few senators who had remained at Rome ; and he chose his subordinates with skill. He could not prevent Pompey and his forces from crossing the sea ; nor could he interfere, while a great army was enrolled and trained near Dyrrhachium, the chief harbour on the west of Greece. He had no fleet, and time was needed to make one. But he used the interval to fall upon Pompey's army in Spain and shatter it. A similar attempt in Africa was unsuccessful.

Thus in the autumn of 49 B. C. the advantage was all with Pompey. He had an immense army at his disposal, great pecuniary resources, and a powerful fleet. Caesar had any number of men but little money. Yet he determined not to await Pompey's return but to transfer the war to Greece. He succeeded in landing, first a part of his army and then the whole of it, at Apollonia, and then made an unsuccessful attempt to blockade Pompey in his camp near Dyrrhachium. Pompey broke through the lines, and Caesar, cut off from his supplies, was forced to retreat to the fertile plains of Thessaly. Here he, in his turn, was blockaded by Pompey at Pharsalus and would have lost his whole army, if the Senate had not insisted on accepting the decisive engagement which Caesar tried to force upon him. Pompey was utterly defeated in the battle. But he had still an army and a fleet in Africa. He counted also on the support of Egypt, where the king, Ptolemy XIV, was greatly indebted to him. But his hopes of a hospitable reception were disappointed : the king, fearing complications, put him to death by treachery.

The war did not end, however, with Pompey's death. Caesar followed his rival to Alexandria. He needed money, and Ptolemy was in debt to Rome. Here the conqueror, quite unexpectedly, had a narrow escape from destruction. He took part in a local dynastic contest between the king and Cleopatra his sister and consort. He took the side of Cleopatra, and it must be supposed that he hoped to be rewarded, not only by the queen's caresses but by a supply of the indispensable sinews of war. The army and the population of Alexandria sided with the king and besieged Caesar in the palace. Reinforcements, hurrying from Asia Minor, arrived just in time. Next he was obliged to hasten off to Asia Minor, to settle accounts with Pharnaces, a son of Mithradates, who was seeking, under cover of the general disorder, to restore his father's kingdom in the East. Meanwhile the remains of Pompey's army and the senatorial fleet collected in Africa, where the ranks were filled up with fresh recruits and detachments of African allies. This imposing force Caesar met, when at last he led his army to Africa in 47 B. C. Once more his military genius decided the issue in the battle of Thapsus in the following year, and the resistance of the Senate was finally broken. A fresh attempt on the part of Pompey's sons to form an army in Spain forced Caesar to fight one more battle against the Pompeians at Munda in 45 B. C., where the last survivors of the senatorial forces were defeated and destroyed. Caesar was left alone, without a rival, with a new Senate chosen by himself and entirely subservient to him, and with an army admirably trained and absolutely devoted to their leader.

XII

THE DICTATORSHIP OF CAESAR. THE THIRD
STAGE OF CIVIL WAR: ANTONY AND OCTAVIAN

AFTER his victory over the Senate, gained in Africa in the
year 46 B. C., Caesar became the head of the Roman state,
and held that position till his death on 15 March 44 B. C.
He did not consider it necessary to strengthen his position
by resorting to the methods of Marius and Sulla ; nor did he
set to work to destroy all those who had fought against him
or whom he might suspect of disaffection. Such a course
was repugnant to him ; and he probably considered that
a reign of terror was an unsuitable means of supporting any
kind of power. On the contrary, he summoned to work with
him all of the hostile faction whom he thought able to serve
the state, including a number of active politicians, such as
Cicero, Cassius, Marcus and Decimus Brutus. He did not
look upon himself as bound by his democratic past. He never
dreamed either of restoring the Senate to power or of recognizing the sovereignty of the Roman rabble. His activity as
head of the state lasted less than two years, and was interrupted
by the troublesome Spanish campaign of 45 B. C.

It must be remembered also that he did not consider even
his military task as complete. He was convinced that the
frontiers of the state must be made safe against foes from
without, before the foundations of a new system of government could be finally laid down. The most pressing problems,
and those which called for an immediate settlement, were
these. Greece, Macedonia, and Epirus must be protected
against the assaults of their Thracian, Illyrian, and Celtic
neighbours ; and the frontiers of the new Eastern provinces
annexed by Pompey must be secured—the frontiers, that is,
of Syria, Palestine, and Bithynia with Pontus. The provinces,
near and far, were in great danger. On the Danube a powerful
Thracian kingdom was growing up under the sceptre of
Byrebista, which threatened to swallow up, first of all, the
Greek cities on the western coast of the Black Sea. In
Mesopotamia the Roman arms had suffered a shameful

defeat at the hands of the Parthians; and the conquerors, not content with their victory, were preparing to fall upon Syria and Asia Minor, and thus to restore the great Persian kingdom of which they were the heirs. Rome could not stop half-way on the path of an imperialistic policy: her natural boundaries as a world-power she sought in the ocean and the desert. Caesar therefore planned a campaign in the East, first against Thrace and then against Parthia, and gathered in Illyria a great army of sixteen legions. His immediate departure to join the army was definitely fixed and probably hastened his end.

The situation made it unnecessary for Caesar to settle at once the fundamental question of his relation to the military forces of the state. He was the leader of the army, the only leader whom it recognized, and this army was still in the field and on the eve of a campaign. We do not know what form his relation to the army would have assumed on the conclusion of the great expedition which he had planned. One thing is clear, that with regard to the composition of a Roman army he was prepared to develop the plan instituted by Marius. He certainly did not consider it indispensable that his army should consist exclusively of Roman citizens. As the army of a world-wide state it was to contain representatives drawn from every part of the population capable of bearing arms. Such was the army which he bequeathed to his successors. It contained Roman citizens but also many natives of Gaul, Spain, and even Asia Minor. His armies were stationed outside Italy, in the provinces; at Rome he kept only a small detachment of his praetorian guard, that is, of the bodyguard who attended on him as the bearer of the supreme command; and even this detachment he dismissed shortly before he was murdered. His power was supported in Rome, Italy, and the western provinces by his veterans, some of whom had already received, and others were expecting, grants of land; the latter class lived meanwhile in large groups at Rome or in the Italian towns.

But the internal affairs of Rome called for some kind of organization, even if it were only a makeshift. The machine of government must be such as to go on working in Caesar's absence. As I have said already, all Caesar's actions prove that he looked on the existing constitution as useless and obsolete. His hostility to the Senate was shown by his persistent struggle against it. The popular assembly, made up of the city rabble, he regarded merely as a convenient instrument for carrying on that struggle. There is no doubt that Caesar intended to make radical changes in the constitution ; and though he never completed his reforms, the main lines are unmistakable. External forms and appellations were left untouched ; but the Roman state as ruled by him was essentially and radically unlike the Roman state as it had been governed by the Senate.

His first business was to secure to himself supreme control over all public affairs, and to do this in such a way that no external change was obvious. Here he was following a plan which had been adopted long before by the tyrants in Greece. Like them, Caesar kept the old names of institutions but infused into them a new element which changed them beyond recognition. This new element was his own power, the power personal to Caesar himself. This power was a kind of mosaic, made up out of many pieces. Each of the pieces was of Roman origin and bore a Roman name ; but the name in most cases covered something new. His power, supreme and incommensurable with that of the other magistrates, found expression in the title of 'dictator', which he bore for a time in 49 and 47 B.C., and which was conferred for ten years by the Senate and the people in 46 B.C., and, in the following year, for life. A permanent dictatorship was contrary to the principles of the Roman constitution. There is no doubt that the Roman title of 'dictator' was in this case a mask for what was called 'tyranny' by the Greeks, and 'monarchy' by the nations of the East.

Caesar first introduced into public life the principle that one man might hold several offices together when in 59 B.C. he had been simultaneously consul in Rome and proconsul in the Gauls. This precedent had been followed by Pompey in 52 B.C., when he was consul in Rome and proconsul in Spain, and Caesar now made a regular practice of holding several offices simultaneously. From 48 B.C. he was elected consul annually ; from the same date he received from the people the 'tribunician power'; that is, without being a tribune, he enjoyed all the rights of the tribunes, including their inviolability, which the people granted to him by special resolution in 47 B.C. As early as 63 B.C. he was elected

Pontifex Maximus, and in 48 B. C. he became a member of all the patrician priestly colleges. This accumulation of titles and powers was contrary to all Roman political tradition, but fitted in with the theory that the people has a sovereign right to create new forms of power. To this extent Caesar was a consistent democrat.

Many other powers which had no precedent in Roman constitutional history were piled up on this foundation. A special law handed over to Caesar the supervision of morals (*praefectura morum*) which had formerly been part of the censor's duties ; and Caesar made use of this office in order to threaten with expulsion from the Senate or the equestrian order all who fell under his displeasure, on the plea that their conduct was such as to disgrace their rank. Other special laws conferred on Caesar the right to appoint magistrates for the provinces, and to recommend to the people for election half of the magistrates to hold office at Rome ; the right (granted in 48 B. C.) to conclude peace and declare war ; the right of voting first in the Senate ; the perpetual right of commanding the army and disposing of the public money ; and, finally, the right to issue edicts, confirmed beforehand and without discussion by the Senate, while the magistrates on entering office had to swear obedience to these edicts.

This great accumulation of miscellaneous powers, accompanied by a long list of ill-assorted titles of honour, created for Caesar an entirely exceptional position in the state. The Senate, packed with his partisans, was his council ; the popular assembly met merely to vote laws that had been previously accepted, and never even attempted to take any active part in public affairs ; the tribunate of the people showed no sign of life whatever. Caesar was in fact a monarch, superior to all control of every kind. Whether he intended to accept the title of king is uncertain. His enemies asserted it, and his most fiery partisans, such as M. Antonius, apparently desired it. Caesar himself never explained his view on this point definitely ; and his actions and casual allusions are contradictory, and may be explained in different ways. It was also widely believed that he intended to move the capital from Rome to the East. Gossip said that he intended to marry Cleopatra, the queen of Egypt, and to adopt Caesarion, the son whom she had borne him : he did summon her from Alexandria and gave her a residence in Rome.

Whatever may be thought of these rumours, which belong to the kind of gossip often called forth by a political crisis, it is certain that Caesar considered his power to be hereditary. Just before his departure for the East he made a will, by which he adopted his nephew, Gaius Octavius, and bequeathed to him the greater part of his fortune. This was a clear proof that he regarded Octavius as his heir and inheritor of his position. Octavius had been with Caesar in Spain and was then sent to Illyria to complete his general education and military training.

Caesar found support for his autocratic power not only in his army, his veterans, and the powers granted him by the people : fascinated by his personality, the masses regarded him with a kind of religious awe. To them he was not merely the favourite of fortune and the military genius but also a superior being. The religious ideas of antiquity drew no hard-and-fast line between the divine and the human ; and they were ready to recognize Caesar as a super-man, a hero in the ancient religious sense of the word. Far from resenting this attitude, Caesar even encouraged it. He made no protest when the Senate passed decrees which tended towards his deification : thus they instituted a special priestly college of Julian *Luperci*, built a temple to Caesar and the goddess Clemency with a special priest for this new cult, and changed the name of the month *Quintilis* to *Iulius*, or July.

Apart from the establishment of his own personal autocracy, it is difficult for us to distinguish the outlines of the transformation which Caesar intended to accomplish in the state. But one point is not doubtful : he meant to extend the Roman and the Latin franchise as widely as possible among the inhabitants of the provinces. Cisalpine Gaul and Narbonese Gaul were to become parts of Italy ; a number of Roman colonies were founded in Spain and Africa ; the Latin franchise was freely granted to provincial communities—in Sicily, for instance. It is remarkable that the same plan was followed also in the East : colonies of veterans were sent to Sinope and Heraclea, the chief commercial centres on the south coast of the Black Sea. It is possible, however, that this measure, and also his policy of friendliness towards the Crimea, were dictated by Caesar's wish to secure his rear during his coming campaign in the East. Still more notable is the restoration of Carthage in Africa and Corinth in Greece—the two great commercial cities which had been destroyed by the Roman oligarchs ; in both places it was provided that the new Roman colonists should find room for the native population. Most of the Corinthian colonists were manumitted Greeks.

All this indicates that Caesar intended to get rid of the sharp distinction between Italy and the provinces, and to create in all parts of the empire a class who should enjoy the same rights as Roman citizens in Italy. The Senate was reformed in the same spirit : it was now to become a body representative not merely of Rome and Italy but of the whole empire, and therefore Caesar appointed his friends and loyal supporters without regard to their origin or previous career. His other measures were, more or less, of the nature of make-shifts. His correction of the calendar was important, his partial reform of the civil and criminal courts was less so. There is a law still extant which is called by his name, and consists mainly of regulations for the organization of local government in the Italian communities. These regulations were intended to form part of a code which should lay down the form of municipal institutions in the different towns. My personal impression is this—that Caesar intended first to carry out his great military expedition, which aimed at the creation of a world-wide Roman Empire, and then to take in hand the business of permanent constitutional changes. It is possible that he intended after his return to change the nature of his own position entirely.

In what he did Caesar failed to take account of one thing ; and that was the strength of the senatorial order, which was still by no means convinced that its social and political activity had come to an end. The appointment of upstarts to the Senate, the lavish distribution of the Roman franchise, the refusal to recognize the privileges of the ruling classes—these things certainly contributed in no small degree to Caesar's end. The noble senators would not resign without a battle the privileges which their order had enjoyed for centuries ; and, as we shall see later, their struggle in defence of these privileges was victorious. When a conspiracy was formed in 44 B. C. by a group of senators, its success was no doubt a matter of accident ; but when we remember that the senatorial party gained a large number of adherents and, even when defeated, was able to force Octavius, Caesar's adopted son, to pay regard to its wishes, we must allow that Caesar went too far, and that the time for a decisive transformation of the Roman state had not yet come.

On the Ides (or 15th) of March in the year 44 B. C. Caesar was murdered at a meeting of the Senate by a band of conspirators, among whom Marcus and Decimus Brutus and Cassius were the ringleaders. They had a majority of the Senate on their side but did not meet with the sympathy they expected either from the Roman mob or the army, or even the population of Italy. The automatic transference of power to the hands of the Senate, which the conspirators evidently expected to follow Caesar's death, never took place. Antony, the consul, and Lepidus, the Master of the Horse, possessed a military force, which was entirely devoted to them and enabled them to suppress any threatening movement on the part of the Senate. The position of the conspirators became still more critical when it became clear that the populace of the capital was against them. The rabble was bought over by the gifts bequeathed to them by Caesar in a will which Antony at once made public.

But the position of Caesar's partisans was not stable either. Who was to be Caesar's successor? No one gave a serious thought to Octavius, the boy of eighteen who had inherited Caesar's fortune and name, and was then with the army in Illyria. The situation was approximately the same as after the death of Alexander the Great. But it soon became clear that Antony the consul had more energy and foresight than any one else at Rome. He insisted on patching up an agreement with the Senate. The Senate was prepared to confirm all the Acts of Caesar in general, and his arrangements for the immediate future in particular, including the distribution of provinces among the ex-magistrates. In return for this concession Antony was willing to treat the recent event as a regrettable misunderstanding and to sink Caesar's death in oblivion. But this amnesty was no permanent settlement : each side was in search of means to strengthen their position, or, in other words, of military support.

With this object Antony, who had secured possession of Caesar's treasure and his papers, first passed a law in contravention of Caesar's arrangements. By them Antony was to have the province of Macedonia, while Syria was allotted to Dolabella, the other consul ; but the new law, though it left Dolabella's province unchanged, gave Antony Caesar's old province of Gaul, with the exception of Narbonese Gaul ; and Decimus Brutus, one of the conspirators, was to be transferred from Gaul to Macedonia, but without an army, as the troops there were recalled by Antony to Italy. Contrary to Caesar's intentions the terms of Dolabella and Antony were extended from two years to six. Antony provided for the safety of Spain in his rear by sending Lepidus to carry on war there against Pompey's surviving son, Sextus, who had established himself in the country. The tenure of all these posts was to begin immediately, before Antony and Dolabella had ceased to hold the office of consul. The ex-praetors, Marcus Brutus and Cassius, were got out of the way : they were sent by the Senate to organize the corn-supply in Italy and Sicily. When their praetorship came to an end, they were to have the unimportant provinces of Crete and Cyrene. It seemed as if the Senate was beaten.

But Antony's triumph was premature. Brutus and Cassius found means to make their way to the East, where they won over to their side part of the army quartered in Macedonia, subdued by force all opposition in Asia Minor, and put an end to Dolabella. In Italy Antony's plans were shattered by the appearance of Gaius Octavius. The young man had accepted the position of Caesar's heir with all the obligations it involved, and now demanded that Antony should repay the money he had seized ; he required also, as Gaius Julius Caesar Octavianus —the name he bore after his adoption—that he should share in the government of the state. Antony refused these demands, and Octavian was forced to show that he was capable of defending his rights. The situation became more complicated when large bodies of Caesar's veterans rallied round Octavian and were joined by two of the four legions recalled by Antony from Macedonia ; and the confusion increased when Octavian offered his services to the Senate in the contest with Antony, who was trying to expel Decimus Brutus by force from north Italy. The compact between Octavian and the Senate was actively supported by Cicero, who had become the head of the senatorial party at Rome. Antony accepted the challenge and blockaded Decimus Brutus at Mutina, but was defeated by the senatorial armies under Hirtius and Pansa, the consuls for 43 B. C., and by a considerable army under Octavian, on whom the Senate had conferred the powers of a propraetor. Cicero and his party evidently believed that Octavian would prove an obedient instrument in their hands, and that, after helping them to deal with Antony, he could in one way or another be got rid of. Cicero did not even conceal this intention, and Octavian saw through it.

It was a great misfortune for the Senate when both the consuls fell in the two battles at Mutina and most of their soldiers went over to Octavian, only a few submitting to Decimus Brutus. Instead of leading his army against Antony, Octavian marched upon Rome : the Senate had refused to grant the consulship and a triumph to himself, and rewards in money to his men. The appearance of the army under the walls of Rome broke down all opposition : Octavian was elected consul with Quintus Pedius. First of all they carried a law by which Caesar's murderers were summoned to justice and condemned in absence. Meanwhile Decimus Brutus marched against Antony ; he hoped for support from Lepidus who had been summoned from Spain, and from Plancus, the governor of Narbonese Gaul. But Lepidus made common cause with Antony, Plancus refused to support Brutus, the armies of Brutus melted away, and he himself fled and was killed by barbarians on his way to the East. The Senate's dream of ruling Italy collapsed for ever. The collision which all expected between Octavian and Antony never took place. The three Caesarian leaders, Antony, Lepidus, and Octavian, met near Bologna in north Italy and concluded an agreement, by which the three were to be made commissioners for reorganizing the state (*tresviri reipublicae constituendae*) with unlimited powers. The western provinces were divided among the triumvirs ; Octavian and Antony were to settle matters with Brutus and Cassius, while Lepidus was to guard Italy. All the items of this agreement received the form of law in virtue of a statute moved and carried by the tribune Titius on 27 November 43 B.C. The triumvirs were to retain their powers for five years.

The reorganization of the state began with a reign of terror, which repeated in a worse form all the horrors perpetrated by Marius and the democrats and later by Sulla. There were two objects to be gained by it—the destruction of all opponents and the collection of means to carry on a campaign against Brutus and Cassius. The first of these objects was not attained : though an immense number of victims, including Cicero, lost their lives, a yet greater number made their escape either to Brutus and Cassius in the East, or to Sextus Pompeius who had seized Sicily and created a powerful fleet. Even in their second object the triumvirs were not entirely successful. Confiscation gave rise to wild speculation in land, but the great sums hoped for were not realized, owing to the heavy fall in the value of the confiscated estates. The last struggle of the Senate against military tyranny took place on Greek soil. In 42 B. C. Antony and Octavian met the powerful army of Brutus and Cassius at Philippi in Macedonia. The story of Pharsalus was repeated: Antony was able to force a battle, and his antagonists were unable to decline it and to starve him and his army into surrender. The steadiness of Caesar's veterans and the military skill of Antony prevailed over the republican enthusiasm of their opponents. Brutus and Cassius fell. It is remarkable that both put an end to themselves ; and Cassius at least had no reason for suicide ; for Antony's victory was far from being decisive on the first day of the battle.

Thus the struggle with the Senate ended, but civil war still continued. It was clear that there could not be three masters of the Roman dominions, even if, as was actually done after Philippi, those dominions were carved into three portions. The division, however, was incomplete : Italy was to be ruled by the triumvirs jointly, and the East was not included in the arrangement. The most pressing business was to satisfy the armies who had gained the victory. Money and land must be found for 110,000 soldiers, and the triumvirs had neither one nor the other. Moreover, Sextus Pompeius, firmly established in Sicily, was intercepting the transport of corn from Africa to Italy. An arrangement was made that Antony should remain in the East and collect money, while Octavian returned to Italy to search for land. Octavian carried out his mission : he confiscated the land belonging to the citizens of eighteen prosperous communities in Italy, and handed it over to the soldiers. The dispossessed land-holders either became tenants of the new owners, or went away to live in the towns, or emigrated to the provinces. Many of them waited for the opportunity that a new civil war might offer, of returning to their own farms or seizing those of others. Antony's task was more troublesome. The East had already been stripped bare by Brutus and Cassius ; Egypt alone offered some possibilities. Meeting Cleopatra, the Egyptian queen, at Tarsus, Antony preferred to tap the wealth of Egypt by peaceful means rather than by violence : he became the husband of the queen. It is probable that this step was not prompted merely by susceptibility to Cleopatra's charms : it was a tempting prospect, to dispose of the wealth of Egypt without striking a blow, and still more tempting to have Egypt as a personal possession and not as a new Roman province.

Meantime the situation of Octavian in Italy was far from brilliant. Pompey was master of Sicily, and Lepidus was suspected of keeping up friendly relations with him. Italy resented the ruin caused by the confiscation of land ; and this resentment was kept alive by Antony's friends who dreaded Octavian's growing power. Things came at last to an open conflict conducted by Fulvia, Antony's wife, and Lucius Antonius, his brother. Some of the Italian towns took a hand in the affair, and Octavian had some difficulty in defeating the army of Lucius and starving him into sur-render after a long siege of Perusia in 40 B. C. His wife and brother received no support from Antony : the situation in the East was complicated by an invasion of the Parthians and their seizure of Asia Minor. In such a crisis the assist-ance of Italy was indispensable ; but Octavian was by no means inclined, immediately after the events at Perusia, to admit Antony to Italy for recruiting purposes. When an open rupture seemed inevitable, the friends of the two trium-virs and the veterans of the Civil war contrived that the rivals should meet at Brundisium in 40 B. C. and draw up a fresh agreement. Sextus Pompeius was included in this agreement by the treaty made at Misenum in the following year. Sardinia, Sicily, and Greece were allotted to Pompey ; Antony became ruler of the East and Octavian of the West, with the exception of Africa which was made over to Lepidus. Italy was still to be ruled jointly by all the four magnates, though none of them except Octavian was resident in the peninsula. To confirm the alliance between the rivals, Antony married Octavia, the sister of Octavian. Fulvia had died before this time ; and nothing was said about Cleopatra.

The conditions laid down in these compacts were not carried out. The war with Pompey still went on ; and a fresh collision between Octavian and Antony would have arisen ; but Antony, occupied by his project of driving the Parthians out of Asia Minor, was willing, in return for the right of raising an army in Italy, to abstain from interfering in the struggle against Pompey, and even to help Octavian. A new compact, made at Tarentum in 37 B.C., confirmed the agreement and renewed the powers of the triumvirs for five years more.

In 37 B.C. events took a decisive turn. Octavian with a great effort inflicted a succession of stunning blows on Pompey and drove him to Asia Minor where he lost his life ; and at the same time he stripped Lepidus of his power and his army. When Lepidus landed in Sicily, his troops deserted him and went over to the victorious Octavian. The rest of his days Lepidus spent as a dignified exile in one of the Italian towns. Octavian had now become undisputed master of the West. His hands were untied, and the time for agreements had gone by. Antony also had no further desire for agreements : in 36 B.C. he broke definitely with Octavian and declared Cleopatra to be his wife. From that time he stands forth as the lord and master of the East, while still retaining his claims on the West. The alliance with Cleopatra was a natural consequence of this policy, since it secured him a strong economic and strategic base. The Parthian campaign was to bring him military glory in the East and in Italy, and to prove to all the world that he and not Octavian was the true successor of Caesar ; the same campaign was to create an experienced and well-trained army, and also to provide the means for making war on Octavian. In fact, Parthia was to do for him what Gaul had done for Caesar.

But Antony had not taken into account the complicated nature of his task and the insufficiency of his own strength. Though he escaped the fate of Crassus, yet his two campaigns in Parthia cost him a considerable part of his Roman army and greatly weakened his claim to be an invincible general. Armenia was seized by treachery and plundered ; but that gained him little glory. Still more prejudicial to his influence with the army was his compliance with the demands of Cleopatra—demands which he could not refuse, because it would have been a death-blow to him if she had gone over to Octavian. He made over to her children a part of the Roman provinces in the East. It is possible that to this transfer he gave legal form by making it a provision of his will, which he had conveyed by friends to the Vestal Virgins at Rome for safe custody. But we cannot exclude the possibility, that this will, published by Octavian, was a forgery.

The fact itself, that Roman provinces were transferred to Cleopatra's children, is certain. Previous Roman commanders, such as Sulla, Pompey, and Caesar, had possessed the right to convert provinces into tributary kingdoms or to reverse that process ; but none of them had ever exercised this power so boldly or with such disregard of Roman interests. Antony was evidently coming forward as the direct representative of the Hellenistic kings, and proving to Rome that the plan of shifting the centre of the Roman Empire from Italy to the East was no novelty to him.

Octavian took the fullest advantage of his rival's mistakes and failures. Ingenious, unabashed, and persistent, he sought to prove to Italy and Rome that Antony was the miserable slave of Cleopatra, a man with no will of his own and no sense of honour, and a traitor to those Roman ideas of which Octavian proclaimed himself the champion. If Antony were victorious, Rome would be enslaved by the East, Italy would become a province of Egypt, and the pride of the conqueror would be exchanged for the shame of defeat. To prove his assertions, Octavian published Antony's will and part of their private correspondence. Whether he believed the charges he made, we cannot decide : we do not know whether Antony really aimed at enslaving Italy and Rome. But it is highly improbable that he did so. As an experienced general, he knew the worth of the Roman soldier and his superiority to Eastern troops ; he knew that his position in the East depended absolutely upon armies raised in Italy. Hence he could hardly have thought in earnest of ruling the Roman Empire without holding a solid base in the Italian peninsula.

But Octavian's assertions were effective : they were believed by Italy and by many of the Roman officers and men in Antony's army. The Senate also took the side of Octavian. It is highly probable that in his dealings with that body he bound himself by certain promises. At all events the awful prospect of a foreign conqueror on Italian soil awakened once more the ancient spirit of the Punic wars. The second quinquennium of the triumvirate now came to an end, and the restoration of constitutional government was due. The consuls of 32 B. C., who were partisans of Antony, demanded in the Senate that the triumvirs should abdicate, and promised, in Antony's name, that the old constitution should be restored. Thus threatened, Octavian called upon Italy and the provinces to swear allegiance to himself personally, as the leader of Italy and the whole state against Cleopatra. This oath, on which Octavian now based his authority, was taken by Rome, Italy, and the provinces. Antony, indeed, extorted a similar oath from his army, the Roman citizens resident abroad, and the natives of the provinces ruled by him.

The war began in 32 B. C. Great forces were collected on both sides. Antony had a powerful fleet and watched for an opportunity to cross from Illyria to Italy. But Octavian got the start of him : his huge flotilla of light vessels enabled him to land an army at Actium, close to where Antony's troops were encamped. In order to break through the blockade and, in case of victory, to cut off Octavian from Italy, Antony decided to fight a battle at sea. The details of this engagement are doubtful. Is it true that Cleopatra betrayed Antony by withdrawing the Egyptian fleet at the critical moment ? Is it true that Antony followed her, abandoning his ships to the caprice of fortune ? Or are these malicious fictions, circulated by Octavian in order to blacken his rival ? We do not know the truth. The extant accounts in history and poetry were coloured by the official version of the facts ; we do not hear, and it is probable that contemporaries never heard, what Antony's friends had to say. At all events, the attempt to destroy Octavian's fleet was a failure. Antony's own fleet was destroyed, and with its destruction vanished all hope of a victory on land. The two armies stood face to face in Greece. To retreat into the interior of the country without security for their communications was a most hazardous enterprise ; they were dispirited by the destruction of their fleet ; and a large part of the army deserted to the conqueror's side, while the rest dispersed. Antony and Cleopatra, having broken through the blockade with part of the fleet, sought a final refuge in Egypt. The attempt to raise an army for the defence of Egypt was unsuccessful. When Octavian drew near, Antony put an end to himself ; and Cleopatra, after an unsuccessful attempt to gain the favour of Octavian, followed his example when Alexandria was taken in 30 B. C. Octavian was left alone, the master of the Roman Empire.

XIII

ROME, ITALY, AND THE PROVINCES, IN THE FIRST CENTURY B. C.

THE preceding chapters have set forth the political history of the Roman state in the time of the Gracchi and after their deaths. Let us briefly summarize the facts. The senatorial system of government was attacked by a succession of revolutionary politicians with a definite programme, which was, to transfer all power to the popular assembly, to redistribute the land, and to extend the limits of the franchise. Of this programme the last item only was realized to some extent, and that after a cruel war : the whole of Italy was admitted to the body of Roman citizens. The other two points led to a long political conflict, in the heat of which their real meaning was forgotten. Rome was divided into two camps—the partisans of the Senate, and its enemies. Meantime the need of constitutional reform grew with the growth of the state. The cautious foreign policy of the Senate, which shrank from the annexation of more provinces, gave place first, in the second century B. C., to the selfish policy of the great landowners, and then, in the next century, to a frankly imperialistic policy, which was carried out both by the Senate and by the enemies of the Senate, including the class of business men who were known as ' knights '.

The two highest classes of Roman society, the senators and knights, were supreme in the provinces. The former governed the provinces with almost unlimited powers and were sometimes guilty of scandalous misconduct. The speeches of Cicero against Verres, the governor of Sicily, describe such a case in vivid colours. The knights' chief business in the provinces was to collect the taxes and dues, which the Senate had let out to them through the agency of the censors. By collusion with the governor, by bribing him, by presenting him with shares in the joint-stock companies which were formed for the collection of taxes, the knights found it feasible to oppress the provincials and squeeze the last drop of juice out of them. It was useless to send complaints to Rome. Occasionally, as in the case of Verres, a skilful advocate was willing to plead for the provincials, if he could thereby crush a political adversary or improve his own prospects of advancement. But in most cases the juries, being composed of senators or knights or both together, returned a verdict in favour of those who paid them most.

Another scandal of provincial government consisted in the extensive financial operations of capitalists who lent money, often at usurious rates of interest. The loans were advanced chiefly to the cities of the East, which needed them in order to satisfy the greed of tax-farmers and governors. At the beginning of the civil wars these cities were already hopelessly involved, and each aspirant to supremacy at Rome laid them under contributions which they could not pay. Their difficulties were taken advantage of by the Roman bankers and capitalists, both senators and knights. They were ready to find money but demanded exorbitant interest and all the property of the city as security. If the city was unable to pay, the creditor was backed up by the power of Rome and demanded his money with the help of armed force. The tributary kings were treated no better. The real purpose of many military operations carried out by the Romans in Asia Minor was to enforce the payment of debt. To take a share in the business of tax-farmers and moneylenders was so much a matter of course, that men of the highest character, Cicero, for instance, a man of unstained reputation and an excellent provincial governor, did not scruple to engage in it. Brutus, the murderer of Caesar, invested his money in loans to cities and charged interest at 48 per cent.

The scandalous condition of the provinces provided the democratic leaders and also all ambitious aspirants to power with an effective weapon against the Senate and senatorial government. Nevertheless, neither the triumph of the democratic party, nor the temporary success of individual political leaders, brought about any real change. The democratic leaders and their opponents were alike absolutely dependent upon the army ; and the army now consisted of professional soldiers, who sought by military service to satisfy their greed, first for booty and plunder, and then, when their time of service had expired, for allotments of land. Experience proved that it was impossible to use the army in order to carry out a definite political programme. The army supported

Marius the democrat, and it supported Sulla the aristocrat. About politics it cared little ; but money and land it insisted on having. The two requirements could only be supplied by constant wars and the annexation of province after province. Thus Sulla and Pompey and Caesar and Antony and Octavian were all forced to carry on an imperialistic policy and to extend unceasingly the limits of the state ; and they found support for this policy, without regard to their political objects, among the class of knights and among the senators themselves.

The enormous growth of the state further increased the importance of the army. Without the army the Roman state would have broken up at once. But the army would obey no leader, unless he made them sure of victory and allotments of land. This was clearly seen by all the chief actors on the political stage. Pompey alone tried to avoid this logical conclusion : he wished to make a compromise between the constitution and a monarchy ; he wished to rule as the first Roman citizen, and yet to enjoy the confidence of the people. But he failed and became in the end a tool of the constitution against which he was fighting : he was forced to defend the Senate against Caesar, a more consistent aspirant to autocracy based upon the sword. Caesar frankly confessed that he owed his power to the army ; and the army was the weapon with which Antony and Octavian struck down the last attempt of the Senate to reassert itself. Antony and Octavian alike founded their pretensions to supreme power on military force alone. The military weakness of Antony and his inability to get recruits from Italy settled the dispute for primacy in favour of Octavian.

This same growth of the state, with the annexation of ever new provinces and the increasing number of tributary kings, made it more and more obvious that the Senate was incapable of dealing with a problem which was now forcing itself to the front—the problem of government for a world-wide state. The material well-being of Rome depended on the prosperity of the provinces ; and Italy, tax-free herself except for a small revenue derived from customs, looked to the provinces mainly for support. But the provinces, drained dry by senators and knights, and treated by the leaders of civil war merely as a source from which to draw money, became steadily less prosperous : the economic development of the

West was stopped, and the East was beggared. All this was well known to the chief men at Rome. The central point of Sulla's reforms was this very question, how the state could be governed ; and to Caesar the same problem was of primary importance. But the question was insoluble, if the old order and the ancient constitution of Rome as a city-state were preserved. Here, too, the only possible expedient was to adopt some new form of constitution ; and the only possible form, owing partly to the excessive importance of the army and its leaders and partly to the unwillingness of Italy and the Roman citizens to resign their dominant position in the state, was a constitution based on the military power of an individual—in other words, a system of monarchy was inevitable.

Thus the first century B. C. was an epoch of transition, when the old city-state was breaking up and degenerating into the rule of two privileged classes, the senators and knights, and when a new system of monarchy was growing up. The conception of a family of free and independent states—the conception which the Greeks fought for and which lay at the root of the Roman constitution in the fourth and third centuries B. C.—now gradually gave way to the ancient Eastern notion of a single world-wide state, possessing a uniform culture and ruled over by one man.

During this century the changes in the social and economic life of Italy were not less profound than the change in politics. The rural population in particular suffered greatly from civil war. The policy by which the Gracchi sought to revive the old system of small landholders was attempted more than once during these wars ; but it proved a failure. Repeated distributions of land among the discharged soldiers did nothing to restore the old state of things, though Marius and Sulla, Pompey and Caesar, Antony and Octavian, all carried through extensive measures for this purpose. New landholders were created by hundreds of thousands, and as many were evicted from their holdings to satisfy the needs of the new-comers. We hear little of the way in which the country-side was affected by these tremendous upheavals ; but we know enough to justify the belief that they made no radical alteration in Italian agriculture. Many of the veterans, unaccustomed to peaceful labour, went bankrupt, and their land passed into the hands of capitalists. Others held on to their allotments

VILLA URBANA AND VILLA RUSTICA

1. Part of the mural decoration of a house in Stabiae. A splendid villa built on the seashore, probably in Campania. A quay on arcades projects into the sea. Near it in the harbour is a boat. On the quay some figures are strolling, while a fisherman runs busily about with his fishing-implements. The villa, with beautiful porticoes in front, follows the curve of the shore; behind are other buildings and a park. Scores of similar landscapes among the wall-decorations of the Imperial period furnish splendid illustrations of the descriptions by Horace and his contemporaries, and show that, in attacking the luxury of the Augustan age, he and public opinion in general were not exaggerating. To those who travelled by land and by sea, along the shores of Campania, Latium, Etruria, and the lakes of north Italy, large and beautiful villas were undoubtedly the outstanding feature of the landscape. The owners of these villas were certainly not all members of the Imperial house or of the highest aristocracy, but in many cases rich freedmen. 1st cent. A.D. Naples, Museum.

2. Part of the mural decoration of the House of the 'Fontana Piccola' at Pompeii. A tower-shaped rustic house inside a walled court with a wide entrance-gate. In the court are seen palms and other trees, a shed attached to one of the walls of the house for protection against the sun's rays, and a high building like a pavilion, which perhaps represents the superstructure of a well. On one side of the entrance-gate is a plough, on the other are three women seated on a bench, talking. 1st cent. A.D. Pompeii.

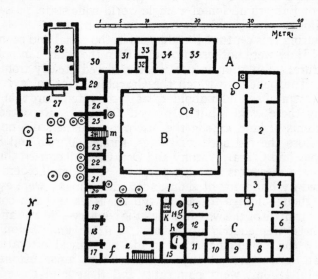

TEXT-FIG. 1. PLAN OF A VILLA RUSTICA NEAR GRAGNANO.

PLATE VII

1. A CAMPANIAN VILLA

2. VILLA RUSTICA, POMPEII

PLATE VII

and either displaced or became part of the old landowning middle class who took the lead in the provincial towns. At all events, the award of land to veterans did nothing to stop the growth of large estates.

For this period, far more than for earlier times, we have plenty of evidence about the immense estates owned by the ruling aristocracy in Italy and the provinces—estates which were cultivated by slaves or by tenants who might be called serfs. I have spoken already of Sulla and his forty thousand freedmen. Pompey's family owned such vast estates in Picenum that he could recruit a whole army among his own clients and freedmen to support Sulla against the democrats ; and Domitius Ahenobarbus, one of the senatorial generals, did the same, when Caesar invaded Italy after his rupture with Pompey. Pompey was not boasting when he said, on the eve of the war with Caesar, that he had only to stamp his foot and legions would grow out of the ground. He was thinking not only of his veterans and their sons, who were now his clients, but of the multitude of tenants upon his great Italian estates. Cicero, though never reckoned a very rich man, possessed villas and estates in many parts of Italy ; and yet he disapproved of land in general as an investment. It is true that land did not remain long in the same hands : changing with the changes in politics, it passed from one owner to another. But it tended on the whole to become the monopoly of a few wealthy capitalists.

During the civil wars great fortunes became commoner : every spasm of the conflict gave birth to new millionaires. Marius, Sulla, Pompey, Caesar, Antony, and Octavian—all these not only became immensely rich themselves but also enriched a vast number of their adherents, some of whom were clever enough to stick to their money. Anarchy in the provinces and inefficiency in the central government increased the opportunities of provincial governors to feather their own nests at the cost of their subjects. And lastly the conquest of the East by Pompey and of Gaul by Caesar enriched the generals and the officers. On the whole, the senatorial class grew richer than poorer during the civil wars, and the number of great capitalists belonging to this class grew larger.

The class of knights also grew richer, and a number of new families were added to it. The title of *equites* was no longer restricted to the eighteen centuries of knights, who were entered on the roll of citizens for mounted service : it was now enjoyed by all fully enfranchised citizens, whose property was valued at not less than 400,000 sesterces. The number of persons so qualified had risen enormously. By collecting the taxes in the provinces, by taking leases of public land, by lending money in Italy and abroad, by supplying and transporting armies, by building ships of war and transports, by buying up spoils of war, especially live stock and slaves, by purchasing confiscated land and other property in Italy during the massacres and proscriptions—by all these means great numbers of enterprising and unscrupulous people, whose parents were in many cases still slaves, had made their fortunes.

This lately acquired wealth was invested in all kinds of enterprises—trade, industry, tax-farming—but chiefly in land both at home and abroad. Cicero's friend Atticus may be taken as a normal type of a rich and respected knight who had given up speculation. His fortune was mainly invested in land situated in Epirus, and he raised live stock there on a large scale. As a man of culture and lover of literature, he put some of his money into a publishing business. He was Cicero's publisher. Sulla's freedman Chrysogonus, who grew rich out of the proscription, and whom Cicero has pilloried, may serve as a specimen of the dishonest and rapacious speculator.

Rome at this period was a vast centre of business and served as an exchange for the whole world. Immense bargains were concluded in the forum, e. g. for the Roman corn-supply and for the Italian export of olive-oil and wine. The shares of the great companies, which contracted for the collection of taxes or the cultivation of state domains, were bought and sold there. Many Roman citizens, especially from south Italy, spent their lives abroad—in Greece or Asia Minor, Africa or Gaul. They carried on commerce of all kinds, with special attention to money-lending and the slave trade. Every large centre of trade and industry in these provinces included a number of Roman citizens, who were united in a corporation of their own and played an important part in the business life of the place. I have mentioned already how Mithradates massacred about 80,000 of these Roman traders with their clerks and slaves in Asia Minor and Greece.

The flow of capital from the East to Rome and Italy

raised the wealth of the peninsula to an extraordinary height, which was not affected even by the horrors of civil war. M. Terentius Varro, born at Reate in the Sabine country, a friend of Cicero and also intimate with Caesar, wrote a treatise on agriculture, a serious and scientific work, for Roman landlords and capitalists ; and in it he gives a rose-coloured description of Italy as the most fertile and best-cultivated country in the world. Now as earlier, this was due chiefly to the scientific farming of the nobles, Roman and Italian. The system was the same as that of earlier times. Most of the work was done by slaves. More and more attention was given to the culture of the vine and olive, to growing fruit and vegetables, to poultry, and to stock-breeding. To these subjects most of Varro's treatise is devoted. The fall of Carthage and the ruined state of the East (of which more will be said below) made Italy the chief producer of wine and oil for the western market. Improved methods applied to vines and olive groves made it possible even to export wine and oil to the East, which had once supplied the whole world with these commodities. Money was made also out of small allotments whose principal produce was grain. The thriving towns of Italy with a constantly rising population demanded an immense amount of corn. Corn imported from the provinces could not compete with the native product except in seaport towns, because the cost of carriage by land was excessive.

It has been asserted that the smallholders were swallowed up by the great landlords, because the former mainly grew corn, which constantly fell in price because of the vast import of cheap corn from the provinces. It is certain that they were swallowed up ; but this was not caused by the import of corn but by other causes—the flow of money to Italy, the eagerness of rich men to invest their capital in land, their willingness to buy land at any price, and the heartless confiscations by which the leaders of revolutionary armies flooded the land market. In fact, if the civil wars brought ruin in their train, the victims were generally men of moderate or small means. Almost all the individuals of whom we know certainly that they were ruined by civil war belong to the class of fairly well-to-do farmers. Virgil lost his estate ; and he was a small landowner at Mantua in north Italy. Horace, as a partisan of Brutus and Cassius, forfeited his property, which consisted of land near Venusia, on the borders of Lucania and Apulia. Many no doubt were thus ruined and forced to take up their residence in the towns, others became tenants of the fields they had owned, and others were forced to emigrate to the Eastern or Western provinces. They were joined there by all who thought it better to sell land in Italy and seek their luck in foreign parts, where they hoped to find a good investment for their capital and labour.

The flow of capital to Italy explains also the expansion of industry there in the second and first centuries B. C. Some kinds of manufacture had flourished from very early times. Etruria had always exported a large quantity of bronze articles; as early as the fourth century the local pottery of south Italy had driven out vessels exported from Attica; and these manufactures were now largely developed. Capua became one of the chief centres for the production and export of bronze and copper vessels. Capua first, and Arretium in north Italy later, supplied all the West with earthenware. In the first century a great manufacture of earthenware lamps was started in north Italy. The fine fleeces of Apulia had long been famous and now became known all over the world, while an excellent wool for coarser fabrics was supplied by the flocks of north Italy.

The provinces, however, were in a much less flourishing economic condition. In the West, Africa produced corn on the vast estates of the Roman nobles, but produced hardly anything else; Spain was slowly recovering from fierce and continuous wars, from the time of Viriathus to Sertorius, and from the time of Sertorius to the conflict between Caesar and Pompey; Gaul was first ruined by the invasion of the Cimbri and Teutones and then weighed down by Caesar's campaigns in the centre and north of the country. Yet even there the influence of Italy, so near and so prosperous, was felt. The whole of Italy had now become Latinized. The language of Pompeii was Oscan before the Social war; at the time of Sulla's death Latin had driven Oscan out. In Cisalpine Gaul the Celtic tongue died out without leaving a trace behind: every one spoke and wrote Latin. Virgil, the greatest of the Latin poets, was a native of Mantua; his rival, Horace, was born at Venusia in south Italy. Latinized herself, Italy began to diffuse the same influence among the Western provinces. Latin culture and Latin town-life took root there.

In the first century the planting of Roman colonies and the immigration of Italians turned southern Spain and southern Gaul into something like districts of Italy. These Italians took with them some of their native capital and their native capacity for business. The settlers took a lively interest in the economic life of these countries and paved the way for future prosperity.

In the East the situation was far different. The war with Mithradates, the requisitions levied by Sulla and the democrats, the supremacy at sea of the Cilician and Cretan pirates, the domineering of the great tax-farming companies, the shameless finance of the Roman bankers, the presence in Greece of Pompey's and Caesar's armies, the unconcealed pillage carried on by Brutus and Cassius and then by Antony —all these causes had finally destroyed the prosperity of the richest districts in the East. The cities groaned under the burden of debt, and the debt rose steadily. The only country not utterly ruined was Egypt ; and even Egypt had suffered severely from the continuous dynastic disputes of the first century, from the greed of her Roman patrons, who willingly advanced loans to the contending parties at exorbitant interest, and from the arbitrary rule of Antony and Cleopatra. It is no wonder that the East was enfeebled not only financially but morally as well. The best men had emigrated to Italy or to the West. The temper of those who remained became more and more depressed ; and men who despaired of the present and of any future on earth sought consolation in religion and in doctrines partly religious and partly philosophic, which held out the possibility of a better life—beyond the grave.

This explains why interest in knowledge and scientific investigation, together with belief in the creative power of human reason, disappears almost entirely at this period. Men withdraw into themselves ; they ponder over moral perfection and union with God ; they try to lead a more intense inner life. Heading this movement with its motto of ' Detachment from Life ', the philosophic schools—Epicurean, Stoic, and Cynic—became more influential. They all taught the necessity of self-concentration, of seeking satisfaction in oneself, of looking at the life of the world as something ' indifferent '. Their methods, indeed, were unlike. Epicureanism lays down a purely materialistic view of things ; Stoicism connects the search for an inner life with religion ;

Cynicism devotes itself mainly to an unsparing criticism of mankind and society. The last great creative genius in science and literature whom the Greek world produced was Posidonius, a Syrian Greek from Apamea, who spent his whole life at Rhodes. A man of vast acquirements and keen intelligence, he was proficient in almost every department of knowledge. He was an excellent teacher of rhetoric ; he was one of the best historians of his time and wrote a continuation of Polybius ; in science he made important original discoveries and founded physical and economic geography, and wrote on tides and volcanoes. As an ethnographer he was the first to study northern Europe, and our first scientific knowledge of the region is due to him. He was famous for his skill in mathematics and astronomy. With all this knowledge he combined a profound religious feeling, and believed in spiritualism and astrology and the possibility of mystical apprehension. When one compares him with such a thoroughgoing rationalist as Polybius, one realizes the vast change that had passed over the East in the interval between them.

In this respect a very different picture is presented by Italy during this period. A vigorous and independent civilization grew up there, a distinct branch of the Hellenistic tree. We have seen already how Greek culture inundated Rome in the third century B. C., and how the next century gave it a Latin aspect. In the first century Roman culture finally ceased to be a thing borrowed from foreigners, and became truly national. This is shown most clearly by the literature. The Latin literature of this age is fresher and more direct than contemporary Greek literature. Among the poets we find such mighty geniuses as Catullus the lyric poet, Lucilius the satirist, and Lucretius the poet and philosopher. These men created the metre and rhythm of Latin poetry, and the poetic vocabulary. They did not invent new forms of verse, but they poured into the traditional forms the brilliance of their youthful genius. The same is true of prose, which was created mainly by Cicero. His predecessors were the great political orators of the past hundred and fifty years, the jurists who had forged the exact terminology of the civil law, and the historians who had celebrated the Roman state and its victorious arms. What they had done Cicero made use of. He proved the capacity latent in the Latin tongue for expressing shades of meaning as abstruse and elusive as those in

LIFE IN ITALY IN THE 1st CENT. B.C.—
1st CENT. A.D.

1. TRADE IN SLAVES

1. Part of a funeral *stele* from Capua. The upper part of the *stele* is occupied by two standing male figures, the Satur and Stepanus of the inscription engraved beneath them: 'M. Publilius M. l. Satur de suo sibi et liberto M. Publilio Stepano. Arbitratu M. Publili M. l. Cadiae praeconis et M. Publili M. l. Timotis.' The lower part of the stone shows the bas-relief here reproduced. A nude man is represented standing on a stone base. On his left a man moves quickly towards him, probably talking and pointing at him; he wears the Greek chiton and chlamys. On his other side another man, clad in a toga, quietly extends his right hand towards him. The scene no doubt represents the slave trade. The nude man is the slave, the man in the Greek dress is the seller, and the *togatus* the buyer. There can be little doubt that the two executors of the will of Publilius Satur intended to represent an episode of his early life—his purchase by his master and later *patronus*—in order to show the modest beginnings of one who became a great man in Capua and whose personality and history were probably known to everybody there. Similar was Trimalchio's idea in adorning the peristyle of his house with pictures which portrayed various episodes of his own life, beginning with the *venalicium cum titulis pictum* (Petron., *Cena*, 29, 3). Late Republican or early Augustan period. Museo Campano, Capua.

PLATE VIII

2. A FUNERAL PROCESSION

2. Part of the sculptural decoration of a funeral monument, found at
Amiternum in Central Italy. A funeral procession is represented. The
deceased, in full dress and as if sleeping, is carried on a litter by eight
men. The body is stretched on a couch; above the couch is a canopy.
The canopy consists of four poles and a mat covered with embroidered
figures of stars and of the half-moon. Before the catafalque is an or-
chestra of flute (*tibicines*), trumpet (*tubicines*), and horn (*cornicines*)
players. The catafalque is surrounded by mourners (members of the
family and friends) bewailing the deceased. Behind is the crowd of
participants in the funeral procession. Early 1st cent. A.D. Museum,
Aquila.

3. Bas-relief from the same monument. The funeral banquet. Two
groups of six persons each are seated around two tables on couches
(*triclinia*). Between them is a table with food and drink. Two slaves
are ministering. Early 1st cent. A.D. Museum, Aquila.

3. A FUNERAL BANQUET

PLATE VIII

which Greek philosophy is so rich. It is remarkable that at this time the chief authors belong to the higher class of Romans and Italians, and that the south Italians of humble origin who laid the foundations of Latin literature have no successors. Among the prominent men at Rome there are few who are not authors. Sulla writes *Memoirs*; Caesar has left to us *Commentaries*, describing his campaigns in Gaul and during the Civil war; Cicero was at once a statesman, an advocate, and a man of letters. Special attention was paid to history, as a handy weapon for political strife and party propaganda. I have spoken already of Sallust's *Jugurthine War*; his other extant work is a narrative of Catiline's conspiracy, equally brilliant in style, and equally devoid of either historical impartiality or scientific method.

Science kept pace with literature. It is true that the Romans paid little attention to the exact and minute discoveries of Greece in mathematics, medicine, physiology, astronomy, geography, and the natural sciences. But grammar, rhetoric, archaeology, jurisprudence, philosophy, the history of religion and law—all these became favourite subjects of study with educated Romans. The works of M. Terentius Varro submitted to a careful scrutiny the development of the national literature, religion, and public institutions; Cicero wrote a number of popular works on philosophy and rhetoric; and Lucretius expounded the doctrine of Epicurus in a poetic form. But perhaps the chief monument of Latin genius is the steady growth of that juristic literature in which the living Roman law is interpreted.

In the domain of art less was accomplished. Greek sculpture, Greek paintings, and the products of Greek art generally, abounded in Italy and Rome; and much work was turned out at Rome by Greek artists. But Roman art was still unborn: it was a child of the empire. The Romans may have contributed something to the development of realistic portraiture; but this can hardly be called an original discovery; it was rather an advance along the path already trodden by the Hellenistic sculptors and painters. Roman architecture, too, showed no originality but contented itself with reproducing Hellenistic models.

The general aspect of life in Italy, and especially at Rome, was almost entirely Greek. Thus Greek was the language of fashionable society; or, at any rate, a knowledge of Greek was indispensable for a gentleman. This external aspect of life is well known to us from Cicero's *Letters*. It was a full life that was lived by the grandees of Roman society. Every self-respecting member of that body owned a splendid palace in Rome with a horde of domestic slaves and hundreds of clients ; and he had two or three or more luxurious country houses, with parks and gardens ; and many of these houses were built on the seashore. A brilliant social life went on there in town and country : there were banquets with music and dancing ; new literary works were recited ; lectures were delivered by philosophers or orators from Greece ; or, if the party was small, gossip and scandal enlivened it. Women were not excluded—indeed they played a chief part on that stage. The tattle of these great people turned on romantic actions and love affairs, on marriages and still more on divorces. Politics were very fashionable. From time to time the thundercloud of civil war fills the sky. But no sooner has it passed by than the old life begins again with all its interests and follows the familiar round. The provincial towns tried to follow the example set by Rome. Of the life led by the lower classes at this time we know nothing ; but it is unlikely that it was specially attractive.

XIV

THE PRINCIPATE OF AUGUSTUS

THE struggle of the Senate against a military despotism was long drawn out. Though it seemed as if the blows dealt by Caesar had brought it to an end, yet, as we have seen, he went too far and too fast in his treatment of the existing system. He refused to take account of the form which had been imposed by the lapse of centuries upon the Roman state ; and, above all, he ignored alike the desire of the citizen body to maintain their privileged position in the empire, and the high position which had been attained by the two leading classes of the community—the senators and the knights. Nevertheless, the Senate failed, for want of military support, in their attempt to restore the old order of things and recover their authority after Caesar's death. In the contest which followed between Antony and Octavian the supreme control of the Senate was no longer an issue : the question had been definitely settled in favour of military leadership. The question, which of the two competitors for power was more acceptable to the people, was only of secondary importance. The really important issues were these : Ought the unity of the state to be maintained ?—And, if it were maintained, what form of authority would be most acceptable to the directing classes of the population, i. e. to the whole body of Roman citizens ?

Two forms of military monarchy were suggested. Caesar, whose view was inherited by Antony, had insisted on a military rule based upon the support of the population throughout the world. He held that Italy, otherwise the Roman citizens, and the provinces, otherwise the subjects of those Roman citizens, must at some time be blended into one body and pay identical allegiance to the supreme ruler. But the higher ranks of society, supported by all Roman citizens, that is, by all Italians and some provincials, while recognizing that the leader of the armed forces of the state must have supreme authority, were unwilling to surrender their privileged position and be swamped among the population of the provinces. The national pride of Italy was aroused. The citizens demanded that the predominance which they had gained by long years of conflict should be recognized as their right. Octavian defeated Antony because he realized the strength of this national feeling and made use of it in the contest with his rival. Relying upon this feeling, he bound himself by an unwritten engagement to maintain inviolate the political predominance of Italy and the essential features of Italian society. The Roman state needed new blood, and a restoration was inevitable, but no more than a restoration : to create a new state on the ruins of the old was not contemplated or desired by any one. The old Rome was not dead, thought the citizens ; why then sing dirges for it before the time ? Such was the conviction that prevailed in Italy, and Octavian probably shared it himself. It is obvious that under these conditions he had not a free hand in making the constitution. His claim to greatness is this—that he not only understood the relation between the various forces at work, but was also prepared to work honestly, in order to draw from the situation the right practical conclusions. I repeat— there is no reason at all to suppose that his actions were dictated merely by calculation, or, in other words, that his political course was merely a concession to the general opinion of the citizens. Beyond doubt, he believed himself that public opinion was right, that Rome was not dead, and that he himself had a call to restore her ancient glory.

This then was his task, to combine the military power inherited from his predecessors and proved indispensable for the restoration and maintenance of peace, order, and good government—to combine this with the strongly expressed wish of Italy and the Roman citizens to maintain their privileged position, if not in a political sense, at least in social and economic relations. On this condition Italy was prepared to accept and support a military ruler who was almost an autocrat. The provinces were ready to acknowledge any authority that secured them peace and order.

The first two years that followed the close of civil war were given up by Octavian to the passing of certain measures which he thought indispensable, if his later and more sweeping reforms were to be successful. He was now the head of the Roman state, and his right to administer it was undisputed. But he showed at once that he had no intention of treading in Caesar's footsteps. The object of his first measures was to reinstate the higher ranks of Roman society and the whole body of citizens, and to restore the city of Rome itself. In 29 B. C. he revised the roll of the Senate and expelled 190 unworthy members partly admitted to the House by Caesar. Their abdication of their title was voluntary, but suggested to them by Octavian. These men had been raised by Caesar's decree from the army to the Senate ; they did not belong to the senatorial class, and many of them had only recently received from Caesar the rights of citizenship. Thus the Senate again came to represent the highest Roman nobility. A year earlier Octavian carried a series of measures, in order to purify the body of citizens and ensure that it should consist predominantly of Romans and Italians. In his opinion, it ought not to be recruited in Caesar's fashion by the admission of provincials, but to grow from within ; and with that object he insisted that every citizen should marry and rear a family, and that the blood of these new citizens should be purely Italian. Marriage with freedmen was forbidden. That these measures were deliberate, and represented a strong conviction in the mind of Octavian, is proved by their confirmation with some changes in 18 B. C. and again in A. D. 9. Special measures were also adopted to prevent misalliances among the higher classes : the prohibition of marriages with freed slaves was strictly enforced in the case of senators, though it proved impossible to impose it upon the whole body of citizens. And lastly, in 28 B. C., Octavian began his task of restoring the capital by rebuilding the most revered temples.

At the same time he endeavoured to bring back by degrees the external forms in which the republican government had once been clothed. Yet he did not, during the early years of his rule, lay down his extraordinary powers : he was still the military chief, whom all the population was bound to obey, in virtue of their oath of allegiance. As such he kept the title which he took as early as 40 B. C., and which indicated his close connexion with the army. It was the custom at Rome to add *Octavianus* to his name of Gaius Julius Caesar and to call him for short by the former name alone. But he did not call himself ' Octavian ' ; and for the name ' Gaius ' he substituted the complimentary title of *imperator* conferred on him by the army. This purely military title, which became with him not only a title but a name, he accepted in order to distinguish him from the other revolutionary commanders whom their armies had saluted in this fashion after a victory, and who used it as a title pure and simple ; and he kept it, even when his authority had ceased to be purely military ; it had become a custom. Moreover, in the provinces this title soon became connected with an idea of the unlimited and universal nature of his power—an idea which he had no wish to upset. This explains why the inhabitants of the Eastern provinces were made to swear allegiance to him personally, when his authority had become definitely established. He was not one of the Julii. Even less desirable was the name ' Octavian ', which showed that he belonged not to the Julian but to the Octavian family. But he kept the name ' Caesar ', because he inherited from Caesar the right of commanding the army ; and he emphasized the connexion with Caesar in another way. Caesar had been deified after death ; and his successor called himself ' son of the deified Caesar '. Therefore his full name ran thus : *Imperator Caesar Divi filius*. But, while retaining his extraordinary powers and revolutionary title, he chose to hold the office of consul, and was elected annually after 31 B. C., together with a colleague ; this election, like that of the other magistrates, was made by the people voting in the ordinary popular assemblies. He ruled the state in his own person but acted through the Senate and popular assembly, which met at the usual times for the dispatch of the usual business.

After two years of transition Octavian considered it possible to crown his work and restore finally the old order of things. At a meeting of the Senate in 27 B. C. he laid down his special powers and formally proclaimed the restoration of the ancient constitution. But at the same meeting the Senate insisted that he should accept a number of new powers, military and administrative, of which more is said below. These powers established his position as head of the Senate and First Citizen or *princeps* ; and that day gave birth to the new form of government which we, after the Romans themselves, call the ' Principate '.

He received on the same occasion that additional title by which he is universally known and which became his personal name. The Senate added to his former style, *Imperator Caesar Divi filius*, the title of ' Augustus '. Previously, this epithet had been applied only to certain gods, to imply that they were 'augmenters' and creators of something different and better—the same idea which is at the root of Roman belief in the religious essence of individual genius. Thus the title was conferred upon Octavian as the restorer and 'augmenter' of the state, and as the man invested with the highest 'authority' (*auctoritas*), a word derived from the same root as the word 'Augustus'. (We shall in future drop the name 'Octavian' for that of 'Augustus'.) The state over which he ruled had long been called by the Romans themselves the 'Roman Empire', i. e. that part of the world where the authority of the Roman people was the supreme law; and the bearer of that authority, after the revolutionary period, became the 'Emperor'.

The year 27 B. C. begins a period during which the steady activity of Augustus created a new constitution for the empire. I shall endeavour to describe this constitution in its entirety, as it took shape after the formal pronouncement of restoration by Augustus. There was nothing startling or revolutionary in it: Sulla, Pompey, and Caesar had all taken a share in laying the foundations for this new construction. But Augustus had the skill to combine into one whole the contributions of his predecessors, while endeavouring to interfere as little as possible with the external forms of public life that had the sanction of centuries. Thus the principate was constructed; and the fact that it stood firm for nearly two centuries proves that Augustus could learn of the past, could estimate the real forces of the empire, and could comprehend the mental attitude of his contemporaries.

It would be useless to search for a single constitutional formula by which to define the results of what Augustus actually did. What was it he created? Was it a monarchy, or a dyarchy shared by himself and the Senate, or a restoration of the old republic? For fifty years past this question of terminology has been debated by scholars, but the debate has been entirely fruitless. The main task of Augustus was just this—by minute and patient labour to efface the distinction between these conceptions, and to smooth away the sharp angles. Hence the constitution he made, though it can be described, cannot be completely defined by a single word or in a brief formula. He wished himself to be regarded as the restorer of the old constitution: this is distinctly emphasized in his account of his own activities which was published after his death by his successor Tiberius at Rome and in the provinces. But Tacitus, when he surveyed the emperor's work, a hundred years after it was completed, from the watchtower of history, and even the contemporaries of Augustus, saw clearly that this account was unsatisfactory. They, like modern historians, were inclined to simplify the question by saying that Augustus created a monarchy. Both views are right, and both are wrong. It is impossible to bring the type of constitution created by Augustus under any single simple formula. To do so would be to misunderstand its essential nature which grew up historically out of various elements.

When Augustus had defeated Antony, his power rested upon his sole command over the armed forces of the state. When he laid down his extraordinary powers in 27 B. C., he abdicated also his command over the army. His purely military title (which was spoken of above) he retained ; and his military power was immediately handed back to him by the Senate. How he would have acted if the Senate had not done this we do not know. It did confer on him proconsular power for ten years in all the provinces where armies were quartered, except Africa and Macedonia. But it is notable that the Senate made no attempt to take this power from him : his connexion with the army was too close to be dissolved by any decree they could pass.

The soldiers who had fought for Augustus or Antony could not be demobilized all at once. Some were discharged and provided with land ; but more than half—about 250,000 men —were kept with the colours and distributed among those provinces which needed military protection. The fleet also it was necessary to keep up ; otherwise the pirates would have become masters of the sea.

Rome needed a well-organized standing army, and yet one which should not say the last word on political questions, but should remain, as far as possible, neutral in such matters. The importance of this point was certainly recognized by Caesar and by Antony, the inheritor of Caesar's ideas ; and they tried to escape the danger by forming an army, not composed of Roman citizens but of the inhabitants of the Empire in general. They readily enlisted provincials in their legions ; and to the best of them, those who rose to be centurions, they threw open a splendid career, which might culminate even in the senate-house itself. But this path was not open to Augustus : his victory was a victory of the citizens over the provinces. The state ruled by him must still be a state in which Italy and the Roman citizens were masters and the provincials merely servants and subjects. And such an empire could only be guarded by an army whose nucleus consisted of Roman citizens.

It cannot be said that Augustus overcame this difficulty in which he found himself owing to the force of circumstances. His organization of the army was a compromise. Here, as in other departments of state, he made a system of a practice introduced during the civil wars. The Roman army became a standing army, not in fact merely but also in theory. Its nucleus was formed by legions of Roman citizens, serving for a period which was fixed in 63 B. C. at sixteen years and raised to twenty years in 52 B. C. In fact, even after twenty years, not every soldier received the *honesta missio*, or ' honourable discharge ' : the difficulty of raising fresh levies, the wish to retain experienced and disciplined men, and also the necessity of providing veterans with land or money—all these considerations induced Augustus and his successors to keep time-expired soldiers with the colours. The principle that the legions should consist of Roman citizens was retained. Under Augustus the legionaries were mainly natives of Italy and Roman citizens from the provinces ; but occasionally, and especially for the East, this rule was relaxed and the practice of Antony was followed. Augustus retained the right of conscription, and every citizen was still liable in theory to service in the legions ; but he and his immediate successors never had recourse to conscription except at a crisis. After the civil wars there were plenty of men ready to join the army ; and to fill the ranks with volunteers for long service was comparatively easy.

From this time onward the legions of the standing army were never quartered in Italy, but in the places where war was actually going on or might be expected to break out—in the provinces of Gaul and Spain, in the Danube country, in Syria, Egypt, and Africa, which had strong and warlike peoples on their frontiers. The soldiers lived as if on campaign in camps that were fortified but not permanent. Such was the theory at least, but in fact many of these stations were converted into permanent camps. A legion was not confined to a particular province, but might, in case of need, be shifted from one to another. The soldiers were naturally forbidden to marry—a flagrant contradiction of the laws by which Augustus had made it the duty of every Roman citizen to rear a family. The system of command was, in general, the same as before. The centurions still represented discipline and tradition; but, for political reasons, they were not permanently attached to a particular legion but went from one to another. The possibility which the centurions had enjoyed of promotion to the two highest classes was not continued by Augustus. Only the very few among them who belonged to the equestrian class could look forward to an equestrian career. The officers all belonged to the privileged classes. As earlier, some of the tribunes were elected and some nominated by the emperor; as a rule, they held their commands for short periods. Superior to them were the commanders of legions, who were called *legati*; they belonged to the senatorial class and had generally held the office of *quaestor* or *praetor*; and like the tribunes, for political reasons, they did not hold their posts long. The supreme command of any provincial army was held by legates of the emperor in imperial provinces and by proconsuls in senatorial provinces; their tenure was seldom prolonged beyond a year. Officers, centurions, and even soldiers had some preliminary training before joining the army. On the emperor's initiative boys and young men of senatorial and equestrian rank went through a course of this kind at Rome; they were formed into special corps for this purpose, and their honorary commander, called *princeps iuventutis*, ' chief of the young men ', was the heir apparent. Gaius and Lucius, the grandsons of Augustus, whom his daughter Julia bore to Agrippa, were the first to hold this title. The other towns of Italy had similar institutions which carried on the ancient organizations for uniting the young citizens of the town in a single club or corps.

Augustus made an innovation, when, in addition to the legions quartered abroad, he formed a large detachment for the special purpose of guarding the emperor's person. A commanding officer on active service had always been attended by such a body, called ' a praetor's guard ', *cohors praetoria*. Since the commander-in-chief was now, contrary to the constitutional practice laid down by the Senate, permanently resident at Rome, it was natural that his guards should be there also, at the head-quarters. Not one but nine cohorts (a tenth was added later) were required by the dignity of the commander-in-chief of all the troops; in each there were 1,000 men serving for twelve years, which were raised later to sixteen; their officers—the praetorian praefect, with tribunes under him—belonged to the equestrian class. In addition to the praetorian guard, there were three 'city cohorts', *urbanae cohortes*, quartered at Rome; they were recruited from among citizens and formed a military police. There were also seven cohorts of firemen, in which freedmen might take service. Both police and firemen were commanded by praefects of their own. Lastly, the palace of the emperor was guarded by armed barbarians, chiefly Germans, who were reckoned not as part of the army but as belonging to the imperial household.

A second innovation of Augustus perpetuated a practice which had sometimes, but only in great emergencies, been resorted to by the Senate in republican times. This was the formation of a second army, consisting entirely of provincials. It contained cavalry and infantry regiments (*alae et cohortes*), of either 1,000 or 500 men, commanded by Roman officers of equestrian rank; after twenty-five years' service the men became Roman citizens. The formation of this army, almost equal in number to the original army of citizens, was a concession to Caesar's ideas and also to the fact that Rome was now an empire; but it held an inferior position. These troops were called 'auxiliaries' (*auxilia*), and were attached to the legions. They were intended to lighten the burden of military service for the citizens, and to make forcible conscription unnecessary. Detachments of soldiers were occasionally sent by allies of Rome, mainly tributary kings, in support of a Roman army.

Another novelty was the creation of a standing navy. One squadron was anchored at Misenum in south Italy, and the other at Ravenna on the Adriatic. The crews were at first slaves belonging to the emperor; later they were citizens of the lowest class, or freedmen, or provincials; the officers were knights. The fleet was not large: probably the number of rowers, sailors, and soldiers did not exceed 10,000. The ships were small and light and were chiefly used for police duty, that is, for hunting down and capturing pirates.

But the chief innovation on the republican system was this—that military affairs were now withdrawn entirely from the competence of the Senate and the popular assembly. Nor were such matters any concern at all of the annual magistrates, the consuls and praetors ; they were reserved exclusively for the emperor to deal with. Augustus had not a monopoly of military power (*imperium*) : in theory, it was possessed by all consuls at Rome and all proconsuls and propraetors in the provinces. But since the armies were stationed, almost without exception, in the provinces governed by Augustus, and since the praetorian guard defended his person, therefore he had complete control over the military forces.

The proconsular power was conferred on Augustus for ten years by the Senate in 27 B. C., in order that he might govern certain provinces—just those provinces which had enemies on their frontier and in which, therefore, armies were quartered; and it was renewed five times for periods of five or ten years. His power over the army included every department of military affairs. He appointed the legates who commanded the armies in the imperial provinces ; he appointed the commanders of legions and of auxiliary cohorts, and the tribunes and praefects who commanded the cavalry. All these belonged to the senatorial or equestrian classes. Even the non-commissioned officers—the centurions, or commanders of the centuries into which the cohort was divided—and the non-combatant attendants of the superior officers, were nominated by him.

Augustus alone was entitled to settle the distribution of troops among the provinces, and to prescribe their tasks, either military or civil, the latter including the construction of roads and bridges. From him the soldiers received their pay, the legionaries getting half as much as the praetorian guards but more than the auxiliaries. And, lastly, their pensions were fixed and paid by him. (The institution of a regular system of pensions was another innovation.) For this object a special treasury was created, the *aerarium militare*, into which Augustus paid a considerable part of his private fortune, and to which some part of the public revenue was diverted. This new system of military organization made Augustus as absolute as Caesar had been : the only difference was this, that his power was disguised under another name and assumed other forms, less repulsive to Roman tradition.

It must, however, be noticed that all the measures described above did not solve for Augustus his fundamental problem.

Neither the supply of troops, nor their fitness for war, nor their detachment from politics was thus secured. The standing army, in so far as it was an army of long-service volunteers, threatened to become a caste, a body of professional fighters, distinct from the rest of the population and disliked by them. Their fighting power was lessened by the political considerations which made it impossible to form a body of officers and non-commissioned officers, well trained and permanently connected with their men. And lastly it was impossible to secure that the army should remain neutral in politics. The imperial guards were bound to exercise a strong political influence ; and even the provincial armies were sure soon to realize that every wearer of the purple must, in the long run, depend upon them for the strength and permanence of his authority.

A matter of no less importance, if we are to understand the system set up by Augustus as *princeps*, is his relation to the finances of the state and the material resources of the empire. The system of taxation was not changed, and the revenue remained as before. Citizens paid no tax on Italian land held by them ; the only taxes levied upon them were a duty of 5 per cent. on the value of slaves manumitted, and a succession duty of 5 per cent. introduced by Augustus late in his reign, in A.D. 6. The state derived its revenue mainly from the domains belonging to it, in which were included the provinces ; but these sources were not sufficient to defray the cost of a great standing army. Hence during the first century B.C. the state paid its way mainly by war : the expense was met out of the booty taken by the troops. The army in the field maintained itself. During the Civil war the leaders of revolutionary armies followed the same system : their troops were maintained partly by confiscating the property of political opponents, and partly by robbing the provinces which were the scene of war.

Such a condition of things could not go on, when the civil wars were ended. Meanwhile the expenses had risen greatly, owing to the formation of the praetorian guards, the establishment of a standing fleet, and the introduction of a regular pension system ; also the regular army was now on a peace footing, and its occasional campaigns, as we shall see later, brought in no revenue. Vast sums were swallowed up also by the buildings which Augustus erected at Rome and by military roads in the provinces ; money was spent on magnificent shows in the Circus, theatres, and amphitheatre ; more was required for the distribution of corn to the citizens at Rome—an institution inherited by Augustus from republican times and now thoroughly established. The normal revenue was insufficient to cover this expenditure. On the other hand, it was imprudent to introduce new duties in Italy or to increase the burden of taxation in the provinces : Italians and provincials, the latter especially, had suffered severely from civil war, and the only consequence would have been universal discontent. It was possible to increase the revenue gradually by a more orderly and systematic method of collecting the taxes, by a strict control over the tax-farming companies, and by substituting eventually, for the collection of the land-tax by tax-farmers, a system of collection by state officials. A preparatory step in this direction was a general census of property owned in the provinces; this was started by Augustus and admirably carried out in Gaul by his stepson Drusus ; and perhaps the same thing was done in Galatia, Syria, and Palestine, the newly annexed provinces in the East. But all this took time, and an immense sum of money was wanted immediately. The Senate was aware of its helplessness in the matter : the *princeps* alone could do anything.

Augustus understood the advantages of his position. After the Civil war he was the richest man in the state. How he acquired his colossal wealth we do not know. The limit between private and public property was not carefully observed by any revolutionary leader in that troubled time ; and no inconvenient questions were asked. The personal wealth of Augustus grew even after peace was established, chiefly by legacies from wealthy men, who bequeathed to him part of their property, either from personal attachment or from a wish to establish doubtful titles—after the Civil war almost all titles to property were doubtful—by giving the head of the state a direct interest in their validity. His fortune assumes still more impressive proportions, if we accept a rather vague statement of our authorities, to the effect that Egypt on the death of Cleopatra became the private property of Augustus. Though contrary to all the traditions of Roman public law, such an arrangement is quite consistent with the Hellenistic theory, according to which Egypt was the personal property of the Egyptian kings. At all events, it is unlikely that the position of Egypt was precisely defined from the point of view of Roman public law. Theoretically, she was one of the Roman provinces assigned to Augustus that he might govern them ; for Roman legions were stationed there ; but in point of fact the troops in Egypt were not commanded by a senator, according to the constitutional rule and the practice in other provinces, but by a knight, who inherited all the royal rights in his capacity of the emperor's personal lieutenant.

In the possession of this immense wealth Augustus found a new means to make himself indispensable to the state. At the repeated request of the Senate, he came to the rescue of the treasury more than once. He undertook the cost of new buildings in Rome ; he paid for grain to be distributed among the inhabitants ; he contributed the money to assure the soldiers their pensions ; he provided the pay for his guards, bought land for the veterans, gave largesses to the soldiers and the populace, and celebrated splendid games. It is unlikely that the state was put to any expense for the upkeep of the imperial provinces—those which were ruled by Augustus, and in which the Roman armies were stationed. The revenue of these provinces was supposed to cover the expenditure on the troops ; but it was probably insufficient, and Augustus paid the difference out of his own pocket.

Hence the Senate abstained altogether from interfering in the finance of the imperial provinces. The treasuries of these provinces became branches of the emperor's private treasury, and the combined offices received later, under the successors of Augustus, the name of *fiscus* (*fiscus* is the Latin word for ' a money-bag '). The *fiscus* and the emperor's personal property (*patrimonium*) generally were managed by his confidential slaves and freedmen. They also, in the emperor's name, collected the taxes in his provinces and managed his property in the senatorial provinces—those which were governed in the name of the Senate by Roman magistrates. The superintendent of his accounts, the manager of his personal property, and his agents in the provinces all bore special titles : the first was called *a rationibus* (' in charge of the accounts '), the second, *a patrimonio*, and the third, *procuratores* (agents, attorneys). He had also a number of confidential secretaries, known as *ab epistulis*, who attended to his private and official correspondence.

Under these conditions the part played by Augustus personally in the finance of the state was of the highest impor-

tance. Without his aid bankruptcy was inevitable, or a resort
to the predatory methods of republican times. As a matter
of course the Senate gladly agreed that he should organize
the collection of the succession duty, which was very distasteful to the citizens, that he should control the management
of the public treasury in the temple of Saturn, and that his
procurators should keep an eye on the proconsuls, propraetors,
and quaestors sent out by the Senate to govern the senatorial
provinces. At the end of his life and rule Augustus was really
the manager of the Roman Empire, the careful steward of
her property, and the owner of immense wealth which he spent
mainly upon the state. The budget of the empire was to
a large extent identical with the budget of the ruler.

The army and finance were the two main pillars on which
the personal power of Augustus rested. An important addition
to these was the general satisfaction caused by the order he
established. The provinces were contented ; after the disturbances of civil war, the new system of government controlled by the emperor, which checked the arbitrary behaviour
of the tax-farmers and regularized the collection of the direct
taxes, gave them a breathing-space and a chance of recovery.
It is no wonder that in the East men began, as early as
29 B. C., to pay divine honours to Augustus. The position in
Italy was more complicated. Italy was also glad to rest
after the horrors of civil war ; but she was not content with
that. Every section of the population had its own claims
and its own hopes. But Augustus managed to satisfy all these
sections, more or less successfully. First of all, as I have
said already, Italy remained the dominant country : there
was no talk of merging its identity with that of the provinces,
and the Roman people was still master of the Roman Empire.
Nor was there any hint of removing the distinction between
the different classes of citizens : the old division into classes
remained and was even more sharply defined than before.
An ordinary citizen could not become a knight, or a knight
a senator, except by favour of the emperor. The candidate
for promotion must possess a certain fortune and a stainless
character, and also must gain the emperor's consent to enter
his name upon the list.

The senators were less satisfied with the settlement than
any other class, though Augustus made concessions which
were generous when compared with Caesar's treatment of

that body. The Senate continued to exist, as the supreme council of the magistrates and, in particular, of the emperor. Augustus treated it with great respect. All important public business was discussed by it ; and it still managed the government of certain provinces ; and the governors of these provinces, and of most imperial provinces, were senators. Augustus generally appointed senators to represent him at home and abroad in commissions entrusted to him by the Senate and people. None but senators could command the legions. The sons of senators began their military service not as common soldiers but as officers. Members of the senatorial families alone were eligible for the Roman magistracies ; and the seats in the House were filled mainly by these magistrates when their term of office was over.

For all this, the senators knew very well that, though they might discuss business as the emperor's council, the decision rested with him, not with them ; and they were aware that the future of each one of them depended absolutely upon the emperor. The people elected as magistrates only those candidates whom he approved. From time to time, by special commission from the people, he revised the list of senators and struck out the unworthy. As he chose, he could appoint this or that senator to the command over part of the army or to be governor over an imperial province ; even a senatorial province could not be obtained if the emperor objected. In the province itself, the governor no longer felt himself a free man : he knew that far away at Rome a steady attentive eye was watching all that he did ; he knew also that he would do well to be content with the large salary fixed once for all for provincial governors, rather than run the risk of returning home to be tried by a really impartial court, in which the emperor once more was the real judge. And lastly, Augustus was ready to give pecuniary assistance to impoverished senators, if they were devoted to him ; and property, valued at not less than a million sesterces, was a necessary qualification for any one who hoped to be elected to the Senate and remain a member. Thus the Senate and the senatorial class were entirely dependent on Augustus. They submitted to this painful necessity ; but they would not have submitted had he not left them in full possession of their social privileges.

The second class in the empire, the class of knights, not only accepted the position of Augustus but backed him up in every way and proved his most trusty supporters. This powerful class of business men, which had come out stronger from the civil wars and much more numerous, in spite of the many victims whom the wars had claimed, could not fail to be satisfied with the treatment it received from Augustus. The disreputable past which dogged too many of these men was forgotten : the class was officially declared to be the second class in the state and a hereditary branch of the aristocracy. The knights received definite rights in public life, as members of the jury-courts, officers in the army, financial agents of the emperor, and governors of certain provinces, such as Egypt and the newly organized provinces in the Alps. There were certain drawbacks : the sphere of their activity was gradually restricted, and, in particular, they lost entirely their former absolute control over tax-farming transactions ; Augustus might confer the privileges of the class on individuals or withdraw them, as he saw fit ; and they found that military service as an officer was not merely a right but a duty. But on the whole this class gained far more than it lost.

Nor had the population of Italy, not included in the two highest classes, any reason to be discontented. Its numbers had been much reduced during the civil wars, and its composition was greatly changed. Many once well-to-do people had been robbed of their land, and discharged soldiers had taken their place. But this took place long before the end of civil war ; and those who had lost their property had adapted themselves as best they could to the new conditions. The allotments of land granted after the battle of Actium were less hasty and more systematic : the land for the veterans was not taken by force but paid for. No fierce hatred was kindled by the transaction. Above all, the time of uncertainty about the morrow had gone by, and men could breathe freely once more. The constant raising of recruits was at an end ; and yet the ranks were open to all who wished to serve. The armies no longer moved about the country or were billeted upon the people ; there was a respite from pillage and from the burden of forcible requisitions. Life had returned to its ordinary course ; and there were excellent prospects for Roman citizens residing in Italy. Members of the provincial aristocracy and bourgeoisie might acquire Roman citizenship and even be promoted to the equestrian rank by the emperor's power or by service in the army and in the municipal administration. Flourishing trade and industry enriched the active and stirring class of freedmen ; or, if they chose to serve the state, they had excellent opportunities in the navy, or the fire brigade, or the financial offices.

The Roman proletariate must also be briefly mentioned. They soon reconciled themselves to the loss of political importance. About 200,000 were maintained by the state, receiving a ration of corn. The rest Augustus kept in good humour by giving them employment together with a constant supply of amusements and occasional doles of money.

The authority of Augustus rested partly on his military position and his control over the revenues of the state, and partly on the popularity with the masses of the new constitution. The precise form in which he clothed his directing position in the state was a matter of secondary importance. In defining his relation to the former instruments of government—the magistrates, Senate, and popular assembly—Augustus avoided all appearance of unconstitutional action. He would not hear of a dictatorship, either for a limited period or for life ; nor would he accept the title of 'guardian of laws and morals'. Whatever exceptional powers he possessed he resigned in 28 and 27 B.C., and by so acting restored the constitution just as it had existed before the dictatorship of Caesar. In theory, Rome was governed once more by the magistrates, the Senate, and the popular assembly.

If Augustus, who was himself one of these magistrates, was the real ruler of Rome, he was so in virtue of his personal charm and moral authority and the clearly expressed desire of the Senate and people. From this point of view he was a second Pompey : he was what Pompey had wished to be. A decree of the Senate had conferred on him as proconsul control of the army ; the tribunician power he, like Caesar, had received from the people ; he was elected consul in the ordinary way year after year till 23 B.C., after which, though pressed by the electors to stand, he only held the office at long intervals and in exceptional circumstances. In the eye of the law the state was governed, as of old, by the Senate, except the imperial provinces which the Senate itself had transferred to Augustus, and except those departments of government which also the Senate and people had begged him to undertake, such as the supply and distribution of foreign grain, the maintenance of the roads, and the order and safety of the capital. If in fact it was Augustus, and not the Senate and popular assembly, that ruled the state, then the Senate and popular assembly, without any visible pressure from Augustus, were content that it should be so.

The firm and sensible foreign policy of Augustus also did much to strengthen his principate. The system of distributing the standing armies wherever the frontier was threatened with danger proved advantageous : it secured peace and a possibility of economic development both for the provinces and for Italy. Frontier warfare still went on ; but its purpose now was to strengthen and rectify the frontiers. Where it was necessary to do so, new territory was conquered and annexed to the existing provinces. Thus, after a long and exhausting war the still independent part of Spain was conquered, and the whole country divided into three provinces—Baetica governed by the Senate, and Tarraconensis and Lusitania governed by Augustus.

The position was more complicated on the eastern frontier of Gaul, i. e. on the Rhine, and also on the Danube, in the country fringing Macedonia and the Roman province of Illyricum. Gaul had now been thoroughly subdued and pacified, and was divided into four provinces—Narbonensis ruled by the Senate, and Aquitania, Lugdunensis, and Belgica ruled by the emperor. Thus, it was possible for the emperor to give serious attention to the northern frontier, in other words, to the relations between Rome and the German tribes. It is not likely that he ever thought of including all Germans in the Roman state. Most of them lived in such a primitive and barbarous fashion, altogether untouched by Graeco-Roman civilization, that to turn their forests into part of a Roman province would have been out of the question. His plan was more modest. He wished to bring within the empire all the Thracian and Celtic tribes to the south of the Danube, and all the German tribes to the west of the Elbe, who had already come under Roman influence, and so to create a natural frontier, easy to defend and as short as possible, running from the Black Sea by the Danube and the Elbe to the North Sea.

The conquest of the countries south of the Danube and east of the Rhine was early taken in hand by Augustus and carried on systematically. In 35 and 34 B. C., while he was triumvir, he waged in person a long and obstinate war against the Illyrian tribes of Iapodes and Dalmatians, and thus gained for Rome a strip on the eastern shore of the Adriatic with all its Greek and half-Greek cities, where contact was beginning to be established with the new Roman colonies and settlements on the upper Danube. A further step was taken when the Alpine districts were subdued and pacified by Tiberius and Drusus, the stepsons of Augustus. Augustus himself had fought there in 35 and 34 B. C., and had subdued and exterminated the Salassi in 25 B. C. The process was completed by his stepsons between 15 and 13 B. C., when the Alpine regions were annexed and divided first into military districts, and later into small provinces governed by the *procuratores* or personal agents of the emperor. Still earlier, in 29 to 27 B. C., M. Licinius Crassus, the governor of Macedonia, by a series of successful campaigns had moved forward the frontier of the empire as far as the lower Danube, and forced the native tribes of Thracians and Illyrians to submit to Rome. His work was carried on by Marcus Lollius and C. Calpurnius Piso with important results : the submissive and tributary kingdom of the Odrysae in Thrace was strengthened ; Rome became the protector of the Greek cities on the western shore of the Black Sea, and established a connexion with the Greek colonies on the northern shore ; and a military station was established also on the lower Danube in Moesia.

At the same time the subjection of Germany south of the Elbe, and its conversion into a Roman province, was carried on systematically. The task was entrusted to Drusus, the emperor's stepson and governor of Gaul together with the Rhine country. Operations began in 12 B. C., and were successful. There was no serious opposition on the part of the Germans. But in 9 B. C., before his enterprise was completed, Drusus, while returning to the Rhine, was fatally injured by a fall from his horse. His task was continued for two years more by his elder brother, Tiberius, whose chief exploit on the Rhine, the destruction of the Sygambri, caused a great sensation at Rome. In 6 B. C. a coolness between Augustus and Tiberius caused the latter to give up for a time his public functions, and the governors of the Danube frontier directed the foreign policy of Rome on the north Danube and the Rhine. Further campaigns in Germany followed. L. Domitius Ahenobarbus, a skilful general, who was long in command of the Roman troops, nearly succeeded in conquering Germany south of the Elbe and carrying the frontier to the Elbe and the Danube; all that remained to be done was to shatter the powerful kingdom of Maroboduus in what is now Bohemia. In A.D. 6 preparations were complete for a great campaign commanded by Tiberius who had returned to the Rhine command two years before, when the Romans were overtaken by one disaster after another, which finally destroyed the patient work of Drusus and his successors in Germany.

The Pannonian tribes south of the Danube, whom Augustus had partially subdued in 35 and 34 B.C., now raised a formidable rebellion in the rear of the army, and were soon joined by the Dalmatians. The war was so alarming and the success of the rebels so great that Italy prepared for another barbarian invasion, and Augustus hastily mobilized all the forces of the empire, even having recourse for the first time to a compulsory levy. The danger was averted by the well-planned and consistent operations of Tiberius; Germanicus, the youthful son of Drusus and afterwards famous, served on his uncle's staff. Hardly had the rebellion been crushed, and Roman control of the Danube been established, when a fresh disaster took place on the Rhine. In A.D. 9 the legions commanded by L. Quintilius Varus were making their annual military promenade in Germany for such purposes as making roads and fortifying new camps. Some German tribes, headed by Arminius, a prince who had received a Roman military training, managed to lure Varus and his men into a trap in the Teutoburg forest, and surrounded them. Varus himself fell; three legions and a number of auxiliary cohorts were destroyed almost to a man. All the work of Augustus in Germany was undone for the time. The Romans, though they held fast to the Danube frontier, were forced to withdraw from the Elbe and concentrate their efforts on fortifying the Rhine. And, as we shall see later, what seemed in the reign of Augustus to be a temporary retreat became a permanent arrangement.

In the East Augustus refrained from any forward policy. Egypt, as I have said already, had been annexed after the death of Antony and Cleopatra. Expeditions, made from Egypt by Gaius Petronius into Nubia, and by Aelius Gallus into Arabia, promoted Roman trade with central Africa, Arabia Felix, and India. In 20 B.C. an agreement was made with the Parthians, by which they returned their Roman prisoners and the standards captured from Crassus and Antony. In Armenia Augustus was content to exercise an indirect influence through the native kings, who sat on the throne by Roman support and favoured their supporters. Gaius, the grandson and heir of Augustus, lost his life while establishing one of these Roman nominees on the throne of Armenia. In Asia Minor Augustus carried on the policy of his predecessors, Pompey and Caesar : some districts continued to be tributary kingdoms, while others, such as Galatia, were converted into Roman provinces. Augustus was never obliged to wage a regular war in Asia ; for such a name cannot be applied to the pacification of predatory tribes in the mountains of Pisidia.

The population of the Roman Empire took less interest in foreign affairs, the more those affairs and military control were concentrated in the hands of Augustus. The danger of foreign invasion had disappeared ; wars were undertaken merely to strengthen the frontiers ; even the frontier provinces ceased to fear the irruption of neighbouring tribes. And thus the prestige of Augustus, as the defender and guardian of the state, rose to an unassailable height.

XV

RELIGION AND ART IN THE TIME OF AUGUSTUS

FOR more than forty years Augustus was the undisputed head of the Roman Empire, known as *princeps* to the civilian population, and to the army as *imperator*. During this time the troubled sea of civil commotions sank to rest. Peace and prosperity returned and took up their permanent abode in the empire. But the grievous period of the civil wars could not pass by without leaving its profound traces on the Romans. The mental attitude of the directing classes had undergone a complete change : men ceased to take an interest in the state and public affairs, which had been of vital importance to them for centuries. After the horrors of civil war, the idea of civic freedom—an idea closely connected by the Romans with the idea of the state—had become, in the minds of most men, inseparable from the anarchy and confusion which were still so fresh in the memory of the generation contemporary with Augustus. The old idea of political freedom found nothing to replace it. It is hard to believe that the gospel preached by Horace in his ' Roman' odes— the gospel of submission and silence and steady work for the state—could inspire the citizens and fill the place of the old ideal. The official and the subject were new and not very welcome features of daily life, and not easy to idealize. It is natural, therefore, that a dark shade of pessimism covers all the thought and literary production of this period.

In the ancient world the mass of the population never attained, either in the East or the West, to a scientific and rationalistic way of thinking. Even in the educated section of Graeco-Roman society such a habit of mind was rare ; and religion still governed their general view of life. I have explained already how philosophy, especially Stoicism, adapts itself to religion. From this connexion new doctrines arose, such as neo-Pythagoreanism with its mysticism and predominant interest in a future life. By degrees these doctrines and even rationalistic Epicureanism were converted into systems, with every detail scrupulously worked out and accepted by its followers as absolutely true. Philosophical inquiry tended more and more to become what we call ' dogma '. Moreover, both Stoicism and neo-Pythagoreanism gave a distinctly religious form to their dogmas, and reduced philosophy to a system decidedly more religious than philosophical. Dogma by degrees became theology.

Of these two systems Stoicism was the more widely diffused in the Augustan Age. Stoic doctrine was exceedingly flexible, easily adapting itself to new conditions ; it was clear, logical, and easy to master. Long familiar to the Romans, it had at one time adapted itself to their belief in the perfection of their constitution, that is, in the perfection of the system by which the oligarchy of the city-state ruled over the world. But now, under the influence of the changes which had taken place in the Roman Empire, Stoicism reconstructed its teaching on politics, and reverted to the principles of Zeno and Chrysippus, the founders of the school. It ceased to take an interest in the state. Forms of government it treated as unimportant ; but it held that monarchy, especially if the monarch is the best man in a state which includes all mankind, offers the largest amount of inward freedom to the individual. But the state is a thing of secondary importance ; what really matters is the moral improvement of the individual, with unfailing and unremitting self-discipline, a strong sense of duty towards himself and his fellow men, and indifference to the ordinary business of life as a thing of secondary importance. The Stoic ideal was *ataraxia*, the perfect equilibrium of the soul. If he can attain this ideal, man does not fear even death. In case of necessity he is free to take refuge in suicide. The supreme guide of man's personal life is the deity, the incarnation of universal reason, single in spite of his many forms, who rules and penetrates the whole world.

This philosophical, moral, and religious theory, profoundly rationalistic in its essence, was widely diffused, especially among the highest classes of Roman society, but could not satisfy the majority of those who sought consolation in philosophy. High and low alike had suffered shocks of such severity that they could not easily find peace in the abstract *ataraxia* of the Stoics : for a long series of years every citizen had been confronted almost daily with the spectre of death by violence. Thus, men's thoughts turned to the mystery of a future life, and they appealed to philosophy and religion for an answer to their questions. But Stoicism was dumb. It is not surprising, therefore, that a great number turned aside to neo-Pythagoreanism with its mystical eschatology and preoccupation with a future life. Related to this there were purely religious currents, Greek in origin and little affected by philosophy : I refer to the Eleusinian mysteries, which were permeated through and through with Orphic doctrines, and in which the revelation of a future life was so prominent. The decoration of many Roman tombs in the Augustan Age and later shows the influence of neo-Pythagorean and Orphic ideas. Virgil was the most typical and most gifted interpreter of the soul of his age ; and it is important to note how his poetry is saturated with eschatological fancies drawn from these sources. Nor is it surprising that many were attracted by astrology, with its pretensions to science, its doctrine of universal 'sympathy', and with the possibilities it offered of looking into the future.

Side by side with these religious and philosophical tendencies we find a different attitude—of men who do not trouble their heads with high matters but simply enjoy life ; and enjoyment of life had now been made possible by Augustus. This materialistic view is glad to shelter under the terms and phrases of Epicureanism ; but it is as far removed from the actual teaching of Epicurus as from the scientific and rationalistic position, which also it sometimes adopts as a disguise. Ovid and many other Augustan poets are typical examples of this hedonism ; and so is Trimalchio, a rich and illiterate freedman of south Italy, and the hero of a novel written by Petronius in Nero's reign.

These different currents of opinion all reveal an instinctive impulse to return to a purely religious position, to a formula of some kind that will answer all difficulties and calm all doubts and fears. This is true even of the materialism which borrows the name of Epicurus. A religious wave, rising by degrees, catches hold of a larger and larger number of hearts, and gains one victory after another over rationalism and science. The process is perhaps most clearly seen in the growth of divine worship paid to the emperors. Two currents meet here, one coming from above and the other from below. I have spoken already of the fundamental ideas current in the ancient world, which led to the worship of deified men, especially of Alexander the Great and his successors. Neither ancient religion nor ancient philosophy drew a hard-and-fast line between the divine and the human. Hence the belief in a Messiah—in the incarnation of divine power in a human form on earth, in order to save and regenerate perishing humanity. Hercules and Apollo were legendary saviours of this type. The Sibylline books, closely connected with the worship of Apollo and influenced by the Messianic ideas of the East, spoke of the possibility that they would come again. It was believed that some critical moment would bring back the man-god, the Saviour or *Soter*. He might appear in the form of a god suffering for man ; or he might appear as the divine conqueror of evil, flooding with light the darkness in which humanity is sunk. The famous Fourth Eclogue of Virgil and some Odes of Horace show how firmly men believed in the possibility of such an Advent, and how deeply this idea, combined with astrological and neo-Pythagorean fancies, had entered into the minds even of educated men.

Such were the ideas in which the contemporaries of Augustus, who had survived with him the horrors of civil war, had been brought up. When, after decades of anarchy and internecine strife, the victory of one adventurer over another—and how many such had that generation seen !— was suddenly and quite unexpectedly followed by peace, and when the storm of civil war was laid all at once, it seemed natural to see in this a miracle, an interference of divine power in earthly affairs. It was easy to connect this miracle with the person of Augustus, and to behold in him the incarnation of the divine power, the Messiah, the Saviour. The figure of Augustus, so prosaic and so far from divine, was hidden from men's eyes behind a veil of mysticism and glamour. A new Apollo, he conquered the powers of darkness and restored peace and civilization. The cloudy prophecies of the Sibylline books had come true : Messiah had appeared, bringing with him a new era in human history, a new Age of Gold (*saeculum novum aureum*). Augustus the Saviour recalled Apollo, the triumphant conqueror of evil, rather than the martyred gods Hercules and Dionysus. In Augustus, as the creator of peace and prosperity some found the features of the kindly god Mercury, the bringer of wealth and civilization, the divine messenger who proclaims to the world the new era ; but Apollo had the preference, as one of the ancestors from whom the Julian house traced its descent, and as the ally of Augustus in his victory over Antony.

Whether Augustus thought himself to be an incarnation of divinity, whether he believed in the divine protection of Apollo, we do not know and probably we shall never know. But it is certain that he was perfectly aware of the current of opinion so unmistakable in contemporary society, and consciously turned that current into a definite channel. The temple of Apollo on the Palatine beside his own residence ; the temple of Venus Genetrix in Caesar's forum, recalling the divine origin of the Julian house ; the temple of Mars the Avenger in the forum of Augustus, whose legend was bound up with the history of Rome's origin and also with the annals of the Julii ; the ceremony of the Secular Games, to signify the end of confusion and the beginning of a new era ; the altars of Peace and Favouring Fortune on the Field of Mars— all this was well suited to the ideas and hopes of Rome and Italy in the Augustan Age.

And everywhere, side by side with the deity, we see the figure of Augustus. In his person religion and the state were combined. Roman citizens and provincials had long been accustomed to worship the divine power of the state under the form of the great goddess ' Roma ', who was represented in art in the likeness of Athena, the great goddess of Greek civilization and organized society. Beside Roma stood the mysterious and shadowy form of Vesta, symbolizing the hearth of the great Roman ' house ' and the undying fire of that hearth. And now to these was added one more symbol and source of Rome's greatness, the *genius*, the divine creative power (*numen*) belonging to Augustus, the head of the great Roman family. This combination was quite in harmony with the religious conceptions of the Roman citizen : he remained faithful to the primitive creed of his race—the belief in gods of the domestic hearth, in the *genius* of the house-holder, in the *genii* of men united in religious societies, and in the *genius* of the great victorious family of the Roman state.

From these two sources, the mystical belief in a Messiah and the belief that a divine *genius* dwells in man, proceeded the worship of Augustus—a worship inseparably combined with that of the state. In the East the belief soon grew up that Augustus was an incarnation of divinity, and his image took its place beside that of the goddess Roma, who had long been worshipped there. In Italy and among Roman citizens inhabiting the provinces the worship of the *genius* of Augustus was naturally included among the objects worshipped by families, corporations, and communities, and lastly by the unions of these communities in the Romanized provinces of Spain, Gaul, and Africa. And everywhere the same idea prevailed—the identity of the state and its chief in their divine essence. Augustus could not fail to perceive and make use of this frame of mind, which built a religious basis for the throne he had usurped. But neither he nor the poets whom he patronized invented this belief and forced it upon Italy and the provinces ; essentially, it was not opposed to the forms of religious and philosophic thought most widely diffused among the highest and most intelligent classes of Roman society ; and it was firmly held by the general population of Italy and the provinces.

The prevailing temper, however, especially among the directing classes, was one of profound pessimism. No one took the new era to be a heaven on earth. The contemporaries of Augustus were more inclined to find the Golden Age in the past than in the present or future. This pessimism underlies the imaginative literature of the Augustan Age ; and it underlies all the restoration undertaken by Augustus, especially in the sphere of religion. The poetry of Virgil and his contemporaries uses imagination to idealize the distant age when Rome was sound ; and the historical literature of the age, especially the great history of Livy, ' From the Foundation of the City '—a work of literature as much as of history—breathes the same spirit ; and it appears even in the antiquarian works of the period, dealing with the early constitution and primitive religion of Rome.

Quite in harmony with this literary movement is the action of Augustus in restoring ancient shrines from ruin and rescuing primitive rites from oblivion. The same flavour of archaism hangs about his restoration of public morality, his sumptuary laws, and his laws about marriage. It appears even in the education of the young nobles : the physical and military training necessary for those who were to serve the state was disguised in forms drawn by Augustus from the forgotten past. Boys showed their horsemanship in the ' Trojan Game ', an ancient pastime half military and half religious.

The young men were reviewed on the square before the temple of Mars the Avenger, the protector of the army in ancient Rome; and the military exercises of the boys and young men were performed on the Field of Mars. Similar corps of young men were formed in the provincial towns, under the patronage of the ancient Roman and Italian gods.

But this revival of the past covers new developments as well. Fresh construction goes hand in hand with restoration, and expresses itself in creating a new art for the Empire—an art whose chief triumph is the imperial city itself. System and order were now introduced into the chaos of buildings, some of them splendid, erected at haphazard by the revolutionary leaders. Rome becomes the real capital of the world, in which the republican past is combined with the monarchical present—the city of a sovereign people with a residence for the head of that people. Augustus gave special attention to the heart of the ancient city—the Forum and the parts of the city adjacent to it. The Capitol with its temples rose as before above the Forum ; but side by side with it, and also dominating the Forum, a residence was built on the Palatine for the *princeps* to dwell in, in close proximity to the temple of Apollo and the shrine of Vesta. There, too, the relics of Rome under the kings, connected with the Palatine from time immemorial, were carefully preserved : the Hut of Romulus, the earliest seat of divination, and the Cave of the Lupercal. In the Forum, Augustus was not content with restoration, but perpetuated his own memory and that of his deified father in a number of new buildings. The temple of the Divine Julius, and the Basilica bearing his name, added a quite new and personal aspect to the impersonal centre of political and business affairs in republican Rome. A second adjacent forum was added, consecrated to the deified father of Augustus, and containing the temple of Venus Genetrix ; and then a third, bearing the name of Augustus himself, and built round the temple of Mars the Avenger, who had punished Caesar's murderers and thus created the new order of things.

But the chief site of the emperor's building operations was the Campus Martius, itself a new and splendid city of his construction. Here also sacred buildings predominated, but there was no restoration : the buildings were new and intended for the worship connected with the principate. Conspicuous among those erected by Augustus himself were a graceful altar to Peace, an altar to Fortune, and the Mausoleum of the emperor and his family, surrounded by a park. Near these were stately piles raised by his friends and coadjutors, or members of his family : the Pantheon of Agrippa, where the statue of Augustus, modestly placed in the vestibule, was associated with the images of the supreme gods in the temple itself ; palatial baths for the people, also built by Agrippa ; the theatre of Marcellus, the emperor's nephew, not far from the splendid theatre of Pompey ; a great building for meetings of the people, dedicated to Caesar's memory. These buildings and many others, correct and classical examples of the new architecture and sculpture, all glorified Augustus in one way or another : they commemorated his services to the state, his patriotism, his munificence, his piety, and his mighty acts. A long inscription, written by Augustus himself in simple and precise language, served to tell the same story ; and every Roman could read it after the emperor's death upon the entrance to the Mausoleum, his monument and temple. The same theme was repeated in the reliefs (still extant) on the altar of Peace, and in the sculpture of other contemporary monuments dedicated to the glorifica-tion and worship of Augustus or to the worship of his family and kindred. The artistic quality of these monuments is in keeping with their purpose : they are in the true style of im-perial art—cold, stately, majestic. A single idea, the greatness of Rome and of Augustus, is everywhere predominant.

There is nothing that need surprise us in this wealth of art. We must not forget that much was accomplished in Rome and Italy even under the unfavourable conditions of the republican era, and that the best Greek and Hellenistic artists had now found a refuge in Italy. It is therefore not surprising that in literature also Roman genius shows no sign of exhaustion. The Augustan Age produced worthy rivals of Cicero and Catullus. Most conspicuous is the group of great poets connected with Augustus through Gaius Maecenas, a passionate lover of literature and art, and the emperor's friend and minister.

This group, which was adorned by the names of Virgil and Horace, it is the custom to describe as a group of court poets, whose business was to glorify Augustus. Most of them had been ruined by the revolution and depended for support upon Augustus and his intimate friends. But it is not likely that Augustus forced them to accept his views. They did not owe it to his patronage that they were recognized as classics in their own lifetime by all who spoke the Latin language. In this matter also Augustus showed his knowledge of human nature and his sensitiveness to prevalent feeling. He knew that Virgil and Horace could not help writing in his favour ; he felt that their genius would express in a succession of unforgettable images the fundamental ideas of his reign. It is impossible that the burning words which we read on many pages of the *Aeneid* were suggested to Virgil by Augustus : they poured forth from the poet's own heart, and they found sympathetic and enthusiastic hearers and readers, not only in Augustus and his family, but among Romans everywhere. The greatness of Rome and of Augustus is the main theme of the poem. That greatness was felt by others than Virgil : the temper of Horace is cooler and more sober ; yet he, too, recognizes Augustus as a saviour and the creator of a new era, and willingly pays him a tribute of recognition and reverence. It is remarkable, however, that not one of the Augustan poets, except Virgil, dedicated a great work to Augustus himself. When Augustus suggested that they should celebrate his exploits in verse, they all politely declined in almost identical terms, and we can still read their refusal. Even in Virgil we must read between the lines to find the name of Augustus : his hero is a different person—that pious and conscientious Roman, Aeneas of Troy.

Most of the Augustan poets eschew long and serious poems on political subjects. They prefer personal detail ; they are interested in their own emotional experiences, or incidents that have happened to themselves or their friends. Their attitude to the rest of the world is condemnatory and somewhat contemptuous ; or, at least, it is ironical, as we see in the *Satires* and *Epistles* of Horace. For religion they care little : not one of them wrote anything to rival the noble hymn addressed to Venus by the sceptic Lucretius. Their treatment of this subject is generally fanciful, and sometimes, as in the *Fasti* of Ovid, archaeological ; the only exceptions to this rule are found in Virgil with his neo-Pythagorean ideas, and in those odes of Horace which reflect some aspects of native Italian beliefs. All their work—Virgil again is exceptional—repeats the same refrain—' Live and enjoy your life ' ; but this motto has lost the joy in life which breathes in early Greek poetry : one feels behind it the pessimism that marks all this period. Ovid, the youngest of the group, is also the most careless and light-hearted ; but he skims over the surface of life, as if afraid to look deeper. Even calamity does not make him feel seriously the profound tragedy of life. Augustan Rome appears to live a full life and a life of great creative activity ; but the poets themselves seem to surmise that their song is no prelude but rather the final chord of a paean in honour of the Golden Age.

XVI

THE JULIAN AND CLAUDIAN DYNASTIES

AUGUSTUS died in A.D. 14, when he had ruled the Roman state for more than forty years of peace. He regarded the principate not as a temporary arrangement which must end with his own life, but as a permanent institution; and he intended his power to be hereditary. Because his health was not strong and he had many illnesses, he was careful during his whole reign to keep beside him some one person, whom he himself treated as his heir and signalized as such by admitting him to a share in the proconsular power and investing him with the inviolability of a tribune. The first of these was his nephew Marcellus who married the emperor's daughter Julia; but he was a sickly youth and died in 23 B.C. His next heir and intended successor was Agrippa, who married Julia after the death of Marcellus. Then Agrippa gave place to Gaius and Lucius, his sons by Julia. But these also died young; and towards the end of his reign Augustus was obliged, against his own will and under the influence of his wife Livia, to adopt the only member of his family who was fit to undertake the burden of government. This was Tiberius Claudius Nero, the son of Livia by her first husband. His brother Drusus, who died in 9 B.C. during his victorious campaign in Germany, had left a son Germanicus, a youth of much promise, who was now by the wish of Augustus adopted by Tiberius. In this way Augustus tried to provide that after the death of Tiberius, who was over fifty in A.D. 14, the succession should pass not to his son Drusus but to Germanicus.

The personal authority of Augustus, and the universal feeling that the existence of the principate was indispensable for the maintenance of peace and order, made it possible for Tiberius to take over the reins of government without dispute. The army recognized him as emperor and swore allegiance to him immediately after the death of Augustus; and later the Senate conferred on him all the special powers which had made Augustus master of the state. From this time down to the suicide of Nero the throne was occupied by members of the Claudian house, the first two of whom were adopted into the family of the Julii. The transference of power from one member of this family to another, the personal character of each, and the incidents of their reigns, have been described by Tacitus, the last great Roman historian, in his *Annals*. His *Histories* depict the fall of that power and the time of confusion which ended in the elevation of another family, the Flavii, who were not even distantly related to Augustus. The genius of Tacitus is wonderful, and his penetration into the minds of the different rulers and those who stood round the throne is profound. If any one wishes to learn the characters of the immediate successors of Augustus, he may and must read what remains of these two works. All that has been written later about this period by ancient or modern historians is either a faint reflection of his genius or dry and lifeless extracts from his writings.

Of the successors of Augustus it cannot be said that the conditions under which they lived were wholesome. They all felt that they were rulers, not because of their own virtues or services to the country, but simply as the inheritors of the popularity, authority, and divinity of Augustus. Not one of them possessed either genius or personal charm. Their connexion with Augustus was their only claim to the position they held. Tiberius was a competent general of the old Roman type—strict, methodical, and sincerely devoted to his country ; and he showed the same virtues as a statesman and ruler. But he lacked the creative energy which inspired every action of his predecessor ; nor did he possess the remarkable power of Augustus to get on with other men, to fascinate them, to make them serve him, and also to choose out the best brains for his service.

Caligula succeeded Tiberius and reigned from A. D. 37 to 41. The son of Germanicus, he had grown up in constant fear for his life, surrounded by palace intrigues, and associating with corrupt young Hellenistic princes, who were resident at Rome either as hostages or to press their claims to one or other of the Eastern crowns. Chancing to survive all his brothers, he was the only member (by adoption) of the Julian family alive on the death of Tiberius. His elevation completely turned a head which was weak enough before. His short reign gave definite proof of mental derangement.

Claudius followed his nephew Caligula and reigned from A. D. 41 to 54 ; his father Drusus, the brother of Tiberius, died in the reign of Augustus. He never belonged to the Julian family and had no expectation of succeeding to the throne. But when a few conspirators had made a violent end of Caligula, the praetorian guard proclaimed Claudius emperor, for want of a better. His actions showed the devotion to duty and the patriotism traditional in the Claudian family ; but weak in body and weak of will he became a mere tool in the hands of his wives, Messalina and Agrippina, and his freedmen.

Nero, the last emperor related to Augustus, reigned from A. D. 54 to 68. His mother was Agrippina, daughter of Germanicus and second wife of Claudius. Nero was her son by her first marriage to Cnaeus Domitius Ahenobarbus. He had great natural gifts and a strangely mixed character. His succession also was irregular : it was brought about by his mother's boundless ambition and her crime—for she poisoned Claudius. In order to retain his power, he was compelled to trample on the corpses of his half-brother and his mother.

Such were the conditions under which the successors of Augustus rose to the throne. Not one of them was convinced of his right to rule ; they all lived in the steadily waning light of the charm exercised by the founder of their line. Hence the chief anxiety of all the emperors in the first century is to secure their position ; they all dread rivals whose right is equal or superior to their own ; they are all haunted by the spectre—a spectre indeed, for it has no substantiality—of a Senate restored to power. Their lives are therefore filled with palace intrigues, in which the women of the imperial family, more ambitious and abler than the men, play a large and sometimes a decisive part. Plots, real or imaginary, are constant and give birth to crimes, of which some are actually committed, while others are attributed to the emperors by the hundred tongues of rumour in Rome, the capital of the world, where the centre of interest is the person and family of the ruler.

All these emperors feared not only their personal rivals but also the attempts of the Senate to reassert itself. The Senate was still an imposing and impressive body, and it cannot be denied that some senators still nursed the hope of recovering their old position ; but it is certain that as a body they took no definite steps to prepare for such a consummation. That it would come about of itself some day was the hope of a few ; but the majority were sceptical and took no actual step in that direction. Nevertheless, the rulers were so uneasy that every sign of opposition in the Senate was immensely exaggerated, and every plot, whether real or imaginary, led to a regular massacre among the prominent members of the aristocracy. Thus one by one the noblest families vanished from the scene for ever, and carried with them their dreams of restoring the ancient constitution with the Senate at its head.

The atmosphere which surrounded these princes was indeed heavy with guilt and crime. Tiberius, the best of the four, was already embittered and depressed by the cold unfriendliness of Augustus, and found himself from the beginning of his reign in a very awkward situation. Beside him stood the imposing figure of Livia, the widow of Augustus, to whom he owed his accession. The great body of those who had been prominent in the previous reign, together with many of the Roman aristocracy, were hostile to him. They disliked his pride, reserve, and coldness, and refused to recognize his right to rule. The opposition knew that he was unwilling to pass over his son Drusus in favour of Germanicus whom he had been obliged to adopt, and therefore they praised up Germanicus, who was a general favourite, till they made him out more than human. Life at court became quite impossible when Germanicus died in the East, where he had been sent to govern. He probably died a natural death ; but the natural death of a young man was incredible to that generation. The wife and children of Germanicus, and also the people of Rome, were convinced that he was the victim of a crime engineered by Tiberius and Livia.

It is not surprising that Tiberius left Rome, where he was surrounded by intrigue and hatred, and settled at Capri. From there he tried to rule the empire. The one man whom he trusted was Sejanus, the praefect of the praetorian guard. Him he left as his representative at Rome, and allowed, for the security of his position, to quarter his men in special barracks in one of the suburbs. Thus Sejanus became the virtual ruler of the city. Meantime, as a matter of course, the palace intrigues and the rivalry between the relations of Germanicus and Drusus went on without a break, till Sejanus resolved to make use of these quarrels for gratifying his own ambition. He hoped himself to succeed Tiberius. There followed a long series of dark and horrible crimes—the murder of Drusus, poisoned by his wife whom Sejanus had seduced ; the destruction of Agrippina's children, one after another ; the banishment and death of Agrippina herself ; and finally the discovery that Sejanus was plotting against the emperor, and his execution, followed by a period of gloom and horror which carried off guilty and innocent alike.

The history of Tiberius is typical : it is repeated in the case of all his successors. The madman Caligula lived in constant dread of plots, and destroyed without mercy every one whom he feared. He went so far that the people of Rome were actually disgusted. Brought up among young princes, scions of the autocratic royal families of the East, he demanded divine honours, and declared himself to be not merely *princeps*, that is, first citizen of Rome, in theory at least, but 'lord and god' (*dominus et deus*), and aroused the anger of his people by introducing Hellenistic customs at his court. He formed open connexions with his own sisters and proclaimed one of them as his wife and goddess. It is no wonder that he soon fell a victim to a plot contrived by some of the officers of the praetorian guard.

The same atmosphere surrounded Claudius. During the first years of his reign he was a mere puppet, at least in his relations with the Roman aristocracy, in the hands of Messalina, his frivolous and corrupt wife. His favoured freedmen opposed Messalina with all their might. Terrified by the spectre of conspiracy, fearing that Messalina would put Silius, one of her lovers, on the throne, and pressed by his freedmen, he consented to the death of Messalina. But at once he became a puppet in the hands of another imperious woman, his niece Agrippina, whose only motive for marrying him was that she might dispatch him to a better world and set her son, the young Nero, on the empty throne. The principate, which had become cruel and terrible in the last years of Tiberius and under Caligula, Claudius made ridiculous and terrible at the same time. Last comes Nero. Beside him stands, as a constant menace to his power, his half-brother, the boy Britannicus, the son of Claudius by Messalina and the rightful heir to the throne. Nero begins with the murder of Britannicus. Then his imperious mother tries to keep down her no less imperious son and to make of him a tool in her hands. To escape from her control becomes a fixed idea with Nero ; and his favourites encourage him in the attempt. His second crime is the dastardly murder of his mother. Now he rules alone, but he is hampered by Seneca and Burrus, who had brought him up and taught him and wished to guide his youthful steps. They also are removed, and now he comes into collision with the hostility and contempt of those around him ; he has to meet the silent but stubborn opposition of the classes who take the lead in society. A reign of terror follows, and the massacre of all whom Nero suspects to be out of sympathy with himself and his methods of government. The principate is still formidable, but now it excites feelings of disgust and horror.

Increasing disgust for the foulness of the court strengthened the opposition, and for once they found courage not only to die bravely but to strike a blow. Nero, who relied entirely upon the praetorian guard, never showed his face to the armies in the provinces, and the legions were disaffected. The opposition took advantage of this. The armies were informed of Nero's conduct and flagrant breaches of Roman tradition—especially his passion for the theatre and appearances on the stage, and his marked preference for Greeks over Romans. The generals who were in actual command as Nero's legates had a strong personal influence over their men, and an armed rebellion against the emperor broke out in Gaul. Their war-cry was ' Down with the tyrant '. The rebels were willing to put in his place any one who would follow in the footsteps of Augustus—preserving the form of constitution devised by Augustus, and acting within the limits of the constitution as a *princeps* ; the tyrant, the ' lord and god ', they could no longer endure. The new ruler could not fail to be constitutional, because he was to be closely connected with the Senate. In this cause the standard of rebellion was raised by Vindex in Gaul. The legions in Germany, understanding that the movement was aimed not at Nero but at Rome, suppressed it ; but even they did not wish that Nero should go on reigning. The emperor was forced at last to commit suicide.

Now came the question of a successor. Who was to restore the ' freedom ' which the tyrant had suppressed, a nominee of the praetorian guard, or the commander of a provincial army ?

The provinces seemed at first to prevail. When Verginius Rufus, commander of the legions in Germany, refused to reign, Galba was proclaimed emperor by the army in Spain and recognized as such by the other armies and by the Senate. But when he came to Rome, the praetorians, fearing the loss of their privileges, made away with him and placed Otho on the throne. The legions in Germany rebelled and raised Vitellius to power. He marched on Rome and conquered the praetorians on the plains of north Italy. But now a fourth candidate appeared in the field—T. Flavius Vespasianus, put forward by the armies in the East. The army of the Danube declared for him and overthrew Vitellius. Vespasian came to Rome and by his experience, coolness, and firmness founded a dynasty which lasted for a considerable time. So A. D. 69, the year of the four emperors, came to an end, and the principate triumphed once more, as a standing institution, as an idea ; but it was clear that the ruler must be a constitutional ruler, and that the time had not yet come for an unconcealed military despotism.

This triumph of the principate as an institution found expression in a law specially proposed by Vespasian and accepted by the Senate—the *lex de imperio Vespasiani*, or law to define Vespasian's powers. It was in fact more comprehensive than the name implies. It was the first attempt to define in writing the relations between the *princeps* and the state. It contained nothing new : Vespasian merely brought together all that had been adopted in practice for nearly a century. The rights and duties of the ruler, upon which Augustus had built up his supremacy, and which had been altered in some details by his successors, were here enumerated one after another. Thus the troubled ' year of the four emperors', as the year A. D. 69 is called by our authorities, did not lead to a military tyranny exercised by a favourite of the soldiers, but to the re-establishment of the principate as devised by Augustus.

During the hundred years which divide Vespasian from Augustus, the principate, as such, had kept its main foundations unshaken. Except for the attempt of Caligula to convert it into an absolute monarchy, all the emperors held fast to the policy of Augustus in domestic and foreign affairs. When the election of magistrates was transferred by Tiberius from the popular assembly to the Senate, he was only summing up a process complete even under Augustus, by which the assembly of the people at Rome lost all political importance. In the reign of Claudius his freedmen were the civil service which governed the empire ; and the growing importance of these functionaries was a natural consequence of the control exercised by the emperors over all public business. In the same way the personal influence of the ruler upon affairs tended to concentrate the management of finance in his hands, or in the hands of officials, either knights or freedmen, who were his personal subordinates. But this control gradually loses its personal character and becomes a part of the government machine. The line between the private property of the ruler and the property of the state becomes fainter and fainter.

In foreign policy also the tradition set by Augustus held good. Circumstances had forced Augustus to adopt a defensive policy on the frontiers—in Germany, on the Danube, and on the Euphrates—and the same policy was consistently carried out by Tiberius. It aimed at creating a strong military frontier, with a chain of legions and auxiliary forces, at all times capable of attack as well as of defence. Tiberius and his successors made no attempt to gain territory in Germany. The plan of an Elbe frontier conceived by Augustus was finally dropped. But Germanicus demonstrated the power of the Roman arms by several campaigns in the interior of Germany ; and the diplomacy of Tiberius sowed discord between the tribes so ingeniously that a general alliance under a single leader, such as Arminius had formed with some success, was for long impossible.

The same policy was maintained on the Danube by Tiberius and his successors. The frontier there was linked up with the Rhine frontier by the new province of Rhaetia, part of what is now Switzerland, and with Macedonia by including the tributary kingdom of Thrace among the Roman provinces. The first of these measures was carried out under Tiberius, and the second under Claudius. Between Greece and Dalmatia (formerly Illyricum) a new province of Epirus was formed in Nero's reign. In the reign of Claudius a Roman army and fleet appeared for the first time in the Crimea, in order to support the Bosporan kingdom and the city of Chersonese in the contest with their Scythian and Sarmatian neighbours, who were Iranians, and to make war on the pirates that infested the Black Sea. In the north Claudius began the conquest of Britain with the intention of including all the Celtic peoples in the Roman Empire.

In the East the situation was more complicated during the first century. The task of the Roman emperors here was to strengthen the Euphrates frontier. For this purpose the chief necessity was to introduce uniformity and order into the organization of Roman possessions in Asia Minor and Syria. Both these countries were by degrees entirely converted into a series of Roman provinces, and the remaining tributary kingdoms became Roman possessions. This policy was carried out with special energy under Claudius and Nero, and led, in the reign of the latter emperor, to a long and bloody conflict in Judaea. The conquest of Judaea was carried on by Vespasian and, after he had been proclaimed emperor, by his son Titus. There was long warfare crowned by victory in Armenia, where Nero's general, Corbulo, distinguished himself by his talents for war. Near the end of his reign Nero dreamed of realizing a vast plan which Caesar probably had been the first to conceive : this was to annex the entire coast of the Black Sea, and to convert Armenia, Georgia, and the Crimea into Roman provinces. In the year of his death he was preparing a great army with a view to this campaign. Nero's plan was abandoned by Vespasian, whose Eastern policy centred on the creation of a really strong military frontier against Parthia. Armenia, Georgia, and the Bosporus continued to be vassal kingdoms.

Lastly, in Africa the main object was the security of the frontier in the Roman provinces of Africa and Numidia, and in Mauretania (now Morocco). They needed protection against the warlike tribes who occupied the plains in the southern part of the province of Africa, or the mountains of Aurès and Morocco. These enemies were harassed by constant expeditions, and their lands were gradually annexed to the Roman provinces. Finally, the southern frontier of the empire was advanced to the edge of the desert, and in the west the province of Mauretania was annexed in the reign of Claudius.

The work done by the emperors in regulating the government of the provinces, both imperial and senatorial and especially the latter, was highly important. For one thing the personal control of the ruler by means of his financial agents was strengthened ; for another, the meetings of representatives from the different cities, which were held in order to perform the worship due to the emperor, made it possible to complain to the Senate and the emperor at Rome, in case the provincial governors misused their powers. A third point of importance is the gradual disappearance of the tax-farming companies who levied the direct and indirect taxes. Their place was taken by the imperial officials or procurators, who were employed in the emperor's name in all the provinces, both imperial and senatorial. These men, except those filling the highest positions, were almost all either imperial slaves or imperial freedmen ; they had offices for collecting the taxes in the chief town of the province and branch offices elsewhere ; and all the threads of this network of finance were gathered up in the personal treasury of the emperor at Rome of which we have already spoken. Thus the financial administration of the empire was gradually converted into an elaborate bureaucratic machine, governed from the centre by the emperors. In the government of the empire the Senate had little to do, in addition to the management of Italian business : it might recommend to the emperor candidates for provincial governorships, or investigate complaints against these governors, or alter laws affecting the senatorial provinces, or consider such questions of foreign policy and provincial government as were referred to it by the emperor.

This administrative machine worked smoothly and steadily; the foreign policy of the emperors was consistent, and their defence of the frontiers was firm ; serious attention was paid to the security and convenience of communication throughout the empire, both by building armed fleets to police the seas, and by steadily extending the network of military roads ; and all this had a strong effect upon the popular imagination. Men felt no fear of the morrow but believed that the existing state of things was secure and permanent ; convinced that the system devised by Augustus answered its purposes, they were ready to support it in every way ; and the result of this conviction was a vastly increased activity in all departments of economic and intellectual life.

The effect was visible both in intellectual life and in art. Eagerness for education was never so widely spread in the ancient world as then. In East and West alike thousands of schools taught the children of the towns Latin or Greek, and some, especially in the West, taught them both languages. Books newly published by the booksellers at Rome became known at once in the provinces of Spain, Gaul, and Africa. Every educated man in the West knew the names of the great writers of the East, of the leading men of science, professors, and philosophers. In spite of the use of two languages the culture of the empire became more and more uniform. Italy was still the main centre of literary production. The East had not yet had time to recover from the injuries of the civil wars, though even there signs of a renascence were observable. One of the chief men of letters of the time was Dion, a native of Bithynia, an orator, philosopher, and politician; he was surnamed Chrysostomos or 'Golden-mouthed', and took an important part in resisting the tyranny of Domitian. But the West produced a regular succession of great poets and prose writers. Seneca, the tutor of Nero, poet, philosopher, and publicist; Persius, the satirist; Lucan, the author of an epic poem on the Civil war, put to death by Nero; Petronius, another victim of Nero, though once a favourite, an elegant and witty writer and a keen observer of daily life—all these were eagerly read throughout the empire. The chief poets of the Flavian period, Martial the epigrammatist and Statius the writer of epic, began to be famous. This literature belongs entirely to the present : it depends upon the topics of the day or often of the hour; it avoids serious and abstruse subjects, except philosophy; it portrays the seamy side of life, but shrinks from all profound investigation of social and moral questions ; it is lively, elegant, perfect in form, and completely adapted to the taste of its readers. Of the historical literature of this period, which expressed the temper of opposition pervading the higher classes, we unfortunately know hardly anything, because it was almost all destroyed by the blind anger and exaggerated fear of the rulers. Yet the echo of it is still audible in many a page of Tacitus. Tacitus, a great historian with a profound knowledge of human nature, has left us a wonderful gallery of characteristic portraits—the emperors, the members of their families, and the most prominent figures in the high society of the first century. Tacitus is the last great Roman writer. His style, trenchant, brilliant, and tormented, reflects faithfully the feelings of the high senatorial class to which he belonged.

In art also, especially in the great imperial architecture initiated by Augustus, there was a great development in this period. A succession of stately buildings rose in Rome, Italy, and the provinces. We may particularize the colossal *thermae* or bathing establishments of Nero and Titus, with their vast halls and luxurious colonnades, huge cupolas and vaulted roofs, while their internal arrangements were remarkable for generous design and brilliant colour. The Colosseum, the noble amphitheatre of the Flavians, is universally famous. Not less remarkable are the many triumphal arches, covered all over with historical and allegorical reliefs, and crowned with the statue of an emperor riding on horseback or driving a chariot. These reliefs carry out the essential purpose of the monument, and at the same time represent a great advance in purely artistic accomplishment. They are the best evidence of the skill attained by sculpture in the first century. The relief becomes for the first time a real picture, full of life and movement. The distribution of the figures on the different planes, the reality and variety of the grouping, the play of light and shade—these give the relief a remarkable expressiveness, which is in sharp contrast with the cold and monotonous stateliness of an earlier period. It is enough to compare the sculpture on the Altar of Peace already mentioned with the triumphal arches of Claudius and, still more, of the Flavian emperors. In particular, the reliefs on the Arch of Titus, representing a triumphal procession after the conquest of Judaea, rank among the highest achievements of Roman imperial art.

XVII

THE AGE OF ENLIGHTENED DESPOTISM: THE FLAVIANS AND ANTONINES

THE power exercised by the successors of Augustus was merely personal, and their manner of life more than questionable; the atmosphere of their court reeked of intrigue and crime and foul scandals. Hence there grew up among the directing classes of the empire a strong opposition to the principate as an institution. The preachers of Stoic morality, whose influence over the enlightened section of society increased steadily, brought forward a theory which clashed with the view held by the emperors who followed Augustus. Each of these rulers regarded his authority as a personal right, founded upon his relationship to Augustus; but, according to the Stoics, it was false to consider the principate as a thing merely intended to gratify personal ambition, or as a despotism founded upon violence and force: power, they said, was entrusted by God to that man who was morally and intellectually superior to the rest of the community, and the proper exercise of it was a duty laid on him by God, a heavy personal obligation. The ruler, prince, or king was not a master, according to Stoic teaching, but the servant of mankind; and he should work for the welfare of all, not for his own interests and the maintenance of his power.

This theory was not new: invented and maintained by the Cynics, it had passed on to Stoicism and was shared by many of the best rulers in the Hellenistic Age. It was also, in some degree, the foundation of that new morality which Augustus dictated by the mouth of Horace to his contemporaries and especially to the class who served the empire created by him. It was by degrees adopted by almost all Roman society, and its supporters forced it upon the attention of the rulers. This point of view was boldly defended by many of the victims who perished in the reign of terror under Nero.

The events, however, which followed Nero's death, proved afresh that monarchy in some shape or other was inevitable, that this form of government alone was recognized by the people at large and especially by the army, and that a campaign to restore the old senatorial system was not merely useless but infinitely harmful, because it could lead only to a revival of civil war with all its horrors. Hence the appearance of a new dynasty on the throne, however much it owed its elevation to chance, aroused no protest from Roman society. Men hoped that the regenerated principate would really show the world an example of power in the hands of ' the best ', exercised with due regard to established constitutional forms and without prejudice to the privileges enjoyed by the upper classes.

This hope was not altogether disappointed by the reigns of Vespasian and his elder son Titus. We have seen that Vespasian, in theory at least, regarded his rule as a continuation of the principate of Augustus ; and the latter really approximated to the Stoic ideal. But in fact Vespasian's power relied entirely upon his connexion with the armies. This is proved by the title of *imperator*, which he, like Augustus before him, adopted as his personal name, thus asserting his command of the soldiers and also the hereditary and unlimited nature of his authority. This may be inferred from his persistent attempts to confine the succession to his own family. His scheme was vigorously contested by all the opposition : they held that the heir to the throne should be ' the best of the best '—in other words, the best among the senators—and that relationship to the actual ruler should be ignored. Such a claim led to strained relations even in the lifetime of Vespasian. But he and his son Titus reigned for only twelve years. They were fully occupied with the task of re-establishing the state, and especially its finances, which had been ruined by the insane extravagance of Nero and the cost of civil war in A. D. 69 and 70 ; and therefore they refrained from pressing the dispute to a final issue, and kept as far as possible within the limits of the Augustan constitution.

Domitian, the younger son of Vespasian and the third Flavian ruler, made all compromise impossible. He rejected the theory of the ' best man ' as ruler of the state ; and more than this, he drew the inevitable logical conclusions from that rejection. Taking the path laid down by Caesar and followed by Antony and Caligula, Domitian emphasized in all his actions the absolute nature of his power and the sacredness of his person. He demanded blind submission and relied upon the army alone, which he bribed by a considerable addition to the pay of both officers and men. There were, however, as we shall see later, military motives as well as political for this increase.

The attempt to make himself an autocrat of the Hellenistic type ran counter to the hopes and views of Roman society and met with sharp opposition from all classes. Disaffection in the Senate was suppressed with great cruelty, under a pretence of prosecuting ' philosophers ', in other words, all who maintained and preached the new theory of the right relation between the ruler and his subjects. But the temper of opposition was not confined to Rome : it spread to the provinces. The Hellenic world and Alexandria, its intellectual capital, had long been seething with discontent. A number of Greek philosophers, some of whom, like Dion Chrysostomus, had been expelled from Rome, were eloquent in attacking ' tyranny' and defending the true theory of kingly power as expounded by the Stoics. Apollonius of Tyana, philosopher and prophet, clairvoyant and miracle-worker, became their idol. In the end Domitian fell a victim to a palace plot. Though the occasion of his death was accidental, it was undoubtedly brought about by growing resentment against his policy.

As Domitian's successor the Senate and the armies proclaimed Gaius Cocceius Nerva, who belonged to an ancient and noble Roman family. The change of rulers was effected without bloodshed. Nerva, who was much respected but a very old man, reigned from A. D. 96 to 98. He began by making concessions to public opinion. One of his first actions was to adopt Marcus Ulpius Trajanus, one of a Roman family resident in Spain, who was universally recognized as an able and experienced general and also as a sincere believer in the Stoic theory of government. With Nerva and Trajan begins a new chapter in the history of the principate, in which the leading feature is the good understanding between the supreme authority and the community. The community, once for all, recognized the principate as indispensable and was ready to serve it. In return, the *princeps* accepted the Stoic theory of imperial power in its full extent, and tacitly bound himself to spare the feelings and maintain the privileges of the directing classes ; he also undertook to respect the ancient constitutional forms, and to act, in appearance at least, not as a monarch with unlimited power, but as the first and best citizen freely acknowledged as such by the state.

No essential change in the principate resulted from these concessions. On the contrary, the power of the *princeps* was increased by his reconciliation with the community : it became less restricted and more autocratic. The senators, gratified by retaining their class privileges and their high position in the state, were ready in return to submit to necessity and become merely a body consulted by the emperor. Nevertheless, the emperors were morally bound by having accepted, under the pressure of public opinion, the Stoic theory of a ruler's duty— bound all the more because they all accepted the theory without reserves and made their personal behaviour conform with it. This is clearly shown by the fact that they renounced the idea of a hereditary empire, transmitted in a single family. It was the easier to do so as several successive emperors lacked direct heirs. Adoption therefore took the place of inheritance, and the emperors honestly tried to choose for their successors the best men or the most promising youths among the aristocracy.

This system of adoption produced excellent results. Rome never had such a succession of rulers, able, honest, hard-working, patriotic, and conscientious, as in the first seventy-five years of the second century. The emperors differed in character, temperament, and origin : some belonged to the Italian nobility, others to the provincial ; but they all consistently carried out the same principle and put first the duty of labouring for the state and the empire, for the benefit of all their subjects.

After the short reign of Nerva, the foundations of the new policy were laid by his successor, Trajan, who ruled from A. D. 98 to 117. Of all the successors of Augustus, Trajan is the most remarkable. He was a great military genius and a far-sighted statesman who clearly realized the immediate problems before the empire and the dangers which threatened it from without ; and besides all this he was an excellent administrator, entering into every detail of government and personally directing his subordinates, whom he chose with care from the governing aristocracy. His correspondence with Pliny, a typical member of a well-born, highly educated, and conscientious Civil Service, affords a notable instance of honest collaboration between a ruler and his subordinates for the welfare of the state.

Trajan was succeeded by Publius Aelius Hadrianus, also a Spaniard but a ruler of a different type. Though belonging to a family of Roman citizens resident in Spain, Trajan was always a rigid upholder of ancient Roman traditions; like Augustus he was, first and foremost, the ruler of Roman citizens. Hadrian, who reigned from A. D. 117 to 138, represented a different tendency. He was a cosmopolitan emperor; he represented the bilingual civilization of the empire, based upon the parallel and sometimes indistinguishable development of both East and West for many centuries past. He was a great traveller and visited every part of the empire. Wherever he went, he studied the remains of antiquity with eager attention; he tried to master the mysteries of Egypt, that cradle of civilization; he lived for a long time at Athens and in Asia Minor, where he associated with the best representatives of the learned class in Greece, was initiated into the Eleusinian mysteries, and showed a profound interest in the best Greek art. But in spite of all his cosmopolitan sympathies and antiquarian interests, he was, above all things, a Roman emperor, and commander of a Roman army, with which he shared the hardships of camp life, and from which he demanded strict discipline and a high professional standard. He was also the head of the civil service, directing their activities and keeping a strict eye upon them during his travels; he was the careful manager of the public purse and was deeply concerned in the economic condition of his subjects generally. In all his actions he kept in view the empire as a whole, and endeavoured, without lowering the status of Roman citizens or undermining their theoretical superiority, to increase the rights and improve the finances of the provincial population.

Of his successor, Antoninus Pius, who reigned from A. D. 138 to 161, we know much less. But we do know that he was greatly valued by the general population of the empire, and may therefore suppose that his policy was that of a man devoted to the welfare of the state. We are much better informed about his successor, Marcus Aurelius, who reigned from A. D. 161 to 180. In the difficult conditions of his reign, when external danger on the frontier threatened to sweep everything away, and when a frightful plague weakened the Roman power of resistance, he stands before us as the truest representative of the Stoic theory, that royal station is a duty and something like a martyrdom. Taking little personal interest in politics or war or administration, he was absorbed in the workings of his own mind. His real attention was reserved for the problems of philosophy, especially those which touch on morality and religion. Here he feels himself at home : he teaches, divines the truth, and tries to convince others of it. But his personal tastes he sacrifices to his duty and devotes himself to the saving and strengthening of the Roman Empire. In his *Meditations* he has left us a picture of his inner life, his seekings and sufferings and those decisions which gave him strength to live ; and his reign proved how sincerely and consistently he sacrificed the interests and tastes of the philosopher to the duties of the leader and ruler.

Physically weak and not remarkable for strength of will, he was accessible to external influence and formed a faulty estimate of those with whom he lived—his wife, his dull and indolent colleague, Lucius Verus, and especially his son, Commodus. His worst mistake was to surrender his power to this son, who had no sympathy with the ideals of his father or his father's predecessors. Commodus, who reigned from A. D. 180 to 192, repeated the excesses of the bad old times— the despotism of the first century and the military absolutism of Domitian.

The age of the Antonines, as we call it, is especially conspicuous for a rupture in Roman foreign policy. During the whole century that policy had been defensive without being passive, and occasion had been taken more than once to rectify the frontiers by annexing districts to the existing provinces and creating new provinces. The object was to find a frontier which should be easy and convenient to defend. At the same time there was an inclination to incorporate in the empire all peoples that were fit to receive the Graeco-Roman civilization. Thus the policy, while remaining defensive, did not hesitate to annex new territory, when it could not be avoided, or to carry on preventive warfare in the enemy's country.

At the same time the work of organization was coming to an end—that work begun by Sulla, Pompey, Caesar, and Augustus, which was intended to convert Rome into one world-wide state, divided into military and administrative districts. This Roman Empire was surrounded by a ring of military fortresses—in Britain ; on the Rhine, Danube, and Euphrates ; in Arabia, Egypt, and Africa. As the process of organization became complete, the question of the relations between Rome and her neighbours, the Germans and Parthians, forced itself to the front. A century of proximity to the Roman Empire had left its mark upon them. The Germans had learned much from the Romans, had borrowed to some extent their military tactics, and knew that there were weak points, as well as strong, in the Roman system of an armed frontier. The Parthians had convinced themselves that Rome was by no means invincible, and that the Euphrates was by no means an impassable barrier. Hence it is not surprising that the German tribes on the Rhine and the Danube increased their pressure in the reign of Domitian. The prolonged struggle with these Germans explains much in the treatment of his armies by this emperor. Service had become more difficult and dangerous, and the flow of willing recruits had fallen off, so that it was necessary to abandon the principle of filling up the legions from the urban population alone, or at least from natives of Italy, and to make the army more attractive by a rise in pay.

Domitian's campaigns in Germany, though not unsuccessful on the whole, proved to his successors the complicated and troublesome nature of the task. They had two courses open—either to fall back on a purely defensive policy, or to continue the work of Caesar and Augustus and demonstrate afresh to their neighbours the power of the Roman arms. The time seemed suitable for a forward movement, especially in the East and on the Danube. The Roman Empire was prosperous, its resources were apparently inexhaustible. Parthia, on the contrary, was suffering from dynastic disputes ; and, while becoming Hellenized, she was losing her former military strength and solidarity. The Germans were disunited, and their attempt to combine in larger political units could easily be defeated. Dacia in Thrace thrust a wedge into the heart of Germany, and was therefore marked out as a natural and convenient base, from which to renew the policy of attack combined with defence. By these considerations the foreign policy of Trajan was shaped. His Dacian and Parthian campaigns were the beginning of a fresh advance, and their object was to extend the frontiers of the empire to their farthest limit. His operations were crowned with success : in two campaigns he broke the power of Dacia and made it into a Roman province ; in the East he annexed Arabia Petraea and won two great victories over the Parthians, which not only crippled Parthia but enabled him to conquer Armenia, Assyria, and Babylonia. But his further designs in the East were arrested by a rebellion in Mesopotamia, a rising of the Jews in Syria and Egypt, and also complications in Africa and Britain ; and then he died suddenly, and all his Eastern policy was left in suspense.

Hadrian took a very different line in foreign affairs. He obviously thought that the forces of the empire were not sufficient to carry out the vast projects of Trajan in the East and West. He preferred the defensive to the offensive and tried the effect of diplomacy upon neighbouring peoples. He restored to Parthia almost all Trajan's Eastern conquests, with the exception of Arabia. For defence he built armed fortresses on most of the frontiers, and behind these the legions and auxiliary troops were distributed. It is hard to say which of these two emperors was right. It is possible that Trajan over-estimated the forces of the empire and overlooked the immense difficulty of the task which he imposed upon them ; he may have been blind to the risks involved in the extension of the empire to the north and south-east. The conquest of Germany would inevitably have ended in collision with the Slavs and Finns ; and the conquest of Parthia would have brought Rome up against the other Iranians and the Mongols. It is possible that Hadrian gauged more exactly both the difficulty of the task and the incapacity of Rome to perform it. Perhaps he was the first to note the signs that the creative force of the ancient world was failing ; and perhaps his policy of defence postponed the catastrophe with which Rome was threatened. At any rate, that policy secured for the empire another interval of peace—an interval which covered his reign and that of Antoninus Pius, his successor.

But the same problems rose again in a more insistent form to confront Marcus Aurelius. Trajan's purpose was not accomplished by the annexation of Dacia : that was to be followed up by the conquest of Germany and by active measures against the Sarmatians who were pressing towards the Danube from south Russia. The peace policy of Hadrian and Antoninus Pius was certain to be interpreted by Germans and Sarmatians as a sign of weakness and an invitation to the invader. And this actually took place in the reign of Marcus Aurelius. The Germans and Sarmatians fell on the Danube frontier with terrific force, and a wave of them rolled as far as the Italian frontier and reached Aquileia, the great centre of Roman trade on the Adriatic. The invasion was unexpected. The Roman armies were busy on the Euphrates, repelling a Parthian attack on the south-eastern provinces of the empire—a most difficult task, which was successfully performed by Avidius Cassius, an able general associated with Lucius Verus, the emperor's brother, who was the nominal chief of the expedition. Also the armies brought back with them from the East a plague which raged continuously for several years in Italy and some of the provinces ; and this was a further hindrance to the campaign in the north.

In these difficult conditions Marcus Aurelius shouldered the burden and marched in person against the Germans and Sarmatians. Winning battle after battle, he was able to drive them beyond the frontier and then to deal them a succession of blows on the Danube and in Dacia. He was prevented from completing his task by military complications in Africa and Egypt, and also by a formidable mutiny headed by Avidius Cassius in Syria. Before he could overcome these perils, war broke out again on the Danube, and again a long and exhausting struggle was begun ; but Marcus Aurelius never brought it to an end; for he died on the Danube (near Vienna) in A.D. 180. It is highly probable that the force of circumstances would have compelled him to revert to the policy of Trajan, and to extend the northern and eastern frontiers of the empire. But this arduous enterprise was declined by his son Commodus, who preferred to sacrifice the interests of his country and make peace with Germany—a peace which only postponed for a short time a renewal of the contest.

Except for the troubled reign of Marcus Aurelius, the Roman Empire under the Antonines enjoyed profound peace, broken only by distant wars on the frontier. Within the empire life appeared to be, as it had been in the first century, a steady forward movement for the diffusion and enrichment of civilization. The creative power of Rome seemed to have reached its zenith. There was, however, one disquieting symptom : after the brilliant age of the Flavians we note an almost complete sterility in literature and art. After Tacitus, and after the artists who worked for Trajan—the splendid craftsmen who carved the reliefs for the monument on his tomb, the famous column which still stands in Rome, whose reliefs commemorate his Dacian campaigns, and yet others on similar buildings, such as the triumphal arch at Beneventum—the decades that followed failed to produce a single great writer or a single notable monument of art.

Hadrian, indeed, was a connoisseur and a great lover of art. He did much building both at Rome and in the provinces ; Athens in particular owed to him a number of splendid edifices. A number of monuments in honour of Trajan who had adopted him were completed in Rome and Italy during his reign. Every one knows his temple of Venus and Rome in the Forum, and his magnificent villa at Tivoli. But the art of his time has no original ideas and no novelty of style. For all its technical perfection, it is marked by cold classicism and eclectic archaism.

Even before the time of war and pestilence in the reign of Marcus Aurelius, we mark in the whole of intellectual life not merely a pause but even a backward movement. The only exception is a revival of Greek rhetorical prose, perfect in form but monotonous in substance. Its chief representative is the sophist and rhetorician, Aristides, and his best work is his *Panegyric* on Rome. The *Dialogues* of Lucian are witty and interesting ; he was a sceptic and a humorist who mocked all ideals both new and old. In the West there are only two names to be quoted, that of the satirist Juvenal, a gloomy and bitter observer of the dark side of human life, and that of Pliny the Younger, a shallow orator and a brilliant representative of the epistolary style. The rest both in Greece and in Italy are writers of handbooks, text-books, and of miscellaneous collections of entertaining stories for the amusement and instruction of the reader. We shall meet with the same backward movement in economic life, of which more is said below ; and it contains the explanation of that apparently unexpected catastrophe which befell the Roman Empire in the third century.

XVIII

THE PROVINCES IN THE FIRST AND SECOND CENTURIES A. D.

AUGUSTUS and his successors actually realized what had seemed to the ancient world before their time an unattainable ideal, namely, permanent peace without constant shocks from foreign war and internal revolution, and a life regulated by the orderly conditions of a civilized state. This peace and order was created by the Roman Empire, not for a single inconsiderable aggregation of men but for all who were more or less influenced by civilization. A second great benefit was conferred on mankind by the Roman Empire, when it consciously and consistently carried out the mission bequeathed to it by the Hellenistic Age—the mission of admitting the greatest possible number to the civilization planted by the East, watered by the Greeks, and then accepted and developed by the Italians. Two centuries of peace under the rule of the Roman emperors made it possible to inoculate with this civilization nations of the West and, in a less degree, of the East, which had hardly been touched by it in the earlier period of development. Spain, Britain, Gaul, part of Germany, the northern part of the Balkan peninsula, the north coast of Africa—all these countries received and absorbed this civilization in its Western, Italian, Latin form. But those parts of the East which were not Hellenized already, central Asia Minor, part of the Black Sea coast, a great part of the Caucasus and Transcaucasia, and parts of Syria, Palestine, and Arabia, took it over in its Greek, or rather Graeco-Oriental, form. This civilizing mission Rome performed not by constraint or violent means, not by arms or by transferring nations from place to place, but by peaceful methods and by the natural attraction of a higher form of life offered by a dominant state and nation.

The Roman Empire never was, nor tried to be, a worldwide state of a national type—a state in which one nation subdues and forcibly assimilates other nations to itself: it became by its constitution more and more cosmopolitan. What gave it strength and substantiality and enabled it, in spite of many radical defects in its political and social system, to hold together even after the severe shocks of the third century, and later also under increasing pressure from its neighbours, was its culture, which all shared and all prized, and which united all the inhabitants of the empire in times of danger. But for some trifling local variations, this culture was the same everywhere. Like our modern culture, it belonged to dwellers in towns and was closely connected with the Greek conception of the city, not as a mere agglomeration of buildings but as an association of men with common habits and needs and interests, bodily and mental, who endeavour by united effort to create for themselves acceptable and convenient surroundings for life. The advantages of such a life were less attainable in the country, where comparatively primitive conditions prevailed. Yet there was no impassable gulf between town and country; and the town more and more attracted the rural population and inoculated them with the taste for town habits.

One of the chief tasks of the empire in its civilizing mission was to spread the urban method of life in places that knew nothing of it until they were conquered by Rome. The town became the basis of social and economic life in all parts of the Roman Empire: in Gaul, Germany, and Britain, where the native population led a tribal life; in Spain, where towns of the Greek or Phoenician type existed only on the south and east coasts—and the same is true of Gaul; in Africa, where the Phoenician cities belonging to the period of Carthaginian supremacy were built chiefly on the coast; on the Danube and in the northern part of the Balkan peninsula, where, as in central Europe occupied by Celts and Germans, the scattered tribes of Illyrians and Thracians lived in villages; and in the vast spaces of the Near East, where the Hellenistic powers had begun to build cities before the Romans came, and to reclaim from the rudeness of tribal life the remoter districts of Asia Minor and Syria.

Of the towns which grew up in these countries very few were founded by settlers from Italy. Most of them owed their existence to the natural desire of the native population for the higher civilization of urban life. A long peace had raised these people to a higher social and economic level;

and they enjoyed the advantage of belonging to a single well-ordered state of vast extent. The state welcomed this desire, and granted freely to these newly formed towns those rights and privileges which Rome had always allowed to her Italian allies who later became citizens. I refer to the right of self-government, which had always been the basis of urban life in Italy, and which persisted and increased in Italy when Rome became the dominating power in the Italian peninsula. Thus there had long existed in the peninsula, first, colonies of Roman citizens and their Latin allies; secondly, allied towns, connected with Rome by treaties varying in their terms; and thirdly, towns called *municipia*, inhabited by Roman citizens who had received the franchise from Rome.

At the end of the Social war in 89 B. C. all Italian towns were inhabited by Roman citizens; and they all had the same measure of local government and the same relationship to Rome. In the provinces, during the republican period, the same process of admission to the Roman franchise went on by stages, the stages being the different degrees of local self-government which had formerly grown up in Italy owing to historical causes. The usual form of community in the provinces was a town inhabited by provincials and under the supervision of the Roman governor, which paid to Rome a poll-tax and regular dues levied on land and other property. The measure of self-government enjoyed by such a town was determined by its past history and the willingness of Rome to take that history into account. There were, however, other provincial towns which possessed fuller rights, especially communities which had formerly been allies of Rome and still preserved certain privileges secured to them by treaty, such as freedom from taxes (*immunitas*), and freedom to govern themselves according to their ancient constitution (*libertas*). Even more favourable was the position of the Roman citizens and Latins whom Rome had sent forth in ancient times to the provinces as colonists.

Such was the historic basis on which the Roman Empire deliberately built. Any provincial community, according to its development and its services to the empire or the emperor himself, had three possibilities before it : it might either be put on a level with the allied communities, thus receiving partial immunity from taxation, and also self-government in theory at least unlimited ; or it might receive the status and rights of a Roman or Latin colony ; or it might be placed in the category of towns enjoying the privileges of Roman *municipia*. One stage led to another, and so by degrees a regular ladder was formed, by which a provincial town could eventually reach the status of an Italian town inhabited by Roman citizens.

Italy and Greece and, to a certain extent, Phoenicia and Syria, including the Phoenician colonies, had once been like islands in a great ocean : in them alone the urban type of life was established, while elsewhere it existed, if at all, in a rudimentary form. But now the Roman Empire was converted into a single state divided into a number of administrative departments, in each of which a town formed the basis of social, economic, and public life ; and with the town was linked a larger or smaller district which was styled its territory. The empire became by degrees a vast federation of self-governing towns and their territories, with a central government at Rome.

The transition to urban life was not, of course, equally rapid in all parts of the empire ; but it was everywhere more or less effective in producing similar conditions, social and economic, and a similar civilization. A division of the empire may be made into four parts, based upon the historic past of the different provinces. First comes a group of provinces in which the population is mainly Celtic: Gaul, Spain, Britain, the Alpine provinces. Next comes what was once the empire or the sphere of influence of Carthage—Sardinia, Africa, Numidia, Mauretania ; then the Danube region, inhabited by Illyrians, Thracians, and Celts, and including Dalmatia, the two Pannonias, the two Moesias, Dacia, and Thrace ; and lastly Asia Minor and Syria, containing a number of provinces—Asia, Lycia, Cilicia, Bithynia, Pontus, Galatia, Paphlagonia, Cappadocia, Armenia Minor, Syria, Palestine, Arabia, and two which were not held permanently, Mesopotamia and Armenia Major. Egypt, as always, stood apart.

We shall consider first the Celtic countries. There before the Roman conquest a tribal system prevailed, and the noble families ruled : they owned the land, and all trade and industry was controlled by them. As is well known, the first Celtic regions annexed and converted into provinces were the south coast of Spain and the south coast of Gaul ; Baetica and Tarraconensis in Spain, and Gallia Narbonensis in the Rhone valley, were the first provinces. A method was here applied which had been started in the Celtic part of north Italy when it was annexed by Rome: 'colonies', that is, fortified towns inhabited by Roman citizens, old soldiers by preference, were established; and the number of these increased greatly during the civil wars. These outposts of civilization by degrees attracted the higher class of natives; and part of the lower class also came into residence there, as artisans and small traders, and to work at such jobs as building and transport. The rest of the native inhabitants went on living in their villages and tilled the land assigned to the colony as smallholders or tenants or labourers for wages.

New and much more extensive annexations were made later —in Gaul by Caesar, in Spain and in the Alpine lands mainly by Augustus, while Britain was first conquered by Claudius and his successors; and the inhabitants of these vast territories lived in the tribal fashion already described. In their case a different system was followed. Italy could no longer supply colonists in sufficient numbers; and also the climate and conditions were too strange to attract a large body of Italian husbandmen. Therefore a new system, originated by Caesar, was adopted. The new territories were divided into administrative districts, each containing many settlements, one or more of which were used for the purposes of central government and also as meeting-places where all the population of the province might unite in the public worship of the goddess Rome and the Roman emperor. Prominent among such provincial capitals were Lugudunum (Lyons) in Gaul, Tarraco (Tarragona) in Spain, Camulodunum (Colchester) and Eboracum (York) in Britain.

In the internal government of these new provinces the empire maintained and strengthened the existing system, social and economic, based upon the clan and the subdivisions of the clan, called by the Roman respectively *civitas* and *pagi*. Within the limits of each *civitas* Rome was satisfied if the taxes assessed on the basis of a Roman census were duly paid, and recruits supplied for the auxiliary troops. The agents employed for these purposes were partly the imperial procurators, and partly the native aristocracy, who served as negotiators between Rome and the people at large and were responsible for the people's behaviour. The aristocracy also, as a ruling class, directed all the local life of the tribes, under the control of the Roman governors, the emperor's legates.

By a natural process, however, these centres, formed for

purposes of administration, trade, and industry in each tribal territory and its subdivisions, were gradually converted into towns, which brought together large numbers of the population—the ruling aristocracy, the native and foreign traders, and artisans. The settlement took shape and came to look like the normal Greek or Italian town, and finally acquired the outward forms and the substance of self-government, as well as the social system of the city-state. Celtic 'vergo-brets' became *duumviri*, and Celtic Druids municipal priests. The Celtic *civitas* evolved into a Roman town and eventually received from the Roman government the title and privileges of a *municipium* or *colonia*.

In Africa a similar development took a different path. Africa also was a site for colonization. A number of Italian settlers—merchants, bankers, manufacturers, landowners— got together by degrees in the Phoenician and Berber towns that existed already. During the civil wars and under the empire some of the towns were colonized with Roman veterans, whom the Roman government presented with considerable allotments, taken from the town territory, of cultivated or cultivable land. Thus there grew up urban centres contain-ing two communities, the original Phoenicians and the Roman new-comers. These communities blended in course of time, and the population became mixed. Eventually, the existing state of things was recognized by the state, and the united community received the name and status of a Roman *muni-cipium* or *colonia*.

The gradual advance of the Roman armies to the south and west opened up fresh territories, which contained no urban centres but were suitable for colonization and cultiva-tion. Part of this land was disposed of under the empire in assignment to veterans : colonies of this kind were settled in rapid succession. Part of it was bought up by emigrants from Italy or enterprising inhabitants of the old Roman-Phoenician towns. Villages, containing markets, temples, and shops, grew up in suitable places, and the landowners, traders, and artisans of the district settled there. The popula-tion increased, the village organized itself like a town and gradually became the natural centre of a more or less extensive territory. As such it was made use of by the state, and received the title and the rights of a *municipium* and later of a *colonia*.

Thus a number of towns with territories belonging to them grew up in Africa. But colonization by smallholders was not the only method by which the continent was developed. After Rome had annexed the territory of Carthage and the cities allied to Carthage, the new province of Africa at once attracted the attention of the great Roman capitalists. They bought or rented from the state immense tracts of land which had formerly belonged to Carthaginian capitalists—the ruling aristocracy of Carthage and the aristocracy of other Phoenician cities. Most of this land was not included in the territory of any city then existing ; and when it became the property of Roman senatorial families, the ruling aristocracy of Rome, these estates remained permanently distinct from territories annexed to cities. The Roman landowners tilled part of this land by slave labour, as they did in Italy ; but they also employed both the native population and settlers from Italy, to whom they granted leases for a short or long term or in perpetuity, if they would convert fallow land into cornfields and gardens and pay a moderate rent to the proprietor.

Each addition of territory to the provinces, wherever the soil was capable of profitable development, increased the number of great estates owned by Roman nobles in Africa. The largest landowners were the revolutionary leaders during the civil wars, and later the emperors. During the early empire, the conflict with the Senate transferred to the emperor the vast estates of condemned or executed senators, till by degrees the emperor owned a great part of the soil of Africa. Inhabited centres naturally grew up within these imperial domains. Slaves lived close to the house of the owner or his agent ; they were joined by tenants cultivating that part of the estate ; a hamlet came into existence, and then a village, sometimes a village of some size and pretensions to being a town. An aristocracy of its own grew up in the village ; and it was a common practice with the emperors, to whom it made no difference whether the revenue they received was called rent or taxes, to convert part of their estates into urban territories, and a village occupied by their tenants into a *municipium*.

We have less information about the development of the Danube provinces. The population of these provinces consisted of Illyrians and Celts in the West, near the Adriatic, and of Thracians in the East, towards the Black Sea. The development of the Illyrian-Adriatic shore was similar to that of Spain and Gaul. Illyricum was one of the earliest Roman provinces. Greek cities existed there before the Romans came; and native fortified towns of refuge soon developed under Roman influence into regular cities. Outside the urban territories life was tribal, and the transformation of tribal into urban territories was slow. It appears to have been a peculiarity of the Thracian tribes that they lived in villages, where the population perhaps owned in common the land tilled by the village. In any case, after the Roman conquest of districts inhabited by these tribes, the prevailing form of settlement was the village, whose inhabitants owned the land belonging to the village and cultivated it. Here we find no trace of the superior landowning class whom we have seen in Gaul. On the Eastern frontier of these provinces, on the west coast of the Black Sea, there had long existed large and prosperous Greek cities with extensive territories. But long peace produced its effects; and even in the Thracian provinces many villages grew into towns and received the institutions and title of a Roman *municipium*.

This gradual conversion of the Roman provinces in western Europe into a network of urban territories, and their gradual Romanization under the influence of urban life, would have been impossible but for one condition. All these territories were surrounded by a series of military frontiers, extending in an unbroken line from the Black Sea along the Danube to its upper waters, and then along the Rhine to the North Sea. A similar fortified frontier defended Roman Britain from independent Scotland, and the province of Africa from the nomads of the desert and the savage mountain tribes of Morocco; and yet another ran along the Euphrates and the edge of the Arabian desert, in the East. These frontiers were not merely a breast-plate to defend Roman civilization, but also served to promote that civilization in the most backward parts of Roman dominions.

These strips of Roman territory along the frontier formed a world of their own, with a life peculiar to themselves. About half a million men, young or of middle age, recruited in Italy and the provinces for a term of twenty to twenty-five years, were stationed at different points along the line. They lived in permanent fortified camps of varying sizes: the larger bases for attack and defence accommodated a headquarters and the bulk of a legion containing five to six thousand men; the smaller camps were held by a cavalry or infantry regiment, or by an auxiliary regiment of both arms, with numbers varying from a thousand to five hundred; and there were even smaller stations where detachments of legionaries or auxiliary troops defended the frontier.

The life in these camps was purely military, the life of soldiers in barracks. But there grew up round them settlements known as *canabae*, inhabited by innkeepers and wine-sellers, and dealers in spoils of war. There were women also, some married, regularly or irregularly, to soldiers, with their children; for army marriages, though illegal, were winked at by the authorities. When a man had served in the same place for a number of years and formed ties there, it was natural that he should lose touch with his own country and prefer, when he received his discharge, to migrate from the camp to the *canabae* where his wife and children were. There he could open a shop in the town, or farm a piece of land in the neighbourhood, given him by his commanding officer. Thus the *canabae* grew into a village, and the village into a town; and such was the origin of the great cities that now stand on the Rhine and the Danube—Cologne, Mainz, Strasburg, Vienna, Budapest.

These towns became important frontier markets and centres of large Romanized territories. In peaceful times their streets and shops were thronged by people from the neighbouring villages, and also by traders from near and remote districts inhabited by independent tribes—German, British, Iranian, and Celtic. Some of these visitors spent long periods in such centres of civilization, where they learned to speak Latin or, in the East, Greek, acquired an external polish of culture, and became better acquainted with their enemies. Then they would go home with their habits changed and their minds stored, and thus contribute to the gradual diffusion of Graeco-Roman civilization.

In the East life was more complicated. Into Greece the Roman Empire introduced nothing new, except pauperization, bankruptcy, and a stoppage of all independent political activity. Greece remained, as before, a country of a myriad cities. Nor did the empire do much for Asia Minor and Syria, where the conquerors found an ancient and substantial framework of civilized society already in existence, and made no attempt to alter it; all they did was to extend municipal institutions over the territories included in the Eastern monarchies. Thus we find there the three kinds of community which existed there earlier : the Greek city ; the Graeco-Oriental or purely Oriental temple, owning lands, slaves, and serfs ; and a vast number of extra-urban districts, inhabited by serfs and belonging to the proprietor of the East —in other words, to the Roman emperor as heir of the Eastern and Hellenistic kings. In Syria and Palestine, however, the typical villager was neither slave nor serf, but a free smallholder, a regular peasant. This triple division the Romans took over from the past and maintained, with some partial alterations. There were few Roman colonies in the East, and the Roman element which they contained soon became Hellenized. Under Roman rule, as formerly under the Hellenistic kings, many of the temples were converted into Greek or half-Greek cities, and many villages grew into towns. The Greek language penetrated somewhat deeper into the mass of the population. But the East was still the East, with its own customs and way of looking at the world and its own characteristic life. It is not surprising that it returned more readily than the West to purely Eastern conditions under the control of its later masters—the Persians, the Arabs, and the Turks.

Nor was there any fundamental change in the peculiar life of Egypt. She remained essentially what she was under the Ptolemies. The Roman emperor, as the heir of the Pharaohs and Ptolemies, was absolutely the master and owner of the country. Hardly any new cities of the Greek type grew up under the empire : Alexandria remained the only great city deserving the name. It continued to prosper and became the second city of the empire, a vast centre of trade and industry. The Greek city Ptolemais, founded by the Ptolemies, kept its Greek self-government, but was otherwise indistinguishable from the villages which passed for towns in that country. In imitation of Ptolemais, Hadrian founded Antinoupolis, with a Greek population and Greek municipal government, in memory of his favourite, Antinous, who was drowned in the Nile. But by the side of these Greek cities, the rest of Egypt retained its own immemorial customs, and dwelt in larger or smaller villages at the administrative centres of the nomes into which the country was divided—the nomes which had once been Thebes, Memphis, and Sais, the proud and splendid capitals of the Pharaohs.

A notable feature of Egypt under Roman domination is the rapid increase of a class already existing—a class of land-owners, traders, manufacturers, and contractors, most of whom migrated from other parts of the empire. The Roman government favoured the development of this class, and opened a wide field for their commercial ability, by relaxing the state control of commerce and resigning the many mono-polies established by the Ptolemies. This new middle class lived either in the towns mentioned above or in the villages, especially the largest, which had been the centres of the Egyptian nomes.

Accustomed to live in a town and bringing with them the requirements of civilized existence, this middle class refashioned the ways of Egyptian villages and settlements to suit them-selves, and converted them into settlements of the urban type universal in Greece. But even in Roman times they were a drop in the bucket of Egyptian life. They all lived upon the native population—the fellaheen, of whom the vast majority lived on plots of land belonging to the state or private owners, paid their rent to the landlord or the state, i. e. the emperor, surrendered to the state a considerable part of their gains in the form of taxes, and continued to believe in their own gods and repair to the temples for their worship. Some few rose higher on the social ladder, became Hellenized and took Greek names, and intermarried with the immigrants. But the mass of the people lived under the Romans just as they had lived under the Pharaohs and the Ptolemies.

XIX

GOVERNMENT OF THE ROMAN EMPIRE IN THE FIRST TWO CENTURIES A. D.

THE government of the empire, whose main lines were laid down by Augustus during his long principate, was developed by his successors in the direction indicated by him, becoming more and more methodical and systematic. The most successful and most fruitful work in this department was done by Claudius with his private staff, by Vespasian, and by Hadrian. By the second century we find in existence a system of government where the main principles were unalterably fixed and the changes introduced were chiefly alterations and improvements of detail that did not affect the general structure.

All the threads of administration met in the hands of the emperor and the Central Office attached to his person, where the different heads of departments assumed more and more the character of ministers for the whole empire. Here were worked out, in adaptation to particular cases, all the principles of administration, justice, and finance ; and from here all the emperor's missives—either direct edicts (*edicta*), or instructions to high officials (*mandata*), or letters (*epistulae*), or replies (*rescripta*) to letters and petitions—streamed out into every part of the empire, where they were either published or preserved in the archives of the recipients. Copies were kept in the imperial archives at Rome and afforded the precedents by which later emperors were guided. Great importance attached also to the decisions of law courts, over which the emperor presided in person, generally sitting as a judge of appeal. Such appeals were put in order by a special department of the imperial offices.

This Central Office was divided into departments for the separate branches of imperial business ; and each department was supervised by a single chief, who was originally a freedman, a personal servant, of the emperor ; but occasionally from Otho's time, and regularly after Hadrian's accession, he was an official of equestrian rank. The most important department managed the finances and property of the emperor, his *rationes*, or accounts ; and the head of this department was styled *a rationibus* ; a subdivision of this department dealt with the private property (*patrimonium*) of the ruler. Other important departments were these : the *ab epistulis* and *a libellis*, which dealt with letters and petitions ; the judicial department (*a cognitionibus*) ; the department of records (*a memoria*) ; and the department for collecting evidence concerning matters of dispute (*a studiis*). All imperial business was recorded in a special journal (*commentarii*) kept by an official styled *a commentariis*.

There is no doubt that, as the principate developed, the administrative activity of the ruler grew more and more comprehensive. But the government of the empire in the first and second centuries was far from being a bureaucracy in the modern sense of the word. The ordinary subject, except the inhabitants of the capital, came much less into contact with the officials of the central government than he does in any modern state except America. The imperial officials or, to put it more generally, the direct instruments of the state in general, including the governors of imperial or senatorial provinces, were a mere superstructure added to self-governing communities throughout the empire. The elective magistrates of these communities were the links that connected the man in the street with the state. They and the municipal councils in Italy and the provinces had entire control over the town and its affairs ; they were also judges of first instance, and gave orders to the police of the town and district ; they acted as government agents in settling and collecting the direct taxes ; and they enforced other obligations on the inhabitants, such as making and maintaining roads, and conveying government officers or stores or the government post. They discharged these duties, not only for the town but also for the district, often very large, which formed the territory belonging to the town. In ordinary cases the agents of the central government merely supervised the municipal authorities and heard complaints brought against them by the local inhabitants.

It is true that the right of interference in municipal affairs, possessed by proconsuls and propraetors, and the imperial legates and procurators, was limited by no law but by tradition only ; and a tolerably free use of this right was sometimes made at a crisis, when these great men issued written edicts or verbal proclamations to their military and civilian subordinates. But, as I have said already, the emperor kept a sharp look-out on the doings of provincial governors ; and the governor knew that the annual meetings in the provincial capital, where representatives of the towns came to do worship in honour of the emperor and to discuss local business, might at any time complain of illegal or violent action on his part and draw down on him the vengeance of the Senate or the emperor. Nevertheless, as the demands of the state upon the towns, both in the way of taxes and personal obligations laid upon the inhabitants, became more onerous, the interference of the central government in municipal affairs became commoner. As a large number of the towns were sunk in debt and incapable of managing their finances, special commissions were appointed by the emperor to report on the facts ; and from Trajan's time permanent inspectors (*curatores*) discharged this office, steadily eclipsing the municipal authorities and reducing them to a position in which they were responsible to the state for the town and its territory, but entirely unable to act freely in town affairs. The same process is observable in Italy : the magistrates were overshadowed by the officials who managed the private property of the emperor in the peninsula and also by the senators who had charge of the roads ; and from the time of Marcus Aurelius special legates with judicial powers (*legati iuridici*) were the real governors of their different districts.

The direct control of the emperor, however, extended only to a few departments of government. He did, indeed, control his own immense and ever-increasing property ; his men of business (*procuratores*) managed his estates, houses, forests, mines, and factories. The number of these agents, very large in the time of Augustus, grew larger steadily. A second swarm of procurators, working in the imperial provinces, collected, chiefly through the agency of the city magistrates, the direct tax paid by the provincials, and supervised both revenue and expenditure, the latter including pay and maintenance for the armies and the cost of managing the state domains. Officials of this kind were especially numerous in the rich country of Egypt. In course of time the emperors thought it necessary to extend their control to the collection of the so-called 'indirect taxes'—the succession duty, the duty paid on liberated slaves and on auctions, and the tax on imports and exports. At first special controllers were appointed to watch the doings of the different contractors and contracting companies ; but later the state took into its own hands the collection of these imposts, and they were managed by officials nominated by the emperor. The distinction between state property and imperial property became fainter and fainter, and the *fiscus*, or treasury of the emperor, became more and more identical with the public treasury. Thus, for example, even in the senatorial provinces the management of the emperor's private estates was conducted in the same office as the management of the state domains.

The emperor therefore eventually found himself at the head not only of an army of soldiers but of another army of officials, who were all appointed, paid, judged, and punished by himself alone. From a very early date the highest official posts were given to members of the equestrian class, while the inferior duties in the innumerable offices were performed by the emperor's freedmen and slaves. Thus a new class in society came into existence, and a new hierarchy, in which the gradations were fixed chiefly by the amount of salary but later by titles of honour as well. Officials of the equestrian rank were styled *vir egregius*, *vir eminentissimus*, or *vir perfectissimus*, according to the duties they discharged, but the title of *vir clarissimus* was reserved for senators. The chief equestrian officials received a salary ranging from 60,000 to 300,000 sesterces ; and such a man might eventually become either commander of the praetorian guard (*praefectus praetorio*), or governor of Egypt, or controller of the Roman corn-supply (*praefectus annonae*) ; or they might command the city fire brigade or the fleets or serve as procurators in the chief provinces. But the privileged few were sharply distinguished from their subordinates. They belonged to the upper classes and had generally served as officers in the army, while the inferior members were slaves or half-free, with no hope of promotion to the superior class, although there were occasional instances of it, especially under Claudius.

The main business, however, of all these officials was the finance and economic progress of the state. But in matters not financial almost complete freedom was left, as

I have said before, to the local self-governing units which composed the state.

As *pontifex maximus* the emperor was the head of the state religion, and worship was paid to him personally throughout the empire. Yet the religious life of his subjects was not affected in its development by any interference on the part of the state : even the worship which he received as chief of the state was managed entirely by the self-governing towns and by voluntary societies of individuals called *Augustales*.

Similarly the emperor had no direct connexion with the administration of justice or with the codification of civil and criminal law. Local courts continued to administer local law in Italy and the provinces. Together with these, Roman citizens, just as in republican times, had access to the tribunals in the capital, which relied upon the services of the *iuris consulti* or specialist interpreters of the law ; while the provincials resorted to other judges who formed part of the governor's staff. At Rome, and still more in the provinces, the Roman law and the local codes, especially that of Greece, naturally overlapped and affected one another, so that an imperial system of law grew up. But this was a slow process, and the praetors at Rome and the provincial governors took a share in it as well as the emperors. Nevertheless, the emperors began by degrees to exert a stronger influence in the sphere of law and justice. The highest criminal court for culprits belonging to the senatorial class was now the Senate itself ; and its action was governed by the expressed wishes of the emperor. As the ruler of many provinces, the emperor, sitting as a court of appeal, gave sentence in the most important cases that were referred from them. As head of the army, he framed the main rules of martial law ; and as head of the financial administration, he employed his procurators and the 'advocates of the *fiscus*' to work out a scheme of legal relations in those cases where, in matters of taxation or in the administration of the imperial *patrimonium*, the rights of the state clashed with the rights of the individual. And lastly, the emperor's decisions, either judicial or administrative, soon acquired the force of law and, as such, became one of the main sources of law. An active part in framing them was taken not only by the imperial officials but also by eminent jurisconsults. Thus by degrees was formed that great structure of Roman law under the empire, which was codified later by two emperors successively, Theodosius and Justinian, and has been preserved to our time in that form.

The protection of the subject and the maintenance of order throughout the empire did not form part of the duties discharged by the central government. The emperor's responsibility was limited to the defence of the frontiers and the policing of the seas. Order within the state was maintained by the municipal bodies by means of the local police. Here, however, we notice again the gradual encroachment of the emperor. The safety and order of the great military roads was not sufficiently assured by the towns through which these roads passed ; and for this reason the emperors entrusted the duty to small detachments of soldiers, and stationed military police (*stationes*) at the most dangerous points. Soldiers were also employed to keep an eye on persons suspected of political disaffection, whom the towns could not be trusted to deal with ; and this secret police, recruited from the army, increased greatly in numbers from the time of Hadrian.

The means of communication, and the construction and maintenance of the great military roads, had long been among the principal concerns of the central government, and became under the empire indispensable to the safety and prosperity of the state. The emperors recognized this fact and achieved one of their chief public services, when, by using the army and spending immense sums from their own pockets, they created such a network of roads as mankind had never before dreamed of. It was the duty of the local authorities to construct the local and less important roads; but even here the emperors quickened the activity of the communities and kept an eye on what they were doing. The postal service and the conveyance of passengers and goods are matters connected with the making of roads ; but these important services the state was never able to perform for the mass of its subjects. A service was organized for officials and official correspondence, and for the conveyance of government stores; but this was maintained with difficulty and by means of requisitions burdensome to the people. The private individual had to arrange these matters for himself.

To provide for the refinement and comfort of life in the capital was a duty which was manfully discharged by the emperors. Rome, the city which we now see in ruins, was their spoilt child. The spacious forums, surrounded by splendid temples and public buildings, were their creation. Following the lead of Pompey, the new lords of Rome converted the Campus Martius from end to end into a range of majestic memorial buildings in a setting of parks. By careful planning, they brought order into the chaotic and haphazard growth of the ancient city, and carried out a series of systematic measures in order to make it, in point of sanitation and police control, reasonably well adapted to its million inhabitants. They controlled and supervised the numerous aqueducts and the drainage ; to protect the city from floods, they straightened the banks of the Tiber and built a stone embankment ; they provided for the scavenging of the streets and maintained order in the streets and public places ; they arranged for the regular and abundant supply of food, and financed and regulated the gratuitous distributions of corn which had become a standing institution. And lastly, the emperors were careful that the people should have a sufficient supply of amusements, and sufficient buildings—bathing establishments which were also clubs—in which to spend their leisure time. All such business the emperors performed through delegates of various ranks—senators, or knights, or freedmen.

The subject in which the imperial government showed least interest was popular education. Just as in America now, the people themselves had to attend to the instruction and education of their children. And it must be admitted that the towns, even more in the East than in the West, did a good deal in this respect. All the towns of the empire possessed gymnasiums and palaestras in which the young received mental and physical training. Public libraries, equipped with a sufficient supply of books, were common. The forums, temples, and other public buildings were museums of sculpture and painting. Games and competitions kept up an interest in athletics, music, and dancing. It is true that all these advantages were confined to the towns and the children of the higher classes ; the municipal authorities paid scant attention to the villages and the children of the poor. For the education of youth the emperors did little. At Rome they maintained a number of libraries ; they supported the library and museum at Alexandria ; and they patronized a few men of eminence in science, literature, or art, who were personally dependent on them. But in general they held aloof from the intellectual life of the state, while keeping up a strict censorship upon all seditious writings. Not until the increasing poverty of the towns endangered the existence of all educational institutions, did the emperors step into the breach and undertake to pay a certain number of professors and teachers.

Such was the system of government in the Roman Empire. Its main feature, inherited from the past, is the way in which the utmost possible power of initiative was conceded to the local unit, that is, to the self-governing town. By degrees, however, a tendency develops in the central government to take the local government under its tutelage, and grows steadily, till it threatens to swallow up the independence of the community and to replace the elected representative of the people by the paid official—the agent and servant of the emperor. This process was beginning in the first two centuries and did not reach its height till after the social and political ordeal which Rome underwent in the third century of our era. (In Egypt alone, where urban self-government was unknown, it was different.)

FAMILY LIFE IN ROME AND THE PROVINCES

1. A ROMAN WEDDING

1. Sarcophagus with two scenes representing a Roman wedding. To the right the bride and the bridegroom are represented as shaking hands (*dextrarum iunctio*) in the presence of their relatives, which followed the drawing-up of the marriage contract. Between them is a Cupid. In the centre the great sacrifice in the house of the bridegroom or before a public temple is performed by the newly wedded *pater familias* in the presence of his wife and of her bridesmaids. In the left corner is a personification of the city. 2nd cent. A.D. Church of S. Lorenzo fuori le mura, Rome.

2. Sarcophagus of a child. The parents have represented on his sarcophagus the various periods of his short life. First he is a baby at his mother's breast, while the father looks on. Next he is a little older and held in the arms of his father. As a boy of six or seven he has received a fine present, a carriage driven by a goat. And finally he begins his education and recites before his father a piece of poetry or prose. 2nd cent. A.D. Louvre, Paris.

3. Part of the bas-reliefs which adorned the funeral monument of a rich merchant at Neumagen near Trèves. Two boys are seated in armchairs with rolls in their hands. Between them sits their bearded master. A third boy is late and makes an excuse while scolded by the teacher. 2nd cent. A.D. Museum, Trèves.

PLATE IX

2. EDUCATION OF A CHILD

3. MASTER AND PUPILS

PLATE IX

I. AUTUMN RELIGIOUS CEREMONY

I, 2. Two sections of a painted frieze which adorned the walls of a
public building in Ostia. The frieze represented, no doubt, the religious
calendar of an association of young boys. The building therefore was
probably the house of this association. The first picture represents an
open-air sanctuary of Artemis or Diana. Some of the members with
torches in their hands worship the goddess; others with baskets of fruit
or grapes and with grapes suspended on their standards are moving in a
procession. Their leader gives them an order. They carry two standards
with portrait busts on them. Gaius and Lucius Caesar, the grandsons
and adopted sons of Augustus, the *principes iuventutis,* are probably
represented. The ceremony takes place apparently in the evening in
autumn at the time of vintage. The second picture represents a religious
ceremony probably at the opening of navigation in spring. A ship is
carried on a wagon. The two priests of the association, crowned with
flowers, are making a libation. A standard with three busts (Augustus,
Gaius, and Lucius) is carried by a boy who holds in his left hand a
wreath of flowers. The time appears to be early spring. 1st cent. A.D.
Vatican, Rome.

PLATE X

2. SPRING RELIGIOUS CEREMONY

PLATE X

BOYS AND GIRLS

I. BOY FREEDMAN OF EGYPT   2. GIRL OF EGYPT

1. Funeral painting of a handsome boy, found in Egypt. His name was Eutyches, and he was a freedman. 2nd cent. A.D. Metropolitan Museum of Art, New York.

2. Funeral painting of a girl, found in Egypt. She wears a pair of ear-rings and a heavy necklace with a medallion probably enclosing a charm or amulet. 2nd cent. A.D. Museum, Detroit.

PLATE XI

3. GIRL OF POMPEII

3. Fresco found at Pompeii. It shows a handsome girl holding a stylus in her right hand and a *polyptych*, or set of wooden tablets, in her left. It may represent a young poetess of Pompeii or one of the famous Greek poetesses, e.g. Sappho. 1st cent. A.D. Museum, Naples.

4. Funeral *stele* of Q. Sulpicius Maximus, found near Rome. The epitaph says that the boy, who died at the age of eleven, was an excellent Greek scholar. In A.D. 94 he took part in the Capitoline contest in Greek poetry and won a prize. Soon after he died of overwork. His parents engraved his prize-poem (a mediocre poem, indeed) on his funeral *stele*. 1st cent. A.D. Palazzo dei Conservatori, Rome.

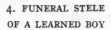

4. FUNERAL STELE
OF A LEARNED BOY

PLATE XI

1. MAUSOLEUM OF THE JULII OF ST. REMY

1. The mausoleum of the Julii of St. Remy (near Tarascon in south France). The beautiful and well-proportioned funeral monument and family grave of some rich resident of southern France, probably one of the veterans of Julius Caesar. It consists of a square base adorned with bas-reliefs showing a hunting scene and scenes of battle between Romans and Gauls; of a so-called tetrapylon—an arch supported by four pillars, and of a colonnaded pavilion with a conical top, where two statues (with modern heads) still stand. The architecture is Hellenistic, not Roman; the monument was built probably by a Greek architect of Massilia (Marseilles). It belongs to the time before Augustus, after the conquest of Gaul by Julius Caesar. 1st cent. B.C.

2. The Pont du Gard, one of the most daring and beautiful constructions by Roman engineers and architects. It is part of an aqueduct which brought water from Uzès to the city of Nemausus (Nîmes). The three stories of arches (160 ft. high) were built across the bed of the river Gard. Late 1st cent. B.C. or early 1st cent. A.D.

PLATE XII

2. THE PONT DU GARD

PLATE XII

I. TRANSPORT OF WINE BY RIVER

1. One of the sculptures on a funeral monument at Neumagen (restored). Found at Neumagen. A rowing barge loaded with four large wine-barrels and manned by six oarsmen and two steersmen, one of whom is marking the time by clapping his hands. The barge, according to the restoration, had its prow and stern adorned with a ram's and a wolf's head. Museum, Trèves.

2, 3. Fragments of bas-reliefs on the funeral monument of a rich merchant of Moguntiacum. Found at Mainz. Three workmen rolling barrels up a plank, which leads apparently to a ship. Four men unloading a ship: one has fallen down with his sack; two are ashore; the other is running down the plank. The ships are laden with wine and corn; and the owner of the monument was probably a large dealer in these products. Central-Museum, Mainz.

4. One of the bas-reliefs of the Column of Igel. Transport of large bundles on horseback over hilly country. Two horses are crossing a hill. At each end of the road is a large building. Igel near Trèves.

5. As No. 4. Two or more men (the relief is broken) are hauling a large and heavy ship loaded with two bales. A steersman is seated on the stern. Igel near Trèves.

PLATE XIII

2. LOADING WINE-BARRELS

3. UNLOADING A SHIP

4. CROSSING A HILL

5. HAULING A BARGE ALONG A RIVER

PLATE XIII

1. THE SHIP OF THE DESERT: THE CARAVAN-CAMEL

1. Bronze statuette of a camel. Found in Syria. A loaded camel stopping on its march across the desert, with its legs set stiff. A typical feature of the Syrian desert. Ashmolean Museum, Oxford. Reproduced by permission of the Trustees.

2. Bas-relief of a sarcophagus. Found at Sidon. The sarcophagus was found intact in one of the subterranean chambers of Sidon. The sides and one of the ends are adorned with garlands suspended from rings fastened in the mouths of lions' heads—a system of ornamentation typical of Syrian sarcophagi, which reproduces in stone the bronze handles and the actual garlands of wooden coffins. The other end is covered with an elaborate design in very low relief showing a sailing merchant-ship floating on the waves of the sea, which is full of fish and leaping dolphins. The ship figured on this monument shows no important points of difference from the ordinary merchant-ships of the Roman Empire in general. It symbolizes, no doubt, the last voyage of the deceased. Museum, Beirut.

PLATE XIV

2. A MERCHANT-SHIP OF SIDON

PLATE XIV

EGYPT. THE DELTA IN TIME OF FLOOD

1, 2. Two sections of the lower part of the mosaic of Palestrina.
Found at Palestrina (Praeneste). The mosaic reproduces the most characteristic features of Ptolemaic and Roman Egypt. The upper part of it
is a sort of zoological atlas of the Egyptian Sudan, with all the fabulous
and real animals of this region and their names in Greek. The lower part
(figs. 1, 2) gives the general aspect of Egypt, especially the Delta, in time
of flood. In the right-hand corner (fig. 2) a peasant's house is visible
with a dove-cote near it. The owner of the house runs out of the door
after his wife, who stands in the garden looking at a boat with soldiers
in it. In the other (left) corner of the mosaic (not reproduced in fig. 1)
are hippopotami and crocodiles. The centre of the lower part is occupied
by two buildings. One of them (fig. 2) is a fine pavilion with a large
curtain, behind which is seen a tower-villa with a large garden in an enclosure. In the pavilion a group of Roman soldiers is ready to celebrate a
festival: a large *crater* and a number of drinking-horns are set out for the
party. At the head of the group a laurel-crowned officer sounds the horn;
he is greeted by a woman with a palm-branch, who offers him a garland
or a diadem; and apparently he gives a signal to a company of soldiers
approaching in a military rowing-boat. (*liburnica*). Near the military
pavilion a party of civilians, including women, gathered under the shade
of a pergola covered with vines (fig. 1), are drinking to the strains of

1.

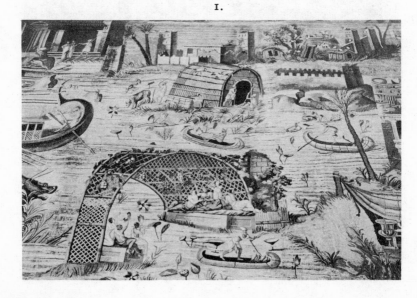

PLATE XV

music: a woman sings a hymn to the accompaniment of the lyre, seemingly in honour of the victorious general. Behind these buildings are two more bands of decoration. In the middle one is seen a small shrine (fig. 2) with a religious procession moving through it; in front, two men carry a stretcher with a sacred symbol on it, and behind are standard-bearers and a congregation of worshippers. A similar stretcher has been found in the ruins of a temple in the village of Theadelphia in the Fayum. Near the temple is a statue of Anubis (the jackal) on a base. Behind the pergola (fig. 1) we see a sacred enclosure and an osier-barn—a μοσχοτρόφεῖον where calves were reared for sacrifice. Before the entrance to the latter two men are talking, one of them with a large fork in his hand, while a third man drives two oxen or calves to the water; round the barn ibises are flying. The last band is filled with large temples. The largest, behind the small shrine (fig. 2), has two pylons and colossal Egyptian statues near the main entrance; in front of it a man riding a donkey, followed by his servant with his baggage. Behind the pergola and the barn (fig. 1) are three other temples: the first is a shrine of ibises ('Ιβιεῖον), the next a typical Egyptian shrine with two towers, and the third a Graeco-Egyptian temple. In the water are seen various animals, flowers, canoes of the natives (one loaded with lotuses), and two large pleasure and hunting boats with cabins (dahabiahs). The whole mosaic is the best and most realistic of the extant pictures which serve to convey a vivid idea of the aspect of Egypt in the Ptolemaic and Roman periods. Palace Barberini, Palestrina.

2.

PLATE XV

XX

SOCIAL AND ECONOMIC DEVELOPMENT OF THE EMPIRE IN THE FIRST TWO CENTURIES

THE Roman Empire of the first and second centuries was beyond all question a brilliant spectacle. It included in one mighty state all that was civilized in the countries fringing the Mediterranean. Nothing was outside it except the savage tribes of Germans, Slavs, and Finns, the nomads of the desert and the negroes of central Africa, and the great Iranian and Mongol population of Asia. Even with these the empire kept up regular and constantly improving relations by commerce and diplomacy, though this connexion was interrupted from time to time by military operations against frontier tribes. Within the empire no pains were spared to secure constant and unhampered communication between its different parts. The population, except the Eastern serfs bound to the soil, could move at will from place to place.

The state did its utmost to make communication safe and easy. The Mediterranean was a Roman lake : from end to end of it, as also on the Black Sea, the great rivers of Western Europe, and the Nile, ships conveyed passengers and goods ; and piracy was kept down by fleets at sea and flotillas on the rivers. Communication by sea with India was fairly safe from Egyptian and Arabian ports, and the voyage along the north coast of Europe as far as the Baltic was practicable ; but in such enterprises the trader had to rely upon his own resources entirely.

Along the high roads which spread out like a fan from Rome and Italy it was easy to travel to the Atlantic, or the North Sea, or the Dardanelles and the Black Sea coast. A similar network of roads covered Asia Minor, Syria, north Africa, and Britain ; and every place resembling a town was linked up with these by branches. Each town kept up the roads connecting it with the main settlements within its territory. The general safety was secured by the armed forces controlled by the representatives of the central power at home and abroad. The self-governing communities and the great landlords, each acting within the limits of their own possessions, organized the local police. The state maintained special detachments of police in Rome, Lyons, and Carthage ; and at Rome there was a brigade of firemen as well.

Municipal life throughout the empire was almost entirely free from the irksome control of the central power. The state was satisfied, provided that no clubs or societies of a seditious nature existed within its boundaries, and that the municipal bodies concerned themselves solely with local affairs. But indeed no community within the empire was ambitious to stray beyond that limited sphere. We hear nothing of any political organizations, either at Rome or within the municipalities abroad, which were regarded as dangerous to the state. The Christian communities alone were prosecuted ; but we do not know whether they suffered as unlicensed associations (*collegia illicita*), or whether the Christians individually were held to account for their refusal to take part in the cult of the emperor which all the empire practised. There were other societies, some professional and some religious. The latter included an infinite number of burial clubs (*collegia tenuiorum*, literally, ' associations of the poor '), whose object was to secure to their members a decent funeral. There were also many other clubs, in which the citizens of the town met according to their ages, and such bodies as philosophic schools, organized like close societies.

Each community lived in accordance with its past traditions, in so far as these traditions were not offensive to the state. In the Greek East, the birthplace of the municipal system, the constitutions or charters of the towns varied greatly both in terms and substance. The Roman government, though indifferent to the details of these charters, supported aristocratic institutions in the larger communities and looked with disfavour on democracy. Hence in most Greek cities the constitution was oligarchical. Alexandria, the capital of Egypt, was treated exceptionally : she had very meagre rights and was strictly controlled by the Roman governor. The cities in the West differed less from one another in their rights and privileges. A few Italian towns still retained their ancient charters based upon historic treaties with Rome.

Most communities of Roman citizens in Italy and the provinces possessed charters bestowed on them by the Roman government. In the provinces a regular colony received its rights from its founder, and other towns from the particular emperor who conferred on them the title of *municipium* or *colonia*. All these charters were drawn up on the same plan. They all provided for the creation of the usual municipal institutions—magistrates, a council of elders or of *decuriones* (local senators), and a popular assembly; they all defined the duties and rights of these bodies, and provided law courts. They contained rules for the election of magistrates and *decuriones*, rules for the proceedings in the council, and rules for the management of the popular assembly. In general they resembled copies of the Roman constitution, in the form which it had taken during the centuries that urban institutions had existed at Rome. Most Italian communities in course of time exchanged their ancient charters for such machine-made constitutions; and it is very probable that they were encouraged to do so by one of Caesar's laws, which prescribed that certain rules should be introduced into the charters of all communities formed of Roman citizens.

Both in the West and in the East the townspeople took a keen interest in their local affairs. Elections to the magistracy or priesthood or council were important events, and there was a lively competition for seats. We see this clearly from the election placards, of which a large number are still extant at Pompeii; these notices were not pasted up on the walls but painted in black or red on the plaster which covered the fronts of the houses. To be elected to the *Augustales*, a corporation consisting mainly of freedmen, was also an honour for which there was keen competition; the *Augustales* had to provide the funds for the worship of the emperor in the country towns. Magistrates and councils were full of local patriotism. In Asia Minor there was an unceasing struggle for primacy among the chief cities, and for the honourable titles of *neocori*, or 'keepers of the emperor's temple'. In return for honours and offices, for statues in the forum and election to the local priesthood, rich citizens were ready to spend large sums on the adornment of the town or on the needs and entertainment of the inhabitants. Most of the public buildings in Italian, Greek, and provincial towns were built out of the private subscriptions of well-to-do or wealthy individuals.

Life at Rome was more complicated. The immense population of the capital, reckoned at more than a million, had no political nor even municipal rights : it was absolutely controlled by the emperor with his ministers and by the Senate. On the other hand, the emperors did all that was possible to make life there convenient and agreeable. I have said already that Augustus made Rome the real capital of the world, and that his successors followed in his footsteps. The city became by degrees the most magnificent in the world, and the pleasantest to live in. Order was secured by the imperial police ; the emperor maintained seven regiments of firemen, who rendered aid also in case of inundations or earthquakes ; special officials attended to the aqueducts, the drainage, the flow of the Tiber, and the upkeep of public buildings, the open spaces, and streets. The public buildings were remarkable for their size, the beauty of their lines, and the elegance of their appointments. Nowhere were there such noble temples, or such richly adorned forums, with triumphal arches, commemorative columns, and a forest of statues; no city in the empire could show such immense theatres, amphitheatres, and circuses ; none had so many public libraries and museums, or such a gallery of statues as Augustus erected in his forum in honour of famous Roman commanders. Peculiar to Rome were the vast and luxurious *thermae*—public baths with athletic-grounds, which served also as clubs and restaurants ; and also the noble halls, called basilicas, which were used for law courts. No Hellenistic capital could rival the public parks, hygienic markets, and splendid shops of Rome. Apart from all this, the palace of the emperors rose on the Palatine, and their magnificent tombs on the banks of the Tiber. Life was easy and cheerful in this marvellous city. About 200,000 of the poorest class were maintained by the state, and the rest could find work in abundance, if they wanted it. Nor was there any lack of amusements, especially under such rulers as Nero, Domitian, and Commodus ; and occasional presents, either in money or in kind, were distributed among the people.

The towns in the provinces, in proportion to their means, kept pace with Rome. And I do not refer to the ancient capitals of the East—Alexandria, Antioch, Pergamum, Ephesus, Athens, Corinth ; nor to the later capitals of the West— Lyons, Carthage, Tarragona, which received from the emperors almost as much consideration and as much generosity as Rome herself. The smaller towns, even the new and unim-

1. TRAJAN'S ARMY FORAGING IN THE ENEMY'S LAND

1. One of the bas-reliefs on the Column of Trajan. In the background is the Roman camp, separated from the scene on the first plane by a range of mountains (the left part of the picture belongs to the preceding scene, where the soldiers are shown entering a recently built camp). The first plane is occupied by a rich cornfield; the wheat is ripe and the crop excellent; the Roman soldiers have crossed the mountains to reap the enemy's fields and transport the corn on mule-back to the camp. Without doubt they would treat their own provinces in the same way, if necessary, especially in time of civil war. 2nd cent. A.D. Forum Traiani, Rome.

2. One of the bas-reliefs of the Column of M. Aurelius. The train of M. Aurelius's army. Heavy carts drawn by oxen and horses and loaded with the impedimenta of the army are moving slowly under an escort of soldiers. The enormous number of draught animals required for the transport of the soldiers' baggage, war material, and foodstuffs may be easily imagined. Most of these animals were certainly requisitioned in the Roman provinces, the enemy's land contributing only a small proportion. 2nd cent. A.D. Piazza Colonna, Rome.

3. As fig. 2. Roman soldiers convoying the war booty consisting of herds of cows and goats and of women captives. The scene is typical and is frequently repeated on the column. Men do not appear among the captives; the booty consists wholly of cattle, women, and children.

PLATE XVI

3. THE BOOTY AND THE CAPTIVES OF WAR

2. THE TRAIN OF M. AURELIUS'S ARMY

PLATE XVI

portant colonies and *municipia* in Africa, Gaul, and Britain, were remarkable for careful planning, cleanliness, and good sanitation. The main streets were straight and wide, the side-streets straight and clean, and all were paved ; the houses were convenient, with drains and a water-supply, with enclosed gardens and conduits. There were large market-places, temples, basilicas, covered markets, buildings for the council and magistrates to meet in ; public latrines built of stone and abundantly supplied with water ; fine public baths with central heating; theatres, amphitheatres, circuses; libraries; hotels and inns. And all this could be found—more or less complete, more or less perfect—in almost every provincial town. The dead were cared for as well as the living. No age in the history of the world comes up to the Roman Empire in the number of beautiful and splendid monuments which it erected in memory of the dead. The roads leading to Pompeii give sufficient proof of this : what variety and what beauty is displayed there ! What then were the roads like that led to Rome ! And the same is true of the provinces. I might point, for example, to the mausoleum of the Julian family at St. Remy in Gaul, to the Igelsaüle near Trèves, or hundreds of other noble monuments still extant in Africa, Greece, Asia Minor, and Syria. Millions were spent upon the dead, tens and hundreds of millions on the comfort of the living. One may say without exaggeration that never in the history of mankind (except during the nineteenth and twentieth centuries in Europe and America) has a larger number of people enjoyed so much comfort ; and that never, not even in the nineteenth century, did men live in such a surrounding of beautiful buildings and monuments as in the first two centuries of the Roman Empire.

Thus, the empire was a world-wide state, consisting of a number of urban districts, each of which had for its centre a well-organized town or city. In these towns, and especially in the capital, lived that part of the population which directed the social and economic life of the empire. The chief place among these many millions was held by Italy with a population almost entirely made up of Roman citizens. But the citizen franchise was by no means restricted to Italy. The successors of Augustus grew more and more liberal, and admitted by degrees as citizens the upper class of every city in the empire. The army, which was still recruited, if not in

Italy, at least in the Romanized or Hellenized parts of the empire, still represented civilization; and through the ranks many persons of middling or inferior station passed into the class of citizens. So the process went on, by which the body of citizens grew larger and larger, till it included most of the upper and middle classes of the urban population in Italy and the provinces.

Together with this extension there was a radical change in the composition of this body, when compared with the republican age or the reign of Augustus. Above all, the old senatorial nobility had disappeared by the end of the first century, partly in consequence of merciless persecution by the emperors, and partly from natural causes : if they married at all, their marriages were generally childless. Their place was filled by a new imperial nobility, natives either of Italian cities or of the provinces. This change is clearly shown in the case of the emperors themselves : the Julii and Claudii belong to the old patrician aristocracy, the Flavii come from a municipal Italian stock, and most of the Antonines belong to the upper class of the Romanized provinces. The new aristocracy was not much more long-lived than its predecessors : after two or three generations families died out and gave place to others of similar origin. The same indifference to the continuation of the name still led to the same result ; and any family which survived for more than two generations was artificially kept alive by the system of adoption.

In the country towns, especially in the upper middle class which aimed at equestrian rank, the same thing is observable —the rapid extinction of families. The equestrian class grows in numbers but is recruited chiefly from without. Here, too, adoption is common, and the adopted son is often a freedman, a former slave of the family. The only class which adds to its numbers is the proletariate in town and country. Of this we have no direct evidence; but it may be inferred from the increasing population of the empire as a whole, which in turn is proved by the steady growth of the cities and increasing area of cultivation in almost all the provinces. It is a marked feature in all the higher classes of the population, that they are unwilling to continue their kind and found a family. Apparently their motive was to secure full enjoyment of their wealth for themselves personally ; and they were not willing to hamper their freedom with the cares of a family. Men struggled for wealth in order to secure for themselves a life of peace and comfort, and in order to rise in the social scale. They cared little what became of their riches : they bequeathed them to the emperor, or to their native city, or to some social or religious institution, or to friends and relations, or to flatterers and freedmen.

The senators were still the richest class of the population. But we find in them no desire to increase their wealth by systematic cultivation of their estates. The rich man's object is to receive a safe and steady income with as little personal exertion as possible. Hence money was invested mainly in land. Estates were managed by slaves and freedmen, and were worked by tenants on short or long leases, the latter being preferred. More life and energy was shown by the class of knights and the middle class in the country towns, especially the lower section of it : the higher section, here too, was apt to rest content with what they had got, and preferred spending to acquisition. A stagnation is perceptible throughout the empire, a paralysis even of the desire for gain. Meanwhile, the composition of the highest classes was constantly changing : men of a lower and less refined type replaced the representatives of traditional culture, and then died out themselves before they had time to appropriate entirely the tastes and interests of their predecessors.

How the lower class of the population lived it is difficult to say. In the towns they enjoyed the same advantages of comfort and good order as the rich. At Pompeii or Timgad in Africa there are no houses which one would not care to live in. Things were probably worse in the poor quarters of the capital cities ; but their inhabitants could enjoy the splendid squares, gardens, basilicas, and baths. Slaves were, of course, less well off than the free population ; but even they, under the empire, attracted more and more the attention and benevolence of the legislator. Of life in the country we unfortunately know nothing. But perhaps this very dumbness is significant. If we hear no paeans of joy, we hear also no complaints. In the troublesome times that followed at the end of the second century and the beginning of the third, the country finds a voice and uses it to complain of its hardships to the emperor. Its silence in the first two centuries is a proof that things were not too bad.

During those centuries the empire was unquestionably rich

and, in comparison with other periods, prosperous. What was the source of this wealth ? What were the forms assumed by its economic life ? These questions are of great importance: in the answer to them lies the explanation of that startling phenomenon in the history of the Roman Empire— the rapid destruction, described in the next chapter, of its prosperity. The material resources of the state were, beyond doubt, immense. She included the richest parts of Europe, Africa, and Asia, on which the prosperity of modern Europe is based. Besides, she developed the resources of Asia and north Africa more thoroughly than is done at present. She commanded fertile districts for cultivation, extensive pastures for stock-raising on the largest scale, virgin forests, mines and quarries almost unworked, rivers and seas abounding with fish. We must admit in fairness that the Romans found out these resources and did their best to make use of them.

Their prosperity was based on agriculture and stock-raising. It is certain that the empire greatly extended the area of cultivation. In modern Africa, for instance, in Algeria and Tunis, immense districts, which were never reached by Carthaginian civilization and contain no traces of Carthaginian cities or farms, and where now, in spite of French colonizing activity, only scanty flocks of sheep and goats wander over the parched plains, were densely populated and thoroughly tilled in the first two centuries, especially in the second. This is abundantly clear from the ruins, which the traveller meets at almost every step, of prosperous towns and productive farms. The origin of that prosperity is revealed by the remains of imposing Roman buildings, intended to make a systematic use of the rain which falls here in abundance during the winter months.

It is certain that Gaul, Britain, and Spain began under the empire to produce for the first time vast quantities of grain for export, after satisfying the local requirements. In the East the area of cultivation did not at least grow smaller, except perhaps in Greece for a reason which will be explained later. The prosperity of the Western provinces is attested by the ruins of many flourishing towns, whose inhabitants were fed by the country and which did not exist before this period. Even stronger evidence is supplied by the ruins of those large and small farms, which have of late years attracted increasing attention from archaeologists. It is surely significant that the soil of Britain is covered, in its level parts, with the ruins of large or small 'villas', which were either farms or the central points of large estates. The same is true of France and Belgium and the Rhine country; on the upper Rhine the *decumates agri*, which were included in the province of Upper Germany between the reigns of Domitian and Commodus, were covered with a network of substantial farms. In Egypt the extension of the arable area is proved by documents found there, and by our knowledge of large irrigation schemes undertaken by Augustus.

It is certain that stock-raising also was vigorously developed, and special attention was paid to the cultivation of vines and olive-trees. For this purpose the empire made use of every suitable district within its boundaries. Modern times can boast of few fresh conquests of this kind. Wine, indeed, is now made in Germany; but on the other hand, the southern part of Tunis, which in ancient times was almost completely covered with olive-trees, is now a bare plain. This acclimatization of valuable products is highly characteristic of the empire, and worked remarkable changes in the aspect of the ancient world. The time was past when Greece, and then Italy, supplied the whole world with wine and oil. Under the empire nearly all the provinces grew enough of both commodities to satisfy their own requirements, and even sought to export the excess. This was certainly a serious blow to the agricultural prosperity of Greece and Italy. Having nothing to export in return for the imported grain, they were forced to revert to a more primitive type of agriculture, and once more to grow corn for their own needs.

In spite of the increase in arable area, and the acclimatization of the vine and olive in Western Europe, there was no improvement, but rather a falling off, in agricultural skill. Columella, who wrote a handbook on farming in the first century, complains bitterly of the decay of scientific agriculture in Italy; and we may be sure that the same was true of the Eastern and Western provinces.

The cause of this regression was an extensive development of small farming, which went on together with the growth of great estates. Slave labour applied to the land was no longer of primary importance, even in the East and in Italy. Slaves became dear and free labour cheap, owing to the increasing numbers of the proletariate. The great landlords were glad to give up the plantation system and let their land to small-holders. The emperors were the first to begin this system on their estates. The East followed suit : the owners of large and middling estates lived in towns and had their land culti-vated by smallholders who were in many cases bound to the soil they tilled. These conditions were unfavourable to pro-gressive and scientific cultivation. In spite of more land and more workers on the land, the quality of the work steadily deteriorated.

The same fact is observable in a different department—in the exploitation of natural wealth of other kinds. The number of mines and quarries in working increased. The knowledge of their mineral wealth was probably the main reason why some new territories were annexed to the empire. We may suppose that this motive, among others, induced Claudius to conquer Britain, and Domitian to annex part of south-west Germany ; and at all events the chief attraction of Dacia was its auriferous sand and wealth in other minerals. Here again, beyond question, the sources of the empire's wealth were added to. But the skill of the workers did not keep up with the development of mines. In mining and metallurgy the Romans did not improve upon the methods of the Hellenistic Age, but even lost ground. The treasury, in other words, the emperor, had worked the mines through substantial contractors employing slaves in great numbers ; but now a different method was tried : the work was parcelled out among petty adventurers who had to rely on their own efforts and the help of a few slaves. Under such conditions technical improvements were of course impossible.

Symptoms of this kind are visible in manufacture as well as in agriculture and mining. Districts which had formerly depended upon imports from the large manufacturing centres now began to take a share in production. Hence, the large centres lost their economic position and grew impoverished. The worst plight of all was that of Greece, whose manufactures disappeared almost entirely from the world's market. A few kinds, indeed, of manufactured articles, some of which cannot be called luxuries, were still produced by special districts and exported thence to the ends of the earth, the vast extent of the Roman Empire being a great furtherance to exporta-tion. Some fabrics were still a speciality exported all over the world by Asia Minor, Italy, and Gaul ; the copper vessels of Campania still competed successfully against foreign imitations ; and Egypt was supreme in the market for linen stuffs and paper. But these special goods, produced for the sake of export only, became more and more exceptional. They were driven out of the provincial markets by similar wares, sometimes not inferior in quality, produced by the local workshops. Thus, for example, the manufacture of earthenware vessels and lamps and of glass was no longer limited to one centre. The first of these products has a history of special interest. Beginning in Greece and Asia Minor the industry passed to Italy : in the second and first centuries B. C. the figured earthenware of north Italy has no rival in the world. In the first century A. D. southern Gaul begins to compete ; in the second half of the century the manufacture moves farther north, and reaches the Rhine in the second century. These vessels now conquer not only the northern and north-eastern markets but Italy as well ; and simultaneously Asia Minor is producing the same article after the same patterns for the southern and south-eastern markets. In the second century A. D. all the provinces, both East and West, are turning out in immense numbers the earthenware lamps which had once been almost a monopoly of the workshops in north Italy. Nothing now, except articles of luxury accessible to few, finds a distant market ; and indeed local imitations of the products from great centres of industry crop up everywhere. For instance, the famous purple fabrics of Tyre were imitated in Asia Minor. Thus, in manufacture also production became more and more diffused.

But at the same time the quality grows inferior: there is less both of mechanical skill and beauty. Technique becomes monotonous and somewhat old-fashioned. In jewellery, for instance, it is enough to compare the charming ear-rings and brooches of the Hellenistic Age with the coarse Roman imitations, and the same may be said of the pottery. It is important also to note this : ruins and tombs have yielded up objects of Roman production by the hundred thousand, and these warrant the assertion that practically no new discovery was made in technique : on the contrary, many earlier discoveries fell into disuse. In point of artistic beauty every one knows that the products of the empire are immeasurably inferior to those of the Eastern monarchies, or Greece, or the Hellenistic Age.

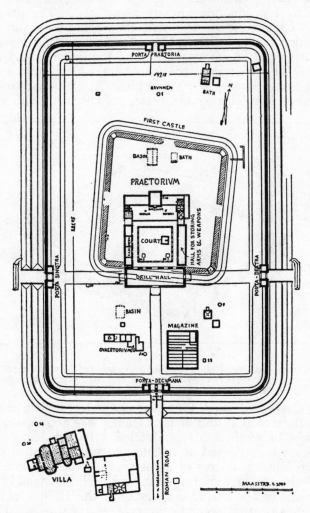

TEXT-FIG. 2.

Plan of the Roman frontier-camp at Saalburg (near Homburg). The earlier camp was surrounded by earthen walls and was later replaced by a well-built camp fortified by stone walls and with comfortable stone buildings inside it. The centre of this camp was occupied by the praetorium which contained a central court, a sanctuary, a drill-hall, and a hall for keeping the arms and weapons. Outside the camp was situated a large villa with an extensive bath. After 'Germania Romana'.

We must seek for the cause of this degeneration in the diffusion of production already mentioned. The provinces had started production to satisfy their own needs, and mass-production at low prices. Thus, the finer and dearer article was driven out of the markets; and the factories and workshops of the purely industrial countries, which found a ready sale in earlier times, now stood idle. At the same time the gradual decline, already mentioned, of culture in the middle

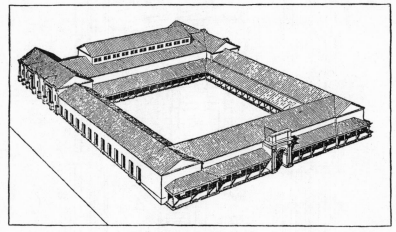

TEXT-FIG. 3.

Restoration of the praetorium of the legionary camp of Vetera (Xanten). It has the same plan as the praetorium of Saalburg. Before the front is a portico. Another portico surrounds the court. After ' Germania Romana '.

classes created a demand for a coarser and less artistic product. This failure of skill and artistic feeling was accompanied by a change in methods of production. The system of large factories, which started at Athens and was developed in the chief Hellenistic centres of industry, had reached some cities in Italy by the first century B. C., but declined steadily after the middle of the second century. In the Italian and provincial towns of the second century A. D., the work was chiefly done by workmen in a small way and in small workshops. A rich manufacturer was a man who owned a number of such establishments; and the hands employed were mainly slaves.

Under the empire, especially during the first two centuries, there was a remarkable development of trade, wholesale and retail, both by land and sea. Regular commercial relations were kept up with the most distant markets—China, India, central and southern Africa, Arabia, central Asia, central and southern Russia, Germany, and even Sweden and Norway. These countries imported manufactured articles in exchange for articles of luxury ; or, more precisely, they supplied the raw material to be worked up in the shops of the Graeco-Roman world, especially in the East. Africa sent gold, ivory, and precious woods ; Arabia sent spices ; pearls and precious stones came from India, silk from China, furs from central Asia and Russia, amber from Germany and Scandinavia.

This foreign trade, however, was not really important for the economic development of the empire. The trade carried on within the empire itself, within the different provinces and between them, was of much greater importance. It grew steadily ; the class of traders grew larger ; and the Semites—Syrians, Jews, and Arameans—became more prominent members of it. Transport between provinces was easy—over the Mediterranean and then along the rivers and highways to the remotest corners. At the end of the third century the Emperor Diocletian published a tariff or list of fixed prices for goods ; it was intended for the Eastern provinces, but it includes, together with the manufactures and products of the East, a great number of articles produced by the West, especially by Gaul. Trade was helped also by the moderate amount, varying from 2 to $2\frac{1}{2}$ per cent., of the customs levied at the frontier of each province. This was a great improvement upon the time when each Greek city or petty Hellenistic kingdom extorted duties from every merchant that entered its territory.

It is certain, however, that the same symptoms which we have already noticed in agriculture and industry were present also in trade. As the provinces became more self-sufficient their need of importation decreased, and the market of every town and village was stocked with local products. In the towns most of the workshops were also shops, and most of the eatables on sale were produced within the territory belonging to the town. This state of things was less pronounced wherever traffic was carried on by river, as in Gaul and Britain, on the Rhine and the Danube with its tributaries, and in Egypt ; but more pronounced in Italy, Africa, and Asia Minor, where this cheap means of communication does not exist.

The expense and delay of transport by road isolated the markets and made them aim at being self-supporting. The same causes hindered the development of large capitalistic enterprises in the sphere of local trade, except for wares carried by sea, or caravan, or rivers. It is an interesting fact that the Emperor Hadrian, who favoured smallholders in agriculture and petty contractors in the mines, tried to put down the middleman in trade, and to connect the purchaser directly with the producer. In spite of this, capitalistic methods were more successful in trade than in any other department of economic activity during the empire. The merchants, together with the great landowners, were the richest men of the time. They formed important trading companies and associations. The merchants interested in shipping, called *naucleri* or *navicularii*, combined in companies of this kind, and became one of the most powerful economic alliances in the empire.

It appears, therefore, that the empire accomplished a great deal in the sphere of economics. Fresh sources of wealth were discovered. Countries which had previously been content with the most primitive commercial arrangements now became accessible to systematic exploitation. Exchange was facilitated by a better system of roads and protection from pirates at sea. The imposts were not burdensome. In the relation between capital and labour the empire, that is, the government of the empire, remained passive and left the problem to settle itself. Its interposition was rare and governed by no system : at one time it favoured capital and great fortunes, at another it took measures to protect the small proprietor and the working man. The emperors of the second century interfered more than others. I have mentioned already Hadrian's defence of smallholders and tenants. It is right to notice the legislation of all these emperors in order to raise the legal and social level of slaves. It must be remembered, however, that the labour question, as we understand it, was unknown to the ancient world. The existence of slavery and the application of slave labour to industry made it impossible for free labourers to combine and fight the employers. Not only so, but the government frowned on any associations for other than religious purposes and would certainly have suppressed them.

Nevertheless, together with a forward movement we have

been forced to notice many disquieting symptoms—the increasing size of landed properties ; the change from scientific farming to more primitive methods practised by small tenants on short or long leases ; the decline of intensive agriculture in Greece and Italy, and of science applied to agriculture—Columella, mentioned above, is the last original writer who treats the subject ; the deterioration of manufactured objects in technical skill and beauty ; and the development of small workshops at the expense of large factories and works.

XXI

THE ORDEAL OF THE ROMAN EMPIRE IN THE THIRD CENTURY A. D.

THE reign of the Emperor Commodus, the son of Marcus Aurelius, ends the period of enlightened despotism and also begins a new period of bloodshed and misery, in which the main feature is the power possessed by the army to settle at will the destiny of the state. The army, once the servant of the empire, became its master, and acted through rulers whom it raised up and pulled down according to its own caprice and for no obvious reasons.

Commodus reigned from A. D. 180 to 192. A second Nero or Domitian, he recalls the worst rulers of the Julian and Claudian dynasties. Entirely absorbed in himself, he spent his life in continuous debauchery, and in gratifying his morbid passion for the gladiator's art. Administration and military affairs were neglected ; he relied entirely upon the praetorian guards, and was hardly at all in touch with the provincial armies. The natural consequence followed : just as under Domitian, a strong opposition arose and took the same line of action. It was the immediate result of a peace concluded by Commodus with the Germans, which was considered by the higher classes of the empire treasonable and shameful. The emperor replied by violent measures : senators were put to death and their property confiscated. This violence led eventually to a palace plot which cost the emperor his life.

As in A. D. 69, the ' year of the four emperors ', the success of the plot led to civil war. The provincial armies took advantage of the death of Commodus to raise their favourites to the throne. The Senate elected M. Helvius Pertinax to the vacant place, hoping that he would restore the tradition of the Antonines. But Pertinax was soon put to death by the praetorians, who had been utterly ruined by the indulgence of Commodus. They then sold the succession to Didius Julianus, a wealthy senator. The provincial armies refused to accept the dictation of the praetorians ; and Lucius Septimius Severus, the commander of the Pannonian armies on the Danube, found it easy, on the pretext of avenging Pertinax, to march upon Rome with his Illyrians and Thracians; he had got the start of his two possible rivals—Clodius Albinus and Pescennius Niger who commanded powerful armies in Britain and Syria. Severus easily defeated the praetorians and took Rome almost without fighting. He cashiered all the praetorians and chose the best men of his own army to fill their places; most of them were Illyrian and Thracian tillers of the soil. He found more difficulty in dealing with his powerful rivals in the north and in the east. But he proved too strong for both of them : Albinus he deceived by promising to make him his heir, and he took advantage of mistakes made by Pescennius in leading his army. Then he settled accounts with all who were not on his side at Rome or in Italy and the provinces by putting them to death and confiscating their property. Thus he became the undisputed ruler of the empire.

Septimius Severus had no intention of restoring the traditions of the Augustan Age. Officially he called himself the son of Marcus Aurelius and brother of Commodus, an Antonine and the successor of a line of Antonines ; but his actual policy was quite different from theirs. His political views are expressed in the last dying words which he addressed to his sons and successors, Caracalla and Geta : ' Be of one mind : enrich the soldiers : trouble about nothing else.' His power was based entirely upon the devotion of the soldiers to his person, and therefore his whole attention was given to the army. He distrusted the Roman aristocracy and kept them at a distance by means of his semi-barbaric guards, and the ' Parthian legion ' which he raised and quartered at Albanum near the capital. He attempted no radical alteration in the system of government, probably thinking it unnecessary; but by his actions he laid down the lines of future development by which the senatorial class was ousted from military commands and provincial governorships, and was replaced by officers of the army. In general, however, he was a conscientious ruler of the state ; and in his dealings with the provinces, after he had defeated his two rivals, he was faithful to the traditions set by the Antonines.

The effects of his policy were visible during his reign and still more after his death. Even in his hands the army was by no means an obedient instrument. The soldiers were losing more and more the taste for war, and took little interest in their business, so that, in spite of his own military capacity, he was unable either to inflict decisive blows upon the Parthians, or to complete the subjection of Britain, where he died in 211 in the middle of a prolonged contest against the highlanders of Scotland. His heir Caracalla at once made away with the brother who shared his throne, but lost his own life as soon as he tried to use his army for a fresh contest with the Parthians on the south-east frontier. The year of his death was 216. The army then proclaimed Macrinus, commander of the guards, as his successor, but betrayed him also, when they found that he intended not only to cut short military operations but also to lower their pay. The ladies of the palace were Syrians, related to Julia Domna, the wife of Septimius Severus, and belonging to the family of the priest kings of Emesa. These cunning and ambitious women took advantage of the discontent among the soldiers. Julia Maesa, sister of Julia Domna, with her daughters Soaemias and Mammaea, won over a part of the Syrian army and by their aid defeated Macrinus. They then raised to the throne the son of Soaemias, whose name before his accession was Varius Avitus Bassianus. But he was the chief priest of the sun-god worshipped at Emesa under the name of Elagabal, and in this capacity bore also the name of his god.

The reign of the Syrian relatives of Severus began one of the saddest chapters in the history of the empire. Elagabal, or Heliogabalus, as the Romans called him, was a religious fanatic who introduced into Rome the manners and customs of his Syrian theocracy. Many of his soldiers were themselves devoted to Eastern cults, and their religious beliefs were not outraged by his proceedings ; but at Rome, even in the depressed and humiliated condition of the upper and middle classes, his innovations met with nothing but disgust and horror. Conscious of this feeling, the Syrian princesses took measures to retain their power, and, when the fanatic Heliogabalus was murdered by the soldiers, they placed on the throne Alexianus, the son of Mammaea, who was more moderate in his views and less Asiatic in his habits ; as emperor he took the name of Marcus Aurelius Severus Alexander. He and his mother endeavoured to reconcile the Roman nobility to their military rule. Some of the ancient forms of public life were restored ; and the Senate was summoned to take part again in public affairs. But the army was more than Alexander could manage.

He did with difficulty repel the danger in the East, when the Sassanian dynasty of Persian kings, fresh from the conquest of the Parthian dynasty of the Arsacidae, invaded the Roman provinces ; but a campaign against the Germans on the Rhine frontier cost the emperor his life : he was killed by his own soldiers in the year 235.

The death of Alexander was followed by a complete collapse. The empire became the chattel of the soldiers. The different armies, one after another, proclaimed their commanders as emperors, deposed them again on the most trifling complaint of their severity or weakness, and used their own strength to plunder without mercy the peaceful and prosperous provinces of the empire. Between A. D. 235 and 285 there were twenty-six Roman emperors ; and only one of them died a natural death. Most of them were men who had a sincere desire for the welfare of the state, good soldiers and good generals, who endeavoured to protect the empire and defend it from foreign enemies ; but their way was always barred by a mutinous rabble of an army ; and they were forced to neglect the safety and integrity of the empire in order to defend themselves against rivals whom the soldiers compelled, often by violent means, to compete for the throne.

Such an internal condition was not likely to make the state victorious over foreign enemies. The frontier was invaded at almost every point. Strong alliances of German tribes were formed, with a plan of seizing the Roman provinces in Europe : the Saxons plundered the coasts of Britain and Gaul ; Gaul was threatened in the north by the Franks, in the centre and south by the Alemanni; the Marcomanni alarmed the provinces on the Danube. A powerful kingdom of Goths and Sarmatians, which had grown up in south Russia, was advancing towards the lower waters of the Danube, and making descents by sea from Panticapaeum upon the Eastern provinces. And lastly, the Sassanian dynasty of Persia, which in the reign of Alexander Severus had taken the place of the decrepit and decomposing Parthian kingdom, was constantly becoming a more formidable foe to the crippled energies of Rome. The lowest depth was touched by the empire under Valerian and his son Gallienus, who reigned from 253 to 268. Valerian was defeated and taken prisoner by the Persians. Under Gallienus the instinct of self-preservation drove the province of Gaul and the rich commercial city of Palmyra in Syria to take the task of defence into their own hands and organize their territories as independent kingdoms. In the year 258 Marcus Cassius Latinius Postumus was ruler of Gaul; at Palmyra, Odenathus fought in defence of the East against the Persians, and his example was followed later by his widow, Zenobia.

The more grievous the condition of the empire, the fiercer grew the pressure of the barbarians upon its frontiers. But at the same time a feeling gathered strength among the people that they must, by some means or other, defend the civilization of the Roman Empire, save its cities from destruction and desolation, and restore the unity of the Roman State. Even the soldiers were stirred by this feeling : they began to show more stubbornness in the struggle against barbarism, and more willingness to submit to the discipline enforced by the emperors whom they themselves had elected. This imperial temper was exemplified by a succession of strong and able emperors in the second half of the third century. It is true that most of them died by violence, and that they were forced constantly to struggle against mutiny at home ; but these difficulties did not deter them. If an emperor was murdered his successor showed, in dealing with the armies, the same firmness which had cost his predecessor his life at their hands : he demanded discipline and blind obedience to his commands in the same uncompromising spirit. The emperors themselves set an example of self-sacrifice—an example which was the more effectual, because most of them had begun their career as common soldiers.

The first of this line of rulers was Claudius, surnamed Gothicus. He reigned from 268 to 270, and inflicted a decisive defeat upon the Goths, by which he arrested for a time their pressure upon the Danube frontier and the Eastern provinces. His successor, Aurelian, reigned five years. He not only defended the Danube provinces and Italy against the Germans but also restored the unity of the empire by means of an army which he welded into one for a time by a discipline of iron : in his reign Gaul and Syria again became parts of the state. His successors—Probus (276–282), Carus, and his son Carinus —fought with success upon the frontiers. After the death of Carus, murdered like Probus by his own soldiers, the army proclaimed Gaius Valerius Aurelius Diocletianus emperor in

284. After a short struggle against Carinus, Diocletian became the undisputed ruler of the empire, and the harassed and exhausted state had rest for a time from internal conflict.

The causes of this terrible crisis through which the empire passed must be sought, partly in the social and economic conditions which grew up in the latter half of the second century, and partly in the organization and feelings of the army. We have seen that economic development took the line of increasing the resources of the empire rather than of making systematic use of them ; that the people were gradually losing their capacity for work and ingenuity in invention ; and that routine became more and more powerful in the sphere of creative production. The real and living interest of the people was not fixed upon social or economic matters but upon questions concerning the inner life of man, and especially questions of religion. This subject is dealt with in a later chapter.

On the other hand, side by side with the higher classes of the community and the active development of urban life, another class, living in the villages and the country, was becoming more conscious of itself : as it gradually rose in civilization, it realized more clearly its own numbers and importance and also the inferiority of its social position. The emperors of the first two centuries did much to develop the self-consciousness of this class, by their treatment of the serfs who peopled by the hundred thousand the imperial estates in the East, and of their multitude of free tenants in the West. The legislation of the early empire endeavours to define precisely the relation of such tenants to landowners on lands belonging to individuals or to the crown ; it defends their interests, when they collide with those of the great landlords ; it supports the class of smallholders as a counterpoise to the rich middle class. In consequence of this imperial policy, the country ceased to be silent and submissive : conscious of imperial support, it found a voice to defend its rights against the pressure of capitalists and the misdeeds of officials.

Another radical change took place at this time in the composition of the army. We have seen that, under Augustus, the army consisted mainly of Italian natives and Roman citizens resident in the provinces. From these two classes the legions were recruited. And though provincials who did not possess the franchise found it less and less difficult to

I. A RICH PALMYRENE LADY

1. Grave *stele*, with a beautiful sculptured and painted portrait of a rich Palmyrene lady, Aththaia, wife of Malchus. Similar portraits are found in masses in the extensive and well-preserved ruins of the rich centre of caravan-trade with the East which was the city of Palmyra. Note the rich jewels of the lady. One of these ladies was Zenobia, the Queen of Palmyra and the rival of the Roman emperor Aurelian. 2nd cent. A.D. Museum of Fine Arts, Boston. Reproduced through the courtesy of the Museum.

PLATE XVII

2. A SASSANIAN KING HUNTING

2. Silver dish, found in Russia, with the figure of a Sassanian king hunting various wild animals. Note the rich horse-trappings and the beautiful helmet and armour of the king adorned with pearls and gems. Note also the excellent rendering of the animals which recalls the most beautiful bas-reliefs of the Assyrian kings. The same pathos is expressed in the figures of dying animals. The king is either Perose (A.D. 459–86) or Khusrau II (A.D. 590–628). The conservative character of Sassanian art vouchsafes, in spite of the late date of our dish, that the scene of the dish may as well illustrate the life and art of the earlier Sassanian period, that of the 3rd and 4th cent. A.D. 5th–6th cent. A.D. Cabinet des Médailles, Paris.

PLATE XVII

gain admission to the ranks, yet most of the legionaries came from the most highly civilized provinces, and the army still represented the most enlightened inhabitants of the empire. Even Hadrian, however, found it impossible to maintain this system any longer. His army was recruited in those provinces where its permanent camps were situated. The urban population shirked the obligation of military service; and hence the army—both the legions and the auxiliary detachments—was filled up by agricultural labourers from the provinces, men who had worked on urban or non-urban territories. At the same time the soldiers' trade became hereditary. The men lived in camps or adjacent settlements; and the children habitually chose their father's profession. In the troublesome times of the later Antonines Rome needed a constant supply of recruits to defend her from the barbarians. Thousands fell in battle, and still more were carried off by pestilence. And further, the civilized classes grew less and less accustomed to military service and sent inferior men to the ranks. Hence the emperors preferred to employ a more primitive section of the population—field labourers and herdsmen from the outskirts of the empire, Thracians, Illyrians, Spanish mountaineers, Moors, men from the north of Gaul, mountaineers from Asia Minor and Syria. And so the army came to represent the less civilized part of the population, the men who lived outside the cities, envying the luxury of the citizen and regarding him merely as an oppressor and exploiter.

The economic prosperity of the state was also affected by the disasters which filled the reigns of the later Antonines. I have said already that the system of taxation was not specially burdensome, even for the provincials. But the expenses of the state were rising: there were more soldiers, and they received higher pay; and the army of officials was growing also. The state had no resource except to increase the taxes. Then the dwellers in towns had grown familiar with comfort and luxury; but their increasing demands could not be met by private generosity, and it was therefore necessary to increase the rates. Both the central government and the towns drew their revenue mainly from dues paid by tillers of the land and breeders of stock, and the higher taxation was not accompanied by any improved methods of agriculture. Therefore the burden fell more and more heavily on owners of land, or, eventually, on those who tilled the soil with their own hands—the smallholders and the tenants on great estates. The country suffered more than the towns from the rise of taxation.

During the wretched period of revolution in the third century all the symptoms mentioned above ripened at a terrible rate. The army and its leaders became the masters of the empire. Conscious of their own strength, the soldiers sought to use it to the utmost. From the puppets whom they had placed on the throne they expected higher pay, large donatives, and leave to pillage with impunity their fellow citizens and especially the wealthy cities, towards which soldiers drawn from the country felt both envy and hatred. The army aimed also at the abolition of the privileges enjoyed by the higher classes ; they demanded that every soldier should have free access to the highest posts, both military and civil. In this point the soldiers were at one with some of their own leaders, who from the time of Septimius Severus grew more and more suspicious of the privileged classes. So by degrees the officers, the last representatives of a higher culture, disappeared from the army : they became indistinguishable from the rank and file, and as rough and coarse as their men. These officers, when they had served their time, were often given civil posts ; and so the highest officials grew barbarized by degrees, and adopted in their administrative action those violent and arbitrary methods which had become rooted in the dealings of the army with the civil population.

The emperors nominated by the army needed money more than anything for success in the political conflict. The only means of getting money was to increase taxation, especially the taxation of landowners. In the constant wars and movements of troops, provisions, arms, and means of transport were indispensable. If there was no money, these things must be taken by force from the people. Thus taxation rose steadily in the third century ; and also extraordinary requisitions for the needs of the army became a regular custom. The demands of the emperors and their troops were not submitted directly to the taxpayer, but to those bodies which had always collected the taxes and were responsible to the state for their payment in full. The same bodies were responsible also for the receipt in full of dues levied in kind by the state in addition to the taxes ; and when forced labour was required, it was their duty to see that it was forthcoming.

The bodies before whom the imperial officials laid their demands were the town councils and their executive officers; in other cases they were guilds of merchants, or shipowners, or artisans. The town councils assessed the tax upon the population of their territory, and their own property was security for payment in full. The guilds were jointly responsible for furnishing such articles of manufacture as the army required, and also for the means of transport. In peace time the burden of these obligations was not grievous to the town councils and municipal magistrates. But as early as the end of the second century, as the demands of the state increased, the taxable capacity of the population grew less and arrears began to mount up. At the same time the supplementary requirements of the state, which were exacted by the same bodies as the taxes, pressed harder and harder upon the people. The position became critical in the third century: the state raised its demands to an excessive height; trade was strangled by constant war and barbarian invasion; industry had dropped its tools; and the armies of the competitors for the throne pillaged every town and village on their line of march. But the emperors and the army needed money, grain, hides, metal, and beasts of burden, and continued to requisition them from the towns. The towns passed the burden on to the country, where it fell chiefly on tenants of land and smallholders; and the enmity between town and country was not lessened by such transactions.

To crown all these calamities, the emperors in their need for money issued a vast quantity of coin. Not possessing enough of the precious metals for these issues, they alloyed the gold with silver, the silver with copper, and the copper with lead, thus debasing the coinage and ruining in the end men who had once been rich. This measure cut at the root of trade and industry. The government mint in the third century became a vast manufactory of base coin. The government, while using this base coin to satisfy its creditors, often refused to take it from the taxpayer.

It is no wonder that a social and economic crisis of extreme severity was brought about by these conditions. The civil population sought an escape from their troubles by supporting one or other of the aspirants to the throne, who, as they hoped, would put an end to confusion and establish order on a firm basis. But the army, greedy of money and plunder, pulled down one emperor after another and made the disease still worse. It must be remembered that the army now consisted mainly of smallholders and crofters; and this class, which suffered more than any other from the financial crisis, attributed their misfortunes to the officials and the aristocracy of the towns, and saw no hope of deliverance except in the power of the emperor. Disappointed in one emperor, they proclaimed another; but their belief in the goodwill and omniscience of the ruler never grew faint. This comes out clearly in some petitions presented by soldiers from their native villages—petitions in which the country people complain of the oppression exercised by town magistrates, officials, and army officers, and expect redress from no quarter except from the sacred person of the emperor.

As this financial and social crisis went on getting worse, the institutions under which the empire had been carried on were changed also. Thus the idea of the principate as power exercised by the First Citizen, and also the privileged position of all Roman citizens, faded away simultaneously. The emperor became a military despot relying solely upon his army. In 212, during the reign of Caracalla, the rights of citizenship were extended to the whole population of the empire; but this measure did not signify any improvement in the legal status of the masses, but the ruin of the Roman State—the Senate and People of Rome. The Senate had no longer any voice at all in public affairs, and the senators had lost all the political privileges which had once belonged to their rank. At the same time the right of municipal self-government faded to a shadow all over the empire. The state was governed by a bureaucratic swarm of imperial officials who had graduated in the school of the army; and they included secret police who took a leading part in terrorizing the subjects. The last signs of civil freedom disappeared: it was the reign of spoliation and arbitrary violence, and even the best emperors were powerless to struggle against it.

At such a time there were naturally few stirrings of intellectual life. The silence of literature was only broken by works of no distinction. Art produced no single work of importance. It must, however, be noted that portrait-sculpture and painting reached a height unapproached till then. The busts, statues, and portraits of this age are characterized by unflinching realism; and we possess in them a remarkable gallery of conspicuous persons and ordinary citizens, some of them sickly and nervous members of the educated class, with the stamp of suffering on their faces, while others are coarse and vigorous upstarts—men who have risen from the ranks of the army, and members of the new semi-barbaric aristocracy of the time. And also, amid the profound decadence of ancient art, a new Christian art lives and grows, which just at this time puts forth its first literary masterpieces (see Chapter XXIV) and works out new types in sculpture and painting.

XXII

THE REFORMS OF DIOCLETIAN AND CONSTANTINE :
THE MILITARY DESPOTISM OF THE EAST

AFTER decades of anarchy and war both at home and abroad, Diocletian, as was said above, restored order for a time in the empire, defended the state from foreign enemies, set bounds to the raging current of passions and ambitions, and carried out a prudent and extensive programme of reform in public and private life. His success was due to the same causes which had helped Augustus to succeed two hundred and fifty years earlier. In himself he was in no way superior to many of the prominent rulers of the century, and every one of his reforms was initiated by his predecessors. Diocletian owed the firmness of his throne mainly to the weariness and disgust with which society and the army were filled, just as they had been filled when Augustus rose to power. The world was thirsting for peace and the chance of returning to a more or less settled life ; and by degrees larger and larger numbers rallied round the emperor in his difficult task of restoring peace and order. I do not mean to deny that Diocletian was a great man. His strength, like that of Augustus, lay in the fact that he realized the temper of the times and was able to make use of it. Like Augustus again, he originated no new principle : he merely brought together what was blindly growing up in the confusion of the age, made it into a system, and gave it the permanence of legal form. His chief aim was not the welfare of his subjects, but the restoration and strengthening of the state : he sacrificed the interests of the people to the public advantage more decidedly than any of his predecessors.

Thus the activity of Diocletian was directed towards three objects : he wished to strengthen the hands of the ruler, to reform the methods of government, and to regenerate the army. It cannot be said that he invested the throne with any strikingly new attributes. By the third century the emperors were already absolute monarchs of the type familiar in the East. Every trace of constitutional government had disappeared. The Senate had sunk to be the town council of the capital and was preserved by the ruler rather as a relic of the past than as a living and working institution. The army alone, together with the emperor, filled the stage of public life; and the emperor, perpetually menaced with abdication and death, had frequently to follow the dictates of his soldiers. Even in the second half of the third century the emperors were in this position; and neither Diocletian nor his successors were able definitely to establish their independence: the army still retained the casting vote in the election of a ruler. But their insolence was curbed to some extent by Diocletian by means of certain measures, dynastic, military, and administrative.

The autocratic power of the emperor, who was called upon to decide every question affecting the world-wide state, had proved incompetent at once to govern the empire and to defend it. For this reason several provinces had tried to cut loose from the state and carry on an independent life under the rule of local emperors. Recognizing that a single ruler could not defend the whole state and establish order throughout it, and also desiring to preserve the principle of unity, Diocletian devised a somewhat artificial system, by which, without sacrificing the identity of the state, the empire and the imperial power were divided. While remaining the single and autocratic head of the state, he introduced as a permanent institution the joint rule which had existed earlier from time to time. He transferred his authority over the western part of the empire to a consort appointed by himself: this was Valerius Maximianus, one of his ablest generals. Thus there was no longer a single Augustus in the empire, but two; and in order to secure the succession, each of them adopted a military leader who was capable of governing and protecting the state. The adopted sons were each given the title of ' Caesar ', and were to succeed the actual rulers, in case of death or incapacity caused by old age. Among these four rulers the government of the state was divided. Each of them had his own capital, his own army, his own executive, and a chief assistant in the person of a praetorian praefect.

This innovation still follows the principles laid down by Augustus as the basis of sovereign power. The imperial throne is still regarded as the chief magistracy of the empire, passing down by adoption from the Best to the Best. But in the nature of that power itself there was a radical alteration. The emperor was no longer merely one among Roman citizens, the First Citizen or *Princeps* : he became once for all ' lord and god'. This is clear from the external ceremonial with which he was surrounded. The devotion paid to the Sassanian kings was reproduced almost exactly for the Roman emperors : all who were admitted to the sacred presence had even to fall on their faces and kiss the hem of the royal raiment.

Nevertheless, the emperor's main function was still to command the army. His regular place was among his soldiers and in close proximity to the dangerous frontiers. The military defence of the empire became the chief business of the ruler, and everything else was postponed to it. For this purpose, the army was first of all reformed on lines that have already been noticed in the history of the third century : the soldiers of Diocletian and his successors were definitely drawn from the most backward peoples included in the empire. The less the soldier had of ancient civilization, the more highly he was prized. The most esteemed of all were the Germans, who were not subjects of the empire at all.

The best troops and the most fit for service—these were generally detachments of barbarians hired by Rome—were kept near the capitals of the rulers, the two Augusti and the two Caesars. These detachments, called *comitatenses*, made up a strong expeditionary force, ready to march to the frontier at any moment. It was developed out of the praetorian guard and was itself a bodyguard, in the wide sense of the word. But for personal attendance on the emperor it was too large ; and special divisions of household troops, called *palatini*, and a still smaller force, called *scholae* and *candidati*, the latter resplendent in white uniforms, were constantly on duty within the palace.

These guards and the expeditionary force quite eclipsed the old provincial army. The last was converted into a garrison force of settlers with a hereditary obligation of military service ; they were called *ripenses* or *riparii* and, later, *limitanei*. Their chief business was to police the frontiers : in actual warfare they were only of secondary importance. A considerable part in the defence of the empire was taken by the fleets at sea and flotillas on the rivers, and also by barbarous tribes (*gentes foederatae*) who were bound to Rome by treaty and more or less dependent upon her. These tribes, paid for their services, helped Rome to protect the frontiers outside which they lived ; in case of need they provided detachments of armed men under the command of native princes, and they allowed the recruiting officers to take men from their territory for the expeditionary force and the guards.

On the whole, the size of the army was greatly increased by these changes. Lactantius, a Christian writer at the end of the third century and the beginning of the fourth, says that the number was quadrupled. This may be an exaggeration, but at least the army was doubled ; and the number of officers rose in proportion. As was said above, the officers as a body changed their character altogether in the third century. At this time any soldier might gain promotion to the guards and then to the rank of an officer commanding a hundred men ; next he might become successively commander of an independent force, commander (*dux*) of all the troops of a single province, and commander-in-chief of an army. The only necessary qualifications were knowledge of his business, courage, devotion to the emperor, and—interest. The noble senators had no connexion at all with the army. A new aristocracy grew up, based upon military and civil service, and regularly recruited from the army and guards, where the most prominent figures were not Italians nor even provincials, but barbarians, mainly Germans, from the strip of territory beyond the frontier. The military career had no need of that general education which was necessary for the civil servant. The chief business of the civil administration was to levy the dues and taxes and organize the finances ; and, in connexion with this chief business, to provide courts of law. Hence the education of these officials was mainly legal : a knowledge of the ordinary law and a ready tongue were needed.

I said above that the army of Diocletian and his successors was predominantly a mercenary army. The best soldiers were recruited among Germans who were either independent of Rome or tributaries. Service in the frontier armies was hereditary : the soldiers were, in fact, serfs of the state, bound to fight in the ranks in return for a fixed reward and the right to occupy land. Nevertheless, the law which required every citizen to serve in the army had never been repealed. Therefore, when Caracalla in the year 212 extended the rights of citizenship to all provincials, every subject of the empire was liable to be called out. During the third century, and still more during the fourth, the emperors kept up this statute, not that they might force all Roman citizens into the ranks, but that they might, in case of necessity, fill up their armies with conscripts. And they had a further object. The law enabled them to lay a fresh impost upon their subjects ; for those who escaped service paid a special tax, called *aurum tironicum*, ' the recruits' gold ', which went to pay the mercenary soldiers.

For convenience of administration generally, and in particular to facilitate the collection of taxes, the whole empire, including Italy, was divided into 101 provinces. These were included in larger groups—the *dioeceses*, of which there were seventeen, and the four *praefecturae*. An Augustus or a Caesar, together with his chief assistant, the praetorian praefect, was at the head of each *praefectura* ; each ' diocese ' was ruled by a *vicarius*, and each province by a governor. The military authority in each province belonged to a special commander called *dux*, and was kept quite distinct from the civil power. Provincial government was controlled by three central offices, which dealt with justice (under a *quaestor*), finance, and the private property of the emperors. Great importance belonged to a carefully organized body of secret police (*agentes in rebus*), who were chiefly concerned with the personal security of the emperor. At the head of the secret police, the palace, and the horde of officials connected with the palace, stood a fourth minister—the *magister officiorum* or ' minister of the court '. The emperor's council (*consistorium*) was composed of the four ministers and certain other members chosen by him.

These military and administrative reforms, which were intended to support and strengthen the empire, increased the expenditure of the state—the military and civil budget. The army, the civil service, the court, the buildings erected by the emperor, the military roads, the frontier forts, the fortification of towns—even in Aurelian's time a stone wall still existing was built round Rome, and by degrees all the considerable cities of the empire were walled in—the fleets for war and commerce, which assured a supply of food to the armies and to the inhabitants of the four distinct capitals— for all these purposes more and more money was required. And the defective education and low morality of the officers and civil servants led inevitably to improper and corrupt practices.

The whole weight of this burden lay on the shoulders of the people, already greatly impoverished by the civil wars of the third century. I have referred above to the increasing taxation of that period. In addition to the ordinary taxes on land and on the profits earned by the exercise of any trade or profession, a special tax (*annona*) was levied in kind for the support of the soldiers and officials ; pack-horses and wagons had to be supplied, to convey state baggage and the state post ; and money must be paid, to escape military service. Either the town councils or the owners of great estates outside the urban territories were responsible for the payment in full of all these taxes and for the performance of this forced labour. I have pointed out also in the preceding chapter, how and why the trade and industry of the empire became disorganized, and how the emperors caused a most serious financial crisis by their insane policy of debasing the coinage.

Matters were not much improved even after Diocletian restored the integrity of the empire and succeeded in establishing a semblance of order in the realm. The world was pillaged and exhausted, a scene of universal violence. It was hoped that Diocletian would bring back normal conditions of life ; but how were normal conditions possible, when the country was reduced to beggary, and when the state, as reformed by Diocletian, laid an excessive burden on the taxable capacity of the people ? His attempt to change existing conditions proved impossible, and all that he did came to this : he gave order and system to the oppression and coercion by which the empire was governed in the third century ; and he simplified the whole machinery of taxation, adapting it to the primitive economic conditions of an impoverished and degenerate state.

The main business of every social and economic centre in the realm was now to serve the state and work for the state. This conception was no novelty to the ancient world : the public life of Egypt in the Hellenistic Age was largely based upon it ; and now Diocletian introduced it throughout the empire. The system of taxation was not much altered essentially, but what had been exceptional in the third century, and only justified by the prevalence of war, was now legalized and made into a regular institution.

A general responsibility was introduced for the payment of all taxes and the performance of all compulsory labour : all the inhabitants of the territory belonging to this or that city were made jointly responsible. This meant that the persons really responsible were the representatives of the community—the town council (*decuriones*) and the magistrates. But since the middle class in the towns was bankrupt already and sought by every means to escape responsibility for the arrears due from the town, therefore service on the town councils and in the magistracies was made compulsory, and the townsmen were bound to reside in their own town and perform this duty.

But the working classes, especially those who worked on the land, were no less bankrupt than the middle class. They, too, strained every nerve to evade the taxes and forced labour. One regular expedient was to change their domicile and occupation ; but when this became a common practice throughout the empire, the state bound the labourers to the soil, whether it was their own or rented, and converted them into government serfs, who, though legally free, had not the right to leave their plot of land ; others served the great landlords on similar terms. Bondage of this kind was familiar in the East ; in the West the way was paved for it by the peculiar social and financial conditions of the second and third centuries A. D., when the great majority of labourers did not own the soil they tilled but were hereditary tenants of the state or the landlords.

In industry and in transport we find a repetition of this arrangement. In each branch of industry indispensable to the state, in the munition factories, cloth mills, and bakeries, the government required the owners to furnish a fixed amount of their products at an unremunerative price, and made the unions of manufacturers, which existed in every town, responsible for carrying out the order. When these unions were unable to supply what was required, the state bound the owners of the shops and their free workmen not to quit their calling but to go on working in the same place. If this measure also failed, the state nationalized certain departments of industry and profited by the forced labour of the serfs so employed. Transport was treated in the same way, the chief victims being the owners of trading ships plying on the seas and rivers.

COUNTRY LIFE IN THE 3rd–4th CENT. A.D.

1. Mosaic found at Carthage. In the centre of the picture is shown a large villa, a combination of a residential house and a fortress. Its dominant features are two high towers at the corners, a massive ground-floor with an arched entrance, giving access to the household apartments and probably to a large court behind, and a handsome loggia on the first floor where the living-rooms are concentrated. Behind the main part of the building are seen two separate buildings—the stable or the *atrium* and a large bath with domed roofs. The villa is surrounded by a park. On the two sides of the villa is depicted a hunting expedition of the master. Two servants lead the way, a beater and a man in charge of the hounds; in the field is the object of the hunt, a hare; while behind comes the master, riding a fine horse and followed by a third servant who carries a bag of provisions. In the upper and lower panels of the picture are scenes of life on the estate. Each season occupies one corner. In the upper left-hand corner it is winter-time. A man carries two live ducks; two boys gather olives; a woman carries a basket full of black olives. They represent the family of a *colonus* portrayed in their relation to the master: they bring the fruits of the season to the lady of the villa, who is seated on a bench, with a fan in her hand, in that part of the park which formed the poultry-yard: on her right a cock is displaying his beauty, and in front of her is a henhouse with chickens before it. The right corner of the same panel, depicting summer, shows the family of another *colonus:* in the background is their modest house, a 'gourbi' (*mapale*), or round hut, made of reeds; in the foreground is seen the *colonus* himself, herding his flock of sheep and goats with the aid of his dog, and holding a shepherd's horn in his left hand. His wife or daughter brings a kid to her mistress (the figure of the lady serves for both scenes). In the left corner of the lower band is pictured spring. The lady of the villa stands in front of her chair, elegantly dressed, amid flowers, with her pet dog in the background; before her stands a servant-maid holding a necklace and a toilet box, while a boy deposits three fish at her feet; behind her a boy-servant or a *colonus* brings a basket full of flowers. The remaining corner represents autumn. The master of the house is seated under the trees of his orchard, which are laden with ripe fruit; behind him lies his vineyard. A *colonus* runs through the orchard carrying two cranes and a roll inscribed *Ju(lio) dom(ino)*, probably a complimentary address or a petition. From the vineyard comes another *colonus,* carrying a basket of grapes and a live hare, which he has probably just caught among the vines. The mosaic gives prominence to the part played by the *coloni* in the economy of the estate: the whole life of the villa is based on their toil and their contributions. 3rd–4th cent. A.D. Bardo Museum, Tunis.

2. Bas-relief of a funeral monument. Part of the sculptural decoration of the Igel column. Six *coloni* in procession bring various contributions in kind to their master's house. They have just entered the court of the house through an arched gate, and they are received before the entrance to the *atrium* (half closed by a curtain) by the master himself or his steward. The gifts, or contributions, consist of a hare, two fish, a kid, an eel, a cock, and a basket of fruit. 3rd cent. A.D. Igel near Trèves.

PLATE XVIII

1. THE ESTATE OF JULIUS

2. *Coloni* BRINGING GIFTS

PLATE XVIII

In this way the urban territories, whose inhabitants the law regarded as free Roman citizens, were converted into districts occupied by state serfs, without any regard to the social position or occupation of the individual or to the stage of civilization which he had reached. Under Diocletian and after him the empire did indeed establish equality among most of its subjects, in the sense that all alike were beggars and slaves.

Things were no better in those districts which did not form part of urban territories but belonged either to the emperor or to members of the senatorial class. The small-holders who were tenants on such estates paid the same taxes : the only difference was that the taxes were not paid to the towns but to the landowner together with the rent. The landowners were responsible to the state for the payment ; but on the imperial estates the responsibility fell on large contractors who rented a great area and managed it pretty much as they pleased. The natural result followed in this case also : the tillers of the soil fell into arrears, and the landlords and tenants of large farms were ruined ; the peasants ran away, and the landlords and large tenants threw up their land, which went out of cultivation and brought no returns. The state had recourse to its regular expedient : it turned the peasants into serfs and required the landlords and large tenants to pay in full the taxes upon the whole area of land.

In some cases, but not in many, the lot of those who lived on large estates was more favourable than that of the labourers who were employed upon urban territories. I refer to those cases in which the estate belonged to a person with influence at court, some great general or high official, who either by pressure or by bribery could evade payment of the taxes and other burdens. Those who could took refuge on such estates, finding slavery to a great man better than slavery to the state. Thus the state was entirely organized on the principles of an Eastern despotism : an autocratic ruler controlled an omnipotent bureaucracy, which suppressed every trace of self-government while professing to retain it, and a population of serfs, living and working principally for the purposes of the government. What a departure from the Graeco-Roman ideals of freedom and self-government!

Such was the manner of life created by Diocletian for his

subjects. Those of his measures which were due directly to the existing conditions, social and economic, held their ground for many centuries and formed the basis on which the empire rested. His reforms in administration, judicial proceedings, finance, and military organization, stood the test of time. He was less successful in dealing with the central authority, in which he tried to unite two incompatible things—a magistracy of the Roman people and a despotism of Eastern type. His arrangements broke down in his own lifetime : after his abdication he lived to see a repetition of civil war between the Augusti and Caesars whom he had appointed.

The conqueror in that war was Constantine ; and to him the empire owed a definition of the central authority which held good for centuries. He gave up once and for ever the notion held by Augustus, the Antonines, and Diocletian, that the emperor was the Chief Magistrate of the Roman people. The throne became hereditary in the family of Constantine, so that in this respect also the government was identical with an Eastern despotism. The dynasty was supported on one side by the devotion of the army, and on the other by religion. Constantine realized that religion is the only conceivable sanction of despotic power. Though all his predecessors, from Augustus downwards, felt this to be true, yet the emperor-worship introduced by Augustus became after his death a mere state institution, hardly connected at all with religion. More is said on this subject in the following chapter. The principate of Augustus and his immediate successors and the principate of the Antonines had no religious sanction : it rested on the connexion of the *princeps* with the Senate and Roman people—upon the fact that the *princeps* was their legal representative. In the third century the connexion was snapped ; and it is therefore natural that the emperors of that age tried to attach their authority to the most powerful religious current of the time—the current which prevailed among the soldiers. But of such currents there were many, and not one bore undisputed sway over the minds of the army. Thus Heliogabalus and Aurelian, in spite of all their efforts, failed to establish any of them as the official religion.

Constantine saw how the land lay : he made a fresh attempt to create a single state religion and at the same time to draw from it support for the imperial authority. His attempt was successful. The cause of this success will be discussed in the next chapter. But the mere fact that Constantine created a despotic and hereditary power, closely connected with the state religion and inseparable from it, proclaims this—that the old Roman state of the Senate and people of Rome ceased to exist in the reign of Constantine, and gave place to a new system which was to rule both East and West for many centuries—a monarchy by the grace of God. The same time saw the death of another fundamental idea of Graeco-Roman civilization—the ideal of citizenship and freedom. In the monarchy that followed Constantine there was no longer any place for the citizens who had peopled the city-states of Greece and Italy : their room was taken by subjects.

XXIII

RELIGIOUS DEVELOPMENTS IN THE EMPIRE
DURING THE FIRST THREE CENTURIES

WE have seen how the rationalistic spirit, originated by Greece and adopted by Italy in republican times, began to lose ground and give way to a religious and mystical attitude of mind. In the East this change took place in the Hellenistic period, in the West not until the civil wars of the first century B.C. I have spoken also of the compromise between science and religion, which Stoicism tried to effect for the educated classes; and of the religious currents which carried away the peoples of both East and West in the first century of our era; though the victory of theology was still incomplete, yet signs of it were visible everywhere and in every section of the population.

Nor did the interest in religion come to an end with the death of Augustus. Its growth may be traced in every part of the empire. The state religion which prevailed throughout the empire was addressed to two objects—the emperor himself, and the trinity of Jupiter, Juno, and Minerva worshipped on the Capitol; and this religion took a definite form, the same everywhere, and became the centre of religious life for the towns and for the army. But this differed from the religion created by the civil wars, and from the deification of Augustus as a Hero and a Saviour, which was so definitely personal and, in Italy, so closely connected with the purely national cult of the *genius* belonging to the family, the cross-roads, the city, and the state. Like the state worship of old Rome, the worship of the emperor and his family, the dead and living rulers of the empire, became more and more lifeless and impersonal. The people met together in the temples of the imperial cult or in the Capitols of the provincial towns, and paid their acknowledgements and tribute of respect to the divine power, through which and thanks to which the empire existed. There was no doubt a certain modicum of religious feeling in such rites; but they offered no help in trouble or consolation in suffering, and answered none of the anxious questions concerning the present and the future life.

Thus the religious consciousness demanded other means of satisfaction than were afforded by emperor-worship. The high educated classes still held on to Stoicism, with its lofty morality and pantheistic theology. But Stoicism grew less and less able to meet the religious needs of intellectual circles : it was too cold, too reasonable and logical, too earthly. And in the domain of superstition, astrology, which used mathematical and astronomical calculation to reveal the future, was unsatisfactory for the same reasons.

It was therefore natural that in the minds of the higher classes Stoic rationalism should give place to a modern version of Platonic and Pythagorean mysticism, and that gnosticism, or the belief in esoteric spiritual knowledge, should flourish abundantly and assume the most varied forms. It is a remarkable fact that from the end of the second century this tendency not only wins over new adherents but produces remarkable personalities, men full of fiery enthusiasm, who preach the new Platonism and Pythagoreanism with all the weapons of dialectic and the power of thorough philosophical training.

During the first two centuries of the empire the chief representatives of religion and philosophy are Stoics—Epictetus the slave, Seneca the senator, and Marcus Aurelius the emperor. The third century is most vividly represented by Plotinus and his disciples—Plotinus the thinker, professor, and prophet. And this school does not confine itself to moral philosophy : it puts forth a full-blown theology and even a mysterious doctrine of the means by which spiritual powers may be forced into the service of man. These, and not the Stoics, are the combatants in the final battle against Christianity and its purely religious view of life.

The middle classes of society either fed on the crumbs that fell from the table of their intellectual superiors, or, perhaps more commonly, adopted the views of their inferiors in rank. Among these, the lower classes, a remarkable increase of religious feeling is observable, and a rapid growth of religious practice. The first two centuries still stand by tradition and the local cults which tradition has sanctified. In Italy a form of religion which had at no time died out is still thoroughly alive—the domestic cult of the *genius*, and of the Lares and Penates, who preserve the life and prosperity of the house and family ; and there are other cults kept up by larger groups—societies, clubs, divisions of the army, and so on. Side by side with this worship the old Graeco-Roman religion lives on: those gods and goddesses who bring prosperity and the chance of peaceful development, such as Fortune and Mercury, are chief favourites with the people of Italy. The symbolical figures of new deities which incarnate abstract ideas are constantly addressed. Many of these are closely related to man's daily life, especially in Rome and the other great cities of the empire—e. g. *Abundantia*, who promises the believer a plenteous harvest; *Annona*, who secures an abundant supply of corn to the capital and other cities; *Justitia*; and *Salus*, who brings health to the family and the state.

A similar resurrection of the old faith is perceptible in Greece and the other provinces. The great deities of Athens, Delphi, and Olympia are living still; and even many old and forgotten cults of local gods and heroes awake from a sleep of ages. In this connexion it is instructive to read the description of the monuments in Greece which was written by Pausanias in the reign of Hadrian. We notice the same process in other provinces also. Old local and national cults were revived and attracted great numbers of worshippers. It is true that the local rites resemble those of the Graeco-Italian religion, and that the local deities assume in statues and reliefs the features of the Olympians.

Though some of the Greek and Roman gods were actually worshipped in the provinces, that goes for little : the really important fact is this, that the provincials did homage to their own local deities. The Celts had their great gods of nature and the state, and their beneficent fairies (*matres*), and their nymphs of the streams and woods ; the Thracians had their god of forests, gardens, and vineyards, a hunter and warrior, to whom they gave the indistinctive Greek name of ' hero ' ; the Illyrians had their god of the hills, and borrowed for him from Greece the name and semblance of Pan ; the Africans had their ancient Berber and Semitic deities—Baal, Tanit, and others—but called them by such names as Saturn, Juno, Caelestis (the Heavenly One) ; the Anatolians worshipped their Great Mother and her divine consort under an endless variety of shapes, and also a ' supreme god ' of the sky and of the thunder ; and the Syrians acknowledged many local varieties of the sun-god. Egypt strictly maintained her ancient religion, though the foreign element of the population forced into prominence Sarapis, the Graeco-

RELIGION. ORIENTAL CULTS. ISIS AND SARAPIS

1. ISIS, SARAPIS, AND
   HARPOCRATES

1. Fragment of a bas-relief found at Alexandria. Three figures and half of a fourth are preserved: the Alexandrian trinity, Isis, Sarapis, and Harpocrates, and half of the figure of Dionysus. The figures of Isis, Sarapis, and Harpocrates are certainly reproductions of fine early Hellenistic statues. 1st cent. A.D. Louvre, Paris.

2. Fresco from Herculaneum. It represents a religious service before the door and on the stairs leading to an Egyptian sanctuary in Campania. The priest (prophet), standing between two attendants, is officiating: he holds in his hands which are wrapped in his white dress a sacred bowl, probably containing Nile water. Another priest is leading the choir of the community which stands in two rows in the court. A priest is performing a sacrifice on a typical Egyptian horned altar, while his attendant is kindling the fire on this altar. Sacred ibises are roaming round. The seated figure to the right represents probably a cymbalist. In the temple court palm-trees and Egyptian bushes are growing. Note that the attendants of the priests are black, while the priests themselves and the congregation are white. 1st cent. A.D. Museum, Naples.

3. Bas-relief found at Rome, probably from one of the Egyptian sanctuaries of the city. It represents a procession in honour of Isis. A priestess of Isis leads the procession. In her right hand is the sacred vessel of Isis (*situla*), on her left arm the sacred serpent (*uraeus*). Next comes the holy scribe (*hierogrammateus*) with his head clean shaved, holding in his hands the sacred book. After him—the 'prophet' with the jar of Nile water (see fig. 2), and finally a girl attendant with the musical instrument of Isis (*sistrum*) and a spoon (*simpulum*). 2nd cent. A.D. Vatican, Rome.

PLATE XIX

2. RELIGIOUS SERVICE

3. PROCESSION IN HONOUR OF ISIS

PLATE XIX

Egyptian god of the Ptolemies, together with a Hellenized version of Isis. Never were more temples built, more altars raised, and more victims sacrificed to these gods.

I have referred already to the fact that certain of these local Eastern cults became prominent, spread beyond the limits of a single country and people, and created religious societies and local churches of their own, till they became cosmopolitan and set forth to propagate their doctrine over the world. Such a tendency appeared as early as the period of Persian dominion ; but it grew stronger in the Hellenistic Age, and began its career of conquest under the Roman Empire. The earliest of these proselytizing religions were Egyptian and Anatolian : the Graeco-Egyptian worship of the trinity including Serapis, Isis, and Harpocrates came from Egypt ; and Asia Minor exported the worship of the Great Mother in a Hellenized form. These were followed by cults of other deities—the Syrian sky-god and the Syrian sun-god, worshipped in various shapes ; Mithras, the warrior-god of the sun, saviour and champion of man and man's civilization ; and Sabazius, the mystical deity of Thracians and Anatolians. Each of these religions, with a view to its diffusion over the world, constructed a definite theology, definite mystical rites, and a definite priestly hierarchy. They spread rapidly over the East, more slowly in Greece and Italy. Earlier than this, when the dispersion of the Jews took place in the Hellenistic Age, the Jewish communities spread far and wide and were followed, under the empire, by Christianity.

These religions, which were only beginning to take regular shape and make proselytes in the early days of the empire, were favoured by the conditions of life due to the existence of a world-wide state. Together with traders and artisans from the East, these beliefs made their way into almost every commercial centre, especially the seaport towns, and there formed close religious societies. The empire put no obstacles in their way. The early emperors paid little heed to religion, provided it was not hostile to their own supremacy. Indeed, enlightened despotism, based upon Stoic principles, was even willing to favour the diffusion of Eastern mysticism, provided always that it was law-abiding and abstained entirely from politics. Thus local and Eastern cults existed side by side in every part of the empire, and the latter found their supporters chiefly in the towns. As a result of this coexistence, we find an attempt to reconcile the different creeds, and to fuse them into one by what is now called 'syncretism', in the minds of their adherents. And such a tendency was welcome to the directing classes of society and suited their pantheistic monotheism.

One of the main centres of religious feeling in Roman society under the empire was the army. That this should be so follows so directly from the working of the human mind that no explanation is necessary. The peculiar form which religion took in the Roman armies gives a true picture of religious movements in the empire generally. At first a purely official worship was paid to the emperor, the Roman god Mars, and the Roman trinity of the Capitol, by the legions and auxiliary troops in all the camps. But side by side with this there grew up a worship of local deities, belonging either to the country where the camp was situated or to the countries from which the soldiers came. Thus in the Crimea the garrison of a remote Roman fortress, who were mainly Thracians, worshipped Artemis, or the Maiden of Tauris, in the chapel and worshipped also outside the walls of their fort their own Thracian deities. Then, when Iranians, Anatolians, and Syrians came as recruits to the colours, they brought with them the religions of the East. Special honour was paid to Mithras, to the Syrian and Anatolian sun-god and sky-god, warriors and rulers, and to Jupiter of the Syrian city of Doliche, a real legionary soldier and armed, like the legionaries, with his attributes of axe and thunderbolt. Their popularity is easily understood : they were gods of strife and conquest, promising to the soldier power and might and victory, and revealing to him a prospect of eternal happiness beyond the grave.

In the darkness and disturbance of the third century these religions flourished abundantly. The Thracians and Illyrians who served in the armies on the Danube bore the image of the Persian god Mithras on the amulets which they wore on their breasts and consecrated in the temples. Mithras was represented on these amulets in the same form as their native Hero—a victorious horseman, subduing and destroying the powers of evil. They had been accustomed to reverence the twin Cabeiri, gods of light and of the sun ; so now they added a twin to Mithras, and united with the pair the Great Mother Goddess, who tempers the harsh creed of the warrior with a female element denoting the productive and nutritive powers

RELIGION. ORIENTAL CULTS. MITHRAS
AND MAGNA MATER

1. Bas-relief found in the subterranean sanctuary of Mithras (*Mithraeum*) at Heddernheim in Germany. The Persian god Mithras, the fighter, the god of light and civilization, the conqueror of darkness and the elemental forces of nature, was worshipped here by the soldiers of the Roman camp, which occupied the place of the modern city of Heddernheim in the Rhine province. The main place in the sanctuary was occupied by this relief. It represents Mithras killing the bull at the bidding of Ahuramazda; out of the blood of the bull sprang up the corn-ears and the vine. The allies of Ahriman—the snake, the scorpion, and the lion— are scared by the dog of Mithras. To the right and to the left of Mithras stand the personifications of the dawn and sunset, Cautes and Cautopates. The scene is represented as taking place in a cave. Over the cave are the signs of the Zodiac. In the medallions which surround the main image are various episodes of the life and passion of Mithras. 3rd cent. A.D. Museum, Wiesbaden.

2. One of the many votive tablets of lead found in the Danube lands. The bas-relief represents the trinity worshipped by the soldiers and the civil population of the Danube country: two equestrian gods in Oriental costume trample under the feet of their horses the symbols of evil (a human figure) and of the elemental forces of nature (the fish) and worship the great goddess who stands in the centre. Behind the riders to the left is Mars, the god of war, and to the right, Nemesis, the goddess of divine Justice. Above is the sun-god in his chariot, and busts of the sun and moon. Below are scenes from the mystic cult of the trinity: the sacred banquet in the centre, the sacrifice of the ram and the initiation of a votary by means of setting on his head the head of the ram to the left, and the initiation of three naked votaries to the right. The lowest panel contains symbols of the cult: the sacred fish on a tripod, the lamp, the lion, the jug, the serpent, the cock. The cult was a mixture of Thracian and Mithraic mysteries. 2nd cent. A.D. Museum, Zagreb.

3. Votive bas-relief, found at Lanuvium in Latium. The bas-relief represents a priest (eunuch) of the god Attis and of Cybele (*Magna Mater*) clad in Oriental garments. On his head a crown adorned with the busts of the great god of Asia Minor (*Sozon*—the Saviour) and two busts of Attis, the lover of Cybele. In his right hand are the symbols of fertility, the pomegranate and three twigs; in his left, a basket with various fruit and a fir-cone. On his breast is the image of Attis. The figure is surrounded by the sacred implements used during the holy service: the whip used for the sacred self-lashing, the cymbals, the tympanum, the pipe, and the flute, instruments used in the ritual music, and a mystic *cista*. 2nd cent. A.D. Palazzo dei Conservatori, Rome.

PLATE XX

1. MITHRAS

2. DANUBIAN TRINITY

EX DONO DVCIS SFORTIAE SFORTIAE

3. PRIEST OF ATTIS AND CYBELE

PLATE XX

RELIGION. ORIENTAL CULTS. SABAZIUS, JUPITER HELIOPOLITANUS, AND BAAL OF DOLICHE

I. THE SABAZIASTS

1. One of the frescoes which adorned the grave of Vibia, a lady, who with her husband, Vincentius, had been initiated in the mysteries of the Thracian god, Sabazius. On the Appian Way, near Rome. Our fresco represents how Vibia, after having been carried off by Pluto and examined by the supreme court of the netherworld (*Dispater* and *Aeracura*), is introduced through a gate (*inductio Vibiae*) by the Good Messenger (*Angelus Bonus*) into the Elysian fields, and how she takes the place of honour at the sacred banquet of the blessed (*bonorum iudicio iudicati*), i.e. those who have been found reproachless by the supreme divine court. Another fresco (not reproduced) shows Vincentius, the still living husband of Vibia, taking part in a banquet, probably in memory of his wife, as one of the seven pious priests (*septe(m) pii sacerdotes*). 3rd cent. A.D. Rome.

2. Bronze statue of the Syrian god Jupiter Heliopolitanus, the Baal who was worshipped in the sanctuary of Baalbek (Heliopolis—city of the sun). The statue represents the youthful god in the primitive form of a *xoanon* (a plank-image) with a *calathos* (symbol of fertility) on his head, dressed in armour with the Egyptian symbol of the sun on the breastplate. In his right hand the god held probably a spear. The seven busts on the body represent the seven days of the week. To the right and left of the statue are bulls, the sacred animals of the god. On the pedestal of the statue is the figure of the goddess Fortune (*Tyche*). Various symbolical bas-reliefs adorn the back of the statue. 2nd–3rd cent. A.D. Private Collection, Paris.

PLATE XXI

3. Bronze triangular plaque, votive, in the form of an arrowhead, found at Heddernheim. The bas-relief represents the Baal of Doliche, a town in Commagene (north Syria). The god, of Hittite origin, was a powerful god of war who was worshipped by Roman soldiers all over the Roman Empire. He is represented standing on his sacred animal (the bull), clad in a Phrygian cap and the armour of a Roman soldier, with a long sword on his belt, an axe in his right and the thunderbolt in his left, crowned by Victory. Above is the bust of the sun; below is the female counterpart of the god, with the sistrum of Isis, a torch and a mural crown, standing on an ass between two figures, probably of Jupiter Dolichenus rising up from rocks and supporting the busts of the sun and moon. In their hands they hold torches in the form of thunderbolts. 3rd cent. A.D. Museum, Wiesbaden.

2. JUPITER HELIOPOLITANUS   3. BAAL OF DOLICHE

PLATE XXI

of nature. The army of the Danube played a prominent part in the political history of the third century, and this trinity whom they worshipped received recognition in the highest quarters : Heliogabalus, priest of the Syrian sun-god and Roman emperor, was only following their example when he solemnly celebrated at Rome a marriage between his god and the Carthaginian goddess, Tanit.

In the troubles of the third century the state was far from ignoring the religious movements of the time. In their search for means to attach the army to their persons, the emperors endeavoured to make the blind forces of religious fervour serve their turn, and to found upon it a close connexion between the army and the throne. The introduction of Mithras at Rome, the worship of the Syrian sun-god by Heliogabalus, the devotion of Aurelian to the single sun-god, are so many attempts to secure this object.

Meantime, among the many religious societies of Eastern origin one became by degrees conspicuous above the rest. This was the Christian Church. It began humbly among a band of disciples who knew and remembered the earthly life of Christ ; then the genius and energy of the apostle Paul changed it into a league of well-organized societies, which were scattered throughout the East and found access even to Italy. Starting from the teaching of Christ, Paul supplied all that was indispensable for a church with a world-wide mission : he laid the foundations of Christian theology, morals, and eschatology, and, what was still more important, the foundations of a universal or Catholic Church.

The Christian communities soon came into collision with the civil power. But the causes of this conflict are not quite clear. Religious persecution was foreign to the customary policy of the emperors, and the legal grounds for prosecution in this instance are not obvious. It may have been caused by the stubborn refusal of the Christians to take part in the worship paid throughout the empire to the ruler ; or perhaps the Christian communities were considered, for one reason or another, to be illegal societies. In any case, even under Trajan, there was a law which made persecution possible.

As time went on, Christianity, though by no means hostile to the state in general, became nevertheless, in consequence of the attitude taken up by the authorities, opposed to the government of the empire. In the conflict that ensued the part of the Church was purely passive, but she gained strength from the ordeal. She developed and improved her organization, and she produced a number of men remarkable for energy and endurance, some of whom lost their lives, but the survivors carried on persistently the work of governing their universal society. At the same time the Christians endeavoured to make their doctrine intelligible, accessible, and acceptable, not only to the common people and uneducated minds, but to a more enlightened class. One of the great geniuses of Christianity and of the ancient world in general was Origen, who established a lasting connexion between his religion and ancient philosophy.

The second century and the beginning of the third witnessed a slow development of the new religion. It was neither recognized by the state, nor systematically persecuted. The third century, a time of political and religious convulsion, marked a crisis in its development. Dropping an attitude of almost complete tolerance, the emperors Maximin, Decius, and Valerian declared open war against the Christians : again and again with feverish activity they persecuted not only individuals but the whole society in the persons of its chiefs and rulers. This change of policy was probably due to the growing influence of Christianity in the army, which threatened to undermine the loyalty of the soldiers.

Many believers fell martyrs for their faith in these persecutions, but the Church was not overthrown. The conflict gave it additional strength. Years of persecution heightened the self-consciousness of the body, and they became convinced that their Church (*ecclesia*) was one and indivisible, a peculiar and mighty institution, a divine state (*civitas dei*) standing apart from the kingdoms of this world. As the state became more decrepit, the Church grew stronger. Membership of the state brought nothing but pain and suffering ; while a member of the Church received from it material as well as moral support. The doctrine of Christ required that each should love and help his neighbour, and the organized Church gave this help to all believers.

When the state emerged from the convulsions of the third century almost entirely deprived of moral authority and relying upon force alone, it was confronted by the Christian Church fully armed in the organization which had been voluntarily accepted by her adherents. The moral authority which the

I. PROPHET   2. PROPHET

1, 2, 3. Frescoes of a grave discovered at Rome in the Viale Manzoni. The grave was a common grave of members of a Christian sect of which the nucleus was formed by the family of the Aurelii. The various subterranean chambers of this grave are decorated with frescoes. Especially rich is the decoration of the main chamber. Here the history of the sect is told in the pictures of the vault, and the prophets or apostles of the new sect are portrayed on the walls. Figs. 1 and 2 show two wonderful heads of these prophets; fig. 3 represents a bearded ascetic figure seated on a rock and reading a book with great attention, while his flock is grazing in the plain. The scene may represent Christ and his apostles. 3rd cent. A.D. Viale Manzoni, Rome.

4. Fresco of the painted grave under S. Sebastiano. The apotheosis of the deceased.

PLATE XXII

3. SHEPHERD AND FLOCK

4. APOTHEOSIS

PLATE XXII

I. MOSAIC OF THEODULOS

Three mosaics of Africa of early Christian time. The date is uncertain.

1. Mosaic found in a private house at Hadrumetum (Sousse) which certainly belonged to a Christian. The mosaic shows the usual Christian symbols: the palm-tree, the vine coming out from a cantharus, the peacocks, partridges, ducks, and pheasants; and it bears the Christian name Theodulos (slave of God). Museum, Sousse.

2. Tomb mosaic found in a Christian cemetery near a large basilica on the island of Tabarka (Thabraca). The mosaic represents the deceased Victoria in the attitude of prayer (*orans*). Near her are a candle, birds, and flowers. Above is a man surrounded by flowers and seated at his desk writing. He is perhaps writing the life of Victoria, who may have been a martyr. Bardo Museum, Tunis.

3. Tomb mosaic found in the same cemetery. The deceased, Jovinus, is a boy. He is represented between two candles surrounded by birds (doves) and flowers. Bardo Museum, Tunis.

PLATE XXIII

2. TOMB MOSAIC OF VICTORIA   3. TOMB MOSAIC OF JOVINUS

PLATE XXIII

civil power had lost was her sole but sufficient support. Battle was offered for the last time to Christianity by Diocletian and his successors. Diocletian tried systematic persecution, that he might compel the Christian Church to submit to the state, as the other social forces of the empire had submitted, and to merge its identity in that of the state. The existence of the Church, as a state within the state, seemed to Diocletian to be, as it certainly was, incompatible with the first principle of the system which he had created—a despotism founded upon the absolute submission of his subjects. The Christians suffered heavy losses, but the battle was lost by the state. The Church had proved herself stronger than her adversary.

This is not the place to examine the intrinsic causes which gave Christianity its immense influence over the hearts and minds of men. The fact has been explained in many different ways ; and it is true of all these explanations that they are convincing to a certain extent, but fail to solve the problem as a whole. One thing is clear : the victory of Christianity indicates a break with the past and a changed attitude in the history of the human mind. Men had grown weary and unwilling to seek further. They turned greedily to a creed that promised to calm the troubled mind, that could give certainty in place of doubt, a final solution for a host of problems, and theology instead of science and logic. Unable and unwilling to direct their own inner life, they were ready to surrender the control to a superior being, incommensurable with themselves. Reason neither gave nor promised happiness to mankind ; but religion, and especially the Christian religion, gave man the assurance of happiness—beyond the grave. Thus the centre of gravity was shifted, and men's hopes and expectations were transferred to that future life. They were content to submit and suffer in this life, in order to find true life hereafter. Such an attitude of mind was entirely foreign to the ancient world, even to the earlier nations of the East, not to speak of the Greeks and Romans. To a Greek the future life was something shadowy and formidable ; life on earth alone was prized by him. But now all this was radically changed; and this change of feeling, more than anything else, proves that the beginning of the fourth century is the turning over of a new page, and a page of strange matter, in the history of humanity.

XXIV

THE DECLINE OF ANCIENT CIVILIZATION

HISTORICAL development knows no interruptions. After the time of Diocletian and Constantine the Roman Empire went on existing for many centuries. But it was now divided into two parts: the Western Empire with Rome for its capital, Rome of the Romans; and the Eastern Empire, commonly called ' Byzantine ', because its capital, Constantinople, or Rome of the *Romaioi*, was founded by Constantine on the site of the ancient Byzantium. I have already described the system of government in this new Roman Empire. Its essential features remained, in both East and West, what they were made by Diocletian and Constantine. The structure they built was, as we have already seen, new upon the whole: it was foreign to Graeco-Roman conceptions of the state and agreed more closely, though not altogether, with the political theories of the Iranian and Semitic East. Some survivals of the former constitution were retained: the ancient formula of *Senatus populusque Romanus* was still used; two Senates, one in each capital, still sat; and some titles of magistrates, such as ' consul ', were kept alive.

The main features in the life of this new empire may be described as follows. The Western Empire gradually breaks up into its component parts, which are Italy and the former provinces; and these parts are eventually ruled by the leaders of different German tribes, who have seized this or that part of the Roman world. This phenomenon is not entirely new; for even in the time of Diocletian, Constantine, and their immediate successors, the Germans were conspicuous in the army and at the imperial court. In the Eastern Empire the process of dissolution is far slower, and old traditions are more tenaciously maintained; but, on the other hand, the influence of the East is stronger, and the government tends more and more to resemble an Eastern despotism. The centre of gravity in the Eastern Empire shifts from the Balkan peninsula to Asia Minor.

At the same time, those countries which had once been the chief centres of political and civilized life fall into decay, and their place is taken by parts of Asia and Europe which had played a secondary part in earlier history. Though the politics and economics of the time may still be called ' Mediterranean ', yet by degrees parts of Europe and Asia, which have no connexion with that sea, gain decisive importance in the history of mankind. These are north Germany, north France, Britain, the Scandinavian countries, and central and northern Russia, in Europe ; Persia under the Sassanian dynasty, and the Mongols, in Asia. In these districts of the north and south-east there grew up gradually political, social, and economic institutions which were destined to determine the future development of the human race.

The history of the ancient centres of civilizations becomes more and more a history of dissolution and decay. The old institutions are replaced by utterly primitive conditions ; in social, economic, and intellectual matters there is an unbroken reversion to barbarism. One feature of the economic condition is especially remarkable—the complete change in agricultural methods throughout the empire. Scientific cultivation backed up by capital and intelligence disappears utterly and is replaced everywhere by a system which merely scratches the surface of the soil and sinks lower and lower into primitive routine. Though estates may be large and great tracts of land are owned by members of the new imperial aristocracy, yet agriculture is based on the tilling of the soil by small cultivators, either owners or tenants. Throughout the world Hodge holds the field, whether the land belongs to the emperor or to great private landowners, whether Hodge himself owns or rents his plot in the area of urban territories. The economic life of the state as a whole and of the ruling classes in the empire and the towns is based upon Hodge. This being the case, there is no longer any question of increasing the area of cultivation : it shrinks instead. In Egypt this process can be traced by written evidence and can almost be proved by figures ; and it is equally present in the rest of the empire.

To provide labour for the land became the chief anxiety of the state and of private owners. Of land itself the quantity was unlimited : the arduous problem was to find farmers who would pay rent and labourers who would till the soil. There was no longer any possibility of basing the industry upon servile labour. The scarcity of labour is a clear proof that the population of the empire was no longer rising but falling. The low birth-rate and rapid extinction of families among the rich, which had caused anxiety in the early days of the empire, was evidently spreading downwards and became a notable feature in the life of the working classes generally. Comparatively less important was the tendency of the agricultural labourer to leave the land; for this was merely a redistribution of the population. The drift of labour to the towns was arrested by the decline of trade and industry, and it is improbable that there was ever any considerable exodus of labour to places outside the empire. The labouring classes were dying out as fast as their social superiors; and their place also was filled by new-comers and foreigners— barbarians from over the Rhine and the Danube, Germans and Iranians, reinforced later by Slavs. This new element was too strong for the existing population to incorporate and assimilate; the foreigners adopted the Romance languages but went no further. Beginning with the fringes of the empire, this inundation of foreign labour covered the central parts, and marked a further decline in agricultural skill and therefore in the productiveness of the land.

Owing to a smaller area of cultivation and a poorer return from the soil, the agricultural class became less and less able to pay taxes, and their purchasing power fell steadily. Each holding aimed at producing all that it needed without recourse to others. The coinage grew less important in the life of the smallholder, or the great landlord, or the state itself. If not in trade, yet in dealings between owner and cultivator, or between cultivator, owner, and the state, payments were almost invariably made in kind, by handing over some of the produce.

The state of trade and industry was equally disastrous. The industrial activity which had prospered so greatly in many quarters under the early empire and worked for a more or less extensive local market, now lessened its output, grew feeble, and died away; and local exchange within the empire died with it. The only branches of industry that were fully employed were those of vital importance to the state. But we have seen already that this kind of business was gradually withdrawn from private enterprise and carried on by the state. It is not clear how far the state undertook the sale of the articles produced in its factories; but it is unlikely that it aimed at a general monopoly of trade and industry.

The exchange of commodities still went on of course between the different parts of the empire and also between the empire and its neighbours. But though the state carried out on a great scale the transport of things required by the court, the army, the officials, and the population of the capitals, trade, with this exception, dealt chiefly with articles of luxury imported from Eastern countries, and naturally fell into the hands of Eastern merchants—Syrians, Levantines, and Jews. They found their best customers in the class of rich nobility and especially in the court which grew more and more oriental in its external aspect. Oriental magnificence with its riot of colour, its overloaded decoration, its tendency to excessive size and weight in personal adornments, had a strong attraction for the German and Iranian elements, which were now almost dominant in the highest ranks of society. Mere massiveness, to the exclusion of refinement, became the fashion of the day at court and among the aristocracy.

The prosperity of the towns was undermined by such economic conditions as these. The great cities and especially the capitals held out longest. As late as the fourth century splendid buildings were still erected at Rome ; but with the next century a gradual process of decay set in. The new capital, Byzantium-Constantinople, grew into a world city, abounding in luxury and adorned with marvellous and imposing architecture, chiefly palaces and churches. The great seaport towns, Alexandria, Antioch, Ephesus, and Carthage, still survived ; and we may class with these the cities where the sharers of the imperial power held their courts—Ravenna, Mediolanum (Milan), Trèves, Nicomedia, Nicaea. But it is noticeable that the rise of new towns in the provinces, which was common enough in the reign of Hadrian, had now ceased. At the same time, in most provincial towns of moderate size the pulse of life began to beat slower and slower. Christian churches and monasteries were the only new buildings ; and the old buildings were kept in repair with difficulty. Grass grew in the cities. The nobles divided their time between the capitals and their villas—villas which stood like regular fortified palaces in the centre of their great estates. When towns, as sometimes happened on the outskirts of the empire, were destroyed by barbarians, it is no wonder that they never came to life again.

The social aspect of the empire corresponded to the

economic changes we have described. It remained just what it was under Diocletian and Constantine, that is, what it became in the critical epoch of the third century. The emperor with his family and courtiers, the officers of the army, the high ecclesiastics, and the bureaucracy—these composed the highest class of society ; they enjoyed all privileges and lived a more or less highly civilized life. All the members of this ruling class had wealth varying in amount, which was mainly invested in landed property. Next came the merchants and speculators, well-to-do men and some of them rich ; most of these were Semites. The urban middle class, such a feature of the early empire, was disappearing. The old middle-class families were dying out ; if they survived, they were lost among the rabble of the great cities, who worked for the state and were maintained by the state, or among the rural population, who worked as serfs for the state or the great landlords. Slavery, though it lived on as an institution, had lost all economic importance ; slaves played no part any longer in agriculture or trade or industry ; their only function was to serve in the great houses of the rich and noble.

Thus energy and power to work dried up, taste grew coarser, and a small privileged group kept on the surface of a sea of destitution ; and from this condition of things we may infer the intellectual condition of the time. The schools still existed and went on working. But they attracted none except from the upper classes and devoted themselves entirely to the task of fitting their pupils for the civil service of the state. The curriculum was unchanged : general elementary education consisted in learning Greek or Latin or both languages, and a knowledge of the chief classics ; and higher education added rhetoric, or training in writing and speaking, and the acquirement of legal knowledge.

In the sphere of jurisprudence there was still life and creative activity. By the labours of eminent jurists, among whom Paul, Papinian, and Ulpian are the greatest names of the third century, the Roman law became by degrees the law of the whole civilized world. Theory and practice still went hand in hand, and one fertilized the other. The general tendency of both was to become more humane ; and a striking example of this humanity is the improvement in the condition of slaves.

Philosophy also lived on but tended to become restricted

to a narrow circle ; and as it blended with religion, it became less and less distinguishable from theology. After Plotinus we find no fresh or creative genius among the philosophers. His restatement of Platonism became, as we have said already, the last refuge of ' heathen ' thought and the last bulwark of ancient learning and scholarship.

Nor was literature dead. Both the Latin and the Greek divisions of the ancient world still produced considerable writers in poetry and prose ; but those flowers were grown in a hothouse. Authors wrote for one another or for a small audience of cultivated and aristocratic readers. Their technique is often almost faultless, but they depend on the repetition of formulas and subjects taken from the past. As typical representatives of this autumnal poetry, so formal and rhetorical, the Latin half of the world offers the following names : Claudius Claudianus, a Romanized Greek and an epic poet ; Rutilius Namatianus, a native of Gaul, who wrote about A. D. 400 an elegiac poem in which he glorified Rome ; and Ausonius, another Romanized Gaul, a master of form, who shows real poetic inspiration in the description of his voyage on the Moselle, written about 370. Still more popular with cultivated society were the purely rhetorical exercises, in the form of speeches and letters, by which Symmachus gained fame for himself and fought a stout battle in defence of the ancient faith and culture. Symmachus was a native of the West ; the East produced about the same time the letters and speeches of the Emperor Julian and of his contemporary, Libanius of Antioch. Nor was history quite dead : in the person of Ammianus Marcellinus (350–400), it produced one more great thinker and observer, who set himself to continue the work of Tacitus. But in all this activity there was no real life : all the authors here mentioned, and dozens of other similar writers, philosophers, and poets, dating from the end of the third century and the two centuries that follow, bear the stamp of weariness, disenchantment, and despair.

Christian literature alone was really alive. The number of readers who were touched and moved by it steadily increased ; it was inspired by a constantly growing impulse, and drew fresh strength from its bloodless warfare against the champions of the ancient world and the dissenters within its own fold ; it was fertilized by ever closer contact with ancient learning, from which it drew all it needed for its own task of giving a Christian education to all the subjects of the empire. In point of form this literature could not rival the champions of the past; but it was full of new ideas and strong in its connexion with the people at large and in the interest they took in it. It was, indeed, one-sided and narrow: religion and theology were its main themes; but it came to include other departments, and sought to Christianize rhetoric and history, and influence the schools. A number of literary schools grew up in the provinces. Among these, in the fourth and fifth centuries, the most prominent figures are the African Fathers, such as Lactantius (about 325) and Augustine (354–430). They were preceded by Tertullian at the end of the second century, and Cyprian a century later. Bright stars that adorn Latin Christianity are the vigorous Ambrosius, who was Bishop of Milan in the second half of the fourth century, and the learned Jerome, who lived from 335 to 420.

Even more vigorous was the life of Christianity in the East. There the fourth century was the culmination of a vigorous and abundant growth of literature. The foundations of Christian theology and Christian poetry were there laid down by Athanasius of Alexandria, Eusebius of Caesarea, Gregory of Nazianzus, and John Chrysostom. It should be noticed that most of these men were born in the outskirts, and not in the centre, of the Hellenistic world. This Christian literature brings before us a new world and new people, whose performances are beyond the scope of ancient history. In the competition with representatives of the past these writers proved victorious; but it must not be forgotten that they also sprang from the ancient civilization and raised their new building upon the old foundations.

The development of the plastic arts—sculpture, painting, and applied art—was not unlike that of literature. The Hellenistic-Roman art still survived. Architecture still flourished. Though the triumphal arch of Constantine is a mere cento, patched together from scraps of similar art belonging to the age of Domitian and Trajan, yet many other buildings—the Baths of Diocletian at Rome, his palaces at Spalato and Antioch, the Baths and Basilica of Constantine at Rome—are both original and impressive; they owe their effect to breadth and freedom of design, to the skill with which abundance of light and air is penned up within colossal walls, and to the singular variety of their vaulted roofs; they impress the spectator also by their conquest over space and by the massive splendour of their decoration with its imposing variety of colour. This cannot be called the noblest product of ancient architecture; but yet one cannot deny to its authors either creative impulse or the power of embodying that impulse in shapely and splendid forms. Nor was the impulse soon exhausted: it was under Justinian that the marvel of architecture which we call St. Sophia was erected. And later still many masterly buildings were raised in the East and the West by an art which was working for both Church and state, but principally for the former.

The decline of originality and power is more clearly marked in sculpture and painting. The portrait-busts of many of the emperors with their sombre magnificence give a vivid picture of the weight and massiveness characteristic of the empire; but sculpture, like architecture, had lost grace, technical skill, attention to detail, and loving treatment of individuality. Of the painting we know little; but here, too, beauty and harmony of composition, with tender consideration for details, were driven out by garish effects of colour.

It appears therefore that the waning of creative power throughout the empire is less marked in art than in other departments of human activity. As in other epochs of history, art pursued its individual course, reflecting with brilliance and creative power the life around it, and the thoughts and feelings of its contemporaries. Its main task, naturally, was to find suitable forms for the chief articles of the Christian creed; and thus the architects aimed at making Christian churches, or houses of prayer, as perfect as possible, with every adornment of painting, mosaic, and sculpture.

This new Christian art, while making use of the technique and the forms of ancient art, moved steadily away from it. Naturalistic figures and subtle ornament, such as marked the Graeco-Roman style in imperial times, and all its symbolism and impressionism, were discarded in the painful effort to find artistic forms that should embody the persons and symbols dear to all Christians. In course of time the central figures of Christian religion and worship, Christ and the Mother of God, found typical expression in shapes, where the old technique is irradiated by a fresh artistic impulse and a fresh and deep religious feeling. At the same time, the advances made by the craftsmen of old were almost all preserved; and fresh progress was made in course of time. We find, indeed, some loss of refinement and elaboration and some conscious or unconscious tendency to archaism; but in all this art there is no savour of death but the stirring and breathing of a new life.

Applied art was less affected by the change of thought associated with Christianity, though the Church naturally demanded its services and adapted the old technique and the old forms to the requirements of Christian worship in its new and more splendid surroundings. But this art was less the handmaid of the Church than of the court and the small group of wealthy men. It was subservient to their changing taste. The new aristocracy could not appreciate the elegance of ancient industrial art : they needed coarser and more highly spiced food. They wished that ornament, dress, jewellery, and furniture should appeal at once to the eye and stun the beholder. For such a demand the East could always cater, especially the Iranian East, which had come less under Hellenistic influence and was therefore inferior to Syria and Egypt in elegance and refinement. Thus the applied art of Irania and Central Asia came in by various routes and defeated all competitors throughout the empire; it proclaimed once more the triumph of massiveness, variety of colour, and sharpness and hardness of lines—in fact, of all the traits peculiar to Oriental art in its early stages.

The ancient world slowly grew old and decrepit and was reduced to dust; but a new life grew up upon the ruins, and the new edifice of European civilization was built on a foundation that had remained firm and sound. The new building rose stone by stone, but its main lines were determined by the old substructure, and many of the old stones were used for further service. Though that world grew old, it never died and never disappeared : it lives on in us, as the groundwork of our thought, our attitude to religion, our art, our social and political institutions, and even our material civilization.

XXV

CAUSES OF THE DECLINE OF ANCIENT CIVILIZATION

IN a book devoted to the history of ancient civilization the reader is entitled to seek an answer to this question: Why did such a powerful and brilliant civilization, the growth of ages and apparently destined to last for ages, gradually degenerate? In other words, why did the creative power of its makers wax faint, with this result, that mankind slowly reverted to primitive and extremely simple conditions of life and then began to create civilization over again from the very rudiments, reviving the old institutions and studying the old problems? It was an effort of centuries to climb up again to the level on which man had lived for a period for many hundred years.

To this question many answers have been given by historians, philosophers, and economists, by students of sociology, physiology, and theology. This is not the place to examine all the methods proposed for the solution of the problem. But one thing I will say: the majority of these explanations take into account only one of the symptoms that announce the steady decline of cultural creation, and declare this to be the cause of the decline as a whole. I shall permit myself, without entering upon polemical discussion, to put forward that solution of the secular problem which I regard as most probable.

What do we mean by the 'decline' of ancient civilization? What lies at the root of this steady reversion of civilized man to the primitive state of barbarism? Wherever we observe this process, we note also a psychological change in those classes of society which had been up till then the creators of culture. Their creative power and creative energy dry up; men grow weary and lose interest in creation and cease to value it; they are disenchanted; their life is no longer an effort towards a creative ideal for the benefit of humanity; their minds are occupied either with material interests, or with ideals unconnected with life on earth and realized elsewhere. In this latter case the centre of attraction shifts from earth to heaven, or from earth to a world beyond the grave.

A process of this kind was repeated fairly often in ancient history. But the plainest and most unmistakable instances are these two—the decline of Greek civilization in the late Hellenistic Age, and the Roman Empire. The history of the East is familiar with the fall of great civilizations. But there the failure was generally due to external causes such as foreign conquest ; thus the Cassites conquered Babylonia, and the Hyksos ruled Egypt ; the Persians destroyed Assyria ; the Hittite Empire was overthrown by Thracians, and the Phrygian kingdom by Cimmerians. Again, it often happened that the decline was temporary and soon followed by recovery ; it was so in Egypt, for example. And further, the transference of civilization is characteristic of the East generally : the Assyrians inherit the culture of Babylonia, which passes next to the Persians, and from them to the Parthians and the Sassanian dynasty ; and the succession is uninterrupted down to our own time. There are longer or shorter interruptions, but there is no definite cessation. It may be that Oriental culture had more staying power, because its creative effort never touched the summits attained by Greek and Roman genius. In the East we never observe that general and permanent change of mental attitude which is characteristic of the West ; and the reason is probably this—that Oriental culture was based on a definite view of religion, which survived all change of circumstances and saved men from falling into the inaction of despair.

But the history of Western culture was different. It belonged to small separate groups, small social and political units, which combined to form a city-state ; and in these city-states it was still an individual thing, confined to the select few. It was born in strife—strife against foreign foes and strife within the state, in defence of certain ideals. The object of the war against foreigners was political independence ; the conflict at home was inspired by the desire for better, more perfect, and juster conditions of life, though each man, no doubt, had his own conception of ' justice '. Belief in the omnipotence of man, in his reason, and in the power of reason to solve all problems, either practical or strictly philosophic and scientific—this belief gave inspiration and made it possible for the best intellects to lay the foundations of what we call the scientific attitude of mind. To this was added a marvellous artistic endowment, which enabled these men to clothe their ideals in visible forms and to produce masterpieces of literature and art.

In the early history of the Greek city-states this culture, created by a minority, was the common property of all the citizens, and even extended to all the inhabitants of the city, not excluding the slaves. But economic development produced in course of time a sharp distinction in society, and divided the population of Greek cities into two constantly opposed groups—'the better' and 'the worse', who may generally be identified with the rich and the poor. Thus by degrees culture became restricted to its creators and the class to which they belonged : it became the culture of the aristocracy alone.

When, after the death of Alexander the Great, the culture of the Greek city-state conquered Oriental culture and took its place—when the inhabitants of the new and old city-states became the ruling class in the East, then Greek civilization flourished more luxuriantly than ever. For the creative activity of the Greek intellectual aristocracy found a wider field with the expansion in the number of cities. But this culture was still confined to the select few ; and this held good of the East especially, where the mass of the people never fully accepted a system that was to them foreign and incomprehensible. In Greece, meanwhile, the class-war became still fiercer ; and this, together with the Greek tendency to separatism, was the reason why the city-states were, on the whole, unsuccessful in their struggle against the monarchs who inherited the power of Alexander. Yet they never made a final surrender to Hellenistic autocracy ; and as time went on, a greater number of Greek cities enjoyed complete or partial independence.

The Greek city-state finally lost its freedom when Greece was conquered by Rome ; and the conquest was preceded by a long period of political and social anarchy. In spite of her superior culture, in spite of her marvellous intellectual and artistic trophies, Greece became the slave of men whom she ranked as barbarians. In the confusion that preceded, and the apathy which followed, the Roman conquest, the chief sufferers were the best men, those who still kept alive the ideals of Greek freedom. Such men, above all others, were subject to that change of mental attitude which I spoke of above. They came to distrust reason ; their ideals were trampled under foot ; and they either sank into the slough of a coarse materialism or sought salvation in mystical religions.

But they found successors in the West—men guided by

the same ideals and intellectual beliefs, and governed by the same political institutions. The Greek city-state was replaced by the Italian town, and by Rome, the head of an alliance between these towns. The Roman aristocracy caught the lamp of civilization from Greece, and carried on the mission of Greece along the same lines, adding, as they worked, the national qualities peculiar to themselves. But Rome was more than a city-state : she was a city ruling over an empire : for every citizen she had hundreds of subjects. In Rome itself the aristocracy who had created the new Italian civilization were forced to endure the domestic conflict by which Greece had been divided. But so long as Rome was fighting for political pre-eminence in the ancient world, the division of classes within the state remained in the background or at least did not cause bloodshed. As soon, however, as she became mistress of the world, the power of 'the best men', the *optimates* or aristocracy, was assailed by the citizens in general. Their war-cry was a better and juster distribution of property, and a more democratic form of government. For eighty years this bloody conflict lasted, and the aristocracy came out of it defeated and demoralized. Its place was taken by the Italian middle class ; and it now became their duty to hold aloft the standard of civilization.

The middle class paid dear for their victory. Though the municipal constitution and the freedom of the citizens were preserved, at least in appearance and for the time, yet a new superstructure, in the shape of the imperial power, towered above the state. It turned out that freedom—not merely political freedom but that freedom of thought and creation which was prized most highly by the noblest spirits—grew steadily less ; and the very conception of freedom was lowered till it meant the voluntary submission of all to one, even if that one was the best among the best, even if he was the *princeps*. And even this freedom belonged only to those who possessed the title of Roman citizens : to the millions scattered over the empire even this shadowy privilege was denied.

The establishment of the empire brought with it a fresh advance of creative genius. But, as I have said already in Chapter XV, this advance lacked the enthusiasm and power which marked the accomplishment of the Greek cities and even that of republican Rome. From the beginning it bears the stamp of weariness and disappointment—the stamp characteristic of a post-revolutionary era ; and later, in the calm atmosphere of peace, order, and prosperity, it grows steadily weaker, and its living energy departs from it. The upper classes, with the exception of the senatorial houses whom the emperors persecuted and exterminated, led a quiet and easy life. Under the emperor's guardianship they had no need to trouble themselves about the morrow. Rome had no rival, and Roman civilization no competitor. That Rome, her civilization, and her political system, were all alike immortal—such was the general opinion. There was no one to struggle with and nothing to struggle for. The ruler himself preached peace and not conflict to the community. What was there to seek for, when all was already found ? Moreover, search was a dangerous business and might bring down much unpleasantness on the head of the seeker.

In this atmosphere of indolent contentment the privileged classes, and especially the urban middle class, came to find their ideals in pleasure, the pursuit of gain, and the attainment, for themselves and their families, of the material advantages of civilization. Men grew selfish and fixed their hearts on idleness and amusement. In such an era of sterility and stagnation the best minds grew dissatisfied with life and found fault with it ; and when they found that this led to nothing, they lost faith in the power of reason—reason which failed them on every hand, while all the time the guardianship and censorship of the ruler was gaining ground. Creative genius dwindled ; science repeated its previous results. The text-book took the place of research ; no new artistic discoveries were made, but echoes of the past were heard, perfect in form but void of meaning ; and also the pen, the graving-tool, and the pencil produced highly spiced work, able to attract and amuse the mind but incapable of elevating and inspiring it.

Those who refused to surrender took refuge in religion. They sought deliverance from the pettiness of real life in the contemplation of God and in communion with the unseen world. Unable to work for others or to strive for the triumph of any great cause, they withdrew entirely into themselves and adopted self-perfection as their ideal, the steady development of their own moral and spiritual being. Under the brilliant exterior of the Roman Empire we feel the failure of creative power and the distaste for it ; we feel the weariness and indifference which undermined, not merely the culture of the state, but also its political system, its military strength, and its economic progress. One symptom of this indifference is race suicide—the refusal to continue the species. The higher classes were recruited from without, not from within, and became extinct before they had time to hand down to following generations the heritage of culture.

But this easy and cultured life was by no means enjoyed by every subject of the empire. The culture was confined to a minority—to the well-to-do urban class. It is true that the members of this minority became much more numerous in that age : new towns sprang up everywhere—among Celts, Iberians, Illyrians, Thracians, and Berbers, in the West; in the hills and valleys of Asia Minor and Syria, and in the plains of Arabia, in the East. But the fact of this increase in numbers must be considered in connexion with other facts. The urban proletariate of slaves and freedmen was growing just as fast, if not faster ; and so was the rural population. Neither of these classes had any share in the idleness and prosperity of their social superiors : their portion was labour and something like beggary. The culture of the town dwellers was not intended for them ; they were fortunate if they could pick up the crumbs. Thus the impotence and idleness of the directing classes brought about a new social and economic crisis in the empire. The most keen-sighted of the emperors realized the danger ; but it was difficult and even perilous for the ruler to arouse the higher classes from their apathy ; and, on the other hand, the stubborn though passive resistance of the 'classes' made it almost impossible to promote the 'masses' freely to superior rank.

The development of these states of mind—apathy in the rich and discontent among the poor—was at first slow and secret. But suddenly it became acute, when the empire was forced, after nearly two centuries of peace and tranquillity, to defend itself against enemies from without. The time called for a great display of enthusiasm. But the rich could not be roused from their indifference ; and the poor, seeing the helplessness and weakness of their betters, and deprived of all share in their idle and indolent contentment, were filled with hatred and envy. Realizing this internal malady of the state, the rulers tried to force their subjects to defend the empire and its civilization. The hand of authority was heavy on high and low alike. In order to save the empire, the state began to crush and ruin the population, lowering the proud but not raising the humble. Hence arose the social and political catastrophe of the third century, in which the state, relying upon the army or, in other words, upon the lower classes, defeated the upper classes and left them humiliated and beggared. This was a fatal blow to the aristocratic and urban civilization of the ancient world.

From this blow the ancient world never recovered. The creative powers of the aristocracy were finally undermined. The indolent and peaceful contentment of the first two centuries gave place to the apathy of dotage, to indifference and despair. In their sufferings men sought deliverance, not in this life but beyond it : they hoped for rest and happiness hereafter. Nor did the lower classes gain anything by their victory : slavery and financial ruin were their portion. They also, after the horrors of the third century, found a refuge in religion and the hope of happiness in a future life. In this impotent condition the empire spent its latter days, ever more and more simplifying its existence and asking less of life. The state, supporting itself upon the relics of past greatness, went on existing just so long as its culture and organization were superior to those of its enemies ; when that superiority disappeared, new masters took control of what had become a bloodless and effete organism. Any creative power that remained turned away from this world and its demands and studied how to know God and be united with Him.

Thus here again, in the case of the Roman Empire, a steady decline of civilization is not to be traced to physical degeneration, or to any debasement of blood in the higher races due to slavery, or to political and economic conditions, but rather to a changed attitude of men's minds. That change was due to the chain of circumstances which produced the specific conditions of life in the Roman Empire ; and the process was the same as in Greece. One of these conditions, and very important among them, was the aristocratic and exclusive nature of ancient civilization. The mental reaction and the social division, taken together, deprived the ancient world of power to maintain its civilization, or to defend it against internal dissolution and barbarian invasion from without.

Chronology

	B.C.
Iron Age in Italy. The Villanovan civilization	1000
The Etruscans in Italy	VIIIth cent.
Alleged date of the foundation of Carthage	814
Colonization of S. Italy and Sicily by the Greeks	VIIIth—VIIth cent.
Alleged date of the foundation of Rome	753
Expansion of the Etruscans in Latium	VIIth cent.
Expansion of the Etruscans in Campania and in N. Italy	VIth cent.
Battle off Alalia. Etruscans beat Greeks	538
Overthrow of the Etruscan domination at Rome	508
First naval victory of the Greeks over the Etruscans. Battle off Cumae	474
Codification of the Law at Rome	about 450
Lex Canuleia	437
Capture of Veii	392
Rome taken by the Gauls	about 390
The Latin war	338
Alliance of Rome and Capua	334
Samnite war	325–304
War with Samnites, Etruscans, and Gauls	298–290
Battle of Sentinum	295
Lex Hortensia. Secession of the plebs	287
War with Tarentum and Pyrrhus	281–272
First Punic war	264–241
Roman invasion of Africa	256–255
First Illyrian war	229–228
Second Illyrian war	220–219
Second Punic war	218–201
Battle of Cannae	216
First Macedonian war	215
Conquest of Syracuse	212
Conquest of Capua	211
Battle of the Metaurus	207
Battle of Zama	202
Second Macedonian war	200–196
Battle of Cynoscephalae	197
War with Antiochus the Great	192–189
Third Macedonian war	171–167
Battle of Pydna	168
Third Punic war	149–146
Fourth Macedonian war	149–148
Destruction of Corinth and Carthage	146
Numantine war	143–133
Slave war in Sicily	136–132
Pergamene Kingdom bequeathed to Rome	133
Tribunate of Tiberius Gracchus	133
C. Gracchus tribune	123–122
Jugurthine war	111–105
Consulships of Marius	107–100
Tribunate of Livius Drusus	91
The so-called 'Social' war	90–88
First Mithradatic war	89–85

	B.C.
Sulla's return to Italy	83
Sulla's dictatorship	82–79
Second Mithradatic war	74–63
Slave war in Italy	73–71
First consulate of Pompey and Crassus	70
Consulate of Cicero. Conspiracy of Catiline	63
The so-called ' first triumvirate '	60
Conquest of Gaul by Caesar	58–51
War between Caesar and the Senate	49–46
Battle of Pharsalus. Death of Pompey	48
Battle of Thapsus	46
Battle of Munda	45
Assassination of Caesar	44
The second triumvirate	43
Battle of Philippi	42
Battle of Actium	31
Augustus	27 B. C.—14 A. D.
Augustus as princeps	17 A.D.

	A. D.
Revolt of Pannonia	6–9
Arminius	9
Tiberius	14–37
Caligula	37–41
Claudius	41–57
Nero	57–68
Galba	68–69
Otho and *Vitellius*	69
Vespasian	69–79
Destruction of Jerusalem	70
Titus	79–81
Pompeii and Herculaneum buried under the ashes of Vesuvius	79
Domitian	81–96
Nerva	96–98
Trajan	98–117
First Dacian war	101–102
Second Dacian war	105–106
Parthian war	114–117
Hadrian	117–138
Antoninus Pius	138–161
Marcus Aurelius	161–180
Parthian war	161–166
Great plague	166
First war on the Danube	167–175
Revolt of Avidius Cassius	175
Second war on the Danube	177–180
Commodus (from 172 co-regent of Marcus Aurelius)	180–192
Pertinax and *Didius Julianus*	193
Civil war : Septimius Severus, Pescennius Niger, Clodius Albinus	193–197
Septimius Severus	193–211
Pescennius defeated	194
Parthian war	195–6
Albinus defeated	197
Second Parthian war	197–199
War in Britain	208
Caracalla (co-regency with Geta 211–212)	211–217
Constitutio Antoniniana	212
Parthian war	214

	A.D.
Macrinus	217–218
Elagabal	218–222
Severus Alexander	222–235
Sassanian Kingdom in Persia	227
War with Persia	230–233
War on the Rhine	234
Maximinus	235–238
Gordian III	238–244
Philip the Arab	243–249
Decius	249–251
Valerian	253–258
Gallienus	253–268
Claudius Gothicus	268–270
Aurelian	270–275
Tacitus	275–276
Probus	276–282
Carus	282–283
Carinus	283–285
Diocletian (286–305 co-regency with Maximian)	287–305
Constantine	327–337

311 - A D

Throug 395 - A.D.

476

327

Bibliography

Cambridge Ancient History, vols. vii–xii (1928–1939), gives a new full-scale survey of Roman history, and full bibliographical listings. Accordingly, these suggestions for further study take account, with some exceptions of only a few recent books, mostly in English. See also the annual bibliographies in *L'Année philologique*.

I. SOURCES (SELECTIONS IN TRANSLATION)

N. Lewis & M. Reinhold, *Roman Civilization*, vols. i–ii, 1951–55 (with a good bibliography of books and articles in English).

Ancient Roman Statutes, tr. by Allan Ch. Johnson *et alii*, 1961.

M. Hadas, *A History of Rome* (Anchor orig. paperback), 1956.

For archaeological illustrative material see the ninety-six plates of the original edition of this book (*A History of the Ancient World*, vol. ii, *Rome*); see also *Cambridge Ancient History*, plates, vols. iii–v.

II. GENERAL SURVEYS OF ROMAN HISTORY

Cambridge Ancient History, vols. vii–xii, 1928–39.

A. Piganiol, *Histoire de Rome*, 4th ed., 1954 (with an excellent bibliography).

G. Gianelli & S. Mazzarino, *Trattato di storia romana*, vols. i–ii, 1953–56 (with a detailed bibliography).

A. Aymard, *Rome et son empire*, 1954.

Textbooks: A. E. R. Boak, *A History of Rome*, 4th ed., 1955; M. Cary, *History of Rome*, 2nd ed., 1954.

J. O. Thomson, *Everyman's Classical Atlas*, Dutton, 1961.

III. ANCIENT ITALY

A. GENERAL WORKS

M. Cary, *The Geographic Background of Greek and Roman History*, 1949.

E. Pulgram, *The Tongues of Italy*, 1958.

G. Devoto, *Gli antichi Italici*, 2nd ed., 1951.

B. PREHISTORY

G. Patroni, *La preistoria*, 2nd ed., 1951.

V. G. Childe, *The Dawn of European Civilisation*, 6th ed., 1957.

C. ETRURIA

M. Pallottino, *Etruscan Painting*, 1952.

Id., *The Etruscans*, Pelican paperback translation, 1955.

R. Bloch, *The Etruscans*, 1958.

Id., *Etruscan Art*, 1959.

D. SICILY AND SOUTH ITALY

L. B. Brea, *Sicily before the Greeks*, 1958.
G. de Miré, *Sicile grecque*, 1955.
J. Heurgon, *Recherches sur l'histoire ... de Capoue préromaine*, 1942.
P. Wuilleumier, *Tarente*, 1939.

IV. THE ROMAN REPUBLIC

A. GENERAL WORKS

Cambridge Ancient History, vols. vii–ix, 1928–32.
Th. Mommsen, *History of Rome*, 1854–56; an abridged Wisdom paperback translation, 1960.
Fustel de Coulanges, *Ancient City* (1863), Anchor paperback reprint.
G. de Sanctis, *Storia dei Romani*, vols. i–iv, 1907–58.
H. H. Scullard, *A History of the Roman World from 753 to 146* B.C., 3rd ed., 1961.

B. MONOGRAPHS

(1) EARLY PERIOD

E. Pais, *Ancient Legends of Roman History*, 1906.
G. Dumézil, *L'héritage indo-européen à Rome*, 1949.
R. Bloch, *The Origins of Rome*, 1960.
E. Gjerstad, *Early Rome*, vols. i–ii, 1953ff., in progress.

(2) PERIOD OF THE CITY-STATE AND OF THE LATIN AND ITALIAN LEAGUE

E. Muenzer, *Roemische Adelsparteien und Adelsfamilien*, 1920.
A. Afzelius, *Die roemische Eroberung Italiens 340–264 vor Chr.* (Acta Jutlandica XIV, 1), 1942.

(3) PERIOD OF THE FORMATION OF THE ROMAN EMPIRE

M. Holleaux, *Rome, la Grèce et les monarchies hellénistiques au III-ème siècle av. J.-C. (273–205)*, 1921.
Id., *Études d'épigraphie et d'histoire grecque*, vols. iv–v: *Rome, la Macédoine et l'Orient grec*, 1952–57.
F. W. Walbank, *Philip V*, 1940.
B. H. Warmington, *Carthage*, 1960.
G. and C. Charles-Picard, *Daily Life in Carthage at the Time of Hannibal*, 1961.
C. G. Starr, *The Emergence of Rome as Ruler of the Western World*, Cornell Univ. Press.
A. Afzelius, *Die roemische Kriegsmacht waehrend der Auseinandersetzung mit den hellenisticshen Grossmaechten* (Acta Jutlandica XVI, 2), 1944.
F. W. Walbank, *A Historical Commentary on Polybius*, vol. i, 1956 (in progress).
P. Meloni, *Perseo e la fine della monarchia macedone*, 1953.

(4) PERIOD OF THE CIVIL WAR

Th. Mommsen, *History of Rome*, Meridian paperback abridgment of the chapters on the Fall of the Republic.
G. Ferrero, *Greatness and Decline of Rome*, vols. i–v (Engl. transl., 1907–9).

Id., *The Life of Caesar*, Norton paperback reprint, (selected chapters from Ferrero, *Greatness of Rome*, see above).

E. Meyer, *Caesar's Monarchie und der Prinzipat des Pompeius*, 2nd ed., 1919.

T. R. Holmes, *The Roman Republic and the Founder of the Roman Empire*, vols. i-iii, 1923.

G. Bloch & J. Carcopino, *La République romaine de 133 à 44 av. J.-C.*, vols. i-ii, 1929-36.

Lily R. Taylor, *Party Politics in the Age of Caesar*, 1949; Univ. of Calif. Press paperback reprint, 1961.

F. R. Cowell, *Cicero and the Roman Republic*, 1948; Pelican paperback reprint, 1956.

H. Frisch, *Cicero's Fight for the Republic*, 1946.

T. R. Holmes, *Caesar's Conquest of Gaul*, 2nd ed., 1931.

Id., *Ancient Britain and the Invasions of Julius Caesar*, 1936.

H. H. Scullard, *From the Gracchi to Nero*, Praeger paperback reprint, 1959.

F. B. Marsh, *A History of the Roman World from 146-30 B.C.*, 2nd ed., 1953.

C. CONSTITUTION AND ADMINISTRATION

Th. Mommsen, *Roemisches Staatsrecht*, vols. i-iii, 3rd ed., 1871-88.

U. v. Luebtow, *Das roemische Volk sein Staat und sein Recht*, 1955.

L. Homo, *Roman Political Institutions* (Engl. transl., 1929).

G. H. Stevenson, *Roman Provincial Administration*, 1939.

A. N. Sherwin-White, *The Roman Citizenship*, 1939.

K. v. Fritz, *The Mixed Constitution in Antiquity*, 1954.

H. W. Parker, *The Roman Legions*, 2nd ed., 1957.

J. H. Thiel, *Studies on the History of Roman Sea-power in Republican Times*, 1946.

Id., *A History of Roman Sea-power before the Second Punic War*, 1954.

F. E. Adcock, *The Roman Art of War under the Republic*, 1940.

Id., *Roman Political Ideas and Practices*, 1959.

H. Hill, *The Roman Middle Class in the Republican Period*, 1952.

D. ECONOMIC AND SOCIAL CONDITIONS

T. Frank, *An Economic History of Rome*, 2nd ed., 1927.

Id., *An Economic Survey of Ancient Rome*, vol. i, 1933.

W. E. Heitland, *Agricola: A Study in Agriculture and Rustic Life in the Greco-Roman World*, 1921.

E. RELIGION

W. Warde Fowler, *The Religious Experience of the Roman People*, 2nd ed., 1922.

C. Bailey, *Phases in the Religion of Ancient Rome*, 1932.

H. Wagenvoort, *Roman Dynamism*, 1947.

H. J. Rose, *Ancient Roman Religion*, 1948.

J. Bayet, *Histoire politique et psychologique de la religion romaine*, 1957.

F. ART AND ARCHAEOLOGY

R. Cagnat & V. Chapot, *Manuel d'archéologie romaine*, vols. i-ii, 1916-20.

E. Strong, *Art in Ancient Rome*, 1928.

A. Maiuri, *Roman Painting*, 1953.

G. M. Richter, *Ancient Italy*, 1955.
I. S. Ryberg, *Rites of the State Religion in Roman Art*, 1955.
I. S. Scott, *An Archaeological Record of Rome*, 1940.
P. McKendrick, *Mute Stones Speak*, 1960.
M. Grant, *Roman History from Coins*, 1958.
H. Mattingly, *Roman Coins*, 2nd ed., 1960.
E. A. Sydenham, *The Coinage of the Roman Republic*, 2nd ed., 1952.

G. LAW

F. Schulz, *Classical Roman Law*, 1951.
Id., *History of Roman Legal Science*, 1953.
H. F. Jolowicz, *Roman Foundations of Modern Law*, 1957.
H. J. Wolff, *Roman Law*, 1951.

H. LITERATURE

See Section *V*, I.

V. THE ROMAN EMPIRE

A. GENERAL WORKS

M. Rostovtzeff, *Social and Economic History of the Roman Empire*, 1926; 2nd ed., 1957 (reprint with some additions).
Cambridge Ancient History, vols. x–xii, 1934–39.
These two works are essential. Both give detailed and classified bibliographies. Accordingly, with a few exceptions, only some works in English published after 1934 are named below.
E. Gibbon, *Decline and Fall of the Roman Empire*, 1st ed., 1776–88; essential parts are available in such paperbacks as *The Portable Gibbon*.
E. T. Salmon, *A History of the Roman World from 30 B.C. to A.D. 138*, 3rd ed., 1957.
M. P. Charlesworth, *The Roman Empire*, 1951.
H. Mattingly, *Roman Imperial Civilisation*, 1957; Anchor paperback reprint, 1959.

B. MONOGRAPHS ON THE EMPERORS

(1) AUGUSTUS

Res Gestae Divi Augusti, Latin text with French commentary by J. Gagé, 2nd ed., 1950; with English notes by R. S. Rogers, 1935; Engl. transl. in Lewis & Reinhold (see above, Section *I*), vol. ii, pp. 9ff.
R. Syme, *Roman Revolution*, 1939; Oxford paperback reprint, 1960.
J. D. Newby, *A Numismatic Commentary on the Res Gestae of Augustus*, 1938.

(2) TIBERIUS

R. S. Rogers, *Studies in the Reign of Tiberius*, 1943.
M. Grant, *Aspects of the Principate of Tiberius*, 1951.

(3) CALIGULA

J. P. V. D. Balsdon, *The Emperor Gaius*, 1934.

(4) CLAUDIUS

V. M. Scaramuzza, *The Emperor Claudius*, 1940.
A. Momigliano, *Claudius*, 2nd ed., 1957.

(5) TRAJAN

F. A. Lepper, *Trajan's Parthian War*, 1948.

(6) MARCUS AURELIUS

E. Renan, *Marcus Aurelius*, 1882; Engl. transl. extant.
A. S. L. Farquarson, *Marcus Aurelius*, 2nd ed., 1952.
M. Hammond, *The Antonine Monarchy*, 1959.

C. CONSTITUTION

J. Beranger, *Recherches sur l'aspect idéologique du principat*, 1953.
M. Grant, *From Imperium to Auctoritas*, 1946.
A. R. Burn, *The Government of the Roman Empire*, 1952.

D. ADMINISTRATION

S. J. de Leet, *Portorium: Étude sur l'organisation douanière chez les Romains*, 1949.
E. Birley, *Roman Britain and the Roman Army*, 1953.
G. Forni, *Recrutamento delle legioni da Augusto a Diocleziano*, 1953.
J. A. O. Larsen, *Representative Government in Greek and Roman History*, 1955.
H. G. Pflaum, *Les Procurateurs équestres sous le Haut-Empire romain*, 1950.
J. A. Crook, *Consilium Principis: Imperial Councils and Counsellors from Augustus to Diocletian*, 1955.
C. G. Starr, *The Roman Imperial Navy*, 1941.
L. L. Howe, *The Praetorian Prefects from Commodus to Diocletian*, 1942.
G. H. Stevenson, *Roman Provincial Administration*, 2nd ed., 1949.
M. Durry, *Les Cohortes pretoriennes*, 1938.
A. Passerini, *Le coorti pretorie*, 1939.

E. ECONOMIC AND SOCIAL CONDITIONS

M. Rostovtzeff, *Social and Economic History of the Roman Empire*, 2nd ed., 1957.
T. Frank, *An Economic Survey of Ancient Rome*, vols. ii–v, 1936–41.
S. Dill, *Roman Society from Nero to M. Aurelius*, 1905; Meridian paperback reprint, 1956.
H. I. Marrou, *History of Education in Antiquity*, 1957.
M. L. Clarke, *Rhetoric at Rome*, 1953.
J. Day, *An Economic History of Athens under Roman Domination*, 1942.
C. G. Starr, *Civilisation and the Caesars*, 1954.
J. Carcopino, *Daily Life in Ancient Rome*, 1941; Yale paperback reprint, 1960.
F. Kenyon, *Books and Readers in Greece and Rome*, 2nd ed., 1951.
W. L. Westermann, *The Slave Systems of Greek and Roman Antiquity*, 1955.
A. N. Duff, *Freedmen in the Early Roman Empire*, 2nd ed., 1957.
M. Wheeler, *Rome Beyond Imperial Frontiers*, 1954; Pelican paperback reprint, 1955.
F. Poulsen, *Glimpses of Roman Culture*, 1950.
J. H. Oliver, *The Ruling Power: A Study of the Roman Empire in the Second Century after Christ through the Roman Oration of Aelius Aristides*, 1953.
U. E. Paoli, *Vita Romana*, 1948 (in Italian; also French and German translations).
E. Barker, *From Alexander to Constantine: Passages and Documents Illustrating the History of Social and Political Ideas*, 1956.

F. THE PROVINCES OF THE ROMAN EMPIRE

Th. Mommsen, *Provinces of the Roman Empire,* vols. i–ii, 1885; Engl. transl. extant.
M. Rostovtzeff, *Social and Economic History of the Roman Empire,* 2nd ed., 1957.

(1) THE WEST

I. A. Richmond, *Roman Britain* (original Pelican Book), 1955.
Antiquities of Roman Britain (The British Museum), 1951.
G. E. F. Chilver, *Cisalpine Gaul,* 1941.
O. Brogan, *Roman Gaul,* 1953.
A. Dopsch, *The Economic and Social Foundations of European Civilisation,* 1937.
J. J. Hatt, *Histoire de la Gaule romaine,* 1959.
F. J. Wieseman, *Roman Spain,* 1956.

(2) ASIA

D. Magie, *Roman Rule in Asia Minor,* vols. i–ii, 1950.

(3) SOUTH RUSSIA

M. Rostovtzeff, *Iranians and Greeks in South Russia,* 1922.
T. T. Rice, *The Scythians,* 1957.

(4) SYRIA

M. Rostovtzeff, *Caravan Cities,* 1932.
Id., *Dura-Europos and its Art,* 1938.
G. Downey, *History of Antioch,* 1961.

(5) EGYPT

J. G. Winter, *Life and Letters in the Papyri,* 1933.
S. L. Wallace, *Taxation in Egypt from Augustus to Diocletian,* 1938.
H. I. Bell, *Egypt, from Alexander the Great to the Arab Conquest,* 1948.
A. C. Johnson, *Egypt and the Roman Empire,* 1951.
R. Taubenschlag, *The Law of Greco-Roman Egypt,* 2nd ed., 1955.
H. A. Musurillo, *The Acts of Pagan Martyrs,* 1954.
G. Charles-Picard, *Civilisation de l'Afrique romaine,* 1959.

G. RELIGION

(1) PAGAN CULTS

F. C. Grant, *Roman Religion,* 1955 (translation of texts).
F. Cumont, *Oriental Religions in Roman Paganism,* Dover paperback reprint.
Id., *Lux Perpetua,* 1949.
Id., *After-Life in Roman Paganism,* 1922; Dover paperback reprint.
I. A. Richmond, *Archaeology and the After-Life in Pagan and Christian Imagery,* 1950.
J. Bayet, *Histoire politique et psychologique de la religion romaine,* 1957.
H. J. Bell, *Cults and Creeds in Graeco-Roman Egypt,* 2nd ed., 1954.
A. D. Nock, *Conversion,* 1933; Oxford paperback reprint, 1961.
F. H. Cramer, *Astrology in Roman Law and Politics,* 1954.

(2) CHRISTIANITY

H. Lietzmann, *A History of the Early Church,* 2 vols.; Meridian paperback reprint.
T. R. Glover, *The Conflict of Religions in the Early Roman Empire,* 1909.
P. de Labriolle, *La Réaction païenne,* 1934.
H. Mattingly, *Christianity in the Roman Empire,* 1957.
E. Stauffer, *Christ and the Caesars,* 1955.

J. Lebreton & J. Zeiller, *The History of the Primitive Church*, vols. i–iv, 1948–49.
C. J. Cadoux, *The Early Church and the World*, 1925.
J. Stevenson, *A New Eusebius: Documents Illustrative of the History of the Church to* A.D. *337* (Engl. transl.), 1957.

H. ART AND ARCHAEOLOGY

(Compare Section *IV*, F)

A. Maiuri. *Pompeii*, 1960.
K. Schefold, *Pompeianische Malerei*, 1952.
R. Meiggs, *Roman Ostia*, 1960.
D. S. Robertson. *Handbook of Greek and Roman Architecture*, 2nd ed., 1943.
A. Boethius, *The Golden House of Nero*, 1961.
L. Lugli, *La tecnica edilizia romana*, 1957.
Ch. Singer (ed.), *History of Technology*, vol. ii, 1956.
L. Homo, *Rome impériale et l'urbanisme dans l'antiquité*, 1951.
C. H. V. Sutherland, *Coinage in Roman Imperial Policy, 31* B.C.–A.D. *68*, 1951.
A Guide to the Exhibition of Roman Coins in the British Museum, 1952.
N. Grant, *Roman Imperial Money*, 1954.
R. Ghirshman, *Iran,* Pelican paperback, 1954.
A. Christensen, *L'Empire des Sassanides*, 1944.
A. J. Arkell, *History of the Sudan*, 1956.
F. Owen, *The Germanic People*, 1960.

I. LITERATURE

(1) GENERAL WORKS

J. W. Duff, *Literary History of Rome*, 2nd ed., 1953.
T. Frank, *Life and Literature in the Roman Republic*, 1931; Univ. of Calif. Press paperback reprint, 1957.
Ed. Norden, *Die roemische Literatur*, 5th ed., 1954.
H. J. Rose, *A Handbook of Latin Literature*, 3rd ed., 1954.
A. Meillet, *Ésquisse d'une histoire de la langue latine*, 6th ed., 1952.
L. R. Palmer, *Latin Language*, 1954.

(2) MONOGRAPHS

F. E. Adcock, *Caesar as Man of Letters*, 1956.
G. Boissier, *Cicero and His Friends* (Engl. transl., 1897).
M. L. W. Laistner, *The Greater Roman Historians*, 1947.
G. E. Duckworth, *The Nature of Roman Comedy*, 1952.
L. P. Wilkinson, *Ovid Recalled*, 1955.
Ed. Fraenkel, *Horatius*, 1957.
L. P. Wilkinson, *Horace and His Lyric Poetry*, 2nd ed., 1951.
G. Highet, *Juvenal the Satirist*, 1954; Oxford paperback reprint, 1961.
C. W. Mendell, *Tacitus*, 1957.
R. Syme, *Tacitus*, 1958.
J. Perret, *Virgile*, 1952.
H. J. Rose, *The Eclogues of Vergil*, 1942.
G. Highet, *Poets in a Landscape*, 1957.

VI. LATE ROMAN EMPIRE

A. GENERAL WORKS

J. B. Bury, *History of the Later Roman Empire,* 2nd ed., 1923; Dover paperback reprint, 2 vols., 1957.

F. Lot, *The End of the Ancient World,* 1931.

A. Piganiol, *L'Empire chrétien,* 1947.

A. Vassiliev, *History of the Byzantine Empire,* 2 vols., 2nd ed., 1952; Univ. of Wisc. Press paperback reprint, 2 vols., 1958.

G. Ostrogorsky, *History of the Byzantine State,* 1956.

B. MONOGRAPHS

A. E. R. Boak, *Manpower Shortage and the Fall of the Roman Empire,* 1955.

S. Dill, *Roman Society in the Last Century of the Western Empire,* 1899; Meridian paperback reprint, 1959.

A. Alföldi, *A Conflict of Ideas in the Late Roman Empire,* 1952.

A. H. N. Jones, *Constantine and the Conversion of Europe,* 1948.

Ch. N. Cochrane, *Christianity and Classical Culture,* 1944; Galaxy Books paperback reprint, 1957.

S. Katz, *The Decline of Rome and the Rise of Medieval Europe,* 1955.

F. W. Walbank, *Decline of the Roman Empire in the West,* 1947.

N. K. Chadwick, *Poetry and Letters in Early Christian Gaul,* 1955.

C. D. Gordon, *The Age of Attila,* 1960.

B. H. Warmington, *The North African Provinces from Diocletian to the Vandal Conquest,* 1954.

M. L. W. Laistner, *Christianity and Pagan Culture,* 1931.

P. Courcelle, *Histoire littéraire des grandes invasions germaniques,* 1948.

E. Demouget, *De l'unité à la division de l'Empire Romain,* 1951.

C. Pharr, *The Theodosian Code* (Engl. transl., 1952).

E. Barker, *Social and Political Thought in Byzantium,* 1957.

Index

Abundantia, 293
Accius, L., poet, 92
Achaean hostages, 92
Achaean League, 58, 67, 72, 73
Acilius, Gaius, 4
Actium, battle of, 145, 177
Adriatic sea, 6–9, 58, 63, 67, 170, 180, 213, 221
Aegean sea, 109
Aelius Gallus, 181
Aelius Syneros, P., 18–19
Aemilii, the, 45; see also Paulus
Aeneas, 4, 15, 191
Aequi, the, 14, 25, 28, 32, 37
Aeracura, 300–301
Aetolian League, 58, 67, 69, 70
Aetolians, 63, 70
Africa, 6, 67, 76, 84, 105, 106, 119, 130–32, 137, 141, 142, 153, 155, 167, 168, 181, 188, 201, 203, 211, 212, 213, 215, 216, 218, 248, 254, 263; colonization in, 220–21; Province of, 77, 81, 221–2; negroes, 248; religion, 293
Agathocles, of Syracuse, 39, 51, 52
Agis IV, king of Sparta, 96
Agrippa, M. Vipsanius, consul, 169, 190, 193; Pantheon of, 190
Agrippina, grandmother of Nero, 197
Agrippina, mother of Nero, 195, 197
Ahenobarbus, Cn. Domitius, 195
Ahenobarbus, L. Domitius, 152, 180
Ahriman, 298–9
Ahuramazda, 298–9
Aix, see Aquae Sextiae
Alalia (Aleria), Corsica, 12
Alba Longa (Albanum), 15, 16, 267
Alban hills, 14
Albanum, see Alba Longa
Albinus, Clodius, governor of Britain, 267
Alemanni, 269
Aleria, see Alalia
Alesia, 127

Alexander I, king of Epirus, 36, 39
Alexander the Great, king of Macedonia, 1, 40, 66, 67, 138, 186, 268, 320
Alexander Severus, see Severus
Alexandria, 130, 131, 135, 145, 207, 224, 232, 249, 251, 294–5, 312, 315
Alexianus, 268
Algeria, 257
Alia, see Allia
Alimentus, L. Cincius, 4
Allia (Alia) river, 29
Alpine provinces, 218, 219
Alps, the, 5, 59, 177
Ambrosius, bp. of Milan, 315
Amiternum, 158–9
Ammianus Marcellinus, 314
Anatolia, 10
Anatolian pirates, 73, 118
Anatolians, 8; religion, 293, 296, 297
Andriscus, 74
Andronicus, 77
Annona, 293
Antinoupolis, 224
Antinous, 224
Antioch, 251, 312, 315
Antiochus III (the Great), king of Syria, 67–9, 70
Antium, 14, 28
Antonines, the, 255, 266, 267, 274, 289
Antoninus Pius, emperor, 209, 212
Antonius, Lucius, 142
Antonius, M., the orator, 107
Antonius, M. (Creticus), son of the orator, 120
Antonius, M., the triumvir, 132, 135, 138–45, 148, 149, 152, 156, 162, 163, 168, 181, 187, 206
Antullius, 102
Anubis, 246–7
Apamea, 157
Apennines, 6, 14
Apollo, 93, 94, 186, 187, 189
Apollonia, 58, 63, 103

337

Cabeiri, the, 297
Cadiz, *see* Gades
Caelestis, 293
Caesar, title, 280, 283
Caesar, C. Julius, 162, 164, 182, 187,
    189, 190, 201, 206, 210, 211, 250
—and Pompey, 122–31
—his dictatorship, 132–45, 175, 178
—and the army, 147–52, 167, 170, 171
—in Gaul, 155, 219
—in the East, 156
—*Commentaries*, 160
Caesar, Gaius and Lucius, 169, 182, 193,
    236–7
Caesarea, 315
Caesarion, 135
Caligula, emperor, 194–5, 197, 199, 206
Camitlnas, Marce, 18–19
Campania, 6–15, 12, 13, 14, 20, 22, 36,
    37, 45, 62, 63, 64, 110, 111, 123, 124,
    126, 150–51, 260, 294–5
Camulodunum (Colchester), 219
Candia, *see* Crete
Cannae, 62, 63
Canuleius, 30
Cappadocia, 218
Capri, 196
Capua, 12, 36–7, 62, 64, 87, 94, 120, 155,
    158–9
Caracalla, emperor, 267–8, 277, 282
Carinus, 270, 271
Carrhae, battle of, 128
Carthage, 800–500 B.C.: 9, 11, 12, 14, 16,
    21, 23
—5th–3rd cents. B.C.: 25, 37, 39, 40;
    and Rome, 50–77, 78, 79, 81, 86; and
    Gracchus, 92, 97, 100, 102, 105
—1st cent. B.C., 136, 154
—1st and 2nd cents. A.D., 218, 221, 249,
    251
—5th cent. A.D., 312
—capitalist system of agriculture, 89, 90
—mosaics from, 286–7
—religion, 302
Carus, emperor, 270
Cassites, 319
Cassius Avidius, 213
Cassius Hemina, 4
Cassius Longinus, C., 132, 138, 139, 140,
    141, 154, 156

Catilina, L. Sergius, 122–6, 160
Cato, M. Porcius, 73, 76, 77, 93, 95
Cato, the younger, 125
Catullus, 157, 190
Caucasus, the, 215
Cautes, 298–9
Cautopates, 298–9
Celtiberians, 75
Celtic language, 8, 155; provinces, 218–
    20; religion, 293
Celts, 8, 12, 23, 74, 106, 120, 126, 127,
    132, 179, 201, 216, 218, 221, 223, 323
Ceres (Demeter), 34
Chersonese, 200
China, 263
Christ, 302, 303, 304–5, 316
Christianity, 292, 296, 302 sqq., 314–17
Chrysippus, 184
Chrysogonus, 153
Cicero, M. Tullius, 123–6, 132, 140, 141,
    146, 147, 152–4, 157, 160, 161, 190
Cilicia, 118, 218
Cilician pirates, 156
Cimbri, the, 106, 107, 111, 155
Cimbrian war, 107
Cimmerians, 319
Cinna, L. Cornelius, 111, 112, 122
Città Lavinia (Lavinium), 300–301
Claudia Quinta, 60–61
Claudia Syntyche, 60–61
Claudian dynasty, 193–204, 266
Claudian law, 88
Claudianus, Claudius, 314
Claudii, the, 28, 255
Claudius, emperor, 18–19, 195, 197, 200,
    204, 219, 226, 229, 259
—*See also* Appius; Clodius
Claudius Gothicus, 270
Clemency, 136
Cleomenes, 96
Cleonymus, 39
Cleopatra, 131, 135, 141–5, 156, 173,
    181
Clodius (P. Claudius Pulcher), 126
Colchester, *see* Camulodunum
Cologne, 223
Columella, 258, 265
Commagene, 300–301
Commodus, emperor, 210, 213, 251, 258,
    266, 267

Constantine, emperor, 289–90, 309, 312, 315
Constantinople, church of St. Sophia, 316
Corbulo, 201
Corinth, 74, 136, 251; gulf of, 7; isthmus of, 74
Cornelia, mother of the Gracchi, 92
Cornelii, the, 45, 116
Corneto, *see* Tarquinii
Corsica, 12, 57, 78
Coruncanii, the, 45
Cotta, Aurelius, 120
Crassus, M. Licinius, 120–22, 124–8, 143, 180, 182
Cretan pirates, 73, 118, 156
Crete (Candia), 118, 139
Crimea, the, 136, 200, 201, 297
Cumae, 12, 22
Cupids, 236–7
Cybele, 60–61, 298–9
Cynics, 156, 205
Cynoscephalae, battle of, 68
Cyprian, 315
Cyrene, 139
Cyzicus, 66

Dacia, 211, 212, 213, 218, 259
Dalmatia (Illyricum), 67, 179, 200, 218, 222
Dalmatians, 180, 181
Danube country, religion, 298–9
Danube provinces, 218, 221, 270
Danube (Ister) river, 6, 8, 132, 168, 179–81, 200, 211, 212, 216, 223, 263, 267, 269, 297, 311
Dardanelles, 248
Decius, 303
Delos, 73, 109
Delphi, 293
Demeter, *see* Ceres
Diana, 33, 236–7
Diocletianus, Gaius Valerius Aurelius, emperor, 263, 270, 271, 279 sqq., 288, 308, 309, 314, 315
Dion Chrysostomos, 203, 207
Dionysius, 35, 39
Dionysus, 34, 93, 94, 186, 294–5. *See also* Bacchus
Dispater, 300–301

Dolabella, 138, 139
Doliche, 297, 300–301
Domitian, emperor, 203, 206, 210, 211, 251, 258, 259, 266, 315
Dougga, *see* Thugga
Drusus, Caesar (Drusus junior), 196
Drusus, M. Livius, the elder, 102
Drusus, the younger, 108
Drusus, Nero Claudius (Drusus senior), 173, 180, 181, 193, 195
Dyrrhachium, 130

Eboracum (York), 219
Ebro, 59
Egypt, 89, 238–9, 246–7, 311, 317, 319
—3rd cent. B.C., 50
—2nd cent. B.C., 66, 67, 69, 70, 74
—1st cent. B.C., 124, 130, 141, 144, 145, 156
—in the time of Augustus, 168, 173, 177, 181
—1st and 2nd cents. A.D., 209, 211, 212, 213, 218, 224–5; government, 228, 229; agriculture, &c., 258, 260, 264; religion, 293, 296
Elagabal, *see* Heliogabalus
Elba, island of, 9
Elbe, river, 179–81, 200
Eleusinian mysteries, 185, 209
Emesa, 268
Ennius, 4, 91
Ephesus, 251, 312
Epictetus, 292
Epicureanism, 156, 183
Epicurus, 160, 185
Epidamnus, 58
Epirus, 39, 40, 72, 132, 153, 200
Etruria, 6, 9, 10, 11, 14, 20, 21, 28, 38, 45, 50, 51, 125, 150–51, 155
Etruscan art, 11, 18–19, 26–7; political activity, 11–12; religion, 33, 34
Etruscan League, 23
Etruscans, 1, 3, 8 sqq., 33, 37, 38, 51
Eumenes II of Pergamum, 70, 72
Euphrates, 200, 201, 211, 213
Eusebius, 315
Eutyches, 238–9

Fabii, the, 22, 45
Fabius Pictor, 4

Fabius, Quintus (Cunctator), 63
Fannius, 102
Fidenae, 32
Fimbria, 112
Finns, 212, 248
Flaccus, L. Valerius, 112
Flamininus, Titus Quinctius, 69
Flavii, the, 194, 204, 255
Fortune (Tyche), 190, 293, 300–301
France, 8, 258, 310
Franks, 269
Fregellae, 96
Frescati, *see* Tusculum
Fulvia, 142
Fulvii, the, 45
Furrina, grove of, 103

Gades (Cadiz), 58
Galatia, 74, 173, 182, 218
Galatians, the, 73
Galba, 199
Gallia Aquitania, 179
Gallia Belgica, 179
Gallia Cisalpina, 118, 126, 136
Gallia Lugdunensis, 179
Gallia Narbonensis, 105, 106, 136, 139, 140, 179, 218
Gallia Transalpina, 126
Gallienus, emperor, 269
Gard, river, 240–41
Gaul (*see also* Gallia)
—geographical connexion with Italy, 6
—aborigines, 7
—Etruscans and, 12
—and the civil war, 105, 108, 139
—Caesar's conquest of, 126–9, 152, 155, 156
—under Augustus, 168, 173, 179, 180
—under Nero, 198
—1st and 2nd cents. A.D., 215, 216, 218, 219, 222, 254, 257, 259, 263
—3rd cent. A.D., 269, 270, 274
—commerce, &c., 90, 153, 242–3, 263; education, 203; monuments, &c., 240–41; religion, 188
Gauls, 8, 28, 35–8, 40, 58, 59, 87, 107, 133. *See also* Celts
Gellius, Gnaeus, 4
Genius, 32, 292
German tribes, 180

Germanicus, 181, 193, 194, 195–7, 200
Germans, 106, 127, 170, 179, 181, 211–12, 213, 216, 223, 248, 266, 269, 270, 281, 282, 309, 311, 312
Germany, 127, 181, 193, 198, 199, 200, 212, 215, 216, 242–3, 258, 259, 263, 310
Geta, 267
Gnosticism, 292
Goths, 269, 270
Gracchi, the, 105, 114, 116, 146, 149
Gracchus, Gaius, 97, 98–100, 108, 123
Gracchus, Tiberius (212 B.C.), 63
Gracchus, Tiberius (triumvir), 96–103, 111
Great Mother, *see* Magna Mater
Greece, 4–8, 10–12, 17, 20, 50, 67–9, 72–4, 77, 81, 82, 110–12, 130, 132, 134, 136, 142, 153, 156, 160, 161, 200, 209, 218, 223, 257, 258, 259, 260, 262, 265
Greek art, 160, 190, 209; culture, 157; language, 160, 202, 313–14; philosophers, 207; religion, 89, 293
Greek cities, 222; colonies, 180; islands, 81
Greek city-state, 320–21
Greeks, 1, 2, 4, 13, 35, 39, 40, 51, 52, 53, 56, 109, 137, 149, 198, 215
Gregory, 315

Hadrianus, Publius Aelius, emperor, 209, 212–13, 224, 226, 231, 264, 274, 293, 312
Hadrumetum (Sousse), 306–7
Hamilcar Barca, 56, 57, 59
Hannibal, 57, 59–64, 67, 70, 72, 75, 88, 93
Harpocrates, 294–5, 296
Hasdrubal (son-in-law of Hamilcar), 57, 59
Hasdrubal (brother of Hannibal), 64
Heddernheim, 300–301
Heliogabalus (Elagabal), emperor, 268, 289, 302
Heliopolis, *see* Baalbek
Helvetii, 127
Hera, 93
Heraclea, 136
Heracles, *see* Hercules

Lycia, 218
Lyons, see Lugudunum

Macedonia, 40, 50, 53, 58, 62, 66–9, 70–75, 77, 80, 81, 106, 132, 138, 141, 167, 179, 180, 200
Macrinus, 268
Macstrna, 18–19
Maecenas, Gaius, 190
Magna Mater, 60–61, 293, 296, 297, 298–9
Magnesia, 70
Mainz, 223, 242–3
Malchus, 272–3
Mamertini, 52
Mamilii, the, 45
Mammaea, 268
Mancinus, Gaius Hostilius, 97
Manes, 32
Mantua, 154, 155
Marcellus, M. Claudius, of Syracuse, 63, 64
Marcellus, M. Claudius, nephew of Augustus, 190, 193
Marcomanni, 269
Marius, Gaius, 106, 107, 108, 110–12, 119, 122, 123, 126, 127, 132, 133, 140, 148, 149, 152
Maroboduus, 181
Mars, 17, 18–19, 32, 297, 298–9
—Campus Martius, 187, 189, 232
Marseilles, see Massilia
Martial, 203
Masinissa, 64, 65, 75, 76, 105
Massilia (Marseilles), 12, 51, 80, 105, 240–41
Mauretania (Morocco), 82, 201, 218
Maximianus, Galerius, 303
Maximianus, Valerius, 280
Mediolanum (Milan), 312, 315
Mediterranean, 117, 118, 120, 121, 248, 263
Megalopolis, 92
Memphis, 224
Mercury, 186, 293
Mesopotamia, 132, 212, 218
Messalina, 195, 197
Messana (Messina), 51, 52, 53
Messapians, 39, 40
Messiah, the, 186, 187

Messina, Straits of, 7, 41, 52, 53. *See also* Messana
Metaurus, river, 64
Metellus, 106
Milan, see Mediolanum
Minerva, 26–7, 33, 93, 297, 300–301
Misenum, 142, 170
Mithradates VI, 109, 110, 112, 118–22, 124, 131, 153, 156
Mithras, 296, 297, 298–9, 302
Modena, see Mutina
Moesia, 180, 218
Moguntiacum, 242–3
Mongols, 212, 248, 310
Moors, 274
Morocco (Mauretania), 201; tribes of, 222
Moselle, river, 314
Mummius, Lucius, 74
Munda, battle of, 131
Mutina (Modena), battles of, 139, 140
Mysia, 77

Naevius, 4, 91
Namatianus, Rutilius, 314
Naples, 6, 12, 13, 35, 36, 39, 51
Narbo (Narbonne), 105
Nazianzus, 315
Neapolis, see Naples
Nemausus (Nîmes), 240–41
Nemesis, 298–9
Neo-Pythagoreanism, 183, 184, 185, 186, 191
Nero, emperor, 185, 195, 197, 198, 200, 201, 203–5, 208, 251
Nerva, Gaius Cocceius, emperor, 207
Neumagen, 234–5, 242–3
Nicaea, 312
Nicomedes III, 119
Nicomedia, 312
Nile, river, 224, 246–7, 248
Nîmes, see Nemausus
Nola, 12
North Sea, 179, 222, 248
Norway, 263
Nubia, 181
Numantia, 75, 76, 92, 97
Numidia, 75, 82, 105, 106, 201, 218
Numidians, 51, 57

Octavia, wife of Antony, 142
Octavian, *see* Augustus
Octavius, tribune, 98
Odenathus, 270
Odrysae, 180
Ogulnii, the, 45
Olympia, 293
Orange, *see* Arausio
Origen, 303
Orphic doctrines, 185
Ostia, 18–19, 236–7
Otacilii, the, 45
Otho, emperor, 199, 226
Ovid, 185, 191, 192

Pacuvius, 92
Padus, *see* Po
Palestine, 132, 173, 215, 218, 224
Palestrina, *see* Praeneste
Palmyra, 270, 272–3
Pan, 293
Pannonia, 218
Pannonians, 181, 266
Pansa, 139
Panticapaeum, 269
Paphlagonia, 218
Papinian, jurist, 313
Parthia, 133, 143, 201, 211
Parthian legion, 267
Parthians, 128, 133, 142, 143, 182, 211, 212, 213, 268, 269, 319
Paul, apostle, 302
Paul, jurist, 313
Paulus, Aemilius, 72, 75
Pausanias, 293
Pedius, Quintus, 140
Penates, 32, 292
Pergamum, 60–61, 66, 67, 69, 70, 72–4, 77, 80, 81, 99, 251
Perose, 272–3
Perperna, 119
Perseus of Macedonia, 70, 72–4
Persia, 133, 310; religion, 296, 297, 298–9, 302
Persians, 224, 269, 270, 319
Persius, 203
Pertinax, M. Helvius, 266, 267
Perusia, 142
Pescennius Niger, 267
Petronius, Gaius, 181, 185, 204

Pharnaces, 131
Pharsalus, battle of, 130, 141
Philip V, of Macedonia, 63, 67–9, 71
Philippi, battle of, 141
Phoceans, 12
Phoenicia, 10, 11, 20, 218, 220
Phoenicians (*Poeni*), Roman name for Carthaginians, 11, 53, 220
Phrygian kingdom, 319
Picenum, 152
Pisidia, 182
Piso, C. Calpurnius, 180
Piso, L. Calpurnius, 4
Plancus, 140
Plato, 2, 89, 92
Platonic mysticism, 292
Platonism, 314
Plautii, the, 45
Plautus, 91
Pliny, 208
Pliny, the younger, 214
Plotinus, 292, 315
Pluto, 300–301
Po (Padus), river, 6, 7
—valley, 8, 9, 12, 23, 38, 58, 75, 87
Poeni, *see* Phoenicians
Polybius, 1, 92, 157
Pompeii, 12, 150–51, 155, 238–9, 250, 254, 256
Pompey (Cn. Pompeius Magnus, the triumvir), 117–31, 144, 148, 149, 152, 155, 156, 166, 182, 190, 210, 232
—his younger son, Sextus, 139, 141–3
Pont du Gard, the, 240–41
Pontus, 74, 109, 125, 132
Porcii, the, 45
Portugal, 75, 118
Posidonius, 157
Postumus, Marcus Cassius Latinius, 270
Praeneste (Palestrina), 16, 20, 26–7, 32, 36, 45, 113, 246–7
Probus, emperor, 270
Ptolemais, 224
Ptolemies, the, 69, 224, 225, 296
Ptolemy Philadelphus, 53
Ptolemy XIV, 130
Puglia, *see* Apulia
Punic Wars, 4, 50–65, 76–7, 86, 90, 91, 92, 93, 94, 109
Pydna, battle of, 72, 73

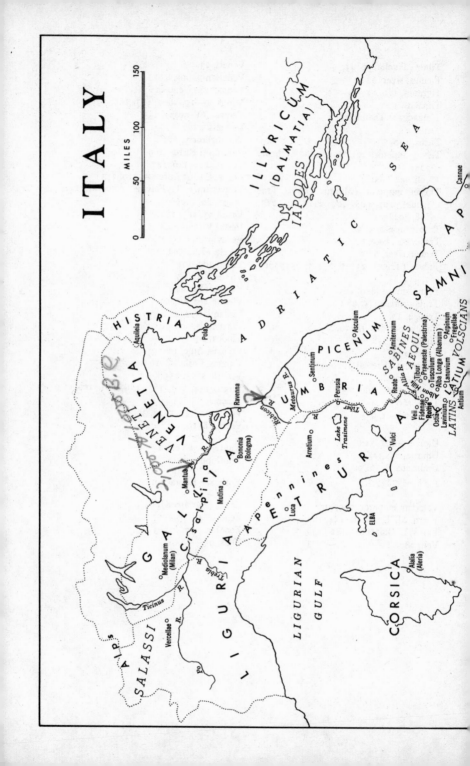

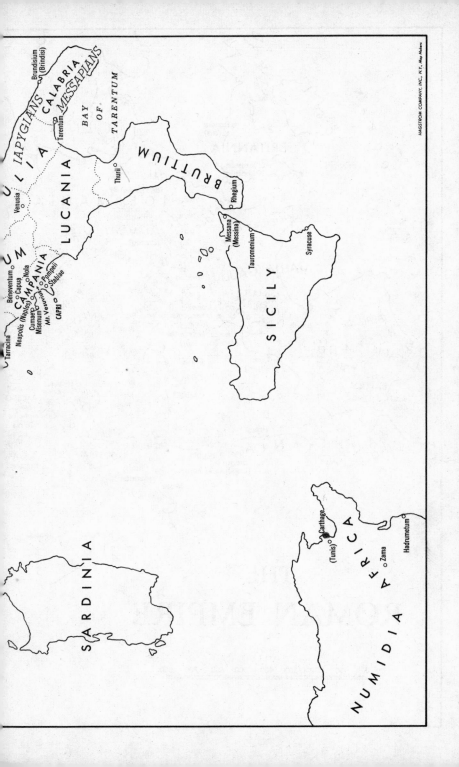

Brundisium
(Brindisi)
CALABRIA
MESSAPIANS
IAPYGIANS
APULIA
Venusia
Tarentum
BAY
OF
TARENTUM
LUCANIA
Thurii
Beneventum
Capua
Nola
CAMPANIA
Pompeii
Stabiae
Neapolis (Naples)
Cumae
Misenum
Mt. Vesuvius
CAPRI
Tarracina
BRUTTIUM
Rhegium
Messana
(Messina)
Tauromenium
Syracuse
SICILY

SARDINIA

Carthage
(Tunis)
AFRICA
Zama
Hadrumetum
NUMIDIA

HAGSTROM COMPANY, INC., N.Y., Map Makers

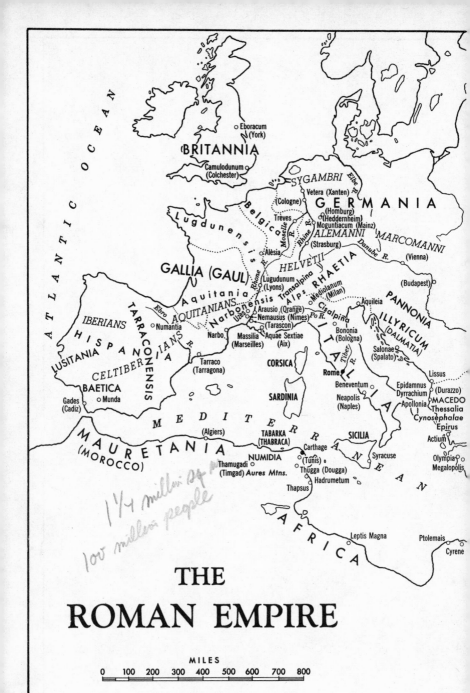

THE

ROMAN EMPIRE

MILES

0   100   200   300   400   500   600   700   800

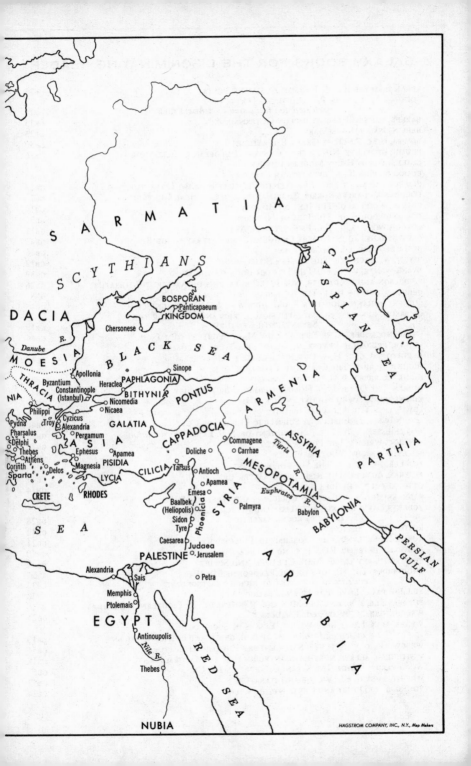

SARMATIA

SCYTHIANS

DACIA

BOSPORAN
Panticapaeum
KINGDOM

Chersonese

Danube R.

MOESIA

BLACK SEA

Sinope

THRACIA

Apollonia

PAPHLAGONIA

Heraclea

Byzantium

Constantinople
(Istanbul)

BITHYNIA

NIA

Nicomedia

PONTUS

Philippi

Nicaea

Pydna

Cyzicus

Pharsalus

Troy

Alexandria

Delphi

Pergamum

GALATIA

CAPPADOCIA

Thebes

ASIA

Ephesus

Apamea

Doliche

Commagene

Carrhae

Athens

Corinth

Magnesia

PISIDIA

Sparta

Delos

LYCIA

CILICIA

Tarsus

Antioch

CRETE

RHODES

Apamea

SEA

Emesa

Baalbek
(Heliopolis)

Sidon

Tyre

Palmyra

Babylon

Caesarea

PALESTINE

Judaea

Jerusalem

Alexandria

Sais

Petra

Memphis

Ptolemais

EGYPT

Antinoupolis

Nile R.

Thebes

RED SEA

CASPIAN SEA

ARMENIA

ASSYRIA

PARTHIA

Tigris R.

MESOPOTAMIA

Euphrates R.

SYRIA

Phoenicia

BABYLONIA

PERSIAN GULF

ARABIA

NUBIA

HAGSTROM COMPANY, INC., N.Y., Map Makers

GALAXY BOOKS FOR THE DISCRIMINATING READER